Democracy, Human Rights and Governance in The Gambia

Essays in Social Adjustment

REVISED EDITION

Aboubacar Abdullah Senghore

Democracy, Human Rights and Governance in The Gambia

Essays in Social Adjustment

Aboubacar Abdullah Senghore

REVISED EDITION

iii

CENMEDRA

Published by CENMEDRA – the Centre for Media and Development Research in Africa

Copyright © Aboubacar Abdullah Senghore 2018

Aboubacar Abdullah Senghore has asserted his right to be identified as the author of this book.

First published in The Gambia in 2018 by CENMEDRA

Revised edition published in The Gambia in 2024 by CENMEDRA

https://www.cenmedra.org

ISBN: 978-9983-94-608-6

Front cover design by Sadibou Kamaso

Front cover image: Copyright@CENMEDRA

The image of a sunrise in the Sahel during the Harmattan symbolizes the penetrative thrust of democratization through the fogginess of authoritarianism across Africa.

Layout design: Fidelis Obieshi Ikechukwu

www.cenmedra.org

info@cenmedra.org

Contents

Dedication   *vii*

About the Author   *viii*

Acknowledgements   *ix*

About CENMEDRA   *x*

Preface   *xii*

Introduction   **1**

Chapter 1
Africa in a Changing World: The Major Governance Crisis in West Africa and the Way Forward   **9**

Chapter 2
Liberal Democracy and Governance in Africa: A Brief Critique   **46**

Chapter 3
Human Rights and Democracy in Africa: Is The Gambia a Democratic State?   **75**

Chapter 4
Press Freedom and Democratic Governance in The Gambia: A Rights-Based Approach   **114**

Chapter 5
The Judiciary in Governance in The Gambia: The Quest for Autonomy in the Second Republic   **171**

Chapter 6
International Human Rights and the Laws of Nations: A Brief Analysis of the Philosophical Foundations, Basic Premises, and Historical Background of Human Rights from the Conventional and Islamic Perspectives.   **213**

Chapter 7
Law Faculties, Ethics, and Legal Professionalism: A Contemporary African Perspective   **260**

Chapter 8
Harnessing Traditional Governance Institutions to Improve Governance in West Africa: A Case Study of The Gambia   **277**

Chapter 9
Towards Arab-African Integration in the Struggle against Western Hegemony and Imperialism: A Critical Perspective   **359**

Chapter 10
Responsible Leadership and Effective Governance: A Prerequisite for Peace, Stability, and Sustainable Development in Africa   **385**

Conclusion   **411**

Note   **414**

Index   **456**

Dedication

This book is dedicated to the memory of my late uncle Alhajie Babu Kumba Njie who insisted I receive education at all costs.

About the Author

Aboubacar Abdullah Senghore, Associate Professor of Comparative Law, is the Deputy Director-General at the Organization of Islamic Cooperation Research Centre for Islamic History, Art, and Culture (IRCICA) in Istanbul, Turkey. He is a former founding Dean of the Faculty of Law at the University of The Gambia and earlier, Faculty of Social Sciences of the same University. He holds a PhD in International Human Rights Law and a master's degree in Comparative Law, both from the International Islamic University in Malaysia, in addition to an LLB in Comparative Law from the International Islamic University, Islamabad, Pakistan. His thirst for knowledge also led him to obtain some post-doctoral certificates in management as well as election observation and monitoring at the Kofi Annan International Peacekeeping Training Centre (KAIPTC) in Accra, Ghana, and an additional certificate in governance at the Council for the Development of Social Science Research in Africa (CODESRIA) in Dakar, Senegal. He worked as a Legal and Research Officer and Head of the Legal and Research Department of the African Centre for Democracy and Human Rights Studies in Banjul, The Gambia. As well as being a founding member of the Association of Deans of Faculties of Humanities and Social Sciences of African Universities, he also served as a Minister of Foreign Affairs and then as a Minister of Higher Education, Research, Science and Technology of the Republic of The Gambia in the Second Republic. In November 2013, he received the Gucci Foundation International Peace Prize. Prior to that, he was named a CODESRIA Laureate in 2005.

Acknowledgements

First of all, I would like to thank all the individuals and institutions that have in one way, or another contributed to the writing of all the articles and book chapters constituting this volume and also to those who contributed to the successful editing and eventual publication of this book. Thus, my sincere thanks go to the editor of this volume Aloa Ahmed Alota and to the editors of all the peer-reviewed academic journals that published most of the articles and book chapters that are constitutive of this volume.

I am equally grateful, most especially, to my long-time secretary and administration assistant Miss Sainabou Ndow who typed most of the manuscripts which have been compiled into this volume. In the same vein, I am sincerely thankful to Mrs Kaddy Jobarteh-Fatty, my former secretary when I headed the Faculty of Social Sciences. She typed a good chunk of my early manuscripts.

Likewise, I am sincerely grateful to the Dakar-based Council for the Development of Social Science Research in Africa (CODESRIA) for giving me the opportunity to attend its 2005 Governance Institute in Dakar. It was during my participation in that training and research programme that I was fully inspired to start my academic writing and research activities. I am also grateful to the University of The Gambia for being the base of my academic career.

Finally, I am most especially grateful to my family - my wives Mrs Khadijatou and Mrs Roheyatou Ndow-Senghore and our beloved children - for their understanding and cooperation.

About CENMEDRA

CENMEDRA – the Centre for Media and Development Research in Africa – is a knowledge centre. Registered as an educational charity in The Gambia on 3 March 2014 it aims to promote, facilitate, and disseminate research in media, communication, and development in Africa. Its activities are focused on five main areas namely media research, researching development, new media and society, education, and publication. In line with its underlying aim of research application, it shares its research results with policymakers, media and development practitioners, media houses, regulators, scholars, politicians, librarians, activists, donors, development agencies, and the wider research community. It has a two-tiered governance structure: a board of trustees drawn from the media, civil society and academia, which provides strategy and policy direction, and an administrative secretariat that is responsible for operations and policy implementation.

MISSION

CENMEDRA exists to foster innovative research that puts Africa on the path of peace, progress and prosperity.

VISION

CENMEDRA envisions an enlightened African society, free from the burden of ignorance, where everyone is able to realize their fullest potential in peace and prosperity.

VALUES

- Integrity
- Openness
- Creativity
- Diligence

Website: https://www.cenmedra.org

Email: info@cenmedra.org

Preface

Efforts that gave birth to most of this chapters in this book began in July 2005 when I attended the 2005 Africa Governance Institute organized by the Council for the Development of Social Science Research in Africa (CODESRIA) in Dakar, Senegal. As part of the requirements for successful participation in the Governance Institute, I had to contribute a book chapter on any related topic of interest, preferably about The Gambia. Thus, I wrote my first-ever peer-reviewed article entitled: "The Independent news media and Democratic Governance in The Gambia: A rights-based approach". It took CODESRIA and the Course Director a very long time to publish the 2005 volume which should have contained various essays contributed by the participants in the 2005 Governance Institute. I am not even sure if the book was ever published. In 2012, I thoroughly revised this chapter and successfully got it published in The Republic of Hungary (*Afrika Tonulmonyok-African Studies Journal*), (Vol. IV 2012, and No.1).

My successful participation in the 2005 Governance Institute and the subsequent intensive research I conducted to write the article referred to above significantly deepened my understanding and sharply increased my interest in the three related areas of democracy, human rights, and governance, which constitutes the substance of this book.

Also in 2012, I published my second peer-reviewed article in the New Jersey-based *Journal of Third World Studies* with the title: "The Judiciary in Governance in The Gambia and the Quest for Autonomy in the Second Republic" (*Journal of Third World Studies* (Vol.27, No.2; Fall 2012, pp.215-248).

The third peer-reviewed article, entitled: "Press Freedom and Democratic Governance in The Gambia: A right-based approach, was also published in 2012 by the University of Pretoria's *African Human Rights Law Journal*. (Vol.12, No.2, 2012)

Thus between 2005 and 2016, I continued to publish peer-reviewed journal articles, to conduct classroom and public lectures and present papers at international academic conferences about democracy, human rights, and good governance across Africa.

In the course of my discussions of human rights and law in the conventional sense, I took some time to address the Islamic perspective of law and rights in general. Similarly, African traditional governance systems, processes and institutions have attracted my research interest. The main thesis that has consistently been projected by almost all this chapters in this book is the need to promote:

• Democratic system of governance across the continent

• Respect for human rights and fundamental freedoms, particularly press freedom

• Respect for the rule of law and supremacy of the authority of the law

• Good governance and responsible management of public resources at all levels of governance in society.

Introduction

When this book was first published in 2018, democracy was gaining traction across Africa. Two years earlier The Gambia, the smallest country on mainland Africa, had experienced a democratic transition of power that ended the 22-year rule of former president Yahya Jammeh who at first came to power in a bloodless military takeover on 24 July 1994. Ever since the end of military rule in 1997, The Gambia has continued to experience peaceful and successful democratic elections, both presidential and parliamentary. It is worth mentioning at this point that despite the fact that the 2016 democratic transition of power in The Gambia was accompanied by a brief political impasse, which lasted for about a month and a half following an election dispute, the transition was successful.

A little earlier Nigeria, the most populous nation on the continent, made history when an incumbent president lost out at the polls and accepted defeat with uncommon grace. A shared quality in the electoral experiences in both countries was the potency of an opposition alliance in removing an incumbent from power, a democratic formula that is proving (in several cases) to be an antidote to entrenched and self-perpetuating incumbency in Africa. In both countries, most particularly The Gambia, defeating the incumbent in an election no matter how democratic, was unthinkable. This was due mainly to either electoral fraud and manipulation as the opposition side and government critics would claim, or lack of sound political maturity and democratic consciousness on the side of the electorate as evidently shown in Gambian elections. Around the same time, a number of open and multiparty elections and leadership transitions happened throughout the continent. This development reinforced hopes of democratic consolidation in Africa.

However, these hopes for return and settlement of democracy have been dealt a severe blow in West Africa when the military struck very recently in Burkina Faso, Guinea Conakry, Mali, and Niger which are now fully governed by juntas. There are also reported failed coup attempts in Guinea Bissau, The Gambia, and Sao Tome and Principe. It is noteworthy that all of this is happening in the West African sub region where the first-ever military coup in Africa took place in Lome, Togo, on 13 January 1963, which ousted the then government of former president Sylvanus Olympio. The resurgence of unconstitutional change of government on the continent and particularly in the sub-Sahara region has puzzled commentators and observers of African affairs, who have been asking themselves: What does this development portend? Is a domino effect of military government imminent on the continent? Is democracy incompatible with the African condition? Or is it that Africa and Africans can only be better governed and can only develop and prosper under military rule?

This unfortunate development in West African politics has turned upside down the remarkable successes recorded by the sub-regional bloc - the Economic Community of West African States (ECOWAS) - in terms of decisively ending civil wars and internal conflicts and restoring some level of democracy and stability in some of the smaller actors of the sub-region over the past two and a half decades. The current situation regarding democracy versus military rule in West Africa is pointing to a very worrying socio-economic, political and security reality on the grounds that the population has to grapple and live with for an indefinite period of time. That is, when it comes to the bigger actors in the sub-region, particularly those vast countries like Mali and Guinea Conakry, ECOWAS has not demonstrated that it possesses both the capacity and the necessary resources to guard or restore, ensure, and maintain democracy, human rights and rule of law in the sub region. Currently, Senegal's story of long-standing and much-talked-about democracy and stability is poised to be severely tested and the outcome could be undesirable especially if the incumbent insists on seeking a third term in the country's 2024 presidential elections. Senegal and its democracy could also be in trouble if the government of President Macky Sall mishandles the ongoing case of the alleged sex scandals against the main opposition leader Ousman Sonko whose national popularity appears to be steadily increasing as the country's 2024 presidential elections are fast approaching.

This book contributes to this broad debate at two levels. At the macro level, it addresses the major governance crisis in West Africa and then offers a critique of liberal democracy in Africa. These two concerns are the main thrusts of Chapters 1 and 2. It argues (subtly) that democracy without constitutional liberalism is hollow and prone to perversion. It thus re-echoes similar arguments made by Claude Ake in *The Feasibility of Democracy in Africa* (2000) and Fareed Zakaria in "The Rise of Illiberal Democracy" (1997). Ake makes a case for social democracy as opposed to electoral democracy. The former, he argues, is marked by the enjoyment of concrete rights and real equality; it also entails mass empowerment of the citizenry. Conversely the latter, which he also terms as minimalist liberal democracy, is characterized by multiparty elections and scarcely guarantees social dividends for the people of Africa. For his part, Zakaria distinguishes democracy from constitutional liberalism, arguing that democracy is about the procedures for selecting a government while constitutional liberalism is the government's goal. Democracy, according to him, involves open and competitive multiparty elections, which should generally be seen to be free and fair. On the contrary, constitutional liberalism entails separation of powers, the rule of law, and the protection of basic liberties such as the rights to free speech, assembly, religion, and property. In Western political tradition, according to him, both democracy and constitutional liberalism are coupled together to form the notion of liberal democracy. He then observes that democracy does not necessarily bring about constitutional liberalism. Constitutional liberalism, however, can strengthen democracy. His observation is pertinent to the African condition, where rights violations are rife in democratic governments. The point is, however, made in Chapter 2 that what is urgently needed across Africa is a change of attitude, not systems. So long as the basic impetus for seeking elective office is self-enrichment and not service to the common good, all forms of political organization are unlikely to guarantee liberty, equality, and prosperity for the African people. While this view is open to contestation as oversimplification of a complex social phenomenon, it is nonetheless an important facet of the governance crisis that is plaguing the continent.

At the micro level, it focuses on democracy, human rights and governance in The Gambia. In Chapter 3, the question is posed if The Gambia is a democratic state. The chapter offers a nuanced response to this question. It notes that democracy is an open concept that should be adapted to fit in with varying social and indigenous cultures. There is thus no unitary democratic template across time and place. Instead, there is a wide variety of democratic conceptions and practices that reflect particular social and cultural contexts. Nevertheless, a common denominator of all conceptions of democracy, as noted previously, is open and competitive multiparty elections. This book thus argues that since elections in The Gambia are normally free and fair, coupled with the existence of constitutional rule, separation of powers, and statutory protection of basic rights and freedoms, the country is arguably a liberal democratic state.

In elaborating this overarching theme of governance, this book also lays much emphasis on press freedom, autonomous judiciary, and human rights, as central tenets of liberal democracy. In a sweeping overview of the evolution of the press in The Gambia in Chapter 4, it notes that the first newspaper established in the country was *The*

Bathurst Times in May 1871. According to the liberal theory of a free press, the press exists (or should exist) as an (relatively) autonomous social institution that holds the government to account on behalf of the people for whom the government bears primary responsibility. While press freedom is protected under the 1997 Constitution of the Second Republic of The Gambia, its enjoyment remains a challenge. This book details instances of press freedom violations ranging from arson attacks on critical media outlets, newspaper closures, to arrest, detention, and imprisonment of journalists, as well as disappearances and murder of outspoken ones. All forms of restraint on press freedom not only have a chilling effect on journalists, but they also distort information flow and debase public discourse. Among the consequences of distorted news is cynicism among the citizens who are deprived of accurate, adequate, and reliable information required to make rational electoral decisions. This ultimately endangers democracy as elections become redundant exercises which are orchestrated to recycle power-hungry politicians. News media ownership structure tends to have similar effects on democracy. Private news media ownership and independent news media are used interchangeably in this book in line with the liberal theory of a free press which recognizes political interference as the major constraint on journalistic autonomy. However, the critical political economy of communication tends to hold a contrary view. According to this perspective, economics (e.g. advertising) is just as detrimental to journalistic autonomy as politics. Edward Herman and Noam Chomsky's *Manufacturing Consent* (1988) is a canonical text in this theoretical tradition. It identifies advertising as a major filter that distorts media content in such ways that it privileges narratives which uphold the interests, values, or worldviews of the dominant or ruling elite.

The independent news media, according to this book, is understood as the print and broadcast media that are not owned, controlled or in any way influenced by the government of the day or by a political party, a pressure group, or any ideologically based organization. It is a term used interchangeably with private news media. It is ironic that private/independent news media ownership proliferated under the difficult political conditions of the Second Republic more than any other time in the history of The Gambia. A possible explanation for this contradiction is that opposition figures, acting through proxies, resorted to the news media as a mechanism of expanding the public sphere to ensure the triumph of rational-critical debates about shared national interests and concerns. This explanation is somewhat consistent with Francis B. Nyamnjoh's (2005) observation that private/independent news media outlets in Africa are largely opposition mouthpieces. Regardless of this rather cynical observation, the significance of the contradictory state of the media in the Second Republic is that there was a certain degree of media pluralism and diversity of viewpoints in the country.

Another dimension of liberal democracy covered in this book is the independence of the judiciary, the subject matter of Chapter 5. Under the doctrine of separation of powers, the three arms of government – legislature, executive, and judiciary - are held to function as checks and balances on one another to avoid the concentration of power in only one arm. Unchecked power, according to this doctrine, tends to lead to absolutism and arbitrariness, authoritarian streaks that are assumed to be antithetical to liberal democracy. As Zakaria argues, the "Western model" of democracy is best symbolized not by mass plebiscite but the impartial judge. This indicates that under this model, premium is laid on the impartiality of the judiciary. This book lays out the institutional structures and processes designed to safeguard and promote the independence of the judiciary in The Gambia. In its assessment, this book concludes that the Gambian judiciary has in many cases steadfastly maintained its autonomy against undue interference by the executive. In some other cases, however, it has fallen far short of what is acceptable.

At the core of good governance is the protection of fundamental human rights. This is a cross-cutting theme that involves the media and the legal professions. In different but interrelated ways, both the legal and media professions strive to defend human rights. Journalists expose human rights violations through the various mass media of communication, while lawyers work to seek redress for victims of human rights in the court of law. In Chapter 6, this book analyzes the concept of human rights from a broad perspective involving the conventional and the Islamic viewpoints. It examines the philosophical foundations, basic premises, and historical background of human rights. Despite variations in the conception, philosophy, history of human rights as well as differing cultural, religious, and political perspectives on human rights, this book concludes that there appears to be a consensus that regards human rights as not only inalienable but also sacrosanct.

A related theme is the role of legal education in fostering legal professionalism across Africa. In Chapter 7, this book argues that the legal profession derives its legitimacy from the institutions mandated to train legal practitioners – that is, law faculties and law schools. It is in these institutions that legal practitioners imbibe the requisite knowledge, skills, expertise, and ethical standards of the profession. Drawing on the specific case of legal education in The Gambia, this book calls for a re-evaluation of the inherited colonial legal curriculum with a view to adapting it to the socio-cultural contexts of Africa.

This book also, in Chapter 8, examines the role and place of traditional governance institutions in order to improve governance in West Africa. In Chapter 9, it maps out the challenges and problems which impede Arab-African alliance as a counter-hegemonic force against Western hegemony. A major remedial step it suggests is for

Arabs and Africans to develop a keen sense of solidarity that de-emphasizes politics of identity, and ethnic, regional, or ideological belonging.

A major revision in this revised edition is the addition of a new chapter - Chapter 10 - which argues trenchantly that sustained peace, stability and development in Africa remains a mirage without responsible leadership and effective governance. In a bold and elegant analysis, it makes the case that the Western and Islamic conceptions of governance share a common concern in their respective emphasis on the respect and protection of the dignity of the individual as well as their welfare and security. In this revised edition, the introduction and conclusion in the original edition have been converted into Chapters 3 and 9 respectively. In their places, a new introduction and a new conclusion are provided. The new introduction synthesizes the broad themes covered in the integrated essays which make up the substance of this book. The new conclusion sums up the main arguments.

Finally, the astute reader would notice that there are minor variations and similarities in style, tone, and mode of citation between some of the chapters of the book. This is due mainly to the fact that each chapter was originally published independently in a different peer-reviewed journal.

Aboubacar Abdullah Senghore, PhD
Istanbul, Turkey
January 24, 2024

1

Africa in a Changing World: The Major Governance Crisis in West Africa and the Way Forward

I.   Introduction

In the few years preceding independence and self-rule in Africa many Africans and their friends all over the continent and beyond had high hopes and expectations that with political independence and liberation there would be a lot of opportunities for the indigenous leaders to prove the worth and dignity of the African people. They expected the entire continent to enjoy the fruits of an effective economic and political governance system which would have ensured sustainable economic growth, lasting peace, and security and that eventually the African people would fully realize all the potential that God has bestowed on them. However, ordinary Africans are bewildered and seriously disappointed by the outcome of several decades of self-rule which is nothing but gross mismanagement of economic resources, rampant corruption, nepotism, political insecurity, decline of state power and authority, endless coups and coup attempts, abject poverty, military, and autocratic rule, overstaying in power and many more. These and other crises have dominated the economic, political, and socio-cultural environment in post-colonial and self-governing independent Africa. In fact, the crisis has now become the order of the day across the length and breadth of the continent. It is very obvious that the majority of West Africans have now lost or are losing faith and confidence in its political leaders and government systems. These disappointing results and experiences have indeed raised serious questions about the quality of the character, mind, and leadership attitude of the post-independent West African leaders.

The crisis, which also includes the absence of respect for human rights and the rule of law, as well as the absence of an effective system of transparency and accountability, has led many Africans and some critics of Africa outside the continent to believe and argue that Africans are incapable of ruling themselves. As such, they emphasized that the colonial powers may have opted out of the continent prematurely. In some respects, certain Africans are calling for or contemplating the return of the colonial powers to salvage the situation.

The most frustrating of all obstacles and problems of African governance are its persistent and chronic domestic conflicts and leadership crisis which have eventually weakened the foundations of the state in countries like Guinea Bissau, Liberia, the Cote d'Ivoire, and Sierra Leone.

Thus, this chapter critically examines the major crisis of governance in post-colonial West Africa, the impact of that crisis on the continent's development in a fast-changing world and the way forward for sub-Saharan Africa.

II.   Nature of the recent conflicts in West Africa

The vast majority of the conflicts in the West African sub-region are multidimensional and multifaceted, as they are either religiously, ethnically, or politically motivated or justified. It is very obvious that the Boko Haram problem and the crisis in northern Mali can be directly attributed to and associated with religion and religious reasoning and justifications. As for those conflicts that appear to be ethnically or even politically motivated they are also firmly anchored in religion and religious sentiments and justifications. If we look at the recent conflicts that took place in the Mano- River Region including the Liberian and Sierra Leonean conflicts and most recently the Ivorian conflict in which people were divided along distinct geographic or ethnic lines, we will find that religion is firmly anchored in the root causes of those conflicts. The geographic distinctions in some of the countries are mainly characterized by (i) a Muslim majority north with a small Christian minority and a Christian majority south with a small Muslim minority; (ii) indigenous Africans of a Muslim majority population or Muslims and traditional animists with a small Christian minority; (iii) a very organized and economically and politically empowered Afro-American or Afro- European Christian minority; (iv) a sizable group with a largely disorganized, uneducated and less developed Muslim majority; or (v) an indigenous African population of a Christian and traditional animist majority with a small Muslim minority. Consequently, it is fair to conclude that the root causes of the majority, if not all of the recent conflicts in our region, are constituted by a mixture of religious, ethnic, and political factors with the former taking centre stage.

However, these three dimensions of the causes of the conflicts in West Africa are interrelated and interwoven in a way that makes it absolutely difficult to distinctly separate them from each other and to be able to allocate fairly and proportionately an exact degree or percentage of the cause of a given conflict to one or the other. In many parts of West Africa particularly in those countries engulfed by the recent conflicts, you would observe that religion, ethnicity and politics are so interconnected and sometimes confused in a way that when one becomes the main cause of a conflict, the conflict will either be fuelled by, or it culminates into the other. Today all the ongoing conflicts, whether religiously or ethnically motivated, have culminated in politically motivated conflicts and characterized as such in the sense that they are transformed into leadership (political leadership) and governance crisis.

III.   The leadership crisis and its various forms

The nature of the leadership problems in West Africa and elsewhere across the continent keeps on changing from one form to another. During the few years that immediately followed independence, Africa was engulfed in destructive and senseless civil wars, whereas throughout the period of the Cold War the continent became a favourite playground for the superpowers. This unfortunate situation produced a unique brand of leadership problem for Africa which aggravated the continent's governance crisis. The leaders of this period gave priority to their own personal or individualistic interests on the one hand. On the other hand, they put the economic, political, and strategic interests of their foreign masters and allies above those of the indigenous people whose interests they were exclusively contracted to serve.

In some cases, the problems were systematic in nature. While some leaders introduced unpopular and failed Marxist economic policies without the consent of their people, others haphazardly pursued western capitalist economic models and as a result they horribly failed their people. There were other leaders, who by their style of leadership engaged their countries in senseless and destructive wars, as a result of which they ruined their national economies. Furthermore, those internal conflicts enabled the leaders concerned to loot their national treasuries, thereby exposing millions of Africans across the continent to abject poverty.

As a result of economic exploitation, political repression and the eventual failure of the social welfare and public service delivery systems throughout West Africa, millions of Africans are exposed to severe economic hardships, political instability, and socio-economic insecurity. Due to the crisis of the 1970s, 1980s and right to the end of 1990s, most economies in West Africa and beyond experienced dramatic decline and eventual collapse. Domestic conflicts and civil wars account for more than 70% of the leadership crisis during this period. In 2001, it was estimated that "there was war in at least one out of three (African) countries and there was only relative peace on the continent and the situation continued to be tense, either due to ethnic troubles or religious disagreements" (Al Mufruki, 2001).

The crisis highlighted above, though sometimes appearing in different forms, continues to exist together with other problems to the present day and they still obstruct West Africa's economic development and progress. These wide-ranging problems of governance in modern-day West Africa include the following: electoral malpractices, disputes over election results, persistent refusal by incumbent leaders to share power with political opponents, the spread of civilian-led autocratic rule and military dictatorships which block all means of democratic and peaceful leadership succession, military coups like the recent ones in Guinea Bissau, Mali, and Niger. Others are the unprecedented rise in the cost of living and basic commodities at a time when only four percent of national budgets is currently spent on agriculture, the dramatic increase in the cost of fertilizer, the continuous rise in the cost of fuel, the instances of daily power cuts because of inadequate generating capacity or the inability of the state to provide enough fuel for power generators, the absence of potential foreign investors from many countries in the sub-region due to poor infrastructure and communication facilities, and poor human rights records of governments across West Africa. The senseless war that Boko Haram is waging against the Nigerian federation represents a new method, level, and timing of religious and ethnic violence in the sub region. These and many more other crises continue to obstruct and sometimes derail the governing process in sub–Saharan Africa (Dowden: 2008) where the removal of entrenched autocratic civilian and military dictators has become a daunting task. Similarly, efforts aimed at the eradication or even substantial reduction of corruption, nepotism, favouritism, and other administrative malpractices have all turned out to be a formidable task holding back socio-economic development and progress in the entire West Africa sub region (Dowden: 2008).

IV.   Few successes

The democratic successes recorded by Ghana, Mali, and Senegal over the past decades recently in achieving democratic and peaceful leadership succession through free and fair electoral processes represent few but limited positive exceptions to the picture painted above. However, the democratic successes just referred to above could not be sustained or properly managed in some of the countries where such successes had occurred. At this juncture let us make a quick mention of recent developments in Mali, Nigeria, and Senegal.

Mali

Since Mali become independent from France in 1960, the West African country has suffered from various destabilizing events which include droughts, a series of coups, 23 years of military dictatorship, internal conflicts and rebellions spearheaded mainly by Tuareg rebels in the north and being completely saddled with a chronic budget deficit making it heavily dependent on foreign aid and remittances by millions working overseas. With all these problems the former Western Sudanese republic (now Republic of Mali) had made significant successes in food production and democratization. Mali is said to be self-sufficient in food production. This is mainly due to the fertile Niger River basin in the southern and eastern parts of the country.

Regarding democratization, Mali was able to break with its long years of military rule when it successfully conducted its first democratic election in 1992. Thus, the first democratically elected president of Mali took power in 1992 and since then the country's democratic credentials and development achievements have continued to grow from strength to strength until the 22nd of March 2012 when Africa's most senseless coup took place in that country. This coup has completely destroyed Mali's new democratic achievements. One of the reasons that make the coup puzzling and incomprehensible is that it came only a few weeks before the country's next democratic elections. The coup leaders justified their action by citing the country's inability to dislodge the Tuareg rebels in the north. In other words, the coup came in the wake of a series of losses suffered by the Malian army in the face of the Tuaregs, who were apparently strengthened following an influx of weaponry from Libya transported there by the Tuareg rebels who fought for Colonel Ghadafi until his death in 2011. (*"Timbuktu's Sidi Yahia mosque attacked by Mali Militants," BBC News, 2 July 2012; "Mali Tuareg rebels declare independence in the north," BBC News, 6 April 2012; Security*

The biggest question here is whether the new military rulers who were now heading to northern Mali have been able to reverse the series of losses the country's army had suffered before the coup, at the hands of the Tuareg rebels? The answer is obviously a definitive "NO"; in fact, the Tuaregs had registered significant successes in the days, weeks and months that followed the coup as a result of the confusion in which the Central government in Bamako has been thrown and which seriously weakened it. Demoralized and rendered ineffective by the absence of a strong, strategically focused, and capable political and military leadership, the Malian army continued to suffer significant losses until France decided to intervene.

Thus, on 6 April 2012, the National Movement for the Liberation of Azawad (MNLA) formed in 2011 mainly by armed Tuareg fighters returning from Libya, proclaimed independence. The MNLA fought together with the Islamist group Ansaradin virtually captured most of the territories in the north including the cities of ancient Timbuktu, Kida, Gau and other towns. It is worth mentioning at this juncture that the Tuareg rebels engaged the Malian army in a series of skirmishes in the vast desert of the nation during the 1960s, the early 1990s, and again in 2006.

To conclude, the 22 March 2012 coup has woefully failed to achieve its stated objective. Thus, as a result of the coup and the ensuing developments relating to the country's chronic leadership crisis, this vast West African country has again been condemned to its usual status of being one of the world's poorest nations despite being Africa's third biggest gold producer. The people of Mali have again suffered serious setbacks in their continuous struggle to end the ever-escalating militancy by the Tuareg rebels who took up arms demanding greater rights for their people since the 1960s and 1970s. As a result of the renewed conflict and the leadership crisis, the human rights situation in Mali remains dire with latest reports revealing terrible incidents of violations and atrocities against both sides; interference with the rights of individuals and groups, including the right to liberty and security of persons; the right to privacy; the right to freedom of movement, assembly, association, and freedom of speech; and other rights violations committed during the renewed fighting in the northern part of the country.

France and its allies have so far failed to bring back stability and return Mali to normalcy and to democratic constitutional rule, while the sub-regional grouping is still undecided about what to do exactly once and for all to end the crisis in that country.

Nigeria and the Boko Haram challenge

Boko Haram is the name of an armed Nigerian Islamist group that is working to implement Islamic law (Shari'a) throughout Nigeria. The meaning of the group's name in Hausa is "Western culture/education – is forbidden". Its full and official name is: *Jamatul Ahlis Sunnah lid Dawda wal Jihad*, meaning the People of Sunnah for Propagation and Jihad. Boko Haram maintains an 18-member Shura or Consultative Council, currently led by the group's Amir, Abu Bakar Shekau, who has two deputies. In addition, in every province in which the group has a presence, it has appointed an Amir for that province. Many of Boko Haram's ranks and files are poor Nigerian youths who have received mainly a religious education, and young people from the neighbouring countries of Chad, Cameroon, and Niger. Boko Haram is thought to be funded by wealthy businesspeople, government insiders, bank robbers and other clandestine groups in Nigeria (International Institute for Counter Terrorism: 2012). Most of its members were students who had abandoned their studies and gathered in northeastern Nigeria, near the border with Niger. Apparently, the group was established as early as 1995 at one of

Nigeria's universities; it became more established in 2002 when Muhammed Yusuf became its leader. Initially, the group did not support violence, but in late 2003 it began a comprehensive rebellion against the Nigerian federation. Boko Haram intensified and confined its attacks to police stations in Nigeria. In July 2009, however, Boko Haram waged a bloody five-day battle against the Nigerian security forces in retaliation for the latter's ruinous campaign to prevent Boko Haram from amassing any further weapons or power.

Muhammad Yusuf himself, and hundreds of his followers, were killed in this battle. Since 2009, Boko Haram has increased, refined, and diversified its attacks on Nigeria. Instead of one-off attacks, it has systematically begun to attack government institutions, security forces, innocent people and the Christian community using explosive devices, guerilla warfare, assassinations, and suicide attacks in public places like mosques, churches, markets, educational institutions, and offices. Boko Haram's stated aim is to overthrow what they describe as a secular regime in Nigeria. It is important to point out at all this juncture that many of those who promote and call for secularism including those who believe that they are secular do not understand the real meaning of the term secularism. According to Al-Attas one only becomes secular when religion ceases to influence one's language and mind. In other words, when religious teachings and concepts do not appear in one's daily language or influence one's thinking (Al-Attas: 1993).

Beginning in July 2009 and up to 2013, the group committed about 200 attacks, killing more than 1000 people. Although its attacks have up to date been centred in northern Nigeria, many fear that it will also infiltrate southern Nigeria, where the majority of the population is Christian. This conflict could eventually reach other parts of West Africa if it is not comprehensively addressed by Nigeria, and perhaps with the support of ECOWAS, the AU, and similar supranational institutions.

Senegal

Senegal is one of the most stable and peaceful countries in West Africa. It is the only country in the sub-region that has not experienced military rule since the country became independent from France in 1960. However, Senegal was, shortly before its last presidential elections in 2012, absolutely engulfed in a wave of political unrest which seriously threatened the country's unbroken democratic record. Coming from a sub-region where presidents seek to be crowned kings or life presidents, it was not surprising at all to see the former president Abdoulaye Wade strongly pushing to break in 2011 the two limits imposed by the constitution sometime to enable him to run for a third term in office as president. Interestingly, when Wade was in the opposition he happened to lobby successfully for a term limit for the presidency. Unfortunately for his country, Senegal's Constitutional Court declared Wade eligible to stand for a third term. This manipulation of the electoral process by the president through amendment of relevant laws and support of the country's Constitutional Court was the reason why political violence broke out in that country in the form of street protests, skirmishes and confrontation between the opposition and the police. Former President Wade's manipulations of the electoral processes in order to stand for a third term constituted a serious violation of Article 23 of the African Charter on Democracy, Elections and Governance which deals with illegitimate change of government.

This issue is further discussed below. The people of Senegal stood firm and chose to reject decisively Abdoulaye Wade's third term bid, and this provided Senegal the golden opportunity to regain its long-standing status of being the bright star of African democracy, with an unblemished record of peaceful presidential transitions since the country gained independence from France in 1960.

It is believed that Senegal has been so fortunate, unlike many West African countries, simply because religion has not in any serious way divided the Senegalese people both in politics and society. There are no tensions between Muslims, Christians, and traditional animists in Senegal, notwithstanding that the West African nation is predominantly Muslim and that its entire Muslim population is united under or behind strong traditional Islamic leaders. Furthermore, its pioneering president who ruled the country for 20 years was a Christian despite the fact that the country is predominantly Muslim. To conclude, the 2012 political and leadership crisis in Senegal and the extent to which they took the country have shown the depth of the seriousness of the fragility, unpredictability, the vulnerability, and un-viability of the processes of democratization and the democratic achievements and the political stability and security of the West African international political subsystem.

Finally, there is a general tendency on the part of many African analysts of viewing Africa's problems in terms of the excesses of individual dictators and autocratic leaders and their wrongdoings. They argue that it was these irresponsible leaders who turned several parts of the continent into killing fields in senseless wars and that only their removal from power, preferably through democratic and peaceful means on a sustainable basis, can make a difference. In other words, a change in government through democratic means is the main pre-requisite for making a fresh start and for attracting foreign investments and economic aid crucial to rescue their economies (Tunde Obodina: 2000). In 1996 alone the international humanitarian mission to Africa cost more than 3 billion US dollars whereas only one third of this money could have been used to address comprehensively the entire economic and developmental problems of the warring countries, while the rest of the money could do a lot of good things towards solving not only the problems of the sub-regions but also tackling the continent's entire economic and development challenges. These analysts focus their minds only on how the continent's inept leaders can be removed from power without critically examining this concept of change in leadership in Africa through democratic means.

The fact of the matter is that there have been changes of leadership, democratic or otherwise, in various West African countries and beyond but the governance crisis either remains intact or becomes worse. In the West Africa sub-region, Nigeria alone has changed the country's leadership for about 12 to 13 times since independence but to no avail. There have been changes of leadership elsewhere in West Africa such as Mauritania, Senegal, Mali, and Guinea Bissau, just to name a few. Despite such changes of leadership in these countries and elsewhere in our sub-region, governments remain corrupt and ineffective as the pace of economic development becomes slower than ever before. Thus, the notion that removing a set of crooked leaders in West Africa is the way forward to solving the sub-region's chronic governance crisis is not precisely correct. In fact, as explained above, removal of inept leaders in many countries only succeeded in shifting power to another set of more corrupt, inept, and ineffective leaders. Let us take Guinea Bissau as an example:

Guinea Bissau

This small actor in the West African International Political Subsystem has so far been the most unstable and underdeveloped territory of the countries of Africa south of the Sahara desert. It appears that Bissau Guinea is not only a failed state but worse than that because it looks as if the foundations of statehood have never been fully established in the country.

According to Article 1 of the 1933 Montevideo Convention on the Rights and duties of states, a territory can only become a state or qualified to be a state when it fulfills the following criteria:

- Definite territory
- Permanent populations

- Stable and effective government
- Legal independence or capacity to enter into legal relations and obligations with other states and non-state actors as well.

Thus, stable and effective government is what the people of Guinea Bissau have not enjoyed since the advent of independence on 10 September 1974. The West African sub-system has also woefully failed to stabilize the situation in Guinea Bissau and therefore becomes unable to help its people establish and maintain the foundations of statehood, the pillars and principles of sustainable democracy and development. This country is probably the only West African territory which had militarily engaged its colonial masters in a prolonged war of independence that lasted for 13 years before its people unilaterally proclaimed their independence in 1974. Since that historic moment, the former Portuguese colony has been going through successive waves of internal conflicts, violence, and insecurity. Bissau Guinea has experienced a period of autocratic and dictatorial rule, four military coups, a civil war, the gruesome murder of its independence leader Amilcar Cabral early in 1974 and four military chiefs of staff and a series of interventions by the West African sub-system. This is a country where no democratically elected leader has ever completed their term in office. After the independence leader Amilcar Cabral was assassinated in 1973, he was succeeded by Luis Cabral who was also overthrown in a military takeover in 1980 led by Joao Bernardo Vieira, the country's longest ruling president. Vieira was also overthrown by the military in the aftermath of another bitter civil war from 1998 – 1999. Vieira bounced back in 2005 when he contested and won the presidential election as an independent candidate. However, he was assassinated in March 2009, and replaced by Malang Bekai Sanyang after winning a presidential election that year. Unfortunately, this president died of a long illness two years after his election. Besides its dark historical past and political instability, Guinea-Bissau is rendered more fragile by a weak economy. It is listed among the poorest countries in the world, with more than 70 percent of the population living on less than US$2 a day. It also has some geographical challenges with over 80 islands in addition to the mainland making it easy prey for drug cartels which have transformed the dysfunctional nation into a narcotic-state (A. Sanyang: 2012).

The efforts of ECOWAS to ensure stability and democracy in Guinea Bissau were dealt a final blow on 12 April 2012 when the military staged one of Africa's most senseless coups in modern times. Following the death of the country's President Malang Bicia Sanyang, a democratic election was held on 18 March 2012 in which the former Prime Minister Carlos Gomez Junior took a slight lead but fell short of the needed majority. Thus, as he and the people of Guinea Bissau, West Africa and the rest of the world were waiting for the second round of election slated for April 2012, the military irresponsibly, irrationally and in total disregard of the authority of the African Union, the ECOWAS and most importantly that of the United Nations, interrupted the democratization process which was expected to confirm the country's commitment to not only stability and political security but also to asserting its democratic credentials (A. Sanyang: 2012)

The 12 April 2012 military coup was immediately and strongly condemned by large sections of the international community including the United Nations through its Secretary- General, the Security Council, and its Peace Building Commission (which has Guinea- Bissau on its agenda, alongside with Burundi, the Central African Republic, Guinea, Liberia, and Sierra Leone). The United States, the European Union, the Community of Portuguese-speaking countries, Canada and the continental powerhouse, South Africa, also condemned the coup, while the World Bank and the African Development Bank suspended millions of development programmes in the country, to increase pressure on the military leaders (A.

Sanyang: 2012) Up until April 2013, the West African grouping, ECOWAS, had not been able to put Guinea Bissau back on track. Although the concept of change in leadership particularly through democratic and peaceful means cannot and should not be totally rejected or discredited, it is high time for researchers and analysts in governance affairs in West Africa to start looking for and focusing on other alternatives.

V.   Cause of the crisis

Political and economic integration whether at the regional or sub-regional levels could be viable alternatives to the proposed idea of change of leadership discussed above. Similarly, constitutional, legal, and systemic reforms and increasing civil society involvement are equally important techniques that could be played to minimize the leadership problems of the sub-region. But like the question of change in leadership, integration alone may not be the key to solving the problem of bad governance in Africa. However, whether we are focusing on change of leadership, or focusing on political and economic integration, or constitutional, legal and systems reforms, or on all and other proposed solutions, we must have a consensus first on the real causes of the crisis. Some writers on African affairs put the blame for the continent's persistent mismanagement, bad governance and under development on ignorance and lack of capacity for effective management and good governance (Obodina, 2008). They explain that this is the reason why there has been a proliferation of capacity building programmes initiated by donors and multilateral agencies over the past decades. The aim of those programmes, this view argues, is to help African countries put in place structures and reforms that will strengthen the rule of law, enhance support for democratic systems and promoting greater accountability and transparency as well as ensuring good governance. This is because the different actors involved believe that poor governance anywhere is due largely to incompetence, ignorance, and inadequate infrastructure and for this, West Africa is not an exception.

While nobody can dispute the fact that bad governance, poor administrative skills, weak judicial systems, inadequate basic infrastructure, and inadequate expertise in almost all fields of development have contributed immensely to the governance crisis in the sub-region and in Africa as a whole, it is also important to acknowledge the fact that these shortcomings are not the main causes of the problems. They cannot explain the instances of constant abuse and misuse of state powers and authority in West Africa. As Tunde Obodina aptly argues, Nigeria for instance, "has a large number of highly trained professionals including accountants and constitutional lawyers" (Obodina: 2000). The same thing applies to Ghana, Senegal, the Cote d'Ivoire, and other countries of the sub-region. There are laid-down budgetary and financial procedures, adequate constitutional and legal guarantees for checks and balances to function and similar facilities on the ground but despite all this, rulers and political leaders in the sub-region have in many instances ignored the provisions of the constitution and the laid-down financial and administrative procedures which were supposed to guide them in the actual working of government.

Thus, abuse and misuse of state powers and authority are, not to a very large extent, due to lack of capacity and knowledge to ensure good governance. African rulers have not been ineffective, inept, corrupt, and tyrannical because they are ignorant or untrained, or incompetent. Similarly, the lack of sufficient administrative or intellectual expertise to formulate and properly execute growth enhancing policies has not been the cause of the governance crisis (Obadina: 2000). African military rulers and autocratic civilian leaders have in recent years demonstrated remarkable political skills to undermine the opposition in their respective countries. They have been successful in tactfully sowing the seeds of confusion and disarray in the ranks of the opposition and eventually making them lose credibility in the eyes of the masses. In some instances, African leaders by demonstrating great political sophistication through the democratic process have peacefully eliminated their political opponents.

Furthermore, the millions of African intellectuals who studied in various foreign universities across the globe and those of them who are working in international organizations and for foreign governments are always outstanding in their respective fields of specializations and experience. It is therefore fair enough for us to conclude that many of the bad economic policies, failed political systems and actions that had entrenched many countries in West Africa in economic under development were deliberately designed and implemented to serve the interests of those in power (Obadina: 2000) The military rulers and civilian autocratic leaders in the sub-region have benefited and are still benefiting enormously from the economic misfortune and the under-developed status of countries across West Africa.

Thus, it would be a great mistake to conclude that West African "political leaders and their advisers are a bunch of idiots, untrained and inexperienced crooks who are ignorant of politics and governance". (Obadina: 2008). This discussion raises a very important question at this juncture - that is, what then is the real cause or reason for this unfortunate situation in West African politics and governance? Why have West African countries been entrenched and engulfed in deep and chronic governance crisis since the beginning of self-rule in the early 1960's to the present day?

To answer this question properly we need to examine the nature and extent of the special interest that the rulers and political leaders had come to serve. In other words, the failure of democracy and economic development in Africa as whole is due mainly to the scramble for wealth and power by the content's political elites who have dominated African politics since the advent independence in the mid-20th century (Obadina: 2008).

According to governance experts in West Africa the sub-region's political elites see political power and the seat of president as a source of personal prestige and wealth accumulation. For them, power and authority are a source of enjoyment, prestige, and wealth accumulation rather than a source of responsibility and accountability. There is high premium on the control of the seat which is the biggest and most easily accessible source of wealth accumulation (Obadina 2008; also A.A. Senghore PhD 2010). That is why when our politicians seek power they use all means to attain their goal and when they get it they resort to all means and techniques that would guarantee their stay in power for as long as God wishes. Such means and techniques would include hand picking and employing people from the same ethnic, religious, or geographic group so as to consolidate their political position on one hand and orchestrating ethnic sectarianism and political repression to distract the attention of the critics at home and that of the international community on the other. This analysis clearly indicates that the real reason for the governance crisis in our sub-region is deeply rooted in the attitude of the people concerned including the successive political leaders in various parts of the sub-region and beyond. This makes the problem more complicated and more difficult to solve. Despite the availability of different factors such as capacity, knowledge, and infrastructure to ensure good governance, the situation has not changed. West Africa does not lack the necessary facilities to ensure good governance which simply means "the effective exercise of power and authority by government in a manner that serves to improve the quality of life of the populous" and which includes the full development of individuals and of their capacity to control their lives (Obadina: 2000). The real cause of the tragedy is that we have a ruling class in our sub-region which "sees the state solely as a means of expropriating the nations' limited resources" and this class is simply incapable of good governance. So long as the ruling class in West Africa and other people in and outside government continue to be motivated by objectives that have very little to do with the common good of the people, governance and economic crisis of the sub-region and elsewhere across the continent will continue to exist. In fact, the ruling elites will, by their character and mission, continue to abuse and misuse the seat of president, the position of power and authority and apply all available methods and techniques including political repression, corruption, electoral malpractices, introduction and application of draconian laws and ethnic separatism to maintain the status quo which has always been bad governance, under development and maladministration.

The impact of the governance crisis on the development of the subregion

The West African subregion has experienced profound leadership crisis over the past two decades. The four countries of the Mano River Union i.e. Liberia, Sierra Leone and Guinea together with Cote d'Ivoire (which used to be the economic powerhouse of the sub-region) have gone through serious conflicts and severe crises which literally destroyed their economies and eventually brought down the state as a whole. Thanks to systematic military interventions by the Economic Community of West African States (ECOWAS), the United Nations and France, the conflicts were militarily brought under control. Given the central position of the Cote d'Ivoire in West Africa, as it used to be the economic powerhouse of the sub-region, the conflicts there left wide ranging severe economic and political consequences not only for the country but more importantly for its neighbouring states and for the whole of West Africa. Indeed, Cote d'Ivoire shares more than 3000 kilometres of land frontiers with five West African countries. The states directly affected are Burkina Faso (584 KM borderline), Ghana (668 KM), Guinea (610KM), Liberia (716KM) and Mali (532KM). More than 4million of the 16 million inhabitants of the Cote d'Ivoire during the civil war were immigrants or descendants of immigrants from those neighbouring countries. About a half of these 4 million immigrants were from Burkina Faso (2.5 million) whereas more than one million of them originated from Mali. Similarly, there were 300,000 immigrants from Guinea, 200,000 from Ghana and 100,000 from Liberia. Countries such as Senegal, Nigeria, Niger and Mauritania and other nations also had many of their nationals living in that country (A UN report 2004). This is why the Ivorian conflicts left serious impact on various national economies of the West Africa sub-region. It was by all standards a sub-regional conflict directly or indirectly affecting the whole of West Africa.

This is because the new environment generated by the Ivorian conflict continues to affect the dynamics of economic cooperation and regional integration among the key actors in the sub-region, particularly the Francophonic countries. This large number of immigrants from all over West Africa, who had settled in the Cote d'Ivoire from all over West Africa, had to be on the move or become economically nonproductive as a result of the war. Consequently, hundreds of thousands of families and millions of people who relied on those immigrants for their daily subsistence were rendered helpless and they had to experience unprecedented economic hardship.

The economic impact

According to a 2004 UN Report on the economic, political, and humanitarian impact of the Ivorian conflict across West Africa, the crisis threatened the entire socio-economic fabric of the sub-region. This is because the Cote d'Ivoire was the second largest economy after Nigeria in ECOWAS and by far the most prosperous country in the West Africa Economic and Monetary Union. It is the principal gateway to the world for landlocked countries like Burkina Faso, Mali, and Niger.

In terms of revenue generation, Cote d'Ivoire represented a substantial source of income for many West African countries whose expatriates form important communities in that country. According to the UN report before the outbreak of the civil war in September 2002 "migrant workers from Burkina Faso in Côte d'Ivoire, sent home about 70 billion CFA Francs in remittances each year." Other countries such as Mali, Senegal and Niger drew important revenue from the same country. As indicated by the then Governor of the Central Bank of the eight Francophonic West Africa Monetary Union, the Ivorian leadership crisis is a major source of "macro-economic instability for the entire West African Monetary Union and that the uncertainties it raises has derailed the dynamics of integration. (The UN report: 2004). In addition to the monetary consequences of the Ivorian crisis, its economic impact in West Africa is also strongly felt in the areas of business, trade, and other commercial transportation, particularly with regard to landlocked countries of Mali, Burkina Faso and Niger which were heavily dependent on Abidjan, the second biggest harbour in West Africa.

Before the crisis more than 85% of the external trade of these countries passed through Abidjan. Likewise, 57% of total imports of those countries were shipped through Abidjan. Similarly, the Ivorian capital was before the war, a major air transit point for flights shuttling in and outside the sub-region particularly those bound for the Middle East, Europe, Southern Africa, Asia, and Latin America and elsewhere across the globe. As a result of the war both sea and air traffic across the sub-region had to be re-oriented. Thus, Abidjan had to lose its supremacy as the central sea and air hub in West Africa. Another negative impact of the crisis on the national economies of the sub-region was the sharp decrease in intra-regional trade and business between Cote d'Ivoire and its neighbours. The annual percentage of exports from Cote d'Ivoire to the sub-region and of imports into the country from around West Africa had significantly dropped from 13.43 – 5.20 and 169.37 32.18 or 421.11 – 288.49, in some cases respectively.

Political crisis

Finally, the civil wars and internal disturbances caused by the leadership crisis in other West African countries like Sierra Leone, Liberia, Guinea Conakry, and Guinea Bissau had in the same way left negative consequences on various national economies of the sub-region. I now move on to the next section which examines integration as the way forward for the sub-region to once and for all overcome its chronic governance and leadership crisis.

Regional integration as the way forward

While there is a high degree of consensus among academics, researchers, governance and political experts in West Africa that political and economic integration for the sub-region could be a good and a very effective way of resolving its long standing and deeply rooted leadership crises and also that African integration is at the moment more realistically achievable at the level of various sub-regions such as the case with the ECOWAS, there could be serious challenges to the realization of integration. Thus, this section first examines the challenges and obstacles to the realization of the proposed political and economic integration project for West Africa and for other sub-regional grouping elsewhere on the continent.

Obstacles to African integration

VI.   Colonial legacies

The advent of independence from colonial rule around the middle of the 20th century did not usher in a complete break with colonial institutions and legacies. One of the most difficult obstacles that impeded Africa's integration in the post-colonial period is the impact of different legacies left behind by colonial powers. English and French colonial rules, for instance, left behind their respective legacies in the legal and economic systems, political institutions, and other aspects of Western civilization. The existence of bitter rivalry and imperial ambitions among European nations and rulers seeking to occupy different portions of African territories resulted in the apportionment of the continent by the colonial powers into so many colonies, protectorates, and settlements. Since the colonial powers came from different socio-cultural backgrounds, spoke different languages, and followed or applied different practices and systems of government and administration, it was inevitable that they would leave behind different legacies in their respective colonial territories. These differences in their colonially inherited values and systems impeded efforts aimed at nation building, economic progress, and political integration on various parts of the continent. Issues like language and colonial partition of territories constituting the same geographical, historical, and ethnic region and planting the seeds of separatists' movements in some regions are among the Western colonial legacies that continue to effectively prevent any form of serious economic and political integration across the African continent. Let us take the Senegambia Region and the State of Cameroon as examples.

32

Senegambian integration: A lost cause

Senegal and The Gambia constitute one natural geographical unit, they belong to the same geographical, historical, cultural, and ethnic region given that Senegal actually sandwiches the tiny but naturally beautiful Republic of The Gambia. The two entities therefore have every opportunity to be united and as Awasom aptly argues "The Gambia is right inside the belly of Senegal and nowhere else is union more required and easier to achieve in Africa than between these two States given that almost every Gambian has a Senegalese blood relative" (Awasom 2006: 94 – 95). But due to marked differences in their colonially inherited values and legacies i.e. languages and economic and political systems, the question of union between the two states has proven to be out of the question. The Senegambia region was carved into two distinct territories by the French and British colonial authorities in 1889 and placed under separate administrations (Awasom 2006: 95).

During the few years that preceded the Gambian independence, many efforts were made on both sides to integrate the two entities and such efforts were apparently supported by the two colonial powers particularly Britain. But such efforts ended in vain because the parties were not prepared to make the sacrifices necessary for the success of such a laudable venture. Gambians were not willing to surrender certain principal areas to the proposed union executive. They made it clear that in the event of union with Senegal the key areas of internal administration, the police, the civil service and local government matters, the legal and educational systems, and the question of maintenance of close ties with Britain and the Commonwealth were to remain under Gambian control (Awasom 2006: 97). Senegal too was not prepared to part with any of the main colonial values it has inherited from France for the sake of a union with The Gambia. On the other hand, one could also ask whether Britain was really genuine in her support for The Gambia to be united with Senegal. This is because The Gambia achieved its independence from Britain in 1965 and full sovereignty with republican status in 1970 without the question of integration with Senegal being given a definite answer or addressed in any concrete form.

Thus, despite signing dozens of collaborative treaties by the two countries since The Gambia became independent in 1965 and despite making a concrete attempt to establish a form of loose union between them in 1982, that was when the Senegambia Confederation was formed, Senegal and The Gambia are still far apart. As the two countries continue to guard jealously their respective colonially inherited values and systems, there is, as yet no sign of readiness and sincere commitment on both sides to integrate into a single union republic.

The case of Cameroon

The State of Cameroon was subjected to the same European experiences starting from the last quarter of the 19th Century when it became a German protectorate in 1884. Awasom explains that "during the First World War in Africa, German Cameroon was conquered by the Allies and divided disproportionately into the British (Western) and French (Eastern) spheres" with Britain acquiring just one-fifth of the territory formally occupied by Germany (Awasom 2006: 90 – 92). Many of the ethnic groups of Cameroon who are separated by the Anglo-French partition of the country are situated on both sides of the territory particularly in the Anglophone North-West and South-West provinces and the Francophone West and Littoral provinces (Awasom 2006: 91) Thus the Anglo-French partition of Cameroon and the differences in their colonially inherited values and systems have created difficult identity crises, which pose a serious threat to efforts aimed at nation building, economic progress, maintenance of peace and order and sustainable development in that part of Africa.

The experience of other African countries

In North-East Africa, Somalia and Sudan were subjected to similar European colonial or imperialist experiences. Somalia was partitioned into five territories namely, British Somaliland, French Somaliland, Italian Somaliland, the North Frontier District in Kenya, and Ogadin in Ethiopia. This was followed by the Italian proclamation in 1936 of the establishment of Italian colony in East Africa, which was called "Africa Orientale Italiana" or the Italian East Africa. The move merged and reconfigured the territories of Eritrea, Somalia, and Ethiopia along ethno-linguistic lines into one colony (Zewde 2006: 54 - 55).

Elsewhere in Sudan, the British government, which was said to have supported the unification of Somalis, followed a diametrically opposite policy. There, Britain planted the seeds of separatism in Southern Sudan, which after independence became one of Africa's longest and most destructive civil wars. The British government effectively sealed off Southern Sudan from the Northern part of the country and the Northern traders were barred from the South. Their declared objective was to protect the Southerners from the habitual raids and exactions of the Northerners. In pursuance of this hegemonic policy, the British government excluded Arabic language in favour of Southern languages, and mother tongues, closed Islamic schools and banned Muslim preachers in the South. At the same time, Christian missionaries were encouraged and given every available opportunity to flourish in Southern Sudan.

However, it was later understood that the real objective of the colonial administration in Sudan was to stop the spread and prosperity of Islam in the South and also to sow ultimately the seeds of Southern separatism (Zewde 2006: 56). In this part of the continent religion was used by the colonial authorities to divide the Africans in Sudan and keep them apart. This policy, arguably, did not serve the interests of the two religions (Islam and Christianity) separating the two peoples in Sudan. Rather the policy only brought about confusion and misunderstanding among a people who belonged to the same ethnic, cultural, and geographical identity.

With southern Sudan achieving independence in July 2011, the war of independence, which was waged by the South against the North, was over and one would have thought that the two independent countries would now put their bitter and painful history behind them and lead their peoples into a new era of peaceful coexistence, good neighbourliness, and friendly bilateral relationship. However, it is very unfortunate, devastating and heart breaking to watch the South and North Sudanese begin a new era of wars and conflicts between their two sovereign states. This time is not a war of independence but rather a war or conflict over borderlines separating the two countries. It is another destructive war over who owns what territory and who should have a legitimate claim and sovereign right over a few oil fields and other natural resources along the borderlines separating the two countries.

Finally, the present configuration of the African continent into so many nation states is another legacy of Western colonialism, which like those highlighted above will definitely block any serious effort or attempt to actualize any meaningful form of Arab African integration aimed at making a united stand against Western hegemony. Thus, unless Arabs and Africans who happened to be victims of Western colonial rule are willing and morally prepared to break with the values and systems they have colonially inherited from the West, they will never be able to unite themselves and their efforts to effectively challenge Western hegemonic and imperialist policies against Islam and the Islamic world in particular and the African people in general.

Let us now move on to consider another difficult issue, which like colonial legacies will definitely be a major obstacle to Arab African integration as it has been proven to be in the past when efforts were made to achieve regional or sub-regional integration in many parts of the continent. That is the issue of identity and politics of belonging. This is what the next section explores.

VII.   Identity and politics of belonging

Ethnic and regional politics is an increasingly ongoing phenomenon in Africa's political processes. References to race, ethnicity, religion, political ideology, people of different backgrounds, district or province of origin have in many cases prominently featured in the daily languages of politicians and political elites, community leaders and the main actors of other interest groups in African societies. Trade unions, political parties, service delivery organizations, socio-cultural groups, economic interest groups and political and think-tanks on various parts of the continent have always been dominated by a particular ethnic, tribal or religious group or proponents of a given political ideology. In Africa today, the politics of identity and belonging has even entered the realm of the African academia. Some Cameroonian academics argued that democracy in Cameroon should be more of an ethnic right than simply an issue of one man one vote. That is because there are small and big tribes and small and big ethnic groups all over the continent. Thus, as a real entity, each of these groups should be taken into consideration in a well-conceived democracy. A Cameroonian academic argued that when a demographically superior ethnic group is part of the picture, there is a big temptation that in applying the principle of democratic free choice the ethnic multitude would express itself in favour of the strong ethnic group, which in this way would stifle those ethnic groups who are demographically weak (Mono Ndjona 1997: 102 – 103). The argument is that although it may be fair enough to recognize the one-man-one-vote democracy principle, this democratic principle would defeat itself when, through that vote, only one ethnic group expresses its hegemony. This amounts to self-contradiction since democracy in this sense would be serving the totalitarian interests of those it has enabled to raise (Nyamnjoh 2006: 236). Academics are among the cream of society not only in Africa but elsewhere too and if some of them are beginning to envisage a democracy of ethnic groups as long as those groups remains a reality, that shows how seriously the continent is affected by the politics of identity and ethnic belonging.

Many parts of Africa particularly, the North-eastern, Central and Western regions, have been ridden with inter-state and intra-state conflicts since the beginning of the second half of the last century due mainly to the clash of identities and excesses of the politics of belonging. The Rwanda-Burundi conflicts, the wars that ravaged Liberia and Sierra Leone during the 1990s, the Eritrea-Ethiopia conflicts and the ongoing Darfur conflicts are good examples of inter-state and intra-state conflicts caused mainly by the clash of identities and the excesses of the politics of belonging. Somalia represents the most unfortunate case of all these conflicts. This is perhaps the only African country where the population is constituted by the same people (black Africans) speaking the same language (Somali) and they profess the same religion (Islam), follow the same school of thought in Islamic jurisprudence and located within one geographical unit.

Somalis are bound together by the necessary elements or values that constitute the major expressions of identity (i.e. religion, language, and ethnic origin). Thus, as it was observed regarding the Senegambia case, in Somalia too, I would say, 'nowhere is unity more required, urgent and easy to achieve in Africa than in that country'.

Elsewhere-in North-East Africa, the conflict in the Western Sudanese province of Darfur is another unfortunate mark in African political history. Like Northern Sudan, the Western part of the country has a Muslim majority population, the so-called Arab African divide is invisible and where it exists it does not justify the war of unprecedented ferocity characterized by massive destruction of life and property and mass displacement of people and animal that the conflict has led to. Thus, the question as to "What unique identity or set of values are the warring sides in Darfur defending or protecting against each other" has not been and probably will never be satisfactorily answered. Similarly, identity politics lay at the root cause of the prolonged civil war that ravaged the Southern part of Sudan. Finally, with the politics of identity and ethnic belonging still raising its ugly head all over the continent, any meaningful form of Arab African integration aimed at making a united front to challenge effectively Western hegemony is very unlikely to happen.

VIII.   Arab disunity

With Arabs deeply divided over several key questions in international relations and world politics such as the Palestinian and Iraqi conflicts, the Arab-Israeli relations and America's attitude towards the Islamic World, the current Syrian conflict and the overall question of the legitimacy of the Arab Spring Revolution, the deeper involvement of the Arabs and the level of their commitment to efforts aimed at creating a continental or sub regional union executive, the level and the depth of their involvement in regional and sub-regional peace keeping missions/ operations as well as the crises in the level and the depth of the Arab's recognition of and commitment to their African identity and the question of how much priority they will give to the programmes of the proposed integration in relation to their local programmes particularly those that touch on culture and tradition, there is little hope that the Arabs will ever be in a position to form a continental or sub-regional union executive working hand in hand with their fellow Africans to face effectively the challenge of governance and development across the continent. The inability of Arabs to agree among themselves and make a united stand in the international political arena is one of the saddest stories of their contemporary history. Arabs are held by non-Arab Muslims in high esteem, they see them as role models and look up to them for an Islamic global leadership that will one day free Muslims, their political leaders and service delivery institutions from the conspiracies and hostile policies of European and Western hegemony. One would often ask why is it that the North Africans are still unable to unite themselves into one Great Maghreb Union despite the fact that they have every opportunity to do so. With the exception of Libya, the North African Arabs do not have different colonial legacies rather they were all colonized by France and therefore their colonially inherited values and systems are one and the same, they share the same language (Arabic / French), religion (Islam), ethnic origin (either Arab or Berber) and constituted by the same geographical unit. Despite possessing all the necessary unifying elements or values, which are the major expressions of a nation's identity, there is no sign of the North Africans' readiness or even willingness to form one Great Maghreb Union. The withdrawal by the Islamic Republic of Mauritania from ECOWAS and that of Morocco from the African Union some years ago are a typical example of the crises in the African identity of the Arab countries in Africa and the level of their commitment and reorganization of that identity.

Thus, unless Arabs particularly African Arabs are able to put their house in order, there is no hope of realizing any form of an Arab-African union, which can realistically stand up to face the enormous challenges posed by Western hegemonic and imperialist policies and conspiracies against the Third World.

IX.   The ineffectiveness of international organizations

There are many international inter-governmental and non-governmental organizations comprising various regions, groups, and cultures from across Africa in their membership. The existing organizations of this type, such as the Organization of Islamic

Conference, the Arab league, the African Union, and the Group of 77, the Eastern and Southern African economic groupings, the Sahel group etc. are all weak and ineffective actors in the international political arena that their voices are not heard of at all in the world's major political events. They cannot make any impact on or influence decisions and major events in the international system, neither can they shape major policies and processes of today's international politics and global governance.

Modern international organizations are playing a major role in the current international political system. The more usual image of the role of international organizations today is that of an instrument being used by members for the articulation of specific objectives. This is particularly the case with international intergovernmental organizations where members are sovereign states with powers to do many things to serve the interest of their respective people. Another important image of the role of international organizations is that they can be used as an arena or forum within which members can act in pursuance of their own interests. In this case, the organizations provide meeting places for their members to come together to exchange views and pursue their respective interests (Archer 2006: 68 – 96). Thus, in this modern age of global governance, international organizations do not only assist the functioning process of the international political system but also they are capable of bringing huge returns and benefits to their members. In conclusion with the type of weak and ineffective international organizations of Africa today, it is clear from the above exposition that there is little chance for them to be able to use those organizations as an instrument or arena for the articulation and eventual realization of their common objectives in the international political system. In view of this political reality of the African international organizations one may be justified to suggest that one important step in their drive to tackle collectively the difficult question of Western hegemony and imperialist policies and conspiracies against them is to strengthen those international organizations by way of giving the sacrifices and concessions necessary for the effective functioning of such institutions in the modern world. However, with the new directions that ECOWAS is taking today to address the critical questions of sub-regional peace and security, human rights, good governance and democracy as well as the question of legitimacy of the government of the day across the sub-region is giving West Africans a high hope that if things continue to work the way they are expected to go, West Africa may be on course to realizing a form of economic and political union for the people of the sub-region.

X.   Different faiths and beliefs

Another major issue which can be considered a critical and fundamental obstacle to the realization of African integration is the presence of different faiths and beliefs throughout the continent. Undoubtedly, the enemies of Africa and the opponents of African unity would definitely attempt to exploit the Muslim-Christian or other religious divide among Africans to perpetuate the hegemonic and imperialist presence of the former colonies and their allies on the continent. Notwithstanding that in some part of the continent, like the Senegambia region African Muslims and Christians have been living together in peace and harmony for several centuries.

XI.   Absence of political will and effective leadership in Africa

There is almost a total absence of sincere commitment, political will and effective political leadership in Africa including the Arab and the Islamic worlds which are closely interwoven with Africa and African affairs to organize the continent, or even West Africa into a viable force capable of challenging Western hegemony and European economic imperialism in the present international political system.
42

The former Libyan leader Muamar Ghadafi was known for his pan-Africanist tendencies and attitudes in the continent's modern-day politics and development drive. He loved Africa and the African people, and his country spent billions and billions of dollars in the cause of the continent's development and eventual unification. Ghadafi lacked the necessary support from his fellow African leaders and the necessary moral legitimacy and credentials to actualize the long-awaited dream of African integration and eventual unification. Most importantly, he missed the opportunity to actualize his dream of a United States of Africa. Now that Ghadafi is gone the continent is waiting to see the birth of new pan-Africanists who will succeed the likes of Nkrumah, Patrice Lumumba and Muamar Ghadafi of Ghana, the democratic Republic Congo and Libya respectively.

Political and economic integration can be pursued either through the intergovernmental or supranational approach. Under the intergovernmental approach there is no sharing of sovereignty, and each member state of the union effectively retains its sovereign authority, which means that each state can veto the application of regional agreements. This method requires close coordination of national policies of the integrating states. There is, however, one obvious weakness of the intergovernmental approach - that is, the lack of enforcement mechanisms to ensure that all states abide by the common rules. As for the supranational method, it implies arrangement under which member states agree to surrender some part of that sovereignty to the central authority. Under supranationalism sovereignty is substantially exercised jointly and that laws passed at the regional level over those matters on which the region has competent jurisdiction shall prevail over national legislation and they will be binding directly on member states and citizens of the union irrespective of their regions of origin. This is known as the principle of "direct effect". Supranationalism is a steppingstone to a federal structure or even a confederation. However, the EU experience envisages a more diversified political outcome in which power is shared at various levels and states interact in complex ways. It is neither a typical federal structure where state power and authority are concentrated at the central level, nor is it a confederal system which is a looser form of union. There is an obvious advantage for the EU model of supranationalism - that is, it ensures the democratic participation of stakeholders, the transparency of supranational decision processes and the accountability of regional institutions. In the absence of those balancing elements/factors, the supranational method will have the obvious weakness of shifting sovereignty to supranational bodies. This will definitely weaken democratic control of individual member states and strengthen the political influence of groups that are able to organize effectively at the regional level. This may have negative consequences for poverty and food security.

Whether West Africa adopts the EU model of supranationalism or the intergovernmental method, political and economic integration could do a lot of good for the entire sub-region. It is thus high time for Africa South of the Sahara Desert to take concrete steps towards integration. This is because during the long years of the African leadership crisis particularly in the 1980s, the continent has significantly been losing ground.

The economic and political situations are still fragile and too bad for Africa to regain the ground it has lost. Growth rates are still very low in many countries, poverty is still rampant and widespread, national economies of the majority of countries are fragile and therefore vulnerable to domestic and external shocks, domestic savings are very low, many countries continue to depend to a large extent on foreign products for their basic communities. There is gross inadequacy of support for, and poor management of the agricultural sector and the continent is still unable "to reap the full benefits of globalization – a process that could increase the resources available for productive investment that west Africa needs so badly (Alhassan Outtara, 1999) with the sub-region integrating its political and economic systems and institutions all those and many other problems could be a thing of the past. With political and economic integration becoming a reality in West Africa, government institutions and the entire governing process will be too big and sophisticated to be manipulated or dominated by the military, for a particular ethnic group or tribe or ideology or by a group of few corrupt politicians. Thus, military coups, civil wars, manipulation of the electoral process by ruling elites, political repression, economic exploitation of the masses, ethnic discrimination, overstaying in power and rampant and outrageous corruption and corrupt practices will soon be a history in West Africa. Political and economic integration if well thought about, carefully planned, and judiciously implemented and managed will definitely guarantee effective, efficient, transparent, accountable, and responsive governance process in West Africa. It will also ensure separation of powers, rule of law, an independent judicial process, respect for human rights and fundamental freedoms popular participation in the political process, equitable sharing of economic resources and sound macro-economic policies and good financial and management systems, political stability, food security and stable and rational regulatory and highly motivating framework supported by effective control and supervision mechanisms. The end result of all this will be the full realization of good governance and its accompanying benefits for both the public and private sectors. Thus, the main thesis of this chapter is that political and economic integration is the way forward for Africa's long standing and deeply rooted leadership crisis to be resolved once and for all. At present, integration is more realistically achievable at the level of various sub-regions and therefore the process can quite easily and smoothly move to the regional level.

2

Liberal Democracy and Governance in Africa: A Brief Critique

I.   Introduction

"It was not until the intensification of popular struggles for democracy in the 1980s that African scholars turned their attention specifically to the question of democracy on the continent" (Archie Mafeje: 1999).

According to Archie, the above is not to say there was no awareness of democracy prior to the 1980s, but rather for the purpose of highlighting the emergence of its dramatic proportion as a result of the growing euphoria for democracy among African scholars. Hence the clamour for liberal democracy by Africans was a somewhat reactionary attempt against the growing ruthlessness and despotic manifestations by many African governments with their actions devoid of any anticipated positive payoff of breaking from the colonial yoke. Such actions included the institution by many of one-party systems, characterized by limited rule of law, dwindling economies, growing abject poverty, domestic conflicts; the absence of popular participation, and where it exists, sometimes in the form of elections, they are marred by intimidation, fraud and so on. Consequently, the agitation for "second independence" as Ake puts it was all the more desirable by many Africans. It served as a catalyst for a more deepened call for democratic pluralism around Africa as the answer to the continent's governance vis-à-vis development problems. (Ake C. 1996).

However, as indicated above, liberal democracy was embraced by Africans to offer 'heavenly solutions' to Africa's governance and development predicaments. Therefore, against the foregoing, this chapter examines liberal democracy by highlighting its nature and form taking due cognizance of its practice in Africa. Second, it assesses the extent to which liberal democracy has delivered on its anticipated objectives in Africa amidst high hopes to restore the shattered anticipated development and prosperity that post-independence was meant to usher in. Finally, this chapter tries to suggest a possible solution to the existing problems of the systemic and the managerial aspects of African governance.

II. Liberal democracy as a system of government

- *Theoretical and conceptual background*

Democracy has been defined in various ways using different approaches. Seward argues that the best approach is to look at those countries known to be democratic and define the concept according to the main features of their practice (Seward 1994:6-2 1). For Beetham, who takes a different approach, the core principles of a democratic system are those embodied in the historical conception of democracy as "rule of the people" i.e. popular control or sovereignty and political equality (Beetham 1993:6). Conversely, according to Holden who constructs a conception of political democracy, inclusive citizenship and political equality are basic principles of a democratic system (Holden 1974:7-9). For his part, Seward develops the assumption that in a democratic system "all citizens are equal with respect to their right to decide the appropriate political course of their community" (Seward: 1994).

The definitions reviewed above seem to agree that there are four basic elements or core values of a democratic system – that is, equality, sovereignty, control, and inclusiveness. These include majority rule and participation, equality, freedom, consensus, coercion, competition, pluralism, constitutional rule and more. It is important to state here that the basic characteristics of democracy are just more than the three-core principles highlighted above. The pillars of democracy include:

• Free press

• Respect for human rights

• Constitutionalism

• Free and fair elections (regular)

• Separation of powers

• Popular participation

• Majority rule with respect for the minority

• Pluralism

With these entire pillars one can then argue that many political systems across the continent are, at least structurally, democratic. This definition of democracy has been re-emphasized by Western donors viz: IMF/World Bank since the 1980s when democracy in the sense of popular participation, good governance and respect for human rights including press freedom were a prerequisite for obtaining their assistance. It is based on this equality assumption that Seward develops a general defining rule of democracy "within the theory of democracy." Thus, according to this rule, "substantive policy and politics and administrative actions performed under substantive policy must correspond to the expressed preferences of a majority of citizens." In other words, there should be necessary correspondence between acts of a government and the equally weighted expressed wishes of citizens with respect to those acts. This is what Seward calls "responsive rule" and for him "a political system is democratic to the extent that and only to the extent that it involves the realization of the responsive rule" [Ibid].

The problem of the "responsive rule" definition is that it appears to suggest direct, rather than, representative forms of decision-making as the favourite. This is because direct decision-making processes are certainly more responsive than the representative forms. But in Africa in general and in West Africa in particular, what obtains is the representative mechanisms of decision-making. To remedy this shortcoming of "the responsive rule" definition, which he himself acknowledges, Saward identifies some core principles or minimal conditions and describes them as "the logically necessary conditions of democracy". These principles are basic freedoms, citizenship and participation, administrative code, publicity, and social rights. So, for a political system to be democratic at least from the liberal democracy point of view, it must observe and respect the basic freedoms of the individual and it also must have a common and standardized form of legal membership compatible with basic freedoms. There should also be appropriate codes of procedure for employees in public bodies, for decisions to be taken into effect and a constant formal process of public notification of decisions, opinions, arguments, issues, and outcomes of all these conditions or basic principles of democracy.

The author is more concerned with basic freedoms, popular participation, and publicity as a means of actualizing the right to freedom of expression and press freedom and as a way of characterizing democratic governance as a fundamental human right. This is because human rights, particularly press freedom, as basic components of democratic governance are always violated in various parts of the African continent. In fact, human rights violation is one of the major crises in African governance in contemporary times.

According to Seward, there is another view which believes that democracy, being the rule of the people by the people and for the people implies, in political terms, the right of the people to freely choose their representatives. In his opinion "a democratic administration is one in which the people, all the people, are enabled to express a free choice on all matters affecting them" (Seward 1994:6-21). However, it should be noted here that this view also recognizes the practical difficulty of operating a system of direct expression of the will of the people as implied by the "responsive rule" definition.

For Hague and Harrop, liberal democracy, particularly in contemporary times, means that citizenship is no longer an elite status but is now extended to the vast majority of the adult population. Likewise, today's democracies are representative rather than direct (Hague and Harrop 2004: 38-39). Thus, elections under this system are regarded as an expression rather than a denial of democracy. According to this view, the meaning of democracy in contemporary times is contrary to what the ancient Greeks viewed it to be. For the Greeks, elections were used as an "instrument of aristocracy"- that is, a "device for selecting qualified people for technical tasks which required an unfortunate departure from self-government" (Hague and Harrop 2004: 38-39). The modern meaning of liberal democracy also includes a system of government based on a liberal philosophy in which the scope of state powers is restricted by the constitution. Thus,

50

under liberal democracy the constitution is supreme and then followed by the legislature (ibid). This is a direct reference to the modern concept of the "rule of law" which emphasizes the supremacy of the authority of the law. The rule of law in this sense is one of the basic components and essential ingredients of democratic governance under the liberal democracy construction. According to the liberal democratic construction, both the rule of law and constitutional rule are essential for a system of government to be truly democratic, and the two principles are further explained below.

The rule of law

By the rule of law is meant the supremacy of the authority of the law that all people and institutions are equally subjected to the control and dictates of the law. The principle of the rule of law emphasizes the equality of people before the law and equal protection of the law, the legality of the administrative acts of the political authorities and fairness or constitutionality of the legal authority backing the legislative and administrative activities of the government of the day. In other words, it is not only enough to govern by law, but the law that is used to govern must be just, fair, and reasonable.

Constitutional rule

The principle of constitutional rule as a core element of a democratic system can only be effective if the constitution enjoys a supremacy status within the political system. The concept of constitutional supremacy teaches that the constitution is the supreme law of the land and all other laws, executive decisions, and administrative activities of the government of the day must be in conformity with the constitution; otherwise, they are declared null and void by a court of competent jurisdiction. This principle is established in Section 4 of the 1997 Constitution of the Second Republic of The Gambia. Constitutional supremacy also ensures a more conducive environment for the observance of the rule of law and the independence of the judiciary.

• A human right-oriented definition

The rights-based approach to defining democracy as a system of government is one which cherishes and advocates the principles of constitutional rule, respect for human rights and fundamental freedoms particularly freedom of expression and press freedom, respect for the rule of law, independence of the judiciary and the legal profession, free and fair participation of multiple political parties in the political life of the state, free and fair elections organized at regular intervals, direct or indirect involvement of the populace in the affairs and political process of their country, the principles of accountability and transparency, and separation of powers between the three main organs of government. These principles constitute the core values or characteristics of a democratic system. Thus, by democracy it is understood a political system that adheres to the principles of constitutional rule, respect for human rights and fundamental freedoms particularly, the freedom of expression and press freedom, respect for the rule of law, independence of the judiciary and the legal profession, free and fair participation of multiple political parties in the political life of the state, free and fair elections organized at regular intervals, direct or indirect involvement of the populace in the affairs and political process of their country, the principles of accountability and transparency, separation of powers between the three main organs of government. These principles constitute the core values and major characteristics of a democratic system based on the liberal democracy construction. This brief explanation of the nature and characteristics of liberal democracy as a system of government is necessary because it clearly shows that the problems of African governance are not originating from this system of governance. Rather, they are mainly due to the poor and irresponsible attitude of most post-independence African leaders.

III.   Democracy and Good Governance

• *Governance and Government*

While government refers to the machinery and institutional arrangements for the exercise of sovereign power for serving the internal and external interests of the political community, governance implies the process as well as the result of making authoritative decisions for the benefit of society (Mander and Asif 2004:11). Thus, governance means the act or process of governing, specifically, authoritative decisions and control (Webster's Dictionary), whereas governance is the interaction between formal institutions and those in civil society. Another definition describes governance as "a process whereby elements in society wield power, authority and influence and enact policies and decisions concerning public life and social uplift" (Mander and Asif 2004: 12). For the World Bank, governance is the way power is exercised in the management of a country's economic and social resources for development. Consequently, the term governance includes public sector management, accountability, the legal framework, transparency, and information. Many governments, international organizations, and multilateral and bilateral donor agencies including the Asian Development Bank share this World Bank's understanding of the notion of governance (World Bank Governance and Development 1992: 9 and Mander and Asif 2004: 12). Consequently, governance refers to "the exercise of economic, political, and administrative authority to manage a country's affairs at all levels. It comprises the mechanisms, processes, and institutions, through which citizens and groups articulate their interests, exercise their legal (or human) rights (and fundamental freedoms), meet their obligations, and mediate their differences" (Mander & Asif ibid). The act of exercising economic, political, and administrative powers of the state to manage its affairs at all levels becomes democratic when the exercise is conducted and the mechanisms, processes, and institutions through which such authority is exercised are created and functioned in accordance with the spirit of the basic principles of a democratic system identified above (Senghore 2010). In other words, a democratic government must be guided by a constitution, the principle of respect for human rights and the rule of law and free participation of citizenry in the government of their country. Modern international human rights conventions have guaranteed the right of every citizen to participate freely in the government of their country and to have equal access, based on non-discrimination, to the government and its services (Articles 2 1 of the Universal Declaration of Human Rights 1948 and 13 of the African Charter on Human and Peoples' Rights).

However, beyond defining the concept of democracy as a participatory system of government, the emphasis from the 1980s was on good governance, a concept that involves bottom-top participation from the election and empowerment of officials of the local governments to the legislature and executive. The free press is underscored to create an atmosphere of transparency. It is expected to inform and expose shady deals, corruption, nepotism, ineptitude, electoral malpractices, etc. It is therefore intended to play the role of a watchdog. Press freedom is therefore not only a basic component of democracy, but it is also a central element of good governance. This brings us to a very important question that needs to be addressed viz: What is good governance? Is it the same as democratic governance? And has liberal democracy been able to ensure good governance for post-independence Africa? (Senghore, ibid)

• What is good governance?

The above discussion on the nature of governance implies that governance has three major components namely, process, content, and deliveries. Factors such as transparency and accountability are included in the process, while values like justice and equity are included in the content of governance. The third element (deliveries) ensures that the citizens especially the poorest have the basic needs and live a life of dignity. It needs to be clarified at this juncture that being able to deliver does not by itself constitute good governance. There is no doubt, for example, that a dictatorship that delivers basic needs to the citizens is better than a dictatorship that does not, but this is not enough for a dictatorship to be termed as practising good governance (Mander and Asif 2004: 14-15).

Good governance, on the other hand, implies an administration that is sensitive and responsive to the needs of the people and is effective in coping with emerging challenges in society by strictly adhering to and implementing the principles of democracy discussed above. For the World Bank, good governance "is epitomized by predictable, open and enlightened policy making, a bureaucracy imbued with a professional ethos, an executive arm of government accountable for its actions and a strong civil society participation in public affairs and all behaving under the rule of law." This description of good governance by the World Bank obviously captures the democratic principles of transparency, accountability, participation, respect for the rule of law and separation of powers. The European Union believes that "in the context of a political and institutional environment that upholds human rights, democratic principles and the rule of law, good governance is the transparent and accountable management of human, natural, economic and financial resources for equitable and sustainable development" (Mander and Asif 2004:15). This envisages a situation where there are clear decision-making procedures at the level of public authorities, transparent and accountable institutions, the primacy of law in managing and distributing resources and capacity building for elaborating and implementing anti-corruption measures. The Government of the Netherlands adds the elements of security, decentralization, and participation of civil society to the EU's definition of good governance. It argues that good governance must allow "a responsible economic and financial management of public and natural resources for the purpose of economic growth, social development and poverty reduction in an equitable and sustainable manner, with the use of clear participatory procedures for public decision-making, transparent and accountable institutions, primacy of law in the management and distribution of resources, effective measures to prevent and combat corruption, support for leadership and empowerment of men and women," (Mander and Asif 2004:15).

These two definitions of good governance by the EU and the Government of the Netherlands substantially incorporate the principles and basic characteristics of democratic governance already alluded to. However, it is obvious from the exposition of both democratic and good governance that sometimes emphasis is laid on the managerial aspect of governance, while at some point the focus is on the systemic aspect. The former is a characteristic of the definition of good governance, whereas the latter is a natural outcome of the definition of democratic governance. Whatever the case maybe, for the government of the day to be both good and democratic, the two aspects of governance (systemic and managerial) must be adequately enforced. In other words, the system within which one governs must be based on the core values of democracy, while the style and manner of managing the resources and affairs of a country are not only transparent, accountable, or effective but also equitable and sustainable. However, it is important to note at this juncture that the system highlighted above can only be followed and exhaustively utilized if African leaders demonstrate positive and responsible attitude in the governing process of their respective jurisdictions.

• **Human rights and democracy**

In the modem art of governance, the linkage between democracy and human rights is not only real but is also genuinely crucial. The two are not necessarily the same but it is fair to say that any struggle for democracy, particularly in Africa, is, in essence, a struggle for human rights. Furthermore, human rights hardly exist, much less prosper in undemocratic societies.

Arat, for example, argues that "where a political system falls on the scale of democracy largely depends on the extent to which it recognizes and enforces civil and political rights. The more strongly civil and political rights are reinforced in a society the more democratic it becomes" (Arat 2000:2-4). The international human rights movement has, both in theory and practice, always emphasized democratic principles. The global and regional instruments have identified several democratic principles as fundamental human rights. These include popular participation, multiple political parties, freedom of expression and press freedom, and equal access to public services, periodic and genuine elections. Democracy is about these values, and they are also fundamental human rights. This explains why human rights basic values for a genuine democratic system of governance under the liberal democracy construction are.

In view of the above argument, one may conclude that democratic governance itself is a fundamental human right. To conclude, liberal democracy as depicted in this section is undoubtedly a sound system of governance and regardless of my criticism of the concept below democracy, if applied the way it is explained, could substantially resolve many of the current crises and complications of African governance. It follows from this exposition that the problems of governance in Africa are not as a result of the system of government adopted by the post-independence leaders, but they are as I have already alluded to, due to the attitude of leaders and politicians from all over the continent.

The section below briefly examines the nature and types of political and leadership crises in post-independence Africa.

IV. Nature of the governance crisis under liberal democracies in Africa

The nature of the governance problems in Africa keeps on changing from one form to another. During the few years that immediately followed independence, Africa was engulfed in destructive and senseless civil wars, whereas throughout the period of the Cold War the continent became a favourite playground for the superpowers, namely the United States of America and the defunct Soviet Union. This unfortunate situation produced a unique brand of leadership problem for Africa which aggravated the continent's governance crisis. The leaders of this period gave priority to their own personal or individualistic interests on the one hand. On the ither hand, they put the economic, political, and strategic interests of their foreign masters and allies over and above those of the indigenous people whose interests they were exclusively contracted to serve.

In some cases, the problems were systemic in nature. While some leaders introduced unpopular and failed Marxist economic policies without the consent of their people, others haphazardly pursued Western capitalist economic models and as a result they horribly failed their people. There were other leaders who by their style of leadership engaged their countries in senseless and destructive wars, as a result of which they ruined their national economies. Furthermore, these internal conflicts enabled the leaders concerned to loot their national treasuries and expose millions of Africans across the continent to abject poverty. As a result of economic exploitation, political repression and the eventual failure of the social welfare and public service delivery systems throughout Africa, millions of Africans are, today, exposed to severe economic hardships, political instability, and socio-economic insecurity. Due to the crisis of the post-independence period particularly during the 1970s and 1980s most economies in Africa experienced dramatic decline and eventual downfall (Al Mufruki, 2001).

Domestic conflicts and civil wars largely accounted for the leadership crisis of this period. In 2001, it was estimated that "there was a war in at least one out of three (African) countries and there was only relative peace on the continent. The situation continued to be tense, either due to ethnic and regional troubles or religious disagreements" (Al Mufruki, 2001).

The crisis highlighted above, though sometimes appearing in different forms, continues to exist together with other problems, to the present day and they still obstruct Africa's economic development and progress. Those wide ranging problems include the following: electoral malpractices, disputes over election results, persistent refusal by incumbent leaders to share power with political opponents, the spread of civilian-led autocratic rule and military dictatorships which block all means of democratic and peaceful leadership succession, the unprecedented rise of the cost of living and basic commodities at a time when only four per cent of national budgets is currently spent on agriculture, the dramatic increase in the cost of fertilizer, the continuous rise in the cost of fuel, the instances of daily power cuts because of inadequate generating capacity or severe shortage of fuel for heavy duty generators, the absence of potential foreign investors from many countries on the continent due to poor infrastructure and communication facilities, and poor human rights records of governments across Africa. These and many more other crises continue to obstruct and sometimes derail the governing process in Africa (Richard Dowden, 2008), particularly in those countries where the removal of entrenched autocratic civilian and military dictators has become a herculean task. Similarly, efforts aimed at eradication or even substantial reduction of corruption, nepotism, favouritism, and other administrative malpractices have all turned out to be a formidable task, holding back socio-economic development and progress in the whole of Africa.

The economic and political situations are still fragile and too bad for the continent to regain the ground it has lost. Growth rates are still very low in many countries, poverty is still rampant and widespread, national economies of the majority of countries are fragile and therefore vulnerable to domestic and external shocks, domestic savings are very low, many countries still continue to depend, to a large extent, on foreign products for their basic commodities and human rights violations and abuses are still rampant. There is gross inadequate support and poor management of the agricultural sector, and the continent is still unable "to reap the full benefits of globalization – a process that could increase the resources available for productive investment that Africa needs so badly" (Alhassan Outtara, 1999).

The democratic successes recorded by Ghana and Senegal recently and also Mali before its current political crisis in achieving democratic and peaceful leadership succession through free and fair electoral processes are few but positive exceptions to the picture painted above. There is a general tendency on the part of many African analysts of viewing Africa's problems in terms of the excesses of individual dictators and autocratic leaders and their wrongdoings. They argue that it was these irresponsible leaders who turned several parts of the continent into killing fields in senseless wars and that only their removal from power, preferably through democratic and peaceful means, can make a difference. In other words, a change in government through democratic means is the main pre-requisite for making a fresh start and attracting foreign

60

investments and economic aid crucial to rescue their economies (Tunde Obadina, 2000). In 1996 alone the international humanitarian mission to Africa cost more than 3 billion US dollars, whereas only one third of this money could have been used to address comprehensively the entire economic and developmental problems of the warring countries, while the rest of the money could do a lot of good things toward solving the continent's entire economic and developmental problems.

All these crises are happening under liberal democracies of various forms with periodic elections taking place everywhere across the continent. Thus, it is genuine to ask at this juncture whether the governance crises in Africa are as a result of the adoption of liberal democracy as a system of government in most part of the continent or such problems are originated in the negative and irresponsible attitude of leaders of post-independence Africa. The latter, as suggested by many governance and legal experts, human rights advocates, researchers, and academics from across the continent, are being described as the main cause of the governance and developmental problems of post-independence Africa (AA Senghore, PhD: 2010)

V. Democracy as an ideology or an instrument of social progress

"It is correct to generalize that after the collapse of the Soviet Union the majority of the world perceived democracy as an instrument of social progress" (Lumumba-Kasongo: 2005). This strong assumption includes Africans, too. However, this drive towards democratization, to be specific, liberal democracy has produced mixed results for Africa. Thus, at this juncture, it will be imperative to reflect on the democratic project in Africa. Many African countries, after independence, were engulfed in a wave of democratization as the perceived magic formula for the achievement of their development agenda, justice, freedom, equality, and economic independence.

However, there emerged stumbling blocks to the achievement of such grandiose ideas that were anticipated. As a result of ideological warfare between the Capitalist West and the Communist East (Soviet and the former Eastern Bloc), the democratic project was hijacked and as indicated above Africa became an ideological battleground for these competing powers. The institutions that were intended to serve this purpose for the achievement of justice, freedom, equality, and development were turned into agents of manipulation for the furtherance of their agendas. The resultant polarization contributed to the establishment of the most notorious dictators in Africa, including Idi Amin of Uganda, Mobutu of the Democratic Republic of Congo, and Eyadema of Togo (Lumumba-Kasongo: 2005). Also, and as explained above, the fulfilment of frequent renewal of mandate for legitimacy purposes as a democratic principle has proven to be another stumbling block to the sustenance of democracies in Africa. This, where it exists at all, it happens in the form of elections which are often marred by violence and often generates enough potential for a country to slide into conflict as was the case in Kenya in 2007 during its post-election skirmishes and in Egypt between 2012 and 2013.

Another challenge to this effort was the disintegration of an "independence consensus." This consensus cuts across ethnic boundaries and availed the independence movements around Africa a unified front to attain independence. However, this consensus broke up shortly afterwards and posed a serious challenge to the existence of the state itself and consequently the democratic project in Africa. This is clearly demonstrated by the bloody conflict in Somalia in the Horn of Africa and before in Liberia and Serra Leone in the Mano River Region of West Africa.

The objective of this enumeration, however, is not meant to be exhaustive, but to avail us the picture of the democratic process in Africa, and some of its challenges as a lead up to discussing the variants of liberal democracy.

VI. The liberal democratic imperative

The form of liberal democracy we have today may not, in fact, be synonymously represented by what has been propounded by the enlightenment philosophers. According to this small group of intellectuals, human actions should be guided by reason and underpinned by principles of liberty and equality. This whole idea of liberalism was to counter the widely held notions like divine kingship or absolutism. The questioning of such rulership was regarded as blasphemous. These awkward notions led to the birth of liberalism and subsequent institution of systems of government as counter measures against aristocratic and monarchical rule. Efforts at the institution of liberalism can be traced to the French and American Revolutions. Their resultant governments represent a prototype liberal government. It met stiff resistance from the royal houses or traditional monarchy. In the face of this resistance, nonetheless, it was able to mainstream itself by the end of the nineteenth century and since then has become the dominant theory of government, enjoying the endorsement of a myriad of the political spectrum.

However, it is worth noting that the symbiotic relationship between democracy and liberalism has not been an all rosy one, given their points of emphasis. It is argued that liberals are not necessarily democrats (Kilcullen: 2000). According to Kilcullen, liberalism, in its classical form, is highly individualistic and democracy is often viewed as a collectivist ideal concerned with the empowering of the masses.

In the early 19th Century, when liberalism was in its heyday, the term liberal democracy would have seemed paradoxical or even contradictory. Liberals were frankly against democracy, because they believe it was incompatible with freedom and that it was even more important than freedom (Kilcullen: 2000).

This shows a dichotomy between the two concepts. Notwithstanding, liberalism and democracy have all come to mean one and the same thing, thus the term liberal democracy (Bo Li, 1991): As for the meaning of constitutionalism, I can say that for the purpose of this chapter, the term refers to the system of representative democracy as propagated in and followed by the West and Westernized systems across the world.

Today, however, liberal democracy has become a household name around the world including Africa. The classical notions of liberalism provided suitable grounds for the emergence and adoption of liberal democracy around the world. The phrase liberal democracy can be best described as fuzzy, given the multitude of its variants that are practised elsewhere and in Africa. Furthermore, despite this problem of inconsistency in its philosophical foundation and basic premise, liberal democracy, both as a concept and a political system, has managed not only to survive but also to function effectively as a viable system of governance and administration.

The post-independence era saw a trying moment for Africans in terms of instituting governance systems. This was manifested by the fact that newly independent states adopted several forms of governance systems at given periods of their statehood. However, one thing that was certain was that liberal democracy came to outplay any other form of governance system. Hence, many governments began to cast themselves from the shadows of other competing ideologies they had bought into. However, if the embracing of liberal democracy in Africa was to salvage the failings of African governments, many have been disappointed.

Another factor was the position of the West in order for Africans to benefit from their aid and loans. It was widely lamented by the West, as espoused by World Bank policies, that Africa's underdevelopment and many other crises were because of lack of democracy and competitive markets on the continent. This impliedly shows that it is democracy that can bring prosperity and glory to Africa. This resulted in a 'wild goose' chase by Africans to institute democratic governance (i.e. liberal democracy). This was described by Michael Huntington as the third wave of democratization. These measures included the introduction of multipartyism, conduct of frequent elections, constitutional liberalism, and emphasis on rule of law, more economic liberalism, and creation of political parties to provide for popular participation. All these measures are to usher in renewed hope in the minds of Africans who have already or might be suffering at the hands of their incapable and ineffective leaders.

In the light of the foregoing, the critique will examine how African governments have delivered on such grandiose objectives that liberal democracy promises. Against that background, I will be looking at the processes and their ramifications to highlight the contradictions between the theory and the practice of liberal democracy and a subsequent discussion of its strengths and failures in Africa to propose, as already noted earlier, a possible alternative or solution that would address Africa's governance ills.

The twin ideals of popular participation and limited government are, in many African countries, under an increasing threat posed by the selfish and irresponsible attitude of leaders across the continent. Multipartyism as a fundamental tenet of liberal democracy that is at providing that framework for popular participation saw a widespread institution in Africa in the 1990s amidst the demise of the Cold War. This liberal tenet reinforces the classical idea that power to make government and rule lies in the hands of the sovereigns. This is deemed to enable the populace to hold their leaders accountable to the electorate. Therefore, multipartyism provides room for public discourse capturing a myriad of opinions that are held by independent people. This marks a leap in the democratization process in Africa.

However, despite this perceived leap forward in Africa's democratic transition, multipartyism has not developed to a stage where all political groups agree to compete with one another on a level playing field (Oliver de Sardan, 2000). Parties are created to partake in elections to avail citizens the choice to elect their rulers. However, election exercises in fulfilment of this basic tenet of liberal democracy, most often in Africa, defeat their purpose. The rationale of elections, serving as a check on elected officials, fails in many instances where these officials in essence become so powerful because they are actually chosen by invisible hands. This is manifested through governments personalizing state resources to influence election outcomes in their favour. However, it may be worth noting that this may not be a problem peculiar to Africa alone, but many democracies around the world. Cassen and Clairmont also expounded (cited in Kasongo, 2005) that the holding of multiparty elections is nothing, but a pretext aimed at qualifying them for the benefits of an already flawed individualistic system. African governments in their bid to curry favour with the donor countries give in to their conditionality, allowing for the West to plunder the crucial natural resources and African markets. Hence an election in Africa becomes a qualifying criterion for accessing donor money which has so far failed to solve any of the continent's chronic governance problems. The economic and political situations are still fragile and too bad for the continent to regain the ground it has lost. Growth rates are still very low in many countries, poverty and corruption continue to be rampant and widespread, national economies of the majority of countries are still fragile and therefore continue to be vulnerable to domestic and external shocks, domestic savings are very low, many countries still continue to depend to a large extent, on foreign products for their basic commodities. Thus, elections have so far failed to address or resolve the problems of governance in Africa.

Instead, elections have become sources of conflicts around Africa, as observed most recently in Kenya, Madagascar and almost Senegal and, early on, in Ethiopia. Also, political party support in Africa has always been galvanized along ethnic, tribal and regional lines. This

66

serves as a potential source of outbreaks of violence. The Kenyan post-election violence between the Kikuyu and the Luos, and the Shona and Ndebele case in Zimbabwe are a clear manifestation of ethnically and regionally charged politics in Africa. Election induced violence and political persecution are contributing factors for Africa's becoming the world biggest refugee generating continent. Thus, more than ten million of the world's fourteen million displaced persons are currently from Africa (US State Department Website). Another limiting factor to the realization of the rationale behind liberal thinking about elections is the high illiteracy levels in Africa, where the majority of electorate are illiterates, as in The Gambia and elsewhere in West Africa where illiterates constitute about 60% of the populace (National Census of The Gambia - 2003). Therefore, they cannot understand the programmes of their candidates. This simply suggests that they may be voting based on sentiments, which does not help in making a rational and informed choice or decision.

The biggest problem of the electoral process is that the outcome does not truly reflect the will of the people and that it always leads to establishing elective dictatorships. According to the leader of the then Green Revolution in Libya, the electoral process always culminates in the victory of a candidate with only a simple majority i.e. about 51% of the total number of votes cast. This is dictatorship established in the guise of a democratic process because the remaining 49% of the electorate who did not vote for the winning candidate would be governed by a government that they never like and never voted for but it is being imposed upon them. Al Ghadafi pointed out in the Green Book another serious flaw in the electoral process. According to him, the parliament as an arm of government instituted as a result of the electoral process is essentially established in the name of the people. Yet this underlying principle is in itself undemocratic since democracy means the power of the people and not power vested in elected members of parliament in the name of the people (Al- Ghadafi 2005- latest edition 2008).

Another fundamental tenet of liberal democracy is the rule of law. Liberalism espouses the avoidance of governmental tyranny through a limited government. This is to ensure that life, liberty, and individual properties are protected. However, these objectives remain a major challenge to African governments. Nevertheless, in the wake of the so-called "third wave" of democratization, Africans have tried to mitigate such problems with the adoption of liberal constitutions. However, this attempt is stifled by the growing tendency for personal government i.e. monopolizing power by incumbents. Constitutional amendments, promulgation of draconian laws, and the hounding of the media are tactics employed by such leaders. Also, the economic liberalist policies that are promoted by the West through their agencies, the IMF, and World Bank in the form of policies like the unpopular Structural Adjustment Programmes (SAPs) then, and now the European Union's Economic Partnership Agreements (EPAs) and Bush's Africa Growth and Opportunity Act (AGOA) are all exploitative instruments of the West in disguise. Given Bush's AGOA initiative, small countries like The Gambia, and other beneficiaries of the initiative, have little to profit from the venture. For instance, in the Gambian case, it is given a quota on all textile exports when, in fact, The Gambia hardly exports textile or if any, it exports on a very minimal scale. Also, the catastrophic SAPs and the calls by the IMF and the World Bank for African countries to open up their markets all wreaked havoc on Africa's economies. And by implementing such policies, people's fundamental rights are curtailed; for instance, access to basic necessities such as health, education, electricity, and water, thereby contributing to lower levels of living. The theory of economic liberalism advocates individualism which runs counter to the collectivist mindset of Africans. Collectivism has provided a social security system for many Africans. The ramifications of such development led to the disintegration of families that were led by one bread winner in the wake of the SAPs.

Liberal democracy, like all other systems, has both strengths and weaknesses. Meanwhile, the liberal democracy enterprise in Africa has succeeded in providing citizens with the platform for the exercise of their political rights, which range from participating in elections to selecting their representatives to exercising choice in belonging to associations. It is a more desirable outcome to authoritarian regimes. In furtherance of the ideals of liberal democracy a good number of sub-Saharan African countries have enjoyed debt relief under the Highly Indebted Poor Countries Initiatives (HIPC). Riding on the back of the strong commodities boom, African economies have been growing on average from 5-6%. Also, on the continent people are freer now than they were under the brutal regimes of Mobutu Sese Seko of former Zaire and now Democratic Republic of Congo, Hastings Kamuzu Banda of Malawi, Idi Amin of Uganda, and Emperor Bokassa of Central African Republic (Ake: 1996). In celebration of the foregoing achievements of liberal democracy in Africa, there is still much to be done. Thus, Claude Ake remarks:

Africans are seeking democracy as a matter of survival; they have the belief that there are no alternatives to this quest, that they have nothing I lose and a great deal to gain. This awareness has grown in recent years, as it has become more and more obvious that neither the indigenous political elites nor the multilateral development agencies are capable of dealing with the African crises. In so far as democracy movements in Africa get their impetus from the socioeconomic aspirations of people in Africa yearning for 'a second independence from their leaders', it will be markedly different from liberal democracy. In all probability, it will emphasize concrete economic and social rights rather than abstract political rights; it will insist on the democratization of economic opportunities, the social betterment of the people and a strong welfare system (Ake: 1996).

Africans in their rush to embrace liberal democracy coupled with economic liberalism have failed to model it to mirror African realities. These realities, as indicated above, include poor infrastructure, poor communication networks, high rate of dependency and the cultural realities like the African social networks. Economic liberalism advocates the withdrawal of the state from the activities of the market losing sight of the appalling poverty among Africans. Such withdrawals give the predatory corporations the leeway to maximize profit on the back of widespread misery. Illustrating this argument is the flow of oil in the backyards of the Niger Delta region of Nigeria, yet its people continue to be condemned in abject poverty. Congo may be Africa's richest country resource in terms of resources, but its people are ranked among the poorest people in the world. All these could be attributed to the meddling into the governance arena by Multi-National Corporations (MNCs) with the blessing of their home governments. Governments that are sympathetic to these MNCs enjoy their support, for example, through funding of election campaigns, and supply of arms to fight insurgencies. Where they do not enjoy such sympathy, they instigate insurgencies to avail them of the opportunity to milk away their valuable natural resources. The liberal agenda has helped open up Africa to the advances of global capital. The exploitation of Africa's resources and access to its market could have been possible without the complicity of African governments (Ake: 1996).

VII. Conclusion

• *Main finding*

In the light of the above it is obvious that liberal democracy, regardless of whatever may be the reasons, has grossly failed to deliver the continent from its chronic leadership and economic crisis.

70

Perhaps, liberal democracy is not the magic formula for Africa's developmental and governance agendas. Maybe this is the time for Africa to decide whether it should experiment with the different democratic variations or other systems of governance or whether the real issues are change of attitudes and not systems.

• The alternative system

If Africa at all needs a new system of government then, this should be a social system which can survive without or with least problems and disputes and capable of ensuring justice, equality, and freedom in the best possible manner. This system should be able to liberate the needs of individuals from the control of others. People must be in control of their means of subsistence and survival and their administration must be sensitive and responsive to the needs of the people and also effective in coping with emerging challenges in society and at the same time it should be strictly adhering to and implementing the principles of justice, fairness and respect for the dignity and the fundamental rights of the human being.

• The Libyan experience

The economic system in the former Great Jamahiriya which was ushered in by the advent of the Third Universal Theory introduced by the founder of the then Green Revolution had, according to its architect, proven itself to be a good socio-economic and political system (Muammar Ghadafi: 2005). The Jamahiriya system, according to the founder, had created a happy society in Libya through its liberation of the needs of individuals from the control of others and thereby giving the people true freedom and social justice. On March 2, 1977, the Great Jamahiriya promulgated its first constitutional document known as the Declaration of the Authority of the People. This declaration established that the basis of the political system is the authority of the people. It also emphasized direct democracy and the adoption of socialism including public ownership.

The Green Book which was the theoretical guide of the Third Universal Theory established the authority of the people, ownership based on the wealth of society, landownership and use by everyone, that individual ownership is necessary to liberate human needs from the control of others and people's ownership of means of production in order to liberate themselves from the control of individuals and groups.

Although the question whether direct democracy can work in other Africa societies, particularly those with vast populations, is a genuine one and needs careful consideration. There are obvious reasons showing that even in Libya direct democracy has suffered from serious shortcomings.

• Shortcomings of the Libyan experience

Direct democracy is obviously not as effective, viable and acceptable to the masses particularly to the grassroots as described by Muammar Ghadafi. The advent of the Arab Spring Revolution in Libya revealed many political realities on the ground in that country. The most shocking and dramatic of such realities is the fact that the vast majority of Libyans were not satisfied with what was going on in their country. Apparently, Ghadafi's own choice of direct democracy was not the choice of the majority of Libyans. This raises the fundamental question of legitimacy. In other words, for the four decades that Ghadafi ruled Libya he did not enjoy full legitimacy. Lack of legitimacy to govern is one of the most delicate and chronic problems of Africa governance. Although Ghadafi's version of democracy might have delivered in the area of infrastructural development, many of the principles of good governance such as respect for human rights and fundamental freedoms, observance of the rule of law, transparency and accountability, civil society participation and decentralization of authority were almost completely absent from his system and process of governing.

• **What is the real issue?**

In my view, the real issue in the overall problems of governance in Africa is not the systemic aspect of it. In other words, the particular system of governing followed by one country or the other whether it is liberal democracy as the case is in most African countries or direct democracy as the case was in Libya, or Communism or absolute monarchy or military dictatorship as respectively witnessed in various countries across the continent, is not necessarily the cause of the political or leadership crisis which has not only hampered development and progress in virtually every African country but has also brought the state down and led it to fail in Somalia in the Horn of Africa, and Liberia and Sierra Leone in the Mano River Region of West Africa in the past. Consequently, what is needed in Africa is a change of attitude and not necessarily a change of systems. There are people who believe that for any governance process to be successful; it must introduce liberal democracy as a system which incorporates the good governance principles of transparency, accountability, decentralization of authority, civil society participation / promotion and protection of human rights and above all that the system must be adequately responsive to needs of the masses including the grass roots (Mander & Assif: 2004). Some governance and legal experts believe that these principles are not fully and adequately represented in many governance systems in Africa. Likewise, the Islamists across the continent world advocate the introduction of Islamic rule and the Islamic system of government in those African countries with Muslim majorities. There is no doubt that the Islamic system of governance, which is backed by divine authority or the wholly Quran and the Sunnah or tradition of the prophet of Islam (peace be upon Him) and which is mainly characterized by administrative centralism could be a very good and viable alternative. The centralized nature of Islamic administration was typically demonstrated by the Ottoman Turks, who ruled the whole of the Islamic world under one strong central administration for about six countries (A.A. Senghore, PhD: 2011).

However, whether it is liberal or direct democracy or an Islamic system of governance or absolute or constitutional monarchy or authoritarianism or Communism or a hybrid of any two of these systems is followed by African countries, as witnessed in some instances, the political and leadership crisis will continue to exist if attitudes are not changed.

Africans must stop viewing or considering leadership as a privilege and a source of economic and political empowerment of few individuals. Rather they must acknowledge and accept the fact that leadership is a responsibility in the first and foremost instances. They must realize the need for them as leaders to sacrifice for the progress and betterment of the masses and be truly sensitive to the legacies they will leave behind. Thus, immoral practices like nepotism, favouritism, all sorts of discrimination, corruption, greed, selfishness, irresponsibleness, autocracy, and the like must be completely eradicated from the political and governance arena throughout the length and breadth of the continent.

3

Human Rights and Democracy in The Gambia: Is The Gambia a Democratic State?

Introduction

Human Rights and Democracy are two concepts that have been identified to be mutually supportive both in theory and in practice. The United Nations Human Rights Council recognizes and acknowledges this relationship through resolutions 2000/46, 2000/47, and 19/36.

The Universal Declaration of Human Rights (UDHR) defines Human Rights as the right to life, the right to food, the right to liberty, the right to work, the right to receive education, the right to freedom of expression, and the right to social, cultural, and economic participation. Accordingly, all peoples are entitled to civil and political rights irrespective of nationality, religion, language, race, ethnic origin, sex, or any other status. Thus, this declaration sets the context for democratic governance in which pluralism, respect for human rights and fundamental freedoms, citizen participation, and transparency, become the norms of governance. These principles as enshrined in international human rights law provide the framework for assessing the democratic performance of states. This means that the extent to which a state is democratic is determined by its reputation or track record in protecting its citizens and residents against human rights abuse and facilitating their enjoyment of basic rights irrespective of their political, economic, or cultural origins. Sovereign states demonstrate willingness and commitment to democracy, the rule of law, and respect for fundamental freedoms by ratifying human rights treaties and other international human right agreements. However, the implementation of these treaties is not obligatory on non-signatory member states of the United Nations. In principle, respect for national sovereignty appears to override the demand for compliance with human right conventions by suspect states and regimes. In other words, a state's sovereign concept of its national interests becomes a factor in its decision to join or abstain from ratifying specific human right treaties. Implicitly, a state's willingness to sign and ratify a human right treaty is arguably a demonstration of good governance and good democratic behaviour. Since 1978, The Gambia has signed and/or ratified nine human rights treaties including the Convention against Torture and other Cruel, Inhuman or Degrading Treatments, and the International Convention on Economic, Social, and Cultural Rights. Many of these conventions were signed or ratified in the Second Republic.

Therefore, this chapter is presented in four sections. Following the link between human rights and jurisprudence, the first section presents an overview of the history of human rights. Thus, the first section explores the origin of the philosophy of law and society in relation to contemporary international human rights law. Democracy as a governance system is discussed in the second section. The first section conceptualizes governance, good governance, and democracy. Drawing on this, the second part of the second section argues that democracy is an open-source concept that should be fitted to the social and indigenous political cultures. The latter part of second section puts the Gambian democracy in context by identifying

76

democratic practices in state institutions based on universal democratic norms.

Sections 3 and 4 examine the Gambian judiciary and legislature respectively. Section 3 discusses the judiciary as the watchdog of the constitution, using every-day law cases to demonstrate judicial independence in The Gambia. Section 4 on the other hand examines the oversight functions of the legislature by evaluating the roles of PAC/PEC and the Ombudsman as instruments of democratic accountability in The Gambia.

Conceptual foundation and basic premises

This section presents the background to the main theme of this chapter. Human rights, as a constitutional concept, have its roots in democracy and jurisprudence. Thus, this section explores this background by discussing the origins of constitutional and Islamic jurisprudence in the first section. Following this, the history of human rights and democracy and the emergence of legal and moral rights as features of a democratic society are discussed in sections two and three respectively. The history and features of democracy and a system of governance is discussed in section four thereby setting the context for discussions in the next section.

I.   *Law and rights in general: some theoretical / philosophical foundations*

One of the most obvious features of the seventeenth century natural law philosophy, which has largely influenced the modern concept of law and rights in the West, was the detachment and separation of law from theology and religion. This was accompanied by a great emphasis on the power of reason as one of the distinctive characteristics of man.

Hugo Grotius (d. 1645), one of the most prominent jurists and legal philosophers of the time who is generally regarded as having prepared the ground for secular and rationalistic version of modern natural law, believed that natural law is a dictate of right reason which measures the quality of moral necessity and legitimacy of an act by the extent of its conformity or otherwise with the rational nature of man. So, for him the state was an association of free men who agreed to come together for the enjoyment of their rights and common interests. Thus, the sole purpose behind the creation and formation of the state was to promote, protect and enjoy the natural rights of men who submitted their sovereign power to a ruler. Some of the dictates of natural law in the view of Grotius include the following:

> To abstain from that which belongs to other persons, to restore to another
> any goods of his which we may have, to abide by pacts and to fulfill
> promises made to other persons, to repay any damage done to another
> through fault and to inflict punishment upon men who deserve it. [1]

These, in brief, are the basic moral foundations of modern international law in general and international law of human rights in particular.

For John Locke (d. 1704), the renowned English political philosopher and another believer in natural law, what existed prior to political, and any form of social organization or institution was a state of nature under which people lived together according to reason without any common superior authority on earth. He believed that in this state of nature men lived together under the guidance of the law of nature by which their rights and responsibilities were determined. Like Grotius and many other natural law philosophers of the same age, John Locke, it appears, did not recognize the importance of divine revelation to law and to the determination of the rights and duties and responsibilities of individuals vis-à-vis one another and society as a whole. This is because the law of nature according to him was an objective rule and measure emanating from God but ascertainable by human reason. [2]

Thus Locke, whose political writings, especially the *Two Treatises on Civil Government*, are believed to have largely influenced the English Revolution of 1688 which gave birth to the 1688 Bill of Rights and subsequently influencing the American and French Revolutions of 1776 and 1789 respectively, [3] was a strong advocate of the natural and inalienable rights of man. He argued that even before government existed, men were free, independent, and equal in the enjoyment of those natural and inalienable rights. In his opinion, the most important of such rights were the rights to life, liberty, and property. He, however, appeared to have acknowledged the existence of a serious weakness in that state of nature he was talking about. In other words, Locke realized that the state of nature lacked some central and common authority and machinery. So, there was the tendency that everybody would have executive power over the law of nature, and this made the whole system prone to injustice and partiality or bias especially when one was to become a judge for one's own case and for those of his friends. So, for these obvious weaknesses and inconveniences of the state of nature, Locke suggested that civil government was the best and the most proper remedy or solution for that problem. [4]

Sir William Blackstone (1723-1780), another English devotee to the theory of natural law, wrote that the law of nature is that which could properly be thought of as human law. He ruled out any role for human beings in making this law. Instead, Blackstone argued that the law of nature was dictated by God and for that reason it was binding over the entire globe in all countries and for all time. He further argued that the role and task of the judge was to try to discover or find out, and apply, but not to make and create this law, and that human laws contrary to the law of nature are invalid, while the valid human law derived its force and authority either mediate or immediately from that original law.[5] I have not been able, however, to detect or even sense throughout his discussion of the law of nature, any inkling of recognition by Blackstone of the importance of divine revelation or prophet-hood to the process by which the law of nature was sent down to man. Blackstone, who believed in the existence of natural law and therefore natural rights, divided rights into two types namely: Absolute and relative rights. The relative rights are incident to and due to individuals by virtue of their membership of society; while the absolute rights are those claims, entitlements, and privileges that the individual is entitled to by virtue of being a man. This is what is meant by natural rights. In other words, they are invested in human beings by the immutable laws of nature. The English jurist and political philosopher thought that the principal aim of society and principal view of human laws was to recognize, protect and enforce such rights and their full enjoyment by every individual member of society. [6]

James Wilson, (d. 1798), an American jurist of the late 18th century and a former associate justice of the United State Supreme Court, was another advocate of the theory of natural law and therefore natural rights of men. He argued that the main function of the law was to guarantee, that is, safeguard and protect the natural rights of the individual against any encroachment by the government. To him, natural law which provides a basis for natural rights and illuminates the ends of government was a God-created absolute standard against which individual and community acts must be measured. The American natural law advocate then defined that what he meant by natural rights as the right of the individual to his property, to his character and reputation, integrity and honour, his right to liberty and safety. [7] All of the above concerns the theory of natural law and natural rights. I now consider other theories of law and rights.

As for the utilitarian theory of law, Jeremy Bentham (d. 1832) held that law is a human creation and that a good deal of law is made by judges. According to his utilitarian theory, law whether made by the judge or the legislature should be in accordance with the Utility Principle and the notion of usefulness, happiness, and goodness to society as well as to the individual. So, for utilitarians, every right is an ordinary one. In other words, for the utilitarians, who set out one supreme goal of happiness and preference maximization, they would accept, recognize, and respect rights only if they are able to bring about their goal of the maximum satisfaction of preferences or happiness. Thus, under the utilitarian construction, an act of torture might be accepted so long as torturing suspects could bring about happiness to society.[8] On the other hand, the Austinian theory of legal positivism emphasizes the aspect of command and sanction in positive law or the command theory of law and sanction theory of duty. The positivists believe that the notion of command implies a relation of superiority and inferiority, that is, law "properly so called" is a command from political superiors to political inferiors which, sanctioned with a threat of evil, has to be complied with or obeyed.[9] Thus, under the Austinian doctrine of legal positivism which he developed in his school of analytical jurisprudence which strictly separates law from ethics and morality, the emphasis is on legal rights and there is no talk of any rights in the absence of clear black letter law giving such rights to the individual. This is because legal rights are conferred by statutes and by the decisions of courts. So, in order for such claims, moral or otherwise, and entitlements and privileges to be given legal force there has to be an enactment of specific legal rights sanctioning or legally recognizing such claims or rights. [10] So legal rights, according to the legal positivists, only exist when there is a specific black letter provision guaranteeing them.

Furthermore, somewhere near the positivist construction, but far away from the naturalist theory of law, stands the American theory of legal realism. This theory rejects the idea that there are rules of law that have weight, authority and '*bindingness*' in the law which the judge should look for and apply in any case before the court. Instead, legal realists have placed judges at the centre of law making. They maintain that judges do legislate and that the judicial decision-making process is a creative rather than a mechanical activity. Obviously, the realists would reject the idea of natural and divine law; rather, they hold the view that judges are not bound by any existing rules, but that a rule of law is made as soon as the judge announces his/her decision. So the law of a state is that body of rules laid down by judges in the course of their determination of the legal rights and duties of the people vis-à-vis the state and vice versa.[11] So for the realists, who emphasize the centrality of the legislative role of the judge, rights are actually existent and really meaningful only in the course of the judicial process especially at the moment when the judge decides.[12] Unlike the legal positivists, who attribute the function of law to a central and superior political authority, the legal realists emphasize the central role of the judicial process in making the law and concomitantly giving, defining and protecting the rights of the individual. It is not clear what exactly this school of philosophy is trying to establish. Do the realists want to emphasize the important role of an independent judicial system in the process of defining and the determination of human rights? Or are they attributing to the judiciary, the legislative role of the legislature when it comes to defining and determining the scope of human rights? What is however clearly understood from the realist construction is the centrality of the role of the judge in the process of adjudication, promotion, and protection of human rights. For A.V. Dicey, another English political philosopher of the 19th century, individual rights were secured not by guarantees set in a formal document but by the ordinary remedies of private law available against those who interfered with those rights. In other words, the common law principles of *habeas corpus* (literally meaning "you should have the body" – that is, an individual who is being detained must be produced before a judge or in a court of law to ensure the legality of their detention) and action for damages in tort to be declared by common law judges are the basis of actualization by citizens of their rights and liberties.[13]

These differences in the theoretical foundations of law and rights among those leading Western legal thinkers do not very much affect the modern concept of human rights; although some controversy still exists over the precise nature, scope, and extent of rights. It goes without saying that the modern concept of human rights has been influenced not only by natural law but also, albeit to a greater or lesser extent, by legal positivism, legal realism, and utilitarianism. However, it is believed that somewhere between the thirteenth and the seventeenth centuries the meaning of the term 'right', an equivalent of *jus* in the Latin, shifted from doing right to possessing, owning, and having a right, a claim, an entitlement and privilege. [14]

Despite the fact that some theoretical differences exist among legal experts over the conceptualization of the value of rights, they all seem to agree on two important aspects of rights first that individuals need protection against the state and government of the day is elected by the majority and that rights whether legal or moral are a necessary if not a sufficient means of ensuring that protection and second – that rights are goods which individuals own or have as theirs.[15]

II.   *Legal and moral rights*

Rights that are created and conferred by a constitution or a legal system may be termed as pure legal rights; that is, the right to appeal, the right to make a will, the right to dispose of property that is lawfully owned and the like. However, rights that people inherently own or have whether or not they are recognized in a given statute, constitution or a legal system are called moral fundamental, natural, and inalienable rights of man. They are also called politico-moral rights. These rights are not created by the legal system, but it recognizes them and guarantees their implementation. These rights are said to have possessed a special value because they rest on a moral conception of people as separate individuals of equal worth. They are sometimes called fundamental rights given that they are recognized in the constitution which is the fundamental law of the country. They are by the same reason also called constitutional rights or basic rights of man.

The civil and political rights invoked by the American Declaration of Independence of 1776 and the French Declaration of the Rights of Man of 1789 belong to this kind of politico-moral rights. [16] We now move on to examine the nature of law and rights in Islamic law.

III.   Law and rights from an Islamic perspective

The Islamic concept of law and rights is fundamentally different from what I have been discussing above. It is not utilitarian, neither is it positivist nor does Islam recognize such loose concepts as legal realism and the theory of natural law. Islamic law, on the other hand, has in the first instance to be placed, understood, interpreted, and applied within the context and bounds of the Divine Revelation. Islamic law is of divine origin and its development or growth, and expansion had to be guided by the fundamental principles of that revelation that is, *al-Quran* and *Sunnah* of the Prophet (Peace and Blessing of Allah Be Upon Him - p.b.u.h). Thus, the typical nature of the law of Islam is that it is of divine origin, it is comprehensive and inclusive of all facets and activities of human life, that it addresses itself to both individual interests and those of society at large, that it is suitable for and applicable by all people of all generations and that

84

the Islamic community is under strict divine obligation to put into effect the rules and principles of Islamic law (albeit every generation of Islam does so in the most suitable way for the solution of its peculiar everyday problems). To sum up, the practical rules of *Shari'ah* deduced from the detailed evidence of the divine sources of Islam, constitute the juriscorpos (it is a technical legal term meaning the "the main body") of Islamic law.[17] Consequently, Islamic law is the only source of guidance for everything needed and related to the life of Muslims and is the heart of the Islamic system of life. This is why Islamic law has different branches or areas of discipline ranging from the rules of theology, the science of method and sources of the law otherwise known as legal philosophy; to the rules governing family life such as marriage, divorce and maintenance, the rules governing commercial transactions, the law of inheritance, criminal law, laws governing civil matters, the law of evidence and other procedural accepts of the law.

This specific nature of law in Islam, its intimate relation and interconnection with the Divine Revelation or *Shari'ah* and the special position of *Shari'ah* (being the heart of and source of guidance for Islam as a religion and civilization or a way of life for Muslims), in the structure of Islam as a way of life, has ruled out any possibility for that law to be separated and detached from theology, faith, or religion in a true Islamic society.

So, it is this law of Islam which is inseparable from its Divine Revelation that defines and determines the nature and scope of the rights of human beings in that system. It provides the necessary procedure and the right framework and regulates the process of promotion, protection and actualization or realization of those rights. According to al-Shātibī, the overriding objective of *al-Sharī'ah* is the consideration of public interests or *maslahah*. In his famous treatise, al Muwāfaqāt, this Maliki jurist identifies five basic necessities of life which are essential to the existence of life and the survival and prosperity of the human being. Their neglect, according to him, would result in total chaos and the eventual destruction of human life on earth. These values, whose preservation and protection is what *Shar ī'ah* is all about, are religion *(d īn)*, life, *(nafs)* intellect, *('aql)* lineage or *(nasl)* or progeny and *(māl)* property.[18] These values are to be protected by both positive and negative means i.e. by providing whatever may be necessary for their full realization and enjoyment, on the one hand, and by preventing whatever could cause or lead to their total destruction or disregard on the other.[19]

As for the precise nature of rights in Islam, some contemporary scholars believe that the majority of Muslim jurists did not or have not made any serious attempt to give an exact definition of right or *haqq*. This is perhaps they feel that the term *haqq* which is the Arabic equivalent of the English word, "right" was so obvious that it did not have to be defined. It *(haqq)* was traditionally used to mean truth, obligation and any benefit or interest and entitlement whether material or spiritual or anything that one legally deserves or is entitled to. It is also defined as meaning both reality and truth. So, anything termed *haqq* must conform to the requirements of wisdom, justice, truth, reality, and propriety. It is, however, important to understand, as al-Attas explains, that the term *haqq* or right encompasses both "statement" and "actions, feelings, beliefs, judgments and the things and events in existence." [20] Thus, the values referred to under the concept of *haqq* or right include numerous values and entitlements that are all universal, indivisible, and inalienable. These are what we refer to in modern times as human rights and fundamental freedoms.

Consequently, I would like to support at this juncture the view held by many that human rights and fundamental liberties in Islam are not mere entitlements and privileges that one has to have, possess, and own. Rather, they are necessities of life guaranteed or given not by

86

any human authority but by God the Almighty and must therefore be respected, promoted, and protected under all circumstances. [21]

Thus, human rights, as Islam teaches, must be preserved, promoted and protected under all circumstances for every human being regardless of faith, nationality, social status and any other consideration. In other words, since human rights are necessities of life, their protection becomes a fundamental obligation falling not only upon the Islamic state but upon each and every individual as well.[22] What needs to be noted in this connection is that the concept of rights in Islam is not only placed within the context of the Divine Revelation but that it also has to be understood, interpreted and promoted or actualized under the guiding Principles of Islamic Jurisprudence (Usūl a-Fiqh).

I have already stated that the overriding objective of *Sharī'ah* is the consideration, preservation and protection of human interests and the general well-being of the people. But what has to be remembered here according to Muslim theologians is that one of the five fundamental values and necessities that *Sharī'ah* aims to protect is *din* or religion and according to al-Attas, there are four primary significations for the term *din*. The first two being indebtedness and submissiveness to the will of God. The state of indebtedness requires that one should abase oneself to the service of one's Master and Creator to whom the debt of creation is owed. This means that the individual must obey the laws and commandments of God the Creator and Sustainer of the universe to whom everyone owes the debt of existence. [23] Similarly, the submissiveness to the will of God means total obedience to God's Law i.e. to observe His commands and avoid His prohibitions. The remaining two primary significations of the term *dīn* are:

i. Judicial power i.e. that people's daily routines – commercial and all other transactional activities are to be conducted in accordance with law.

ii. The natural tendency of man to form society and obey laws and establish just governments as well as to obey God the Creator. [24] It, therefore, has to be taken as a fundamental principle of Islamic theology and law that the concept of human rights cannot be separated from and placed anywhere outside the domain of religion.

Consequently, one of the most obvious differences between the Islamic and the Western approaches to understanding human rights is that there is no room for secularism or secularization of human rights in the Islamic system where the whole concept of right is anchored in the heart of Shariah which is the divine law of Islam. This is why Islamic perception of relativism cannot be the same as that of the conventional systems.

According to al-Ghazālī, the spiritual and religious affairs of life of every individual believer have to go hand in hand with the worldly and material aspects or affairs. The two aspects cannot be separated because the basic requirements of *din* include both the spiritual and material well-being of the individual believers.

Human rights are therefore an integral part of the entire structure and edifice of the Islamic way of life, whereas most conventional political, legal, economic, socio-cultural, and state systems of the modern times are premised on the principle of separation of religion from the state and state matters. Finally, what has become clearly visible from this exposition of the nature and the conceptual foundation of law and rights in Islam is that, unlike modern Western and Westernized constitutions and legal systems where there exists the duality of individual rights and state interests, "Islamic law does not proceed from a position of conflict between the respective rights and interests of the individual" [26] and those of the state. Rather, rights of the individual, their promotion and protection form part of the main functions, duties, responsibilities, and interests of the state and moreover, both the state and the individual are, on an equal footing, obliged to follow the rules of *Sharī'ah*. Furthermore, that their mutual relationship is to be conducted in accordance with the dictates of that supreme divine law. The quality of *īmān*, or faith in God, together with its concomitant aspects of piety, justice, honesty, sincerity, and sense of responsibility, should indeed be the foundation of any bill of human rights in an Islamic state. [27]

This precise and concrete nature of rights in Islamic law was perhaps what had impressed a former judge of the International Court of Justice at The Hague, (the ICJ) when he observed:

> Human rights doctrine in Islam was a logical development from its basic postulates, namely the sovereignty of God and the revelation to the prophet. [28]

The former judge of the ICJ, C.G. Weeramantry, explains that from such postulates, the basic principles of human rights, including those contained in modern international human rights conventions and treaties, followed logically as a necessary part of Islamic law.[29]

Finally, a closer look at the five fundamental values that, according to Muslim jurists, *Shariah* has been revealed to protect and preserve, clearly shows that Islamic law has in actual fact adequately guaranteed the protection and ensured the means of actualization of all fundamental human rights and basic freedoms incorporated in the international human rights conventions and treaties of the modern era i.e. the protection of life, religion, intellect, progeny and property has definitely included all the civil, political, economic, social and cultural rights protected by the modern international law of human rights and various national laws of the nation states of the modern time.

This historical overview of the origins of jurisprudence has thus been used to lay the conceptual foundation for the link between human rights and democracy in contemporary political cultures. Thus, the goal of this seemingly detailed overview is not to dwell on the human rights discourse on its own but to draw an analogy on the contributions of jurisprudence to the evolution of democracy.

Democracy as a system of governance: The Gambian perspective

As the number of scholars who view democracy as an "open-source conception that should be fitted within the social and local political cultures" continues to rise, this section presents an account of Gambian democracy against the backdrop of "responsive rule." Thus, the first part of this section conceptualizes democracy and governance in context. This is followed by an evaluation of The Gambia's democratic institutions using evidence on constitutional rule, the rule of law, respect for human rights and fundamental freedoms, independence of the judiciary, and separation of powers. The cited cases and examples have been used as evidence to demonstrate the democratic credentials of The Gambia against the backdrop of the responsive rule philosophy. Implicitly, this facilitates a reflection on the extent to which governance in The Gambia meets universal democratic norms and the extent to which these norms have been adapted to the social and political uniqueness of the country.

I.   Democracy and Governance

It has been argued that democracy and governance are mutually supportive. Thus, Fukuyama explains governance as the *ability to make and enforce rules, and to deliver services irrespective of any*

90

dominant political ideologies.[30] Kaufman and his counterparts, for their part, contend that governance involves a set of institutions and traditions by which authority in a country is exercised.[31] Other sources such as the World Bank's Poverty Reduction Strategy Paper (PRSP) conceptualize governance *as the way power is exercised through a country's economic, political, and social institutions (WB PRSP n.d).*[32] What these definitions appear to have in common is that governance is an institutional concept. This perspective is implicit in the views of scholars who argue that governance is the way in which a country's institutions are used to manage national affairs. Thus, the governance concept incorporates the beliefs and value systems, through which the citizens of a country articulate their interests, exercise their legal rights, meet their obligations, and mediate their differences. Arguably, governance is an instrument of social cohesion. It is, however, important to mention that this view of governance as a pragmatic concept implicitly differs from good governance as a feature in a democratic state. Thus, the democratic governance concept emerges as a system of government where institutions function according to democratic processes and norms both internally and in their interaction with other institutions.[33] As discussed in the second part of Section 3 below, good and democratic governance highlights the normative entitlement of transparency and the rule of law in the way a country's political, economic, and administrative authority is used to manage national affairs.[34] The key word 'normative' is the adjectival form of norms and values and norms are typically sensitive to culture and thus justify the different variants of democratic governance. Hence, the effort to facilitate insight into the concept of democracy as a governance system should begin with an evaluation of the concept of democracy.

Democracy has been defined in various ways using different approaches. According to Holden, the concept of political democracy, inclusive citizenship and political equality are basic principles of a democratic system.[35] Beetham appears to support the views of Holden when he argued that the core principles of a democratic system are those embodied in its historical conception as 'rule of the people', that is, popular control or sovereignty and political equality.[36] As political thought continued to evolve, scholars began to view the emergence of the democratic principle in parallel with the changing societal complexities to which democratic norms had been designed to address. To this end, Saward argues that the best approach to understanding democracy as a social phenomenon is to look at those countries known to be democratic and define the concept according to the main features of their practice.[37] This view supports the assumption that democracy and a democratic system are context-dependent phenomena in which "all citizens are equal with respect to their right to decide the appropriate political course of their community."[38] The definitions reviewed above embody two fundamental insights. First, these definitions seem to agree that equality, sovereignty, the rule of law, transparency, control, ownership, and inclusiveness form the main tenets of a democratic system. Second, they present an implicit view of democracy as a variant of political culture that is universal in its fundamentals but vary in its methodology across national boundaries.

This perspective appears to have provided the philosophical anchor for the general defining rule of democracy and "substantive policy" in which politics, and administrative actions of governance must correspond with the expressed preferences of a majority of citizens"[39] notwithstanding what these preferences may be in contiguous national jurisdictions. In other words, there should be correspondence between acts of a government and the equally weighted expressed wishes of citizens with respect to those acts. This is what Saward calls "responsive rule" and for him, a political system is democratic to the extent that and only to the extent that it involves realization of the responsive rule through free and fair elections, the principles of transparency and accountability, constitutional rule, respect for human rights, prevalence of the rule of law, separation of powers, independence of the judiciary and the legal profession, and freedom of expression.[40] Regrettably, the 'responsive rule' and the implicit malleability of democratic principles have been challenged by views of some interest groups in those countries that mistake the replicability of democratic norms for the standardization of democratic methodology. Such groups appear to favour the exportation of Western democratic traditions to non-western countries. Arguably, this scenario can be synonymous with disenfranchisement and a negation of the 'responsive rule'.

Theoretically, the responsive rule, as advocated by Saward, lays the foundation for different types of democracy. While direct democracy as practised in Switzerland, presidential democracy as practised in The Gambia, United States, Russia, and parliamentary democracy as practised in the UK, Spain, Israel and in other places share the same norms; they differ in methodology based on the expressed preferences of citizens. In fact, countries like Singapore, and Israel which have built enviable and progressive democratic credentials over the years lean towards the Confucian and democratic theocracies respectively. These variants differ from the Western version and yet they have been responsive to the needs and aspirations of the citizens.[41] Kim argues that democracy would be *more effective in East Asia and culturally relevant if it were rooted in and operates on the 'Confucian habits and mores'* with which East Asian societies are still deeply saturated.[42] Thus, Western liberal tradition should not be exported and standardized. Instead, democracy should be fitted to the social and indigenous political cultures as reinforcement to the "responsive rule" philosophy.

Thus, Kim and other contemporary scholars like Tan and Bridge argue that democracy should henceforth be viewed as an 'open source - conception' that can be adapted to different *'cultural architectures to guide the realization'* of a better nation.[43]

II.   *Democratic institutions in The Gambia*

Based on the foregoing, this section conducts a thorough review of Gambian democracy by using constitutional rule, the rule of law, respect for human rights and fundamental freedoms, the principles of accountability and transparency, and separation of powers, as frameworks of analyses. As argued in the literature, these are the universal antecedents of democracy that can be adapted to fit the social and indigenous political cultures.

III.   *Constitutional rule*

The principle of constitutional rule as a core element of a democratic system can only be effective if the constitution enjoys a supremacy status within the legal and political system of the country. The concept of constitutional supremacy teaches that the constitution is the supreme law of the land and all other laws, executive decisions, and administrative activities of the government of the day must be in conformity with the constitution, otherwise, they are declared null and void by a court of competent jurisdiction. In 2005, The Supreme Court of The Gambia, in **Sabally v Inspector General of Police**, nullified several provisions of the Indemnity (Amendment) Act 2001 for contravening the human rights provisions of the 1997 Constitution of the Republic of The Gambia and article 7 of the African Charter on Human and Peoples' Rights which guarantees the fundamental right of the individual to access the courts of the land. *(Sabally v.s Inspector General of Police and others (Civil Ref: No. 2/2001, 1999 to 2001: GR at 883).*[44] This principle has been established in Section 4 of the 1997 Constitution of the Second Republic of The Gambia. Constitutional supremacy also ensures a more conducive environment for the observance of the rule of law and the independence of the judiciary.

IV.   The rule of law

What is meant by the rule of law is the supremacy of the authority of the law that all people and institutions are equally subject to the control and dictates of the law. The principle of the rule of law teaches about the equality of people before the law and equal protection of the law, the legality of the administrative acts of the political authorities and fairness or constitutionality of the legal authority backing the legislative and administrative activities of the government of the day. In other words, it is not only enough to govern by law, but the law that we use to govern must be just, fair, and reasonable. This is demonstrated in everyday cases in The Gambia where individuals have right to fair hearing; and can win cases even against the Government. Some of such cases is the case involving the main opposition leader, Ousainou Darboe and others murder case; and also, in Modou Jobe Vs the Attorney-General of the Republic of The Gambia as mentioned in Section 3. Furthermore, the rule of law in modern times also calls for the prevalence of law and order rather than anarchy, and the supremacy of international law particularly the international human right law to domestic legislation. Another important example of the prevalence of the rule of law is the law-abiding nature of the Gambian people. This was clearly demonstrated in the recent ban on Female Genital Mutilation (FGM) in the country in December of 2015. As a protection of the rights of women and girls, the Government enacted a bill of zero tolerance on FGM as enshrined in sections 32A and 32B respectively in the Women's Amendment Act 2015.[45] Significantly, the Government has continually demonstrated respect for individual right and has equally protected the rights of citizens including vulnerable groups such as children, women, and the elderly. Another good example is the recent addition to the country's environmental law which bans the use, purchase, and sale of plastic bags in the country. In addition to the fact that this law promotes environmental protection and independence of the Gambian Government, the positive response from the Gambian people demonstrates their law-abiding nature in their daily functions. Thus, the prevalence and demonstration of the rule of law in The Gambia is in line with the Government's respect for international obligations as illustrated by Wade and Philips.[46]

V. Respect for human rights and fundamental freedoms

Both the 1970 and 1997 republican constitutions of The Gambia incorporated comprehensive provisions and institutions which provided adequate guaranties for the promotion and protection of human rights and fundamentals of the individual. As for the 1997 constitution, in addition to including a whole chapter (Chapter 4) on human rights and individual liberties, it has provided additional institutions and practice that further strengthened the domestic credentials and the human right promotion and protection mechanisms in the state and governance system of The Gambia.

96

These include the Office of the Ombudsman, the Alternative Dispute Resolution Secretariat (ADRS), the National Agency for Legal Aid (NARA), which provides free legal aid services and the National Agency Against Trafficking in Person (NATIP). Similarly, since the 1980s onwards particularly when The Gambia was awarded the opportunity to host the continent's first ever human rights enforcement mechanism (the African Commission on Human and Peoples' Rights) The Gambia has become a very vibrant regional centre for human rights activism in Africa. Thus, in addition to hosting several national and international human rights organizations, every year Banjul hosts at least one or two major international human rights conferences attended by leading human rights and legal experts from across Africa, Europe and beyond.

VI.   *Promoting the right to education*

The provision of accessible and equitable education for citizens can be described as a promotion and protection of human rights and therefore one of the fundamentals of democratic governance. In The Gambia, the provision of equitable and accessible basic and secondary education is a notable achievement as indicated in the attainment of the Millennium Development Goal (2A) which is about achieving 100% universal primary education for boys and girls. The establishment of the University of The Gambia and empowering students to study the most reserved disciplines such as legal and medical education is the brainchild, and an exclusive legacy of the Jammeh Revolution. Providing access to tertiary and higher education is a demonstration of freedom, democracy, and right to education as contained in the Gambia's Tertiary and Higher Education Policy (2014 - 2023).

VII. *Independent news media and press freedom in The Gambia*

By independent news media, reference is made to both the print and broadcast media that are not owned, controlled or in any way influenced by the government of the day or by a political party, a pressure group, or any other ideologically based organization. An independent press should be able to distance itself from both the government and the opposition parties to be truly independent. This is what is understood by independent news media practice in this chapter. Currently, Gambians have witnessed the rise and fall of several daily, weekly, and bi-weekly publishing tabloids namely, the *Daily Observer, Foroyaa,* the *Gambia Info,* the *Independent, The Point, Daily Express, Today, The Voice, The Standard* and *Daily News.* The only newspapers that fit into the definition of independent news media are the *Independent, Today, The Voice, The Standard* and to a lesser degree, *Daily Express.* However, the *Independent* and *Daily Express* are currently not in circulation. People focused a lot of attention on the *Independent* as it was perceived to be the most independent paper in the country during its days of circulation. This newspaper suffered from one obvious shortcoming, namely it used to take a tougher stance with the Government of the day than the opposition and it was inclined to lay more emphasis on exposing what would appear to the shortcomings of the Government than highlighting its achievements. This argument does not necessarily discredit the *Independent,* as the reason for this attitude might be the absence of a vibrant opposition in The Gambia. As for the *Daily*

Observer[1], it is known to be a pro-Government newspaper, while *The Point* newspaper, though independent is not critical enough in the way it addresses crucial issues. The *Gambia Info* is Government owned, while *Foroyaa* is owned, controlled, and heavily influenced by the political ideology of its founders, which is socialism or communism. However, it is important at this juncture to consider Nyamnjoh's criticism of the independent press or newspapers in Africa. According to him many of the so-called independent press or newspapers are not truly independent, in some cases; they might be the mouthpieces of the opposition parties. While highlighting the shortcomings of the liberal democratic theory for African media, he argues that the private press has assumed a partisan, a highly politicized or a militant role. There is a growing obsession with the politics of belonging, nationality, and citizenship. Consequently, identity politics has become central to the political process even with the media.[47]

Currently, more than 40 radio stations are legally operating in The Gambia, most of these stations are privately owned. There are several of them in the Greater Banjul Area, while others are operating in various towns and urban centres in the provinces. These include the stations in Brikama, Kerewan, Farafenni, Sapu, George Town or Janjangbureh and Brikamaba. There are stations in Basse, the provincial centre of the Upper River Region, Jarra Soma which is a

---

[1] The Barrow administration shut down the *Daily Observer* in 2017 due to its tax liabilities to the state.

major town in the Lowe River Region, Bwiam in the West Coast Region and elsewhere in the country.

This scenario provides evidence of a huge increase, both in number and type, of private news media organizations in The Gambia, print and broadcast alike. If these trends continue for the next ten years, Gambia's ranking in terms of performance around press freedom as an essential component of democratic governance will be one of the best in the whole of the African continent.

VIII. *Separation of Powers*

Within a system of government based on law, the legislature, the executive, and the judiciary distinctly and separately perform legislative, executive, and judicial functions of the state respectively.

This three-fold division of labour between the three main branches of government is a necessary condition for the rule of law in modem society and therefore democratic governance itself.[48] In Africa in practice, the situation is different. What happens in many countries is that the executive dominates other arms of government.[49] Sections 76, 100 and 120 of the 1997 Constitution of the Second Republic of The Gambia have incorporated the principles of separation of powers amongst the three branches of government. For section 76 (subsection 1) the executive power of The Gambia is vested in the President and that subject to the same constitution such power shall be exercised by him / her either directly or through the Vice President, Ministers, or other officials responsible to him / her. On the other hand, Section 100 of the constitution has entrusted the legislative power of The Gambia in the country's National Assembly.[50] According to this section, the legislative power of The Gambia shall be exercised by Bills passed by the National Assembly and assented to by the President. Similarly, section 120 (subsection 2) has vested the judicial power of The

Gambia in the courts of the land and the courts shall exercise such power according to the respective jurisdictions conferred on them by law. There are three categories of courts in The Gambia.

a. superior courts which include the supreme court, the court of appeal, the high court, and the special criminal court

b. the lower courts *i.e.* the magistrates' courts and district tribunals

c. the Cadi courts which deal with issues of matrimonial issues of Muslim parties alone.[51]

As far as separation of powers is concerned, the 1997 constitution which is purely modelled on the American style of presidential executive is obviously more democratic than the 1970 constitution given that the latter was a combination of both Presidential and the Westminster models. In other words, during the lifespan of the First Republic, all Cabinet Ministers and Deputy Minister or Parliamentary Secretaries were members of Parliament. This means that the Executive was heavily leaning on Parliament or the legislature, whilst the President was both Head of State and Head of Government at the same time.

The Constitution of the First Republic (1970-1994), which enjoyed a supremacy status, had 134 articles and its Chapter III guaranteed protection of human rights and fundamental freedoms.[52] The constitution also had provisions that provided for free participation of multiple political parties in the political life of the state and for holding free and fair elections at regular intervals. Free and fair elections were indeed held after every five years interval with the last elections in that republic taking place in 1992. The constitution recognized the doctrine of separation of powers and guaranteed the rule of law and the independence of the judiciary. Article 42 vested the executive powers of The Gambia in the president, while article 56 vested the legislative powers of the country in parliament and part 1 of Chapter 8 entrusted the judicial power of the republic in the courts of the land.[53] The country had during this period maintained many legislative enactments passed by the colonial administration and enacted so many other laws to support the constitution in the governance process.

The discussion in this chapter has presented a critical analysis of The Gambia's democratic credentials. Using the identified democratic norms as frameworks in concert with the responsive rule philosophy, this analysis challenges the views of proponents of the standardization and exportation of Western liberal democratic systems to nations with distinct cultural values. Using empirical evidence in this chapter, it is pertinent to mention that The Gambia has outstanding democratic credentials. This further reinforces the responsive rule and thus highlights how different variants of democracy can be used to pursue social stability and high quality of life in different countries.

The Gambian judiciary and democratic governance

Given the main theme of this chapter, a scholarly discourse on the judicial arm of government is crucial to understanding the relationship between human rights and democracy. Given the history of jurisprudence and evolution of moral and legal rights as discussed in sections one and two, this section gives a succinct account of the role of Gambian judiciary in the propagation of democratic ideals in the country. Thus, the role of the judiciary in democratic governance is explored. Hence, this section sets the context in which specific case laws have been used to illustrate the independence and the constitutional mandate of Gambian judiciary.

I. *The judiciary and the checks-and-balances principle*

The judiciary is that branch of government established to interpret and administer the law. Constituted by the courts and the judges, the judiciary determines "disputed questions of fact and law in accordance with the law laid down by parliament and expounded by the courts".[54.]

The phrase 'Judiciary in Governance' refers to the composition, order of hierarchy and functions of the judiciary within the structure of government as well as the important role it plays and challenges it faces in the governance process. On the other hand, an autonomous or independent judiciary is one that operates to deliver justice without being hindered by any form of interference or pressure, political or otherwise.

For the judiciary to be autonomous, it must be able to carry out its functions independently of the executive and the legislative arms of the government. This principle of independence of the judiciary is one of the pillars of democratic governance. As for government, it means the machinery and institutional arrangement for the exercise of sovereign powers for serving the internal and external interests of the political community. The judiciary occupies a central position within the overall structure of that machinery and institutional arrangement. On the other hand, governance is the process, as well as the result, of making authoritative decisions for the benefit of society. It means the *act or process of governing*, and specifically refers to authoritative direction and control. According to Mander and Asif, governance is a broader notion than government, state and regime and it is the interaction between formal institutions and those in civil society.[55] In other words, the process of governing is specifically an act of making authoritative decisions and control, and the judiciary wields a considerable part of this authority. At common law, the judiciary is traditionally considered the safe protector and guardian of human rights. This is because the role of the common law judge is essentially to interpret and enforce the law. This role of the judge under the common law system is extremely important to the process of governing because the law, whether the constitution or the ordinary law, is what the judges say it is.

Today, the judiciary is recognized as the third branch of government with the executive and the legislature being the first and the second estates respectively. Judges of the courts system act on behalf or in the name of the government of the day. Thus, if the maintenance of the state government on a daily basis is the sole function of the executive, the authoritative interpretation and actual enforcement of the laws passed by the government's legislature is a sole function of the judiciary. Society cannot govern properly, smoothly, and successfully in the absence of an independent, efficient, well-motivated and vibrant judiciary. According to the principle of *separation of powers*, the judiciary should carry out its functions independently of the executive and the legislature so that the former can effectively hold the latter to account. Broadly speaking, there are three methods of ensuring 'governmental accountability' and the most important of these methods is its accountability to individuals through the courts. This is a direct reference to the principle of judicial review of the executive, known as the supervisory jurisdiction of the courts over the administrative or the executive authorities. According to this principle, the courts have power to police the legality of decisions made by public authorities or executive orders of the government and also to determine the constitutionality or fairness and irresponsibleness of any legal authority or legislative instrument made by lawmakers.

Further understanding would have been gained by examining the composition and hierarchy of the courts, the appointment of judges, their tenure, and other matters of relevance to the judicature system in The Gambia. However, these issues are beyond the remit of this chapter.

II.   *Independence of the judiciary*

An independent judiciary is an indispensable prerequisite of a political system that adheres to the principles of the rule of law and freedom of expression. It implies freedom of the judiciary from interference by the executive or the legislature with its exercise of the judicial functions of the state. It is important to explain that judicial independence does not mean that the court or the judges are entitled to act in an arbitrary manner. Rather, it means non-interference by the political authorities and all other interest groups in the affairs of the judiciary.[56] There is plenty of empirical and statutory evidence which support the independence of Gambian judiciary. There have been many instances in which the executive lost court cases to individuals and private organizations. The courts for reasons of contravening the constitution and or its human rights provisions invalidated legislative instruments and executive orders.[57]

The Court of Appeals in its judgement dated 11th May 1981 in Modou Jobe Vs the Attorney General of the Republic of The Gambia invalidated sections 7, 8, 9 & 10 of the "Special Criminal Court Act 1979" for violating the constitutional rights of the appellant.[58] In June 2005 the High Court in a highly controversial murder case filed by the government, acquitted and discharged the main opposition leader Mr. Ousainou Darboe and four others who were accused of murdering a supporter of the ruling party in 2000.[59]

There is no exaggeration in saying that The Gambia's political system has, since the inception of the First Republic in 1970, to a certain extent adhered to the democratic principles highlighted above. The country's degree of adherence to and commitment to such principles varies from one principle to another and as the next section shows the performance of successive governments of the two Republics around press freedom, has been moving from one level to the other for several reasons. But at this juncture, let's briefly examine The Gambia's democratic credentials in the light of the remaining values of a democratic system.

All that has been said about the nature and extent of human rights and democratic governance in the First Republic is generally identical with and applicable to the Second Republic. From 1997 to date, The Gambia is being governed by a written constitution defined by its section four as the supreme law of the land to which all laws, government policies, Executive Orders, decisions, and all other governance activities should conform. The remaining democratic values of protection of human rights and fundamental freedoms, observance of the rule of law, independence of the judiciary, multiple political party participation in the political process of the country, free and fair periodic elections, the doctrine of separation of powers, transparent and accountable government have been guaranteed by the 1997 constitution of the Second Republic of The Gambia.[60]

The current constitution also introduced additional institutions that could only strengthen Gambian democracy under the Second Republic. These include a permanent independent electoral commission, a judicial service commission, the high court system, and an office of Ombudsman to promote effective public service; understanding of the rule of law; and addressing complaints of malpractice or violation of individual rights.[61]

The institutions, processes, and systems discussed in this section, provide evidence of judicial independence and an active democratic culture in the Gambian judiciary. Despite several challenges, the courts have largely asserted their authority and maintained their independence in the interpretation of the law and dispensation of justice in the country.

Democratic governance and accountability in The Gambia

Transparency and accountability are among the many antecedents of democratic governance. Thus, democratic states uphold the virtue of accountability as they strive to deliver varying constitutional mandates. Thus, the accountability concept has become an important metric in the assessment of good governance around the globe.[62] Drawing on legal provisions in national constitutions, different states continually seek to establish processes and procedures that facilitate the delivery of public good on the basis of responsibility, probity, and transparency. Hence, good governance has become a function of not only political and legal oversight regimes, but a function of moral and administrative accountability as well.[63] This section therefore aims to reflect on how the Gambian state has exemplified itself as a beacon of public accountability over the years.[64] This reflective assessment will focus on reviewing the accountability concept and evaluating some of the horizontal instruments that have been used to deliver public accountability in The Gambia. The goal is not to indict or reprimand any of the existing structures and procedures but to use reflection and appraisal to stimulate dialogue on how we can further improve accountability oversight through improved procedures at the sub-committee levels at the National Assembly.

I.   *A conceptual framework*

The instruments and institutions that contribute to oversight on public finance mirror the notion of accountability in different national jurisdictions.[65] Thus, the parliamentary sub-committees responsible for the oversight function on public accounts are thus the products of this conceptual variety both in name and in mandate. For this reason, it is important that we reflect on a few definitions in the literature.

Accountability has been variously defined. The breadth of the variety of definitions in the literature, arguably entrench the type of conceptual ambiguity that has resulted in different accountability governance frameworks that are today used in different national and supranational jurisdictions.[66] Accountability may therefore be explained as a means or a set of processes and procedures that facilitate the efficacy, effectiveness, and responsiveness of government using legal and institutional benchmarks that reflect acceptable norms and values in the delivery of public good.[67] Thus, public and political accountability systems apply rules and norms that highlight the obligations of public managers to give account of their fiscal and, managerial stewardships to recognized and resident legislative sub-committees. Hence, accountability has been referred to as procedures that are designed to align institutional responsiveness with the development aspirations of nations.[68]

As evidenced in the literature, the American accountability doctrine conceptually differs from what pre-dominates accountability literature in continental Europe.[69] Based on normative considerations, American political discourse presents accountability as a 'virtue' that derives the willingness of public actors to act fairly, transparently, and equitably.[70] Thus, it is used as a standard for the evaluating the conduct of public managers. The Anglo-Saxon scholars, on the other hand, view the concept as an 'actor-forum' mechanism that specifies legal and institutional benchmarks with which public servants can be held accountable *ex-post factor*.[71] Based on these conceptual differences, it could be argued that the focus is not so much on semantics but the resulting concept which shapes the accountability governance frameworks in different countries.

II.   *The Gambian public financial management accountability framework*

The 1997 constitution facilitated reforms in the national budget management system. The relevant sectors of the constitution provide guidance and emphasis on fiscal discipline as the precondition for sectoral budget allocations.[72] Thus, Public Financial Management (PFM) reforms are targeted at improving the accountability and reporting standards of government through a multi-pronged approach that involves the National Audit Office (NAO), The National Assembly (PAC/PEC) and non-state actors. Guided by this accountability objective, the Medium-Term Expenditure Framework (MTEF) and National Medium Term Development Plan known as the Programme for Accelerated Growth and Employment (PAGE), the President constituted an implementation committee with members drawn from PAC/PEC and national executive council to ensure a speedy implementation of PAC/PEC recommendations on audited accounts.[73]

III.   *The PAC/PEC legislative framework*

Committees and commissions, ad-hoc or permanent, are important components of modern parliamentary democracies. The Public Accounts /Public Enterprise Committee (PAC/PEC) and the Ombudsman are examples of accountability apparatus in The Gambia. The Ombudsman, which is also known as Public Complaints

Commission (PCC) in some countries, acts as an independent entity within the state's horizontal accountability structures. The main difference between Ombudsman and PAC/PEC is that the latter conducts oversight functions as a parliamentary sub-committee while the former functions as an independent commission that focuses more on social accountability through compliance and observation of ethics and authorized procedures by managers of public enterprises.[74]

In the Gambian context, PAC/PEC draws its legitimacy from the 1997 constitution as well as the rules of Parliamentary Procedure. Thus, section160(c) and section 175 mandate the National Assembly to 'scrutinize' the audited accounts of public financial institutions and public enterprises in The Gambia.[75] These constitutional provisions blend with the rules of parliamentary procedure to grant legitimacy to PAC/PEC.

According to sections 160 (c) of the 1997 constitution, at least once every year, the Auditor General shall audit and report on the Public Accounts of The Gambia, the accounts of all offices and authorities of The Government of The Gambia, the accounts of the courts, the accounts of the National Assembly and the accounts of public enterprises. Thus, inspection of books of accounts of every public institution and public enterprises, where government has interest is a constitutional mandate of the Auditor General in our government system. It is the audited accounts of these public institutions and enterprises that the Public Accounts and Public Enterprises Committee (PAC/PEC) of the National Assembly is mandated to scrutinize. This oversight function of the National Assembly which includes the scrutiny of government expenditure, examination of financial records and statements to ensure compliance with authorized procedures relating to expenditure, is a new democratic principle in the state and governance system of The Gambia. It provides for *"public accountability through legislative scrutiny"*. [76]

It should, however, be mentioned that the mandate of PAC/PEC excludes its rationalization of government programmes which inform the expenditures for which oversight is being provided.[77] This implies that PAC/PEC lacks the constitutional mandate to question the policy rationale of government. Instead, it should be primarily concerned with investigating compliance and efficiency of public officials and making post audit recommendations to the National Assembly on the issues raised in the Auditor General's report.

IV. PAC/PEC's relationship with the Auditor General

The relationship between PAC/PEC and the Auditor General is somewhat symbiotic in nature. The PAC/PEC is the traditional audience of the Auditor General. The symbiotic nature of this relationship is highlighted in the fact that PAC/PEC relies on high quality audit reporting to provide effective oversight while the Auditor General in turn requires an effective PAC/PEC to ensure that points raised in the Audit report are pursued post audit. This point highlights the potency of The Gambia's presidential committee on post audit recommendations of PAC/PEC.

V. PAC/PEC's mandate and oversight functions

Following the discussion in the preceding section, PAC/PEC's work depends largely on Auditor General's report. Thus, PAC/PEC's functional remit focuses on oversight of financial expenditure to ensure among other things that money was used as intended by the National Assembly that payments and receipts were made in compliance with prescribed protocols and procedures.[78] As part of its financial oversights function, PAC/PEC uses key benchmarks like regularity and propriety as benchmarks of assessment. The *'regularity'* benchmark interrogates receipts and expenditure in accordance with legal and regulatory guidelines like budget appropriation Acts and other related performance legislation. *'Propriety'* on the other hand focuses on scrutinizing ethical practices that revolve around evidence of conflict of interest, avoidance of waste, and compliance with due process and open competition frameworks.[79]

As public service delivery continues to evolve from the old and traditional public administration to new public management, the oversight function of PAC/PEC recognizes this shift and thus mandates the Committee to include three additional benchmarks as it scrutinizes audited accounts. In jurisdictions where new public management principles have been fully incorporated into public sector management, the accounts of government agencies and public enterprises would be checked by PAC/PEC using the three *'Cs'* - Economy, Effectiveness, and Efficiency as additional benchmarks.[80] While the National Assembly in such jurisdictions uses the "economy" benchmark to assess the ratio of such operational inputs as staffing and fixed inputs against cost in monetary terms, "efficiency" and "effectiveness" assess the ratio of public service output to financial input, and outcomes (public service impact on society) against output respectively.[81]

The Gambia has been identified as a good example of accountability best practice by both internal and external oversight agencies.[82] Which is in line with global trends;[83] The Gambia Government's Medium Term Expenditure Framework (MTEF); and National Medium Term Development Plan or the PAGE.

Conclusion

The central theme of democracy and human rights has been broadly explored in this chapter. Thus, the pragmatist approach has been used to explore the relationship between democracy, human rights, and good governance in The Gambia. Documentary and empirical evidence of governance practices in The Gambia have been triangulated with the provisions of the Universal Declaration on Human Rights in an effort to appraise democracy in The Gambia. The emerging pattern, however, is that The Gambia is a democracy whose ideals are consistent with the universal norms of good governance as discussed in Section 2. The evidence presented suggests that democracy in The Gambia bears the hallmarks of a state that is guided by its constitution as it seeks to institute measures to uphold the rule of law and a national culture of transparency and accountability based on the doctrine of separation of governmental powers. Thus, the civil and political rights of Gambian citizens and residents are upheld and guaranteed. While this chapter outlines the obligations of states and citizens in the maintenance of the rule of law, the discussion in Section 2 conceptualizes democracy as an open-source concept that should be adapted to fit social and indigenous political cultures. Thus, the guarantee for fundamental human rights and freedoms has been presented as the metaphor for democratic governance in which the beliefs and value systems of a country are used by its citizens to articulate their interests and uniquely mediate their differences. This implies that the evaluation of a country's democracy must recognize the uniqueness of its people and cultures and applaud all institutions and processes that have been used to achieve political and social stability. The institution of the rule of law holds equality and individual rights and freedoms above political, economic, and ethnic inclination. In The Gambia, the mere fact that citizens are enabled to exercise their rights, meet their obligations, and mediate their differences is a clear manifestation of good governance and democracy.

4

Press Freedom and Democratic Governance in The Gambia:

A rights-based approach

Abstract

This chapter explores the relationship between democratic governance and the free and independent press since the inception of the Gambian First Republic in 1970. It is constructed within the logic of the rights-based approach, which perceives the issues of democracy, good governance, and a free and independent press as related to the modern concept of human rights and fundamental freedoms. Put differently, the free and independent press is not only a mirror of good governance but also one of the essential elements of democratic governance. This chapter represents a modest

114

contribution to the existing literature on the questions of governance, democracy, press freedom and human rights in The Gambia.

Introduction

Press freedom is a prerequisite for the establishment of a functioning democratic system of government and fundamental human rights as well. Embodied in the principle of freedom of expression, press freedom is a concern and principle of international and national human rights law and a basic norm of civilized behaviour. It is viewed by many as a fundamental necessity and an essential ingredient of the process of democratic governance. Thus, governments are expected to permit the press, particularly the private press, to function responsibly, without undue obstruction. Press freedom is not only an indispensable pillar of democracy, but it is also important for the long-term sustainability of social and economic development. A free press is a yardstick for the evaluation of good governance just as respect for human rights is a conspicuous mark of the good governance philosophy. The two are essential ingredients of a democratic system of government.

Since the Tocqueville era, the press has become even more central to democratic discourse worldwide. The advent of broadcasting dramatically extended the reach, influence, and scope of the media. The scale of the media operations further increased in the 1980s onwards using global satellite communications and fibre optics technology. Our new millennium is therefore one of a new revolution in the media that is bound to reshape society through the spreading use of personal computers, the Internet and others forms of social media. The media therefore reveals the democratic culture of a given country and the study of its centrality to the question of democracy, human rights and good governance is urgent.

There is a paucity of research on the media and democracy in The Gambia. Amie Bensouda (1999) and Nana Grey- Johnson (2001) respectively undertook an in-depth study of media laws and the history of the media in The Gambia since the colonial days but these authors did not critically establish the link between press freedom, democracy, good governance on one hand and human rights on the other. Perhaps the lone ambitious project to study and monitor progress in practice of democracy and good governance in The Gambia was undertaken by a group of scholars of the University of the Gambia (Faye, Taal and Suso 2004). The research team came up with a huge document that touches upon various aspects and dimensions of the governance system in The Gambia. The document discusses issues like social inclusion in political participation and integral governance, checks and balances in the 1997 constitution, respect for human rights and the rule of law and the restrictive nature of the human rights provisions of the 1997 constitution. However, about the respect for civil and political rights, the document only makes a situational analysis of government's attitude towards the subject. It peripherally addresses the linkages between good governance, the respect for human rights and the autonomy and freedom of the press. Similarly, the section on the media establishes the fact that independent news media is an indispensable element for good governance, but it is neither explicit nor critical. In other words, the human rights dimension of free media participation in politics and its significance in the democratization process is not illuminated.

This chapter attempts to study the linkage between democratic governance and press freedom in The Gambia from a human rights perspective. This will represent a significant contribution to the existing literature on the issues of democracy, human rights, governance, and press freedom in the country. In writing this chapter, the author had to rely on interviews with media houses, court cases and newspaper publications.

This chapter comprises three sections, an introduction, and a conclusion. The first deals with conceptual and theoretical issues.

116

This functional and working definition serves as a yardstick that is to examine critically the nature and level of democratic governance and press freedom in The Gambia. The section considers in detail many of the principles and concepts relating to the human rights perspective of democratic governance. The second section focuses on democratic governance in The Gambia, private news media practice and press freedom across government's interaction with the independent news media. These include a brief account of the historical development of the private press and a detailed description of the incidents, types, methods of the alleged violations of press freedom in the country. The third section addresses the human rights dimension of press freedom in The Gambia. The conclusion is a set of suggestions and recommendations as the way forward for mutual co-existence between the government and the media practitioners as a way of sustaining democracy and human rights. I now move on to the first section which confides the theoretical and conceptual background of this chapter.

I. Theoretical and conceptual framework

Democracy has been defined in various ways using different approaches. Saward argues that the best approach is to look at those countries known to be democratic and define the concept according to the main features of their practice (Saward 1994:6-2 1). For Beetham who takes the second approach the core principles of a democratic system are those embodied in the historical conception of democracy as the "rule of the people" i.e. popular control or sovereignty and political equality (Beetham 1993:6). According to Holden who constructs a conception of political democracy, inclusive citizenship and political equality are basic principles of a democratic system (Holden 1974:7-9). The definitions reviewed above seem to agree that there are four basic elements or core values of a democratic system i.e. equality, sovereignty/control, and inclusiveness. These include majority rule and participation, equality, freedom, consensus, coercion, competition, pluralism, constitutional rule and more.

Saward develops the assumption that in a democratic system "all citizens are equal with respect to their right to decide the appropriate political course of their community." It is important to state here that the basic characteristics of democracy are just more than the three core principles highlighted above. The pillars of democracy include:

• Free press

• Respect for human rights

• Constitutionalism

• Free and fair elections (regular)

• Separation of powers

• Popular participation

• Majority rule with respect for the minority, etc

• Pluralism

With all these pillars one can then argue that the system concerned is democratic. This has been re-emphasized by the Western donors viz: the International Monetary Fund (IMF) and the World Bank since the 1980s when democracy in the sense of popular participation, good governance and respect for human rights including press freedom were a prerequisite for obtaining their assistance. It is based on this equality assumption that Saward develops a general defining rule of democracy "Within the theory of democracy". Thus, according to this rule "substantive policy, and politics and administrative actions performed under substantive policy must correspond to the expressed preferences of a majority of citizens". In other words, "there should be necessary correspondence between acts of a government and the equally weighted expressed wishes of citizens with respect to those acts. This is what Saward calls responsive rule and for him a political system is democratic to the extent that and only to the extent that it involves realization of the responsive rule" (Saward 1994: 6 – 20).

The problem of the "responsive rule" definition is that it appears to suggest direct, rather than, representative forms of decision-making as the favourite. This is because direct decision-making processes are certainly more responsive than the representative forms. But in Africa in general and in The Gambia in particular, what obtains is the representative mechanisms of decision-making. To remedy this shortcoming of "the responsive rule" definition, which he himself acknowledges, Saward identifies some core principles or minimal conditions and describes them as "the logically necessary conditions of democracy." These principles are basic freedoms, citizenship and participation, administrative code, publicity, and social rights (Saward 1994: 6 – 21).

So, for a political system to be democratic it has to observe and respect the basic freedoms of the individual and it also must have a common and standardized form of legal membership compatible with the basic freedoms. There should also be appropriate codes of procedure for employees in public bodies, for decisions to be taken into effect and a constant formal process of public notification of decisions, opinions, arguments, issues, and outcomes of all these conditions or basic principles of democracy. The author is more concerned with basic freedoms, popular participation, and publicity as a means of actualizing the right to freedom of expression and press freedom and as a way of characterizing democratic governance as a fundamental human right. These values will therefore be included in the working definition of a democratic system for the purposes of this chapter.

According to Saward, there is another view which believes that democracy, being the rule of the people by the people and for the people implies, in political terms, the right of the people to choose freely their representatives. In his opinion, "a democratic administration is one in which the people, all the people, are enabled to express a free choice on all matters affecting them" (Saward 1994:6-21). However, it should be noted here that this view, too, recognizes the practical difficulty of operating a system of direct expression of the will of the people as implied by the "responsive rule" definition.

The working definition chosen by the author

In this chapter the rights-based approach to democracy or democratic governance is one which the author has chosen and which advocates the principles of constitutional rule, respect for human rights and fundamental freedoms particularly, the freedom of expression and press freedom, respect for the rule of law, independence of the judiciary and the legal profession, free and fair participation of multiple political parties in the political life of the state, free and fair elections organized at regular intervals, direct or indirect involvement of the populace in the affairs and political process of their country, the principles of accountability and transparency , separation of powers among the three main organs of government. These principles constitute the core values and major characteristics of a democratic system. Thus, by democracy it is understood a political system that adheres to the principles of constitutional rule, respect for human rights and fundamental freedoms particularly, the freedom of expression and press freedom, respect for the rule of law, independence of the judiciary and the legal profession, free and fair participation of multiple political parties in the political life of the state, free and fair elections organized at regular intervals, direct or indirect involvement of the populace in the affairs and political process of their country, the principles of accountability and transparency, separation of powers among the three main organs of government.

Democracy and Good Governance

Governance and Government

While government refers to the machinery and institutional arrangements for the exercise of sovereign power for serving the internal and external interests of the political community, governance implies the process as well as the result of making authoritative decisions for the benefit of society (Mander and Asif, 2004, p.11). Thus, governance means the act or process of governing, specifically, authoritative decisions and control (Collins York New Dictionary, 1997 edition) Governance, on the other hand, is the interaction between formal institutions and those in civil society. Another definition describes governance as "a process whereby elements in society wield power, authority and influence and enact policies and decisions concerning public life and social uplift" (Mander and Asif 2004, p.12) For the World Bank, governance is the way power is exercised in the management of a country's economic and social resources for development. Consequently, the term governance includes public sector management, accountability, the legal framework, transparency, and information". Many governments, international organizations, and multilateral and bilateral donor agencies including the Asian Development Bank share this World Bank's understanding of the notion of governance (The World Bank 1992 Governance and Development report P.1, and Mander and Asif 2004, p. 12). Consequently, governance refers to "the exercise of economic, political, and administrative authority to manage a country's affairs at all levels. [Thus] it comprises mechanisms, processes and institutions through which citizens and groups articulate their interests, exercise their legal (and human) rights (and fundamental freedoms), meet their obligations, and mediate their differences," (Mander & Asif, ibid).

The act of exercising economic, political, and administrative powers of the state to manage its affairs at all levels becomes democratic when the exercise is conducted and the mechanisms, processes, and institutions through which such authority is exercised are created and functions in accordance with the spirit of the basic principles of a democratic system identified above. In other words, a democratic government must be guided by a constitution, the principle of respect for human rights and the rule of law and free participation of citizenry in the government of their country. Modern international human rights conventions have guaranteed the right of every citizen to participate freely in the government of their country and to have equal access, based on non-discrimination, to the government and its services. (Articles 21 of the Universal Declaration of Human Rights 1948 and 13 of the African Charter on Human and Peoples' Rights)

However, beyond defining the concept of democracy as a participatory system of government, the emphasis from the 1980s was on good governance a concept that involves bottom-top participation from the election and empowerment of officials of the local governments to those of the legislature and executive, as well as press freedom which is underscored to create an atmosphere of transparency. It is expected to inform and expose shady deals, corruption, nepotism, ineptitude, election malpractices etc. It is therefore intended to play the role of a watchdog. Press freedom is not only a basic component of democracy, but it is also a central element of good governance. This brings us to a very important question that needs to be addressed viz: What is good governance? Is it the same as democratic governance?

What is good governance?

The above discussion on the nature of governance implies that governance has three major components namely, process, content, and deliveries. Factors such as transparency and accountability are included in the process while values like justice and equity are included in the content of governance. The third element (deliveries) ensures that the citizens especially the poorest have the basic needs and live a life of dignity. It needs to be clarified at this juncture that being able to deliver does not by itself constitute good governance. There is no doubt that a dictatorship that delivers basic needs to the citizens is better than a dictatorship that does not, but this is not enough to be good governance (Mander and Asif 2004).

Good governance, on the other hand, implies an administration that is sensitive and responsive to the needs of the people and is effective in coping with emerging challenges in society by strictly adhering to and implementing the principles of democracy discussed above. For the World Bank, good governance "is epitomized by predictable, open and enlightened policy making, a bureaucracy imbued with a professional ethos, an executive arm of government accountable for its actions and a strong civil society participation in public affairs and all behaving under the rule of law". This description of good governance by the World Bank obviously encapsulates the democratic principles of transparency, accountability, participation, respect for the rule of law and separation of powers. The European Union believes that "in the context of a political and institutional environment that upholds human rights, democratic principles and the rule of law, good governance is the transparent and accountable management of human, natural, economic and financial resources for equitable and sustainable development" (Mander and Asif 2004). This envisages a situation where there are clear decision-making procedures at the level of public authorities, transparent and accountable institutions, the primacy of law in managing and distributing resources and capacity building for elaborating and implementing anti-corruption measures. Government of the Netherlands added the elements of security, decentralization, and participation of civil society to the EU's definition of good governance. It argues that good governance must allow "a responsible economic and financial management of public and natural resources for the purpose of economic growth, social development and poverty reduction in an equitable and sustainable manner, with the use of clear participatory procedures for public decision-making, transparent and accountable institutions, primacy of law in the management and distribution of resources, effective measures to prevent and combat corruption, support for leadership and empowerment of men and women" (Mander and Asif 2004).

These two definitions of good governance by the EU and the Government of the Netherlands have substantially incorporated the principles and basic characteristics of democratic governance already alluded to. However, it is obvious from the exposition of both democratic and good governance that sometimes emphasis is laid on the managerial aspect of governance, while at some point the focus is on the systemic aspect. The former is a characteristic of the definition of good governance, whereas the latter is a natural outcome of the definition of democratic governance. Whatever the case maybe, for the government of the day to be both good and democratic, the two aspects of governance (systemic and managerial) must be adequately enforced. In other words, the system within which one governs must be based on the core values of democracy, while the style and manner of managing the resources and affairs of a country are not only transparent, accountable, or effective but are also equitable, sustainable, and responsive to the needs of the people.

Human rights and democracy

It is clear from the above exposition that in the modem art of governance, the linkage between democracy and human rights is not only real but it is genuinely crucial. The two are not necessarily the same but it is fair to say that any struggle for democracy, particularly in Africa, is in essence a struggle for human rights. Furthermore, human rights do not and cannot exist or prosper in undemocratic societies. According to Zehra Arat "Where a political system falls on the scale of democracy largely depends on the extent to which it recognizes and enforces civil and political rights. The more strongly civil and political rights are reinforced in a society the more democratic it becomes" (Zahra Arat 2000:2-4). The international human rights movement has, both in theory and practice, always emphasized democratic principles. The global and regional instruments have identified several democratic principles as fundamental human rights. These include popular participation, multiple political parties, freedom of expression and press freedom, and equal access to public services, periodic and genuine elections. Democracy is about those values, and they are also fundamental human rights. Human rights therefore are basic values for a genuine democratic system.

In view of the above argument, one may conclude that democratic governance itself is an emerging fundamental human right. Furthermore, the following principles of democratic governance are essential requirements for the full realization and enjoyment by people of their fundamental human rights in any modern society.

The rule of law

By the rule of law is meant the supremacy of the authority of the law that all people and institutions are equally subject to the control and dictates of the law. The principle of the rule of law emphasizes the equality of people before the law and equal protection of the law, the legality of the administrative acts of the political authorities and fairness or constitutionality of the legal authority backing the legislative and administrative activities of the government of the day. In other words, it is not only enough to govern by law, but the law that is used to govern must be just, fair, and reasonable. Furthermore, rule of law in the modern time also calls for the prevalence of law and order rather than anarchy and the supremacy of international law particularly the international human rights law to domestic legislation. In other words, the rule of law means that states and governments most respect their international obligations and give effect to them (Wade and Philips 1997:44-45).

Constitutional rule

The principle of constitutional rule as a core element of a democratic system can only be effective if the constitution enjoys a supremacy status within the legal and political system of the country. The concept of constitutional supremacy teaches that the constitution is the supreme law of the land and all other laws, executive decisions, and administrative activities of the government of the day must be in conformity with the constitution; otherwise, they are declared null and void by a court of competent jurisdiction. In 2005, the Supreme Court of The Gambia, in **Sabally v Inspector General of Police,** nullified several provisions of the Indemnity (Amendment) Act 2001 for contravening the human rights provisions of the 1997 Constitution of the Republic of The Gambia and Article 7 of the African Charter on Human and Peoples' Rights which guarantees the fundamental right of the individual to access the courts of the land. (Sabally vs. Inspector General of Police and others (Civil Ref: No. 2/2001, 1999 to 2001: GR at 883**).** This principle is established in Section 4 of the 1997 Constitution of the Second Republic of The Gambia. Constitutional supremacy also ensures a more conducive environment for the observance of the rule of law and the independence of the judiciary.

Independence of the judiciary

An independent judiciary is an indispensable prerequisite of a political system that adheres to the principles of the rule of law and freedom of expression. It implies freedom of the judiciary from interference by the executive or the legislature with its exercise of the judicial functions of the state. It is important to explain that judicial

126

independence does not mean that the court or the judges are entitled to act in an arbitrary manner. Rather, it means non-interference by the political authorities and all other interest groups in the affairs of the judiciary (A.A. Senghore: 2010).

Separation of Powers

Within a system of government based on law, the legislature, the executive, and the judiciary distinctly and separately perform legislative, executive, and judicial functions of the state respectively. This three-fold division of labour between the three main branches of government is a necessary condition for the rule of law in modem society and therefore democratic governance itself (Wade and Philips 1997:44-45). In Africa in practice, the situation is different, what happens in many countries is that the executive dominates other arms of government (A.A. Senghore: 2010). As already alluded to, the principles of democratic governance just highlighted are all incorporated or embodied within the juries-corpus of the modern concept of human rights fundamental freedoms. This confirms my earlier suggestion that democratic governance is becoming a matter of rights. In other words, democratic governance is an emerging and fast-growing fundamental human right of peoples and communities. I now move on to the second section which examines press freedom and democratic governance in The Gambia.

II. Democratic governance, the independent news media and press freedom in The Gambia

There is no exaggeration in saying that The Gambia's political system has since, the inception of the First Republic in 1970, to a certain extent adhered to the democratic principles highlighted above. The country's degree of adherence to and commitment to such principles varies from one principle to another and as the next section shows the performance of successive governments of the two republics in press freedom has been fluctuating and sometimes very weak for several reasons. At this juncture, let us briefly examine Gambian democratic credentials in the light of the remaining values of a democratic system.

Constitutional rule: The Gambia has since independence been governed by written constitutions both under the First and Second Republics. The constitution of the First Republic (1970-1994), which enjoyed a supremacy status, had 134 articles and its Chapter III guaranteed protection of human rights and fundamental freedoms. The constitution also had provisions that provided for free participation of multiple political parties in the political life of the state and for holding free and fair elections at regular intervals. Free and fair elections were indeed held after every five years interval with the last elections taking place in 1992. The constitution recognized the doctrine of separation of powers and guaranteed the rule of law and the independence of the judiciary. Article 42 vested the executive powers of The Gambia in the president, while Article 56 vested the legislative powers of the country in parliament and part (1) of Chapter 8 entrusted the judicial power of the republic in the courts of the land. The country had during this period maintained many legislative enactments passed by the colonial administration and enacted so many other laws to support the constitution in the governance process. All this is in theory but in practice the chief executive officer of the nation during this period like any other African president incarnated all other arms of government and became the most powerful man in the country. Despite that and as court cases of the period have shown, the judiciary was largely independent and human rights were generally respected and protected. There were many instances in which the executive lost court cases to individuals and private organizations and the courts for contravening the constitution and/or its human rights provisions invalidated legislative instruments and executive orders (Modou Jobe vs. the Attorney General 1984:AC689).

The Court of Appeals in its judgement dated 11th May 1981 in Momodou Job Vs the Anthony General of the Republic of The Gambia invalidated Sections 7, 8, 9 & 10 of the "Special Criminal Court Act 1979" for violating the constitutional rights of the appellant (Modou Jobe Vs the Attorney General 1984:AC689- 700, Kaba Jallow vs. the Attorney General 1972: Not reported).

All that has been said about the nature and extent of democratic governance in the First Republic is generally identical with and applicable to the Second Republic. From 1997 to date, The Gambia is being governed by a written constitution defined by its section four as being the supreme law of the land to which all laws, government policies, Executive Orders, decisions, and all other governance activities should conform. The remaining democratic values of protection of human rights and fundamental freedoms, observance of the rule of law, independence of the judiciary, multiple political party participation in the political process of the country, free and fair periodic elections, the doctrine of separation of powers, transparent and accountable government have been guaranteed by the 1997 constitution of the Second Republic of the Gambia (Sections 4, 7, 17 - 38, 60, 139 — 159, 76, 100, 120 respectively of the 1997 Constitution).

The new constitution also introduced additional institutions that could only strengthen Gambian democracy under the Second Republic. These include a permanent independent Electoral Commission, a judicial service commission, the high court system, and an Office of Ombudsman (Sections 42-45, 145-148, 131-133 and 163-165 respectively of the 1997 Constitution of The Gambia).

Despite several attempts to intimidate and interfere with the work of the judiciary, the courts have largely asserted their authority and maintained their independence. Recently the government has lost important court battles involving high profile cases to political opponents and individuals. In June 2005 the High Court in a highly controversial murder case filed by the government, acquitted and discharged the main opposition leader Mr. Ousainou Darboe and four others who were accused of murdering a supporter of the ruling party in 2000 (A.A. Senghore: 2010).

The above discussions seek to establish that, despite serious lapses in press freedom as shown below, The Gambia has both under the First and Second Republics been generally governed by law and therefore largely democratic.

Independent news media: Definition

By independent news media, reference is made to both the print and broadcast media that are not owned, controlled or in any way influenced by the government of the day or by a political party, a pressure group, or any other ideologically based organization. An independent press should be able to distance itself from both the government and the opposition parties to be truly independent. This is what is understood by independent news media practice in The Gambia in this chapter. Currently, there are several daily, weekly and bi-weekly newspapers namely, the *Daily Observer, Foroyaa*, the *Gambia Info, The Independent, The Point, Daily Express, Today, The Voice, The Standard*, and *Daily News*. The only papers that fit the definition of independent news media are *the independent, Today, The Voice, The Standard* and *Daily Express*. However, *The Independent* and *Daily Express* are currently not in circulation. They are serving an indefinite suspension or closure. However, given the nature of *The Independent* as the most independent paper in the country this chapter focuses a lot of attention on it. This chapter suffered from one obvious shortcoming namely, it used to take a tougher stance with the government of the day than the opposition and was inclined to lay more emphasis on exposing the shortcomings of the government than highlighting its achievements. This argument does not necessarily discredit *The Independent*, as the reason for this attitude might be the absence of vibrant opposition in The Gambia. Similarly, the nature and style of government that governs the Second Republic may be another factor. As for the *Daily Observer* it is known to be a pro-government newspaper, while *The Point,* though independent, is not critical enough in the way it addresses crucial issues. *The Gambia Info* is government owned, while *Foroyaa* is owned, controlled, and heavily influenced by the political ideology of its founders. However, it is important at this juncture to consider Nyamnjoh criticism of the independent press or newspapers in Africa today. According to him many of the so-called independent press or newspapers are not truly independent, in some cases; they might be the mouthpieces of the opposition parties. While highlighting the shortcomings of the liberal democratic theory for Africa's media, he argues that the private press has assumed a partisan, a highly politicized or a militant role. There is a growing obsession with the politics of belonging, nationality, and citizenship. Consequently, identity politics has become central to the political process even with the media (Nyamnjoh 2005:235-237). This criticism by Nyamnjoh of the independent press in Africa does not in any way defeat the purpose of this study, which examines the relationship between the independent news media and democratic governance in The Gambia because no matter how the private news media are described, the fact that they operate as independent or private news media organizations remains a reality of modern-day politics in Africa in general and in The Gambia in particular.

Independent news media practice in The Gambia: A brief historical overview

The independent print media

In May 1871, Thomas Brown, an English entrepreneur, and a member of the legislative council of the colony, founded The Gambia's first newspaper *The Bathurst Times* (Johnson 2004:31-32) This chapter was sent to London for printing and the finished product then sent back to Bathurst by boat for circulation. Although *The Bathurst Times* was privately owned, the colonial government of 1781-1783 used this chapter "to discuss official government matters and to convey messages or explain policies" as the establishment did not have a medium of its own (Johnson 2004: 31 – 33).

On 23 January 1883, a syndicate of African Merchants launched another newspaper, this time Gambian owned. This chapter *The Bathurst Observer and West African Gazette* (Bathurst was before independence the name of the Gambian capital, which is now called Banjul), being privately Gambian was sometimes very critical of the colonial administration. It attacked several government policies and draconian laws, such as the law that allowed a debtor to be jailed for insolvency (Johnson 2004:50-55). Another privately owned newspaper; *The Gambia Intelligencer* was on 31 July 1883, founded by younger elements of Gambian merchants in the persons of Sam J. Forster, Sam Jones, Henry R. Carroll, and A. W. Carroll. According to Nana Grey Johnson, "This chapter was printed by a four-paged monthly journal with shareholders in Bathurst "The Gambia intelligencer" therefore, was "the first paper functioning in the corporate realm. A group of merchants, lawyers and private individuals established the first truly weekly journal for the Gambia in 1934" (Johnson 2004:129-14 1). This chapter, *The Gambia Echo*, lived through the days of the First World War. *The Gambia Weekly News* was another privately owned paper published twice a week. The

132

former founding editor of *The Gambia Echo* founded this chapter in 1940 immediately after his resignation from the latter. *The Gambia Weekly News* was reportedly soft on and friendly with the colonial administration because the founder had for years been desperately hoping for a royal pardon to redeem his image following his conviction in 1918 to serve seven years imprisonment for defrauding the government of more than 590-pound sterling (Johnson – ibid). It is quite clear from the above exposition that the culture of independent print media practice existed in The Gambia almost for a century before the advent of nationhood.

The advent of nationhood in the 1960s accompanied the proliferation of privately owned media organizations. Many of the newspapers during the first decade of nationhood were founded either by individual editors or by political parties and were characterized by the following: While Newspapers of the past were published on conventional machines; the post independent ones were cyclostyled sheets. In the words of Nana Grey-Johnson, they "took on politics as central rationale." In other words, "journalism as a craft and profession had given up the front seat to political exigency" (Johnson 2004:279). The newspapers during this period were, in most cases, run by one man-company possibly because of their inability to employ staff. So, the publisher was also reporter, editor, proofreader, distributor, salesclerk, accountant, and advertising salesman" (ibid). The newspapers of the period included *The Gambia Outlook, The Nation, The Gambia Times, The New Gambia, The Gambia Onward,* and *The Torch,* all of them were established in the 1960s and have since died a natural death. With the establishment of the *Daily Observer* in 1992, by a Liberian born editor, Kenneth Best as the Gambia's first daily newspaper, Gambian journalism and the culture of private print media was sent into "an unprecedented upward spiral" (Johnson 2004:279).

In May 1999, Amadou Samba, a Gambian lawyer turned businessman bought the Daily Observer Company, thus making it finally a Gambian owned daily. This was followed by the establishment in 1999 of *The Independent* by a new and young breed of journalists in the persons of Baba Galleh Jallow and Alhagie Yorro Jallow. Baba Galleh was before the establishment of *The Independent*, editor-in-chief for the *Daily Observer*, a position he resigned on 6 June 1999, in protest over the sacking of his assistant D.A. Jawo who is one of The Gambia's best-known independent news media practitioners in contemporary times. The next part shows that *The Independent* used to be the most independent news media organization in the Second Republic, not only in terms of ownership but also in terms of its editorials and the stories it carried (Johnson 2004:280-283).

Thus, in the period after independence particularly, during the last two and a half decades, the private press in The Gambia has been very vocal about human rights violations and bad governance but this has not happened without a heavy price both in terms of human and considerable material losses. Media houses, writing and publishing equipment including a printing press were occasionally burnt down. Private radio stations closed, and journalists were physically assaulted and, in some cases, murdered. In mid-December 2004, unknown assailants murdered a highly vocal and one of the leading journalists in the country, Deyda Hydara[2], a former editor of *The Point*. Up until now, all investigations into his assassination have so far been fruitless. Around the same period the government promulgated the Newspaper Amendment Act 2004 and the Criminal Code Amendment Bill 2004. The newly amended Acts cancelled all the licences that had previously been issued to the news media and forced them to re-register, while at the same time increasing the cost of a publishing

---

[2] It was revealed at the Truth, Reconciliation, and Reparations Commission (TRRC) in Banjul in 2019 that he was murdered by state security agents in an operation code-named "the magic pen."

134

licence five-fold, from 2, 600 Euro to 13, 000 Euro (US 3000- US 17000). It also forced journalists to adopt a strict code of conduct within six months and imposed sanctions on violators of the new law. Reporters Without Borders after learning that a new press law was promulgated on 28 December 2004, appealed to the international community to put pressure on the government of the Gambia to stop what it called "its mounting crackdown on Gambia's independent news media" (BBC Focus on Africa:27/12-2004).

I now move on to highlight some of the problems that were allegedly faced by *The Independent* and some of its own shortcomings.

The defunct *Independent* newspaper and its problems in the past

The method of using intimidation, physical assault or arbitrary arrest and detention, death threats or arson attacks and assassinations against media practitioners of the independent press in The Gambia, as claimed by the former *Independent*, is mainly a phenomenon of contemporary times. And interestingly enough this newspaper, which was believed and considered by many to be the most independent and most critical of all the privately owned media organizations in The Gambia during that time, had the biggest share of those incidents of alleged attacks, arrests, detention and interference with press freedom over the recent years. Since its inception in 1999, this chapter complained about so many problems with the government of the day. According to *The Independent*, its editors and reporters were repeatedly arrested and detained, beaten up and otherwise physically assaulted. In an exciting brainstorming session, which lasted for more than one hour between the former editor-in chief of *The Independent*, some of its senior reporters and the author, the defunct company was unable to provide an exact figure of such incidents. However, with the help of this chapter's back issues which were carefully kept in its archives we were able to come up with a good picture of the nature and types of the incidents the newspaper had been complaining about and the circumstances leading to some of those incidents.

Alleged attacks on the *Independent*

Registered on 5th July 1999, *The Independent*, which was a breakaway from *Daily Observer*, had allegedly suffered more attacks than any other Gambian private news media organization. The biggest onslaught on the weekly newspaper was the burning down of its US$50, 000 worth printing press in April 2004 by unidentified people. In September 2003, this chapter's offices were put on fire by unknown arsonists. The newspaper claimed that in the past, Mondays, and Fridays (the days of publications) were considered bad days for journalists at its headquarters as security men would be lurking around. This chapter had its first onslaught a few days after it started operations. Its staff reporter, NB Daffeh was arrested and briefly detained by the police at the Bundung Police Station for investigating a story titled "Handicaps [sic] Decry Immigration Maltreatment." One month later, state security agents allegedly raided the offices of *The Independent* and arrested all six staff members who were at work. The agents also ransacked the offices and went away with its official registration papers, thus forcing it to close down publication for three weeks. It was accused of defying an order from the Registrar of Companies not to publish this chapter. Exactly 12 months after operations, *The Independent* had its fourth arrest. In all these cases of arrests and detention, the editors and reporters bore the brunt. In June 2000, there was another complaint by *The Independent* that the state security agents questioned the nationalities of its founders and proprietors – Baba Galleh Jallow and Alagi Yorro Jallow. The following month, Baba Galleh Jallow, chief editor and a staff reporter, Alagie Mbye were arrested. In June 2000, Alagie Mbye was threatened by gunmen who dropped a letter in his house. In July 2001, another reporter was allegedly attacked by a group of soldiers and in August of the same year another was arrested and detained for three days by the National Intelligence Agency (NIA). In November 2001, a senior reporter of this chapter was allegedly arrested and detained for one week, while in January 2003 *The Independent* received death threats from unknown callers. Furthermore, around the middle of the same month Alagi Yorro Jallow received a death threat. The latest onslaught on this chapter allegedly occurred in October 2005 when its former editor-in-chief, Musa Saidykhan, was arrested by the NIA for inviting President Thabo Mbeki of South Africa to help find a solution to the killing of Deyda Hydara. The agents conceived this as hypocrisy because the matter was purely a national affair and did not therefore need an international solution. The editor's nationality and that of his wife and parents were questioned before he was finally released.

(See the following issues of the Independent Newspaper: 23rd – 25th, July 1999; 19 – 22 August 1999; 21 – 23, 28-30 July; and 27 – 30, November 2000. Also, 16-19, 20 – 22 July 2001; 17-19 August and 23 – 25 November 2001. Also, 13-16, January and 22 –25 September 2003; 16 – 18, January and 8-11 April 2004; 24-27, October 2005. This list showing various issues of *The Independent* is not an exhaustive one. Rather, it is only an example of all the issues surveyed, which gave a detailed account of the newspaper's confrontations with the state).

Attacks on other private news media houses

The end of 2004 was marked by the tragic killing of a leading editor and veteran journalist Mr. Deyda Hydara. Mr. Hydara was, on the night of 16th December, driving home from his office when he was shot three times in the head by unidentified gunmen. He was the managing editor and co-owner of *The Point*, an independent bi-weekly paper. He was also a correspondent for *Agence-France Presse*, a former President of the Gambia Press Union, and a known critic of administrative malpractices of successive governments in The Gambia. The reason for his killing is not yet known and killers are yet to be identified. However, his death came only a day after he and a group of Gambian journalists opposed the passing of the controversial National Media Commission Act already alluded to in this chapter. Likewise on 15 August 2004, the former BBC Banjul correspondent Mr. Ebrima Sillah suffered from a terrible arson attack on his home in Banjul. In the early hours of that day unidentified armed attackers broke several windows of Ebrima Sillah's home and poured petrol inside his living room before setting it on fire. Mr. Sillah escaped uninjured, but the fire caused extensive damage to his property. This attack was a serious warning to the independent press in The Gambia as only three days before the attack the Gambia Press Union had received a threatening letter that was thought to have come from a pro-government militia group called "The Green Boys." The letter accused the private news media in The Gambia of being Western agents, who were bent on sabotaging the development programme of the government of the day. The letter then said they "planned to teach a GPU journalist a lesson very soon." This arson attack was also not conclusively investigated, and the culprits are still at large (IPI report, December 2004). Finally, Radio 1 FM in 2000 had its own share of the series of arson attacks on the independent press. The premises of the radio were attacked and burnt down by unknown arsonists who had earlier dropped death threat letters into the private room of one of its programme managers Mr. Alieu Bah. The owner the late George Christensen suffered burns all over his body during the attack.

What all these alleged series of attacks have established is that there was an atmosphere of mistrust and intolerance hanging over the relationship between the government of the Gambia and the independent news media in the country. This misunderstanding and the overall relationship of mistrust and intolerance between government and the private news media in The Gambia has not only weakened the country's performance in the area of press freedom as an essential ingredient of democratic governance but it has also seriously weakened and marginalized press freedom as a fundamental human right. Perhaps this explains why the African Editors' Forum

138

meeting on 15 October 2005, in Johannesburg, South Africa, placed The Gambia together with Togo, the Cote d'Ivoire, Burkina Faso and Sierra Leone on top of the list of countries in Africa with the worst records of press freedom violations (The Independent, Monday, 24-27, October 2005). However, as shown below, this state of affairs between the government of the Gambia and the private news media has now drastically changed and the country's performance in the area of press freedom as a principle of democratic governance has significantly improved.

Views of the critics of the former *Independent* newspaper

This picture of mistrust, suspicion and intolerance presented by *The Independent* newspaper as having dominated the relationship between the government of the day and the private news media does not represent the views of a few but very strong minorities in the academia and other circles. All those complaints of abuse and violations of press freedom made by *The Independent* newspaper against the Second Republic of The Gambia had never been independently verified or proven and neither were they admitted by the government of the day. Rather, critics of *The Independent* totally disagreed with such complaints and described them as baseless and politically motivated allegations with the sole objective of tarnishing the image of the government. Some moderate but sound academics and researchers admitted that *The Independent* had suffered from one major shortcoming - that is, this chapter would most of the time focus its attention only on shortcomings rather than the positive achievements of the Jammeh administration. This, perhaps, was mainly responsible for the poor relationship that existed between the government and The Independent. This chapter's critics further argued that despite some lapses and shortcomings of the government of the Second Republic in press freedom, government in The Gambia has always been largely democratic (A.A. Senghore: 2010) The country is being governed by a clean and democratically structured constitution pronounced by its section four as the Supreme Law of the Land. The Constitution provides in its chapter four comprehensive and adequate guarantees of fundamental human rights; it recognizes the doctrine of separation of powers and guarantees an independent judicial system (Sections 4, 7, 76, 100 etc of the 1997 Constitution.

The political and governance system of The Gambia under the Second Republic has also incorporated the democratic principles of transparency, accountability, and popular participation. Thus, all the essential principles of democratic governance, which constitute a democratic system of government in contemporary times are not only incorporated into the state, political and governance system of The Gambia but most importantly they are practised daily in the process of governing the country (A.A. Senghore: 2010, also: 2005).

The independent broadcast media

As for the broadcast media the situation is different from the print one. The first transmission signals arrived in April 1926 when two officers of the West African Frontier Force, Gambian Company, Sergeant Major Hepworth, and Sergeant T.L Freeman, were granted licences to operate wireless transmitters, in the colony of The Gambia (Johnson 2004: ibid). This type of licence was, before 1926, granted only to commercial firms "needing to communicate with ships delivering or taking away goods from the port of Bathurst" to encourage local broadcasting and it was during the war in 1940 that listeners in the colony began to enjoy a form of radio broadcasting through a Local Broadcast System (LBS) provided with the help of cable and wireless transmissions (Johnson 2004: Ibid).

The British government used the Gambia Broadcast station "Radio Gambia" during the war for Propaganda purposes and war promotion. Thus, after the end of the war the government in London stopped encouraging "Radio Gambia" and wished to concentrate on broadcasting from "Radio Accra" as the official transmission centre. The governor of the day was ordered to close "Radio Gambia" and keep it only for emergency news broadcasts. For more than a decade broadcasting was stopped in The Gambia and it was on 1 May 1962, when Radio Gambia went on the air again broadcasting on 4.82 MHz, on the 60-meter band, short wave. Eight years later a modern and fully equipped radio station complex was opened at Mile 7, Bakau, by the visiting Nigerian Head of State, General Yakubu Gowon (Johnson 2004: Ibid).

Independent radio stations

Currently, about 30 radio stations are legally operating in The Gambia, most of these stations are privately owned. There are many of them in the Greater Banjul Area, while others are operating in various towns and urban centres in the provinces. These include the stations in Brikama, Kerewan, Farafenni, Sapu, George Town or Janjangbureh and Brikamaba. There are stations in Basse, the provincial centre of the Upper River Region, Jarra Soma which is a major town in the Lowe River Region, Bwiam in the West Coast Region and elsewhere in the country. (Brikama is the provincial capital of the country's West Coast Region, while Kerewan is the centre for the North Bank Region. Farafenni is an urban commercial centre in the North Bank Region; Janjangbureh is the provincial centre of the Central River Region, while Sapo is an agricultural training post in the same region).

Some of the private radio stations are temporarily closed by the authorities. The Citizen FM and Sud FM are among those that are affected and the validity of the move to close the latter is yet to be challenged before the courts. This has been the second time for the former to be closed by the authorities; Citizen FM was about ten years ago closed by the government but reopened after a high court ruling to that effect (Baboucarr Gaye vs Inspector General of Police, HC. (2000) 8 Weekly Law Report of Nigeria, pp.189-200)

Most of the private radio stations are purely commercial stations, while the others are community radios sometimes engaging in commercial activities as well. *Radio Syd* was the first independent station to be established not only in The Gambia but also in West Africa as a whole. It was established in 1970 broadcasting 20 hours a day mainly music programmes in English and the local languages. It also provides tourist information in Swedish (Europa World year book1990:1089- 1094). In 1990, *Radio 1 FM* was established in Serrekunda as an independent commercial radio station. The establishment in 1995 of another privately owned radio station *Citizen FM* by a veteran journalist and a former BBC Banjul Correspondent the late Baboucarr Gaye was another significant achievement by The Gambia in terms of increasing the privately owned broadcast media organizations in the country. Like *The Independent* newspaper, Citizen FM had a troubled history with the government of the Second Republic, and this is further discussed in the next section.

Improved relationship

Notwithstanding the above arguments, the relationship between government and the independent news media has improved very significantly over the past few years. The type of incidents and violations of press freedom that were reported by *The Independent* and other private news media organizations are not heard of or read about in any local newspaper anymore. It is quite clear from the pattern of relationships that we see today existing between the government and the private news media that the two are getting to understand each other now better than ever before. Likewise, the two diagrams below have established that despite all sorts of intimidations, violations and abuses of press freedom reported or claimed by "the Independent" and other private news media organizations against the government of the day, there has been a proliferation of private news media organizations in The Gambia over the past 10 to 15 years.

There has been a huge increase both in number and type of private news media organizations in The Gambia, print and broadcast alike. If these trends continue for the next ten years, the country's ranking in terms of performance in press freedom as an essential component of democratic system governance will be one of the best in the whole of the African continent. In that case it would be impossible for any government of the day to manipulate, suppress or intimidate what would be a massive network of independent news media organizations in the country. At this juncture, I need to explain that the performance indicators relating to the functionalization of the principles or essential elements of democratic governance highlighted above only address themselves to the systemic aspect of governance - that is, the system with or according to which governance is conducted. This does not necessarily ensure good governance for the realization of which the performance indicators in terms of sound management of resources and the responsiveness of the process of governance to the needs and aspirations of the masses particularly those at the grassroots level, must be equally positive. In other words, for good governance to be realized both the systemic and the managerial aspects of the process of governing are equally important (Mander and Asif: 2005)

The tables below show most of the media organizations, both broadcast and print, established in the country over the past three and a half to four decades:

Table A – The broadcast media

A list of radio stations in The Gambia

Station	Location	Frequency
GRTS Radio	Mile Seven (Bakau)	648KHZ, 98.6FM, 96.0FM & 102.5FM
GRTS Radio	Basse (URR)	747KHZ
West Coast	Manjaikunda	95.3, 92.1
City Limits	Westfield	93.6
Paradise	Kololi	105.7
KWT	Kairaba	107.6
Vibes	Manjaikunda	106.1
FMB	Brikima	98MHZ
Taranga	Sinchualagie	97.5
Unique Fm	Bakau	100.7
Kora Fm	Kanafing	103.9
Hill Top	Tabokoto	104.7
Radio 1 FM	Banjul	102.1
Jannehkoto FM	Gunjur	-
Paradise FM	Basse (URR)	-
Farafenni Community Radio	Farafanni NBR	-
Bwiam Community	Bwiam (Foni Kansala)	-
Kerewan Community Radio	Kerewan NBR	-
Soma Community Radio	Jarra Soma LRR	-
Brikimaba FM Radio	CRR South	-
Unique FM	Farafenni NBR	-

Paradise FM	Farafenni NBR	-
Unique FM	Basse URR	-
Capital FM	Kairaba Avenue	-
Citizen FM	Kanifing Estate now Closed	
Sud FM	Banjul now Closed	
Radio Syd	Banjul now Closed	

Table B – Some of the print media

Name of Newspaper	Year of Establishment	Status
The Gambia Info	2009	Still in Operation
Foroyaa	31 July 1998	Still in Operation
The Daily Observer	11 May 1992	Now Closed
The Independent	1999	Now Closed
Today	5 July 2007	Now Closed
The Voice	8 August 2008	Still in Operation
Daily News	6 April 2009	Still in Operation
The Point	16 December 1991	Still in Operation
The Standard	11 May 2010	Still in Operation
Gambia Daily (Formally Gambia Weekly established in 1989)	1994	Now Closed & Replaced by Gambia Info
Daily Express	2007	Closed / Defunct
The Gambia News & Report Magazine	February 18th 1992	Still in Operation

AHOOAH Magazine	2008	Still in Operation
The Senegambia Sun (news weekly)	August 1983	Closed / Defunct since 1985
The Gambia Outlook (in miniature)	1922 (in Rufisque – Senegal and then moved to Banjul in 1927)	Closed in 1992
The Nation (Formally Africa Nyaato)	1962	Closed / Defunct
African Unity	1965	Defunct
New Gambia	1962	Defunct
The Gambia Times	1962	Defunct
The Gambia Onward	1966	Defunct
Torch Newspaper	1984	Defunct since 1993
The Vanguard	1958	Defunct since 1960

The number of newspaper organizations listed under Table B above covers more than 97% of the print media organizations that were established and functioned in The Gambia during the period of more than one century ago up to the present time (Johnson: PP 281 – 333).

As indicated above, the significant increase both in number and type of private news media organizations in The Gambia in recent years as shown by the two tables displayed above is a clear indication of a major improvement in the relationship between the independent news media and the government of the day. However, out of all the newspaper organizations shown on diagram / table B only three of them were owned by political parties. The rest were /are independent newspapers. The political party owned papers are: *The Gambia Times* established in 1962 and run by the former People' Progressive Party – the PPP, which ruled The Gambia since independence in 1965 until 22nd July 1994, when the government of Sir Dawda Kairaba Jawara was overthrown by the military in a bloodless coup. The second political party owned newspaper is *African Unity* which was established in 1965 and ran by Garba Jahumpa a co-founder and leader of the Democratic Congress Alliance (DCA). Thus, this chapter, which became the official mouthpiece of the DCA party, was founded by both Jahumpa and J.C. Faye. The third political party owned newspaper is Foroyaa established in 1987 by a newly established political party embracing socialism as its political ideology. The party established in 1986 is called People's Democratic Organization for Independence and Socialism (PDOIS) locally known as DOI (Johnson 2004, PP 316 – 333).

The fact that the vast majority of papers shown on this diagram were / are independent and nonpartisan clearly indicates that the culture of independent news media practice has existed in The Gambia for more than a century and that as shown above many of the media practitioners of this period and before were somehow conscious of the human rights nature of independent news media practice, particularly that of newspaper journalism. Unlike the situation with the independent broadcast media, most of which established during the Second Republic, a large number of the independent print media organizations existed and functioned actively in the First Republic (Johnson: 2004 PP. 281 – 333). This observation does not contradict the above conclusion that there has been a significant increase, both in number and type, of the independent news media organizations, print and broadcast alike, in the Second Republic of The Gambia.

Press freedom in The Gambia

By press freedom it is understood a press which has the freedom to publish anything without any form of censorship, intimidation or interference by the government or the leadership of a privately owned press or of any other organization or institution or individual. As the next section explains, press freedom is a fundamental human right that should be guaranteed and protected by the state. Thus, it is a violation of the right to press freedom for the state or for any other entity, organizations, or interest group to screen, disrupt or in any other way interfere with all news material before publication to decide what may and what may not be published (Feltoe 1993:15-186). However, I must also note here that like all the branches or arms and agencies of the state and individual citizens as well, the press should respect the laws of the land and be strictly governed by it. This is because media practice as a profession or as a method of disseminating information and ideas is a fundamental right and all human rights and fundamental freedoms, their actualizations and enjoyment are guaranteed and governed by law. Thus, the imposition of measures and restrictive regulations intended to ensure that rule of law prevails and life in society is safe and secure and peaceful for all does not necessarily amount to violation of press freedom. It has been argued in the preceding section that the privately owned media are not always truly independent and free of control, rather they may be and indeed they are sometimes controlled by their owners. Their editorials and main stories published often reflect the thinking, ideological and political orientations of the owners. In this way, they must be fair with not only the government of the day but most importantly with society and the media fraternity and make sure that the stories they carry are objectively reported. *Foroyaa* is an example of a privately owned newspaper, which is influenced by the political orientation and the socio-economic ideology and thinking of its founders. This critical observation does not necessarily contradict the working definition of independent news media practice above. Rather, it reflects an attitudinal rather than a theoretical problem of private press in many African countries.

However, in The Gambia and elsewhere on the continent the poor relationship between the state and the independent news media could pose a serious threat to press freedom. Similarly, training of media practitioners, as shown below, could be a major factor to blame for the troubled relationship between the authorities and the independent organizations. Even though the main methods of interference with the freedom of the media in many countries are censorship, in Africa such methods go beyond the scope and level of normal censorship. The methods of interference used in our time across the continent include intimidation, death threats, arbitrary arrests, and detention, beating up and assassination of media practitioners as well as arson attacks on media houses and the closing and burning down of their premises, printing machines and offices. Added to all these, is the introduction of restrictive laws to control strictly the independent news media and probably to be able to track down certain elements of the opposition who would want to use the private news media for political and other purposes

Press laws in The Gambia

The print media in The Gambia is governed by the Newspaper Act 1944. Registration, printing, publication, and distribution of Newspapers in The Gambia continue to be governed by the Act throughout the First Republic (Sections 3, 4 and 5 of the Act). Section 2 of the Act defines newspapers as "any paper containing and reporting any public news, intelligence or occurrences or any remarks, observations or comments thereon printed and published for sale in The Gambia periodically or in parts or numbers but does not include any such paper published by or under the authority of the government". According to this definition, government controlled or owned papers are not newspapers. Thus, apparently the Act is meant to govern the privately owned print papers. Despite a 1990 amendment the main provisions of the Act remained the same throughout the First Republic. Section 7 of the Act provided for a mandatory registration fee of only 1000 (One thousand dalasis about 40 US Dollars) for anyone who wished to establish a newspaper. Similarly, Section 13 imposes a maximum of 1000 Dalasis fine for an offence under the Act. In 1996, the Armed Forces Provisional Ruling Council (the then military government of Captain Yahya Jammeh who ended the life span of the First Republic in a bloodless coup on 22 July 1994) introduced a drastic amendment to that Act. This amendment known as Decree No 71 of (the Newspaper Act amendment No 2, 1996) increased registration fee from 1000 (One thousand Dalasis) to 100, 000 (One hundred thousand dalasis) that is from about 40 US Dollars to about 3500 (three thousand and five hundred Dollars) for anyone wishing to establish a newspaper. This was a crucial turning point in the relationship between the new military government that had set out to establish the Second Republic and the independent news media.

As for the broadcast media, there was no specific legislation regulating private radio and television stations. From the inception of the First Republic to 2005 the privately owned broadcast media continued to be governed by the provisions of the Telegraphic Stations Act 1913, which was very favourable to the independent broadcast media. In July 2001 the Gambian parliament which was dominated by the ruling party, the Alliance for Patriotic Reorientation and Construction (APRC) passed a highly controversial law to be called the National Media Commission Act, as stipulated in Section 210 of the 1997 Constitution. The press cried foul and argued that the new law was too draconian and that it violated the 1997 Constitution. The government, on its part, believed that the passage of the new law was a significant gain in the country's democratization process as it would not only regulate media practice as a profession and a means of communication and expression, but it would also ensure better protection of the freedom of the press including free speech and press freedom in The Gambia (*Daily Observer*: June 2004). The Gambia Press Union then filed a lawsuit before the Supreme Court of The

Gambia challenging the constitutionality of the new Act. Among the most controversial clauses of the Act were the following: there was a provision on the annual licensing of journalists, which also gave the Commission powers to renew or not to renew the operating licences of journalists and media houses. Other controversial provisions were:

• The Power of the Commission to force journalists to reveal their sources of information

• That all decisions of the Commission are not contestable in any local court

• That the new regulations would not be applicable to the government owned or controlled media

• That the composition of the Commission had among its eleven members only two persons with media background who included the director general of the Gambia Radio and Television Services (GRTS) (Johnson 2004:413-416, also see Section 52 of the defunct Act).

The media houses in The Gambia resolutely refused to comply with different deadliness set by the Commission for their registration. On October 19, 2004, the State television announced the government's intention to repeal the Act during the November sitting of the National Assembly. During its sitting in December 2004, the National Assembly finally repealed the National Media Commission Act 2001. The provisions of the Constitution which had provided for the setting up of the Commission were subsequently repealed (Section 210 of the 1997 Constitution). Repealing of the National Media Commission Act did not bring an end to the struggle by authorities to use the law to control the private news media. Rather as a replacement, the National Assembly further amended the Newspaper Act and the Criminal Code Act late in December 2004 and July 2005 respectively. This latest amendment to the Newspaper Act increased the registration fees/bondage of Newspapers / publishers and managers of broadcasting institutions from D100, 000 to D500.000 (five hundred thousand Dalasis) which is about $18, 000. This increase in a country where the average salary for a civil servant range between US 40 and US 70 is deemed by many as unfair and unreasonable thus it is fair to argue at this juncture that its constitutionality can be successfully challenged before the Supreme Court of The Gambia under whose jurisdiction falls the interpretation of the constitution. Sections 3 and 4, as amended, have brought broadcasting institutions (Radio and T.V stations) into the jurisdiction of the Newspaper Act.

Like the 1944 Act, the 2004 Act (amendment) has excluded broadcasting institutions owned or operated by or under the authority of the government from the application of the Act. Similarly, Section 7 has been amended to include broadcasting stations. Now no person shall be allowed to operate a broadcasting station or cause it to be operated unless he/she gives and executes and registers in the office of the Registrar General a bond in the sum of five hundred thousand Dalasis with such surety or sureties as may be required and approved by the Attorney General. Section 7 (a) cancelled any bond given and executed before coming into effect of the newly amended Act in the sum of D100, 000. Furthermore, the Criminal Code (Amendment) Act 2004 has introduced mandatory prison terms for seditious publications, libel, and defamation without the option of fines (Section 52 of the Act). As for the 2005 amendment of the same law, it provides for a fine of not less than fifty thousand Dalasis and not more than two hundred and fifty thousand Dalasis or imprisonment of a term of not less than one year or to both fine and imprisonment, for anyone who is found guilty of seditious publication (Johnson 2004:236-238 and Conateh 2000: paper presented in June of the same year).

This brief survey of press laws in The Gambia has shown that successive governments of The Gambia and the people as well do not recognize or may not necessarily be conscious of the rights dimension of press freedom and of the fact that it is a prerequisite for or a pillar of a democratic system. Many human rights activists and media practitioners have argued that the use of restrictive laws by the state to control the private news media is one of the main reasons why press freedom is very weak in The Gambia.

The press in litigation

It appears from the materials surveyed that taking court action or litigation against journalists was dominantly used as a method to control and interfere with the independence and freedom of the private press in The Gambia, during the years preceding and throughout the period of the First Republic. When the first press laws were passed and entered into force in The Gambia in 1944, with the primary purpose of giving aggrieved parties an opportunity for redress, people and the state started to seek recompense for libel, defamation, and false publication. In 1948, Finden Dailey, a former editor of Gambia's *Weekly News* was sued by Dr Gordon of Bansang hospital for publishing what Dr Gordon would describe as a false story about him (Johnson 2004: ibid). Earlier in 1941, the superintendent of police sued the same Dailey who was then editor of *The Gambia Echo* for a slanderous publication. Likewise, in 1968 a former manageress of Atlantic Hotel in Bathurst sought redress against Baba Musa Tarawally and Muhammed El Habib Sock, editors of *The New Gambia* newspaper for slander and libel. She claimed that the two falsely accused her of racism and financial impropriety in her administration of the hotel. All these cases were decided in favour of the journalists concerned. But in 1969 a former editor of *The Gambia Onward* Mr. R.S Allen found himself in court facing charges of false publication filed against him by the Inspector General of Police. Mr Allen was found guilty but when he appealed against the conviction in 1971 the Court of Appeals acquitted him. In 1981, immediately after the Kukoi Samba Sanyang's coup, former President Dawda K.

Jawara instituted cases against two London-based publishers *West Africa* magazine and the *Daily Express* newspaper. In 1984, the government was in court again, this time action was against Mr. William Dixon-Colley editor of *The Nation* newspaper. Dixon was charged with sedition, but the case was thrown out of court (Johnson 2004: ibid).

The period between 1971 and 1994 witnessed three high profile cases involving the state and the private news media and which are seen as significant and outstanding given their contribution to the human rights jurisprudence of the Gambian courts in press freedom. In the case of Inspector General of Police Vs Baba Musa Tarawallie, 1971 and the state vs. Sanna Manneh, 1988, the two founders — editors of *The New Gambia* and *The Torch* newspapers respectively were charged with criminal libel and slander. In the state vs. Foroyaa in 1994 the publisher was charged with sedition. These cases are important, and they struck the attention of the legal fraternity because the prosecution of criminal libel was indeed a very rare occurrence in The Gambia. In the case involving Sanna Manneh, for instance, he wrote an article in his solely owned, edited, and managed paper — *The Torch*, entitled "cabinet reshuffle inevitable" and he called for the sacking of the ministers of information and tourism, agriculture, and works and communication. The editor accused the three ministers of corruption, mismanagement, and maladministration of funds in their respective ministries and while in court he pleaded not guilty. A magistrate who acquitted Sanna on the first and the third counts found him guilty on the second concerning Landing Jallow Sonko one of the ministers accused but pardoned him. The state then appealed to the Supreme Court, which in turned reversed the magistrates' court's judgement. The editor then appealed to the Court of Appeals, which reversed the Supreme Court judgement on a technical ground - that is, proper notice had not been given when appeal was made to the Supreme Court and therefore the latter lacked jurisdiction to entertain the case (Johnson 2004:238-239; also, section 178 of the Criminal

154

Code Act 2005). In 1998 the *New Citizen Weekly*, another weekly paper founded by the proprietor of *Citizen FM* radio was hindered and it stopped circulating because its editor owner was involved in another case against the state. This case, the IGP vs. Citizen Radio, 1998, is one of few examples in which the state in the Second Republic has used litigation against the private news media (Baboucar Gaye Vs the Inspector General of Police 2000: WLR 189-200).

Closing radio stations

Given the limited number of privately owned radio stations in The Gambia during the First Republic, and that private broadcasting only started in the country in the 1970s, the practice of closing independent radio stations as a method of interference with or obstruction of press freedom, was not as rampant as other methods already highlighted were. Currently, there are only two significant cases worth mentioning and both have taken place in the Second Republic. In 1990, the *Citizen FM* radio, belonging to a veteran journalist and a former BBC Banjul correspondent, the late Baboucarr Gaye, was closed by the state and proprietor taken to court on charges of operating without a licence contrary to Section 5.7 of the Telegraphic Stations Act 1913 and Regulation 4 made under Section 12 of the Act. The Kanifing Magistrates' Court serving as the court of first instance convicted Mr. Gaye and sentenced him to one month imprisonment with hard labour with the option to pay D350, 00 as fine. The court ordered the radio station be forfeited to the state. Thereupon, Gaye appealed to the High Court in Banjul against his conviction and sentence and on 3 July 2000, the High Court reversed the judgement of the magistrates' court. In his ruling the late Justice W.G Grante Jr. decided that the principal magistrate erred in law and therefore he quashed the conviction and sentence and the consequential order of forfeiture passed on Gaye. The High Court then ordered the state to restore to Babouccar Gaye his radio apparatus and property, which were forfeited, within 7 (seven) days for the radio to resume its normal operation. The High Court Judge during his judgement described freedom of expression not only as a fundamental right but also a basic necessity of a democratic system. The High Court's ruling in this case is significant for various reasons including the following:

• That the court was well conscious of the rights dimension of independent news media practice as a basic principle of a democratic system.

• In an outstanding pronouncement, the High Court recognized the fact that the work of the media to seek and disseminate information freely is a cornerstone of a democratic system in every civilized country of the modern world. (Gaye Vs the IGP 2000: WLR 189-200).

• This case posed a serious challenge to the independence of the Gambian judiciary because it provided the latter with yet another golden opportunity to assert its authority and correct and check on an increasingly ever-powerful executive.

The second private radio station to be subjected to closure by the authorities is *Sud FM*, which is jointly owned by a group of Senegalese and Gambian entrepreneurs. The radio, which was shut down early November 2005, is a subsidiary branch of the Dakar-based *Sud FM* and which the Senegalese government in October of the same year also closed. The reasons for the closure of Banjul Sud FM were not indicated even though there is a consensus among media practitioners and the radio audience in Banjul that during its 8 years of operation in The Gambia, *Sud FM* had never had any problem with the government and the public at large. The radio station's manager argued that Banjul *Sud FM* never had any problem with the Senegalese president Mr. Abdoulie Wade, suggesting the possibility of the parent station in Dakar being closed because of a problem between the radio and the Wade administration. Nevertheless, the *Sud FM* Banjul Station Manager thought that the closure of his radio which happened immediately after the return of President Yahya Jammeh from a one-day official trip to Dakar, Senegal could have been the result of an understanding between the two presidents, Wade and Jammeh. Whatever reasons there might be, the closure of *Sud FM* in Dakar and Banjul does not only represent a case of violation of press freedom in the two countries but also it shows the extent of vulnerability of private news media organizations in the Senegambia region despite their obligation under international law to respect, promote and protect the right to freedom of expression and free speech (Articles 19 of the Universal Declaration; 9 of the African Charter; and 19 of the International Convention on Civil and Political Rights). The crisis involving the closure of <u>Sud FM</u> has not yet been resolved and the radio is until now (May 2011) closed. The Gambia Press Union was said, at some point, to be working very hard through negotiation with the government to reach a lasting solution to the crisis but apparently to no avail. Although it was widely predicted that this case may finally go to court for a judicial solution, it seems that all parties have now lost interest in taking legal action for a judicial settlement of this case. Whether they reach judicial or out-of-court settlement there is need for all concerned to recognize and emphasize the human rights dimension of press freedom. This is what the next section sets out to explain.

III) Press freedom - a fundamental right or a political privilege?

The expressions, "press or media freedom, free speech and freedom of information," are synonymous and they all stand for freedom of expression, which is a fundamental principle of both international and domestic human rights law. Human rights and fundamental freedoms, including the freedom of expression, are God-given; they are an in-born attribute of the humanness of the human being. They are not created by the legal system, rather, the law guarantees their promotion and protection by way of providing mechanisms and institutions for their actualization and enjoyment by all and for them to be remedied in the event of any violation. Section 25 (1a) of the 1997 Constitution of The Gambia provides that, "Every person shall have the right to freedom of speech and expression, which shall include freedom of the press and other media." Earlier in the First Republic, Article 22 of the 1970 constitution guaranteed the right to freedom of expression, which included the right to hold opinions, receive and communicate ideas and information without any interference. The provisions of the two constitutions of The Gambia just cited were/are among the entrenched clauses of and therefore forming part of the fundamental law of the land to which all legislative, executive, or administrative and judicial activities of the state must conform.

In 1998, the High Court in Banjul quashed a judgement of the Kanifing Magistrates' Court in which an executive order closing a privately owned radio station and forfeiting its apparatus to the state was upheld. The High Court viewed the whole action as a serious violation of the appellant's right to freedom of expression in general and press freedom in particular. The High Court then made the following outstanding pronouncement: "It is an undeniable fact that the quest for knowledge and information through the media has become the hallmark and pattern of a healthy democracy in all civilized society throughout the whole world" (Baboucar Gaye vs. the IGP 2000: WLR200). This pronouncement has not only confirmed the right aspect of press freedom, but it has also recognized such freedom as a prerequisite for a genuine democratic system and that an independent and free press has a crucial role to play in seeking and dissemination of knowledge and information as part of the process of democratic governance.

Similarly, the underlined objective of regulating media practice in the form of legislation, as is the case with the Newspaper Act, Telegraphic Stations Act, and even with the defunct Media Commission Act one would assume is to facilitate and protect the work and persons of media practitioners in the country. At the international level, The Gambia as a sovereign independent state and a member of the international community of civilized nations is under obligation in international law to respect, promote and protect press freedom and freedom of expression in general. According to section 219 (c) of the Gambian constitution (1997) the Gambian state shall respect international law, her treaty obligations and (d) that The Gambia shall be guided, in international relations, by the principles, and goals of international and regional organizations of which the country is a signatory. Some of the regional and international arrangements that impose obligations on The Gambia as well as other African State to respect press freedom include the following: Principle One of the General Principles on Freedom of Expression and Broadcasting Regulations which is an African regional instrument, and which says:

1.1 Everyone has the right to freedom of expression which includes the freedom to seek, receive and impart information and ideas of all kinds, regardless of frontiers, orally, in print, in the form of art, through the broadcast media or through any other media of his or her choice.

1.2 The right to freedom of expression includes both the right of broadcasters to be free of state, political or commercial interference and the right of the public to maximum diversity of information and ideas in broadcasting.

1.3 Broadcast content should never be subject to prior censorship either by the government or by regulatory bodies. Any sanctions for breach of regulatory rules relating to content should be applied purely after the material in question has been broadcast.

Article 19 of the Universal Declaration of Human Rights provides that everyone has the right to freedom of opinion and expression. This right includes the right to hold opinions without interference and to seek, receive and impart information and ideas through any media regardless of frontiers.

Article 19 of the International Covenant on Civil and Political Rights guarantees the right to freedom of expression in these terms: "Everyone shall have the right to freedom of expression: This right shall include freedom to seek, receive and impart information and ideas of all kinds, regardless of frontiers, either orally, in writing or in print, in the form of art or through any other media of his choice."

Article 9 of the African Charter on Human and people's Right states that:

9.1 Every individual shall have the right to receive information.

9.2 Every individual shall have the right to express and disseminate his opinion within the law.

The African Commission for Human and People's Rights meeting at its 32nd Ordinary Session from 17-23" October 2001 adopted the Declaration of Principles on Freedom of Expression in Africa. Article One of the Declaration says:

    i.   Freedom of expression and information including the right to seek, receive and impart information and ideas either orally, in writing or in print, in the form of art or through any other form of communication including across frontiers, is a fundamental and inalienable human right and an indispensable component of democracy.

    ii.   Everyone shall have an equal opportunity to exercise the right to freedom of expression and to access information without discrimination.

The right to freedom of expression and press freedom is also protected by other regional human rights regimes such as the European Convention on Human Rights and Fundamental Freedoms; (Article 10) the Inter-American Convention on Human Rights. (Article 13) and Article 11 of the Charter of Fundamental Rights of the European Union (Which was proclaimed on 7th December 2000).

Similarly, as early as 1883, when *Bathurst Observer* newspaper was founded in The Gambia, African journalists, and promoters of the newly emerging private press in the colony of The Gambia were conscious of the importance of the right of private news media practice to their freedom and liberation. Sam J. Forster, for instance, former editor of *The Intelligencer* was a strong advocate of press freedom and a regular critic of the colonial administration. Known "as a crusading press man," Mr. Forster was uncompromising in his relentless attacks and criticisms of the colonial establishment for lack of fair play and justice with the local chiefs particularly the way the British planted their authority in villages and provincial quarters across the colony. The editor was once served an arrest order for reporting in his paper that the government was supporting chiefs in Wuli and Jarra who sided with the colonialists to harass Musa Molloh, the king of Fouladou who was opposed to them. Nana Grey Johnson believes that the Gambian press has inherited and assimilated the libertarian theory of journalism (Johnson 2004). He argues that the liberty of the people to have a say in their governance has been the struggle of the founding fathers of Gambian journalism and still characterizes the central pre-occupation of editors and writers in the Gambia. This element of right consciousness and right-oriented influence continued to characterize private news media practice in The Gambia throughout the period between 1871 to the time of independence (Johnson 2004).

Similarly, Gambian media practitioners, legal and judicial experts, opposition politicians and intellectuals of the post -independence era have always perceived and considered private news media practice and press freedom as a matter of right and not a mere political privilege. In the fundamental laws of the two republics, press freedom has been guaranteed and protected because it is a fundamental human right of the citizens on whose behalf the state exercises sovereignty and jurisdiction (Article 22 of the 1970 Constitution and Section 25 of the 1997 Constitution) Thus, it will be fair to conclude from the above vivid exposition that the state is not and cannot be ignorant of the right status/dimension of press freedom. A former information minister, Mrs. Nenneh Macdoll-Gaye, had one time   stated in a speech to the United Nations General Assembly that proliferation of media houses in The Gambia clearly shows government's strong commitment to allowing press freedom (*The Independent* newspaper 2OO5: Friday 28-30 October). At this juncture, one can only assume that the minister knew press freedom is a fundamental right and that her government is under obligation in international law to respect, promote and protect that right and committed to doing so. It is now appropriate for me to move on to the conclusion, which identifies some of the factors responsible for the of the problems and difficulties that the private press in The Gambia, sometimes face, while at the same time mapping out the way forward for independent news media practice in The Gambia

IV Conclusion and the way forward

A brief analysis of the data presented

This chapter has reached the following findings:

• That private news media practice started in The Gambia as early as 1871.

• That although the political system of The Gambia remains largely democratic since independence the country's performance in the area of press freedom as a core value of democratic system, it can be further improved.

• That the problematic relationship between the state and the private news media is partly due to the former's sceptical attitude and misunderstanding towards the latter.

• That lack of proper training and adequate skills on the part of many media practitioners is a main factor to blame for that problematic relationship.

• That attempts by some journalists to hide behind the private press for political purposes could create a lot of problems and hinder understanding between governments and private news media organizations not only in The Gambia but in Africa as a whole. There is, therefore, an urgent need for media practitioners to try to remain strictly professional, neutral and nonpartisan.

• That press freedom is a fundamental human right whose promotion and protection is guaranteed in the national constitution, the ordinary laws of the land and in international human rights conventions to many of which the Gambia is signatory.

• That there has been significant improvement or substantial increase both in numbers and types of private news media organizations in the Gambia under the Second Republic since its inception in 1997 to date.

• That Gambian media practitioners, statesmen and intellectuals have always understood and advocated press freedom as of right and not a mere political privilege

• That while press freedom as a basic principle of a democratic system is well-established fundamental right, democratic governance itself is an emerging right, the crystallization and consolidation of which, the independent news media, has a crucial role to play.

• Despite the uneasy relationship between the private press and the state, the successive governments of the two republics of The Gambia particularly that of the Second Republic, have contributed very significantly to the improvement of life and the betterment of the human person.

Thus, it will be practically useful for us to try to summarize the main factors responsible for some of the above findings:

- The low level of press freedom in The Gambia can or may be related to several factors including unfavourable press laws, blatant lack of professionalism or insufficient skills, and sometimes lack of access to information by reporters.

- As for the use of the laws to discourage the private news media, we have seen in the preceding section how the Newspaper Act has been amended by the government to increase registration fees for a private newspaper from D 1000 to D100.000 and finally to D500.000 (i.e. from US 40 to US 3500 and finally to US 18000).

- This latest increase in the registration fees of the private news media has now made it virtually impossible for most Gambians to embark upon private news media activity.

- Regarding professionalism and the problem of hiding behind the media for political reasons, it is obvious from the style of reporting, headlines, and value judgements we see in this chapters of today that Gambian media practitioners are in dire need of training in the techniques and art of journalism. Most of them are taken straight away from the classroom to newsrooms, television cameras or to the field to send news reports. Very often newspaper articles are quick to report the most popular rumours in town without any objective and well-researched analysis. Similarly, high profile court cases involving top politicians, thieves or suspected murderers are common front-page headlines, and because of being inefficient and inexperienced, reporters are usually "led only by the interest to report and then harvest being plentiful" but quality is always lacking. (Johnson 2004).

- Gambian media practitioners should be trained on various aspects of media professionalism, they should know governance issues, the process of democratization and democratic governance, human rights issues, the law not only that part of it relating to the media but also the general principles of the law and the important role the media must play in the rocky and rough road to development and nation building. At this point in time, university training in journalism could realistically provide the answer to the problems of insufficient skills and lack of professionalism in Gambian journalism. Although the University of The Gambia, which is still in its infancy, has not introduced a degree or even diploma programme in journalism and the country does not have a school of journalism of any kind, but plans are in their advanced stage, for the country's national university to introduce a comprehensive BA programme in journalism and mass communication very soon. In the meantime, a sort of rudimentary training is necessary to provide a short-term remedy to the problem of lack of professional training for Gambian journalists and the Gambia Press Union has a critical role to play towards achieving this objective[3].

- In 2003, a bold move was taken toward achieving this end with the establishment of the Gambia Media Training Institute through collaborative efforts of the Gambia Press Union, Gambia Radio and Television Services, the UNDP, the Gambia Technical Training Institute (GTTI) and the UNESCO'S BREDA Division in Dakar. The training centre "provided remedial courses covering

---

[3] The Gambia Press Union has established a diploma-awarding school of journalism and the University of The Gambia now awards degrees in journalism and communication.

functional English, communication theory, news writing, radio announcing, communication techniques and technology and computer assisted reporting," (Johnson 2004:337). The government of The Gambia takes the credit for the bold initiatives and the Gambia Press Union through its former president D.A Jawo highly welcomed the move and added that government efforts to provide the necessary training for journalists will only serve to render them more professional in their compartment and delivery. (The Gambia News & report 2003: December 28). With all these laudable efforts the author's visit to the Institute and subsequent reading of events taking place there have revealed that there is still a lot to be done as far as the short-term objective of providing a basic and rudimentary training in journalism is concerned.

- African governments' attitude towards the private press – a source for serious concern and another factor to blame. This factor could be related to lack of adequate commitment on the part of the state in various parts of the African continent to allowing press freedom and independent news media practice. This is because an independent and free press is the most feared force to the autocratic rulers and arrogant and undemocratic administrators of the modern-day Africa. Politicians, rulers, and administrators are always very nervous and sometimes reluctant to allow the media to reporting the instances or incidents of rampant corruption, abuses of power and administrative malpractices, which is a fundamental role for a well-functioning independent free press. The state in Africa apparently influenced by the authoritarian theory seems to be laying undue emphasis on loose and open-ended notions of protection of internal security and maintaining law and order to the detriment of press freedom. It is important to explain at this juncture that the state can and should allow press freedom without necessarily undermining its authority or even responsibility to maintain law and order and effectively protect its internal security. Likewise, regulating media activity does not necessarily mean violation of press freedom. In fact, if we are serious about recognizing the media as the fourth estate, the constitution and the other laws of the land should contain elaborate provisions on the composition, functioning, regulations, limitations, privileges as well as immunities and other governing rules of the media. In other words, society must be sensitive to the composition and to the whole question of handling the affairs of the media as it does to that of the judiciary as the third estate. As far as one can see, only people who are well educated in law always handle the judiciary, including both the bar and the bench. Furthermore, the essence of the rule of law is that government, civil society and non-governmental organizations and institutions including private news media organizations and individuals are all subject to the supreme authority of the law so long as the law is reasonable, fair, and just (Wade and Phillips 1977:84-96) or in line with the constitution. In case of The Gambia, the principle of fairness and reasonableness of the law is synonymous with that of constitutionality. In other words, laws aimed at regulating and governing the media must be in conformity with the 1997 Constitution, otherwise such a contravening law will be null and void (Section 4 of The Gambian Constitution 1997). It was for this reason that the repealed National Media Commission Act was viewed by many as draconian and subsequently challenged before the Supreme Court of the Gambia. In 2001 the Supreme Court invalidated several provisions of another controversial Act of Parliament known as the Indemnity (Amendment) Act for contravening the 1997 Constitution of the Gambia and the African Chatter on Human and peoples' Rights. (Sabally vs. Inspector General of Police ibid). Finally, the following few quotations explain African governments negative attitude or cynicism, scepticism, and authoritarianism toward the independent news media across the continent.

In 1972 a former Attorney General and Minister of Justice of the Jawara regime said: "We have a mandate to run this country and we will not allow one man with his pen to overthrow an entire government, what explanation we give to the people who gave us the mandate." This quotation explains its author's negative and suspicious attitude towards the media.

The question that arises here is will it be practically easy for one man to bring down an entire government with his pen? It is easier said or thought of than done. Another quotation from a former Master of the Superior Courts in The Gambia reads: "Instead of being a detractor or an adversary of government, a free press is an effective forum for public debate, a mechanism that facilitates an invaluable two-way communication between the people and their elected leaders. It's the very catharsis of discontent and an antidote to violence." This quotation explains the deep-seated scepticism, suspicion and mistrust existing between some members of the government and the private news media (*Daily Observer* Banjul 2000). In many Africa countries, advocates of human rights and press freedom as well as independent news media practitioners and rights activists are often seen or labelled as anti- establishment or adversaries of the government, supporters of the opposition and sometimes western agents (*The Independent* 2005: Monday 24-27 October).

The early development of rights consciousness in the minds of Gambian media practitioners may be a significant outcome of government's long standing suspicious attitude to and intolerance of the independent news media. This is a very logical explanation because it is natural that when people are suppressed, they become more conscious of their rights and dignity. When The Gambia was placed under military rule in 1994 and throughout the period leading to the inception of the Second Republic to the present day, human rights activism in the country has been intensified, civil society and rights advocacy organizations significantly increased (Senghore PhD 2005: Paper presented at the Management Development Institute).

William Dixon Colley, a former editor in Banjul, was quoted in 1964 as saying: "In a country where people have no facilities to express opinion through the press or the radio, relations between the government and the governed are bound to be strained. Experience has shown that the liberty of the people is insecure if the forces opposed to such liberty remain in power" (Johnson 2004:3 16). Thus, it is this feeling of insecurity that may force the people to revolt either physically or ideologically. Likewise, the advent of the modern international human rights systems and the subsequent active involvement by The Gambia in bringing about the Global and regional human rights revolution could be another significant contributing factor to the development of rights consciousness in the minds of Gambian journalists of the post-independence period.

The way forward

The way forward for democratic governance and press freedom in The Gambia is for the government, the media, and the rest of society to recognize and or consider the following observations:

• That although The Gambia is to a very large extent democratic, the country's democratic credentials in the area of press freedom are in one way or the other weak.

• A functioning responsible democratic governance system cannot be achieved without a free, efficient, and objectively critical independent news media. Objectively critical and responsible writing and reporting of events and issues help the government see or know about its shortcomings, weaknesses or mistakes and subsequently correct itself.

• That the government of the day is urged to relax the existing press laws and make them favourable to private news media practitioners. This measure will strengthen the country's democratic credentials in the area of press freedom.

• For the media to take up its position as the fourth estate and effectively play its role in the democratic governing and nation building process, it is high time for The Gambia to have a school of journalism of its own or a special department of that sort to be opened within the country's University. This will soon be achieved.

• Private news media organizations must respect the laws of the land, the people's culture and all other norms and standards of responsible behaviour.

• That Gambian journalists abide by all the principles of objective, truthful and responsible writing and reporting namely responsibility, independence, sincerity, truthfulness, accuracy, impartiality, fair play, and decency.

• That journalists are human rights defenders and promoters of good governance.

• That governments across the African continent should continue to respect, abide by and be serious with their international obligations to guarantee, respect, promote and protect press freedom, human rights and human rights defenders.

5

The Judiciary in Governance in The Gambia:

The Quest for Autonomy in the Second Republic

Introduction

The justice delivery system of a country is of paramount importance because it guarantees good governance, sustainable development, and poverty reduction.[1] This view is contained in the executive summary of the former United Nations Secretary General's (Kofi Annan) roadmap for the implementation of the UN's Millennium Development Goals (MDGs). In outlining measures that will help promote human security, Kofi Annan cited "strengthening the rule of law and taking action against transnational crime" as being among the most important of such measures. Thus, for peace, security and political, as well as economic stability, to prevail in a country, its justice delivery system must be able to answer decisively the following questions in the affirmative:

- Is public hearing guaranteed?
- Are court proceedings conducted and completed within a reasonable time?
- Do independent and impartial tribunals established by law administer the justice system?
- Does the country's court system have efficacious means of enforcing its judgments and orders?

According to Brobbery,[2] public hearing is important because it "connotes transparency, avoidance of corruption and [ensures] certainty." As for the independent tribunal question, this "entails a court system that is truly and meaningfully capable of operating without executive or legislative influences." On the reasonable time factor, Brobbery argues that it "implies resolution of the dispute within the period that will not frustrate investment programmes." Certainly, if a prospective foreign investor is a party to a dispute affecting his/her investment, he/she will not hesitate to go to another country if the dispute drags on for many years without settlement. On the efficacious means question, no judiciary can be referred to as good and efficient if disputes that it can resolve expeditiously, cannot be enforced effectively because of endless frustrating motions, reviews, and appeals.[3] Thus, like politicians who decide on policies and policy issues in the executive arm of government, the decisions of judges within the judiciary do have important consequences for society. Judges play the critical role of being arbiters between individuals and public institutions or public authorities exercising powers that may affect individuals.[4] On April 3, 2007, in Independent National Electoral Commission vs. Alhaji Atiku Abubakar (Appeal No. CA/A/71//2007), a Federal Court in Nigeria ruled that the Independent National Electoral Commission, a tool of the Executive, had no power to disqualify any political party from contesting an election. The court held that such power is vested in the court as provided for in the laws of Nigeria—Section 32 (5) of the Electoral Act 2006, Laws of the Federal Republic of Nigeria.

Thus, the role of the judiciary to facilitate and control the process of the exercise of power by state agents for the good of society and to prevent or remedy the incidents of abuse or misuse of power is crucial to the governing process. The judiciary, therefore, functions to ensure legality, fairness, accountability, and objectivity in the process of governing.[5] Despite the availability of a plethora of literature addressing various aspects and issues of governance, law, and justice in The Gambia, almost all of that literature tends to focus on issues other than the specific role of the judiciary, its performance, and the problems it encounters in administering justice in governance in the country. Some of these studies have examined questions such as (1) the law and legal profession in serving the community; (2) crime prevention as a precondition for development of international human rights norms in the Gambian legal system; (3) good governance and poverty alleviation; (4) the challenge of law to development; (5) the law and the media; (6) the rule of law as a means of ensuring sustainable economic development; and (7) the Senegalo-Gambian relationship in the context of Gambian diplomacy.[6]

Some other studies have attempted to carry out an extensive analysis of the history and development of newspaper journalism in The Gambia, the media, press freedom and governance, military rule and democracy, as well as the prospect of democratization under Jammeh, and the history and practice of globalization in The Gambia.[7] There is also some literature on the progress and practice of good governance in The Gambia, as well as on the political history of The Gambia, covering issues such as the country's social and economic setting, constitutional changes, partisan politics, electoral politics, external relations, the 1994 coup and the Jawara legacy.[8]

Furthermore, views have been expressed on the juridical foundations of governance in The Gambia, both in the First and the Second

Republic, institutions of the state, its sovereignty, citizenship, the judiciary as an arm of government and its structure, the position of the Attorney General as a political appointee within the judicial system, as well as public finance and local government matters in The Gambia.[9] These studies have produced useful information and detailed analysis of the various issues of governance. However, much of that literature does not specifically address the question of the judiciary, its role, performance, and challenges in governance under the Second Republic of The Gambia. Thus, in an attempt to expand the realm of the existing literature on various issues of governance in The Gambia, the present study focuses exclusively on the judiciary, its performance, and problems.

Theoretical and conceptual framework

The judiciary is that branch of government established to interpret and administer the law. Constituted by the courts and the judges, the judiciary determines "disputed questions of fact and law in accordance with the laws laid down by parliament and expounded by the courts."[10] The phrase "Judiciary in Governance" refers to the composition, order of hierarchy and functions of the judiciary within the structure of government as well as the important role it plays and challenges it faces in the governance process. On the other hand, an autonomous or independent judiciary is one that operates to deliver justice without being hindered by any form of interference or pressure, political or otherwise. For the judiciary to be autonomous, it must be able to carry out its functions independently of the executive and the legislative arms of the government. This principle of independence of the judiciary is one of the pillars of democratic governance.[11] As for government, it means the machinery and institutional arrangement for the exercise of sovereign powers for serving the internal and external interests of the political community. The judiciary occupies a central position within the overall structure of that machinery and institutional arrangement. On the other hand,

174

governance is the process, as well as the result, of making authoritative decisions for the benefit of society.[12] It means the act or process of governing, and specifically refers to authoritative direction and control. According to Mander and Asif,[13] "[g]overnance is a broader notion than government, state and regime and it is the interaction between formal institutions and those in civil society. In other words, the process of governing is specifically an act of making authoritative decisions and control, and the judiciary wields a considerable part of this authority. At common law, the judiciary is traditionally considered the safe protector and guardian of human rights. This is because the role of the common law judge is essentially to interpret and enforce the law. This role of the judge under the common law system is extremely important to the process of governing because the law, whether the constitution or the ordinary law, is what the judges say it is.[14]

Today, the judiciary is recognized as the third branch of government with the executive and the legislature being the first and the second estates respectively. Judges of the courts system act on behalf or in the name of the government of the day. Thus, if the maintenance of the state government on a daily basis is the sole function of the executive, the authoritative interpretation and actual enforcement of the laws passed by the government's legislature is a sole function of the judiciary. Society cannot govern properly, smoothly, and successfully in the absence of an independent, efficient, well-motivated and vibrant judiciary. According to the principle of separation of powers, the judiciary should carry out its functions independently of the executive and the legislature so that the former can effectively hold the latter to accountability. "Broadly speaking, there are three methods of ensuring governmental accountability" and the most important of these methods is its accountability to individuals through the courts.[15] This is a direct reference to the principle of judicial review of the executive, known as the supervisory jurisdiction of the courts over the administrative or the executive authorities. According to this principle, the courts have power to police the legality of decisions made by public authorities or executive orders of the government and also to determine the constitutionality or fairness and responsibleness of any legal authority or legislative instrument made by lawmakers.

For the purpose of this study, it would be appropriate to examine the composition and hierarchy of courts, the appointment of judges, their tenure, and other matters of relevance to the judicature system in The Gambia. Thus, the section that follows looks into these issues.

The judicature of The Gambia

Sections 120 to 148 of the 1997 Constitution of The Gambia deal with the structure, composition, and jurisdiction of the courts in The Gambia. There are two main categories of courts in The Gambia, namely:

- The superior courts comprising the Supreme Court, the Court of Appeals, the High Court, and the Special Criminal Court.
- The lower courts comprising the Magistrates' Courts, the District Tribunals and such lower courts as may be established by an Act of Parliament. This includes the Industrial and the Rent Tribunals.

According to Section 120(2)(a) of the Constitution, the judicial power of The Gambia is vested in the courts of the land and exercised by them according to the respective jurisdictions conferred on them by law. Section 120(3) of the 1997 Constitution guarantees the independence of the courts in the following terms: "In the exercise of their judicial functions, the courts, the judges and other holders of judicial office shall be independent and shall be subjected only to this constitution and the law." According to this provision, the judiciary in The Gambia shall not be subjected to the control or direction of any person or authority outside the judiciary. Subsection 4 of this Section makes it a mandatory duty upon the government, its departments, and
176

agencies to assist the courts as they may reasonably require protecting their independence, dignity and effectiveness. Section 121 (1) states that the Chief Justice shall be the head of the judiciary and subject to the authority of the Constitution; he or she shall be responsible for the administration and supervision of the courts.

Hierarchy of courts in The Gambia and their respective jurisdictions

Since independence from Britain in 1965, The Gambia has had two distinct types of court system. Below, we briefly examine the court system in the First (1970-1994) and Second (1994-2017) Republics.

The courts in The Gambia in the First Republic (1970-1994)

During the First Republic, which lasted from 1970 until 1994, the courts in The Gambia were structured as follows:

- The Judicial Committee of the Privy Council at Westminster in England as the Court of Final Authority for The Gambia (Judicial Committee Act 1833).
- The Court of Appeals—Section 88(3) of the 1970 Constitution of the Republic of The Gambia.
- The Supreme Court, which enjoyed unlimited original jurisdiction to determine any civil or criminal proceedings under any law (Section 89 (1) of the 1970 Constitution).
- Subordinate Courts, comprising of the Special Criminal Court, the Magistrate Court, the Rent and Other Tribunals as Parliament might establish—Section 94 (1).

According to the appeals provisions of the 1970 Constitution, the Judicial Committee of the Privy Council, located in the UK was the highest judicial body and the Court of Final Authority for The Gambia. Next to the Judicial Committee was the Court of Appeals followed by the Supreme Court and the Subordinate Courts at the bottom of the ladder. According to those provisions, appeal could be made from decisions of the Subordinate Courts to the Supreme Court and from the Supreme Court to the Court of Appeals and from the latter to the Judicial Committee of the Privy Council in London (See Sections 95(1)(a)(b), 96(2) and 97(1) of the 1970 Constitution of the First Republic of The Gambia. Furthermore, the Judicial Committee, serving as the Court of Final Authority for any appeal coming from Banjul, enjoyed all the jurisdiction and powers possessed in relation to that case by the Court of Appeals in The Gambia. Thus, its decisions in such cases were to be enforced in the same manner as the decisions of the Court of Appeals.

Structure of the courts in The Gambia in the Second Republic (1994-2017)

The Supreme Court is the highest judicial institution in The Gambia today, followed by the Court of Appeals. The High Court and the Special Criminal Court apparently enjoy equal status and are ranked below the Court of Appeals. As for the Magistrates' Courts, District Tribunals, and other lower courts, they are at the bottom of the ladder, although the former is apparently ranked above the rest. Consequently, an appeal may lie from the Magistrates' Court to the High Court or from the High and the Special Criminal Court to the Court of Appeals and from the High Court and the Court of Appeals to the Supreme Court. The latter may review its own previous decision and depart from it when it appears that it is the right thing to do. In June 2002, the Supreme Court constituted a review panel comprising the Chief Justice and six other judges of the court to review its 2001 judgement in the case involving the Indemnity Act (Act No. 5 of 2001). As a result, the review panel set aside the court's 2001 judgement. All other courts are bound to follow the decisions of the Supreme Court on a matter of law. The Supreme Court has an exclusive original jurisdiction for the interpretation and enforcement of any provision of the Constitution other than Sections 18–33 and Sections 36(5), which relate to fundamental rights and freedoms (Section 127(1)). The Supreme Court has original jurisdiction on the following:

- To determine the question of constitutionality or otherwise of any law made by the National Assembly or any other person or authority or whether any law passed by parliament, or any other person or authority was in excess of the powers conferred on it/him/her by any other law.[16]

- The question whether any person was validly elected to the Office of President or validly elected to or vacated his/her seat in the National Assembly. (Section 127 (1) (c). In July 2005, The Gambian Supreme Court ruled that Mr. Halifa Sallah and three other members of Parliament have, by virtue of creating and joining a new political alliance, different from their original parties, vacated their seats in the National Assembly and as a result, their seats were declared vacant. This is in accordance with Section 91 (1) of the Constitution. Section 91 (1) states that "[a] member of the National Assembly shall vacate his/her seat in the National Assembly if he/she ceases to be a member of political party on whose ticket he/she was originally elected to the Assembly."[17.]

- On any question whether any official document should be produced, or its contents be disclosed in proceedings before a court where such production is resisted on the grounds that its production or the disclosure of its contents, would be prejudicial to the Security of the State or be injurious to public interest (Section 127(1)(d)).

Where any question relating to those matters falling under the original jurisdiction of the Supreme Court arises in any proceedings in any other court, that court shall stay its proceedings and refer the question to the Supreme Court for its determination. The court making such referral shall then give effect to any decision of the Supreme Court on the matter concerned (Section 127(2) and also see Sabally vs. Inspector General of Police and Others (Civil Ref. No. 2/2001, 1997-2001: GR at 878). Proceedings in the Supreme Court on any question whether the production of any document or disclosure of its contents would be prejudicial to State Security or injurious to public interest shall be held in camera (Section 127 (3). Any other matter other than those highlighted above will fall within the appellate jurisdiction of the Supreme Court.

As for the Court of Appeals, it appears that its jurisdiction is entirely an appellate one and it shall therefore have jurisdiction to hear and determine appeals from judgements, decrees and orders of the High Court and such other appellate jurisdictions as maybe conferred on it by the National Assembly. The Court of Appeals shall also have jurisdiction in appeals from decisions of a Court Martial in the manner provided by law (Sections 129–130).

The High Court exercises three jurisdictions namely: original, appellate, and supervisory jurisdictions. Under its original jurisdiction, the High Court shall hear and determine (1) all civil and criminal proceedings; and (2) interpret and enforce the fundamental rights and freedoms as provided for, under Sections 18-33 and Section 36(5) of the 1997 Constitution.

The High Court has appellate jurisdiction to hear and determine appeals from courts subordinate to it other than the Cadi Court, which handles family/matrimonial disputes involving Muslim parties (Section 132).[18] The High Court shall have supervisory jurisdiction over all lower courts and adjudicatory authorities in The Gambia, including Commissions of Inquiry, and Ad-hoc tribunals. While exercising its supervisory jurisdiction, the High Court will have power to issue directions, orders, or writs, including habeas corpus and orders of certiorari, mandamus and prohibition, as the court may consider appropriate for the purpose of enforcing its supervisory powers (Section 133).

The Special Criminal Court, which looks like a special section of the High Court, has jurisdiction to hear and determine all criminal offences relating to theft, misappropriation, and other similar offences, in which public funds and public property are affected (Section 135). This court of law is locally constituted to deal with special financial crimes of serious gravity. The National Assembly passed an Act called "The Special Criminal Court Act" in 1979 to provide/create the necessary framework for the functioning of this court. In 1980, a former employee of the defunct Gambia Commercial and Development Bank, Modou Jobe, who appeared before the Special Criminal Court established under the new Act on charges of stealing the sum of D595, 791.43 and fraudulent falsification of accounts, sought a declaration to the Supreme Court that the Special Criminal Court Act 1979 under which he was being prosecuted, violated his constitutional rights and was ultra vires the 1970 Constitution. The Supreme Court dismissed such claims and entered judgement against Momodou Jobe. Jobe then took the matter to the Court of Appeals, which was the highest judicial authority in The Gambia at the time. The Court of Appeals by its judgement dated May 11, 1981, allowed in part, the appeal and held that Sections 7, 8, 9 and 10 of the Special Criminal Court Act under which the appellant was charged and convicted were unconstitutional and null and void. Jobe was thus freed and the government of The Gambia took the matter further to the Judicial Committee of the Privy Council in London, which was at the time The Gambia's court of final authority. The Privy Council then allowed the appeal and set aside that part of the judgement of the Court of Appeals. This case, which went through all stages of the country's courts system, indicated that the judiciary was independent during that time. This case represents a practical example of the functioning of the special criminal court on one hand and corrects the excesses of the legislature and executive on the other.

(See case concerning Sabally Vs. Inspector general of Police: 1997 – 2001, GR. 861)

Appointment of judges

According to the 1997 Constitution of The Gambia, the President shall appoint the Chief Justice of The Gambia after consultation with the Judicial Service Commission. Section 138 of the Constitution apparently makes it mandatory upon the President to consult the Judicial Service Commission before appointing a person as Chief Justice. This is supported by Section 147(a), which says that the Judicial Service Commission shall, among other things, have the power to advise the President in the exercise of his powers relating to the appointment of judges.

However, the wordings of the provisions of Section 138 do not necessarily establish this understanding. The President, on the recommendation of the Judicial Service Commission, appoints all other judges of the superior courts except for those of the Special Criminal Court. As for the judges of the Special Criminal Court, the Judicial Service Commission, subject to the approval of the National Assembly (Section 134(3)), appoints them. The power to appoint judicial officers and court staff is vested in the Judicial Service Commission. Such officers include[19].

- Master, Registrar and Assistant Registrar of the Superior Courts.
- Magistrates.
- Members of any subordinate court; and
- Such other officers, members of any court, the National Assembly may prescribe. The Chief Justice appoints staff of the courts and such other judges as he/she, after consultation with the Judicial Service Commission, may direct (Section 146 (3).

Tenure of office of judges

Section 141 of the Constitution of The Gambia has provided both for optional and mandatory retirements for a serving judge. According to Section 141(2)(a), a judge may retire or pension at any time after attaining the age of 65 years, while paragraph (b) makes it mandatory upon a judge of a Superior Court to retire on attaining the age of 70 years. These constitutional provisions on the retirement of Superior Court judges are quite generous and safeguard as far as the security of the tenure of judges is concerned. This is because the period between the normal time to begin a career and 65 or 70 years is fairly long enough for a serving judge to achieve a lot. Section 141(2)(c) threatens that security of tenure for the judge by indicating that a Superior Court judge may have his/her appointment terminated by the President in consultation with the Judicial Service Commission. The power of the President to appoint senior court judges and to terminate their appointments in consultation with the Judicial Service Commission consciously compromises the independence of the judiciary as it provides for unnecessary reliance by the latter on the executive. This loophole in the relationship between the executive and the judiciary weakens the latter's autonomy from the former and is usually the basis of interference by the executive in the affairs of the judiciary.

In 2003, a Supreme Court judge had his appointment terminated under suspicious circumstances. The executive terminated the services of Justice Hassan B. Jallow, the only Gambian on the Supreme Court at the time. This move came after Justice Jallow presided over high-profile constitutional cases in the Supreme Court in which several provisions of controversial acts of the National Assembly were invalidated for contravening the 1997 Constitution and the African Charter on Human and Peoples' Rights. Recently, two of the most able and effective foreign (i.e., non-Gambian citizens) judges that The Gambia has ever had, Justices Tahir and Belgore from Nigeria, left The Gambia to return home following the end of their contracts, which the government was, probably, not interested in renewing. The two judges recently presided over high-profile and politically motivated cases in which the government lost to its political opponents. Similarly, the latest non-Gambian Chief Justice who headed the judiciary up to the first quarter of 2006 has had his appointment terminated by the government and this was followed by the appointment, by the President, of the first ever Gambian Chief Justice since independence in 1965. These are all examples of political pressures exerted by the executive, which have resulted in the compromising of the independence of the country's judiciary.

Unlike Section 141(2)(c), sub-sections 4,5,6, & 7 of Section 141 of the Constitution have provided a complicated and relatively rigid procedure for the removal from office of a superior court judge on grounds of inability to perform the functions of his/her office whether arising from infirmity of body or mind or for misconduct. According to Section 141(5), for example, a Superior Court judge may be removed from his/her office if notice in writing signed by not less than one half of all the voting members of the National Assembly, is given to the Speaker setting a motion that the judge concerned is unable to exercise the functions of his/her office on any of the grounds cited above and should therefore be investigated. Upon receiving such a notice of a motion, the Speaker shall forthwith cause a vote to be taken on the motion without delay (sub-section 6). This motion must be adopted by the vote of not less than two-thirds of all the members of the National Assembly (sub-section 7). Thereupon, the National Assembly shall, by resolution, appoint a tribunal consisting of three persons, at least, one of whom is or was a high court judge who shall be chairman of the tribunal. The tribunal will then investigate the matter and report to the National Assembly through the Speaker on whether or not all the allegations specified have been substantiated. If they have not been substantiated then no further proceedings shall be taken on that matter and the judge will resume his/her normal duties.

On the other hand, if the tribunal in its findings reports to the National Assembly that the allegations have been substantiated, the National Assembly will consider this chapter at its first convenient sitting. If during this sitting, not less than two thirds of all the members of the Assembly have voted to support the motion, then the National Assembly resolves that the judge be removed from office and he/she shall immediately cease to hold office (sub-section 7 a, b, c and d). The procedure of the removal of a superior court Judge established in the provisions of sub-sections 4–7 of Section 141 is very transparent and democratic and therefore provides better guarantees and safeguards not only to the security of tenure of judges but also to the independence of the judiciary as well. This is to be compared with Section 141(2)(c), which gives the President power to terminate the services of a superior court judge.

Thus, it may be appropriate to suggest at this juncture that Section 141(2) (c) be repealed and the procedure established in sub-sections 4-7 be adopted as the procedure for the removal of superior court judges in The Gambia. Similarly, the power for their appointment should be vested in the Judicial Service Commission rather than in the President. In other words, appointment of superior court judges should not be a matter for the executive alone to handle, as this will minimize the chances of interference by the latter in the affairs of the judiciary.

The cadi courts

It can be said that The Gambia runs two parallel systems of justice: the common law system, which the country inherited from the British, and an Islamic-based system called the Cadi Courts System. This system of justice is established to deal with matrimonial issues or matters of family life of Muslims in The Gambia in accordance with the teachings of Islam. The history of this system of courts goes back to the colonial days. The British Colonial Administration established it in 1906. The Cadi Court has very limited jurisdiction as it applies Sharia (Islamic law) only in matters of marriage, divorce, maintenance, and inheritance, where the parties involved are Muslims. Despite the restricted nature of the Cadi Courts jurisdiction, it is a complete and independent system of justice of its own. Thus, an appeal does not lie from it to any conventional court in the country. Rather, the new constitution has introduced a "Sharia" Court of Appeal known as the Cadi Appeal Panel to hear appeals from the Cadi Court of first instance.

The quest for judicial autonomy and political interference in judicial decisions in The Gambia

Although the 1997 Constitution has provided for an independent judiciary, there have been two major conflicting trends characterizing the day-to-day functioning of the courts system in The Gambia. These two trends, the struggle by the courts to assert their autonomy on the one hand, and executive power pressures or political interferences in the affairs of the judiciary on the other hand, are demonstrated in different ways and therefore, treated separately below.

The quest for autonomy

Despite several attempts to exert political and other pressures on and interfere with the work of the judiciary since the inception of the Second Republic in 1997, the courts have, to a large extent, managed to assert their authority and demonstrated their independence. The period between 1997 and 2005 witnessed exciting moments in which the executive lost major court battles to political opponents, individuals, and non-state institutions. In October 1997, the Court of Appeals, which was then the country's highest court, overturned the treason convictions and death sentences of four men who led an abortive coup against the government in November 1996. The Court of Appeals also overturned several criminal convictions in less publicized cases during the period. With the reconfiguration of the courts system in October 1998 and with the newly introduced Supreme Court replacing the Privy Council as the ultimate Court of Appeals for The Gambia, judiciary autonomy continues to grow. Despite many efforts by the executive to interfere with judiciary decisions, the Supreme Court has remained firm and continues to function as an institution that is independent of the executive branch of the government. In 2001, the Supreme Court invalidated a controversial act of parliament known as the Indemnity Act, No. 5 of 2001 for contravening the constitution and the African Regional

186

Human Rights treaty. It was held in that case that the new law indemnifies public officers and state agents against all claims in respect of actions undertaken during any period of public emergency, public disturbance, or riotous situations. The court decided that access to an independent and impartial court for determination of one's rights and obligations is acknowledged as a fundamental human right, which also lies at the heart of the enforcement of other rights. Given the importance of the decision in this case to judiciary autonomy in The Gambia, we take a further look at the case below.

Sabally vs. Inspector General of Police

The relevant facts of this case are as follows: On June 12, 2000, Mr. Sabally, (the plaintiff) issued a writ of summons in the High Court seeking, inter-alia, damages from the State (the defendants) for assaults and injuries allegedly caused to him by the State Security Personnel. The claim arose from the events of 10 April 2000, when there were public disturbances during which several school children were shot to death by the security forces. The defendants denied the claim. The trial began before Justice Kabalata of the High Court on 1 March 2001. While the trial was in progress before the High Court, an Act to amend the Indemnity Act was legislated by the National Assembly and assented to by the President of the Republic on 2 May 2001. The new statute contained several controversial issues including the following:

- It had the effectiveness of retroactively depriving or taking away averted rights.
- Section 1 of the new Act provided that the Act shall be deemed to have come into force on 1st January 2000 that is about 17 months before it was enacted.
- The new (Amendment) Act indemnified public officers and State Security Agents against all claims irrespective of actions undertaken during any period of public emergency, public disturbance, or riotous situation. It was for this reason that

counsel for the defendants submitted that Mr. Sabally's action should be struck out.

- The Act ousted the jurisdiction of the regular courts in favour of a claims commission to be established to receive and hear claims and make recommendations to the President for compensation to deserving claimants. The third and the last issues have the effect of blocking access by individuals and groups to an independent and impartial court for the determination of one's rights and obligations.

As a result of the new law, the defendants filed a motion before the High Court to strike out the civil action on the ground that by virtue of the Amendment Act, the plaintiff had no cause of action against them. These controversial provisions of the Indemnity (Amendment) Act 2001 raised serious constitutional questions, the answer to which goes beyond the jurisdiction of the High Court. Thus, acting on the provisions of Section 127(2) of the Constitution and rule 61(2) of the rules of the Supreme Court, the High Court formulated the matter and/or question and referred it to the Supreme Court for determination. According to Section 127(2), if any question or matter belonging to the exclusive original jurisdiction of the Supreme Court arises in any proceedings in any other court, that court shall stay its proceedings and refer the question or matter to the Supreme Court for final determination. Consequently, the referral court shall give effect to any decision of the Supreme Court. A question of constitutionality of any legislation or Act of the Gambian Parliament is among such matters that belong to the exclusive original jurisdiction of the Supreme Court. Rule 61(2) of the rules of the Supreme Court requires such a reference to be formulated by the referral court in the form of a case or statement specifically stating the question or matter to be determined by the Supreme Court. At the Supreme Court level, counsel for both parties addressed the court with the counsel for the plaintiff submitting that the Amendment Act (No. 5 of 2001) retroactively purports to take away a vested right of the plaintiff to pursue his pending civil action before the High Court in contravention

188

of Section 100(2)(c) of the 1997 Constitution which reads as follows: "The National Assembly shall not pass a Bill to alter the decision or judgement of a court in any proceedings to the prejudice of any party to those proceedings or deprive any person retroactively of vested interest or of vested or acquired rights. . . ."

The counsel for the plaintiff further argued that the Indemnity (Amendment) Act 2001 passed by the National Assembly and assented to by the President on 2 May 2001 when Mr. Sabally's civil action against the state was already pending before the High Court, retroactively purported to take away an acquired right of the plaintiff. Accordingly, the learned counsel contended that the amendment was unconstitutional and in excess of the powers of the legislative authority. On the other hand, the counsel for the defendant argued that the amendment was valid and constitutional, and within the competence of the legislative authority and that the deprivation of a vested or acquired right caused by the new Act was justified by the public interest, which it aimed to protect in pursuance to Section 17(2) of the 1997 Constitution, which reads as follows: "Every person in The Gambia, whatever his or her race, colour, gender, language, religion, faith, political or other opinion, national or social origin, property, birth or other status shall be entitled to the fundamental human rights and freedoms of the individual in this charter but subject to respect for the rights and freedoms of others and for the public interest." Thus, counsel for the defendant argued that the human rights and fundamental freedoms enshrined in the constitution are subject to the public interest. In other words, the individual can be deprived of a fundamental human right in favour of the public interest. Consequently, the Indemnity (Amendment) Act (No. 5 of 2001) depriving the plaintiff (Mr. Sabally) of a vested right (i.e., his right to access the court and pursue the civil action he filed against the State) was valid and constitutional and could therefore be relied upon to dismiss Mr. Sabally's civil action for damages.

As deliberations and submissions were being made before the Supreme Court, another important question was raised. The question concerned the meaning of "vested or acquired right." The court simply referred to its decision in an earlier case where it had defined vested or acquired right. In the case of Sait Boye vs. Baldeh (Civil No. 1/2001, 1997-2001 G.R. 861), the Supreme Court had defined "vested, accrued or acquired right" as "a right that is certain, complete, in existence and has matured and one not subject to a condition precedent." Thus, in the instant case, the plaintiff's proceedings instituted against the defendants were a vested or acquired right because, as his counsel explained, these were not subject to any condition precedent. In handing down its judgment, the Supreme Court of The Gambia unanimously held that by instituting legal proceedings for damages from the defendants as a result of assault and injuries allegedly occasioned to him by the State Security Personnel during public disturbances, Sabally had a vested or an acquired right to continue with such proceedings. Thus, "any retroactive legislative measure purporting to nullify his right to do so would be in contravention of the prohibition against retroactive deprivation of vested rights as provided for by Section 100(2)(c) of the 1997 Constitution". The court further held that "[a]ccess to an independent and impartial court for the determination of one's rights and obligations is acknowledged as a fundamental human right, which also lies at the heart of enforcing other rights". The Supreme Court referred to a decision of the African Commission on Human and Peoples' Rights on 15 November 1999 in Communication No. 145/95 brought by the Constitutional Project, the Civil Liberties Organization against Nigeria in respect of measures taken against certain newspapers. In that case, the African Commission decided that legislative nullification of pending judicial proceedings is in violation of Article 7(1)(a) of the African Charter on Human and Peoples' Rights, otherwise known as the Banjul Charter, which guarantees the right of access to the courts. The Commission thus declared: "A civil case in process is in itself an asset, one into which the litigants invest resources in the hope of an eventual finding in their favour. The risk of losing the case is one that every litigant accepts but the risk of having the suit abruptly nullified will seriously discourage litigation with serious consequences for the protection of individual rights. Citizens who cannot have recourse to the courts of their country are highly vulnerable to violation of their rights. The nullification of the suit in progress; thus constitutes a violation of Article 7(1) (a)" (of the African Charter on Human and Peoples' Rights). The Supreme Court then ordered the High Court to strike out the plaintiff's action filed by the defendant on 14th May 2001 and to continue with hearing of the plaintiff's pending action.

By virtue of this ruling of 5 December 2001, the Supreme Court effectively invalidated the Indemnity (Amendment) Act (No. 5, 2001) for contravening several sections of the Gambian Constitution of 1997 and Article 7(1) (a) of the African Charter on Human and Peoples' Rights. The nullification of the new (Amendment) Act for violating the constitution is justified under Section 4 of the 1997 Constitution, which describes it as the Supreme Law of the land to which all laws passed by the parliament or any other legislative authority should conform. Concerning the other ground, which is based on Article 7(1) (a) of the African Charter, The Gambia is a signatory to the Charter and the country is also the host of the enforcement mechanism of the Charter. Under Article 1 of the Charter, all signatory states are under obligation to recognize, promote and protect all the rights and fundamental freedoms guaranteed by the Charter. Moreover, Article 7(1) (a) clearly makes the issue of access to a competent court/tribunal a fundamental human right and it reads: "Every individual shall have the right to have his cause heard. This comprises: (a) the right to an appeal to competent national organs against acts violating his fundamental rights." To have a duly constituted court case nullified by a legislative instrument like the Indemnity Act during the process of litigation, effectively constitutes a clear violation of Article 7(1)(a) stated above. This is because the nullifying legislation will have the effect of foreclosing all possibility of making an appeal to a competent national organ or tribunal against acts violating the fundamental rights of the individual litigant as provided for under Article 7(1) (a).

This case was a major test to the credibility of the Gambian judiciary because the ill-fated Act of Parliament was thought to have been passed by the government just to cover and protect the military personnel who had taken part in a shooting incident in 2000 in which, several school children were shot to death by the security forces following a serious riot masterminded mainly by the country's leading students' union organization. Thus, if the Indemnity Act had been allowed to remain law, it would have had the effect of blocking the fundamental right of individuals to access independent and impartial tribunals. Similarly, in November 2001, the Supreme Court of The Gambia struck down a substantial part of another Act of Parliament aimed at amending several provisions of the 1997 Constitution. In Hon. Kemesseng Jammeh vs. the Attorney General, the Supreme Court partly nullified Act No. 6 of 2001 known as the Constitution of the Republic of The Gambia (Amendment) Act 2001 passed by the Parliament on 15 May 2001, and assented to by the President on 25 May 2001. This is because the procedural requirements for amending the constitution were not properly followed. Section 226(7) has identified several sections and subsections of the constitution as forming part of the entrenched clauses or key provisions of the 1997 Constitution of the Republic of The Gambia. According to Subsection 4 of the same Section, a bill of the National Assembly aimed at altering any of such key provisions shall not be passed by Parliament or assented to by the President unless it has been referred by the Speaker of the House to the Independent Electoral Commission to call for a referendum on the bill within six months of such reference. In this case, no less than 50% of the persons entitled to vote in the referendum shall take part in the referendum and the bill must be supported by at least 75% of those who have voted. Among the affected clauses that Act No. 6 of 2001 aimed at amending was Section (1) of the Constitution, which reads as follows: "The Gambia is a Sovereign Republic" while the proposed amendment would have read: "The Gambia is a sovereign secular Republic." The word secular was the focus of the proposed amendment and this would have had the effect of alienating religion altogether from all the matters of state life in The Gambia where more than 99% of the population are deeply religious. Act No. 6 of 2001 was passed by the National Assembly and assented to by the President without holding a referendum on the Bill despite the fact that it affected some of the entrenched clauses, which can only be amended after such a referendum is held and the proposed bill supported by at least 75% of those voting. It was for this reason that Act No. 6 of 2001 was partly invalidated. According to Section 4, the Constitution is the supreme law of The Gambia and therefore, all laws passed by parliament including amending bills and executive orders must be in conformity with the constitution otherwise such contravening laws and orders shall be null and void.

In 1999, *Citizen FM*, a privately owned local radio station, was closed by the state and the proprietor, a veteran journalist and a former BBC Banjul correspondent, Mr. Babubacar Gaye, was taken to court and charged with the offence of operating a radio station without a licence contrary to Section 5(7) of the Telegraphic Stations Act of 1913 and Regulation 4 made under Section 12 of the Act. The Kanifing Magistrates' Court serving as the court of first instance convicted Mr. Gaye and sentenced him to one-month imprisonment with hard labour with the option to pay GMD35, 000 as fine. The court then ordered the radio station be forfeited to the state. On appeal to the High Court in Banjul against his conviction, the High Court on 3 July 2000 reversed the judgement of the magistrates' court. In his ruling, Justice W. G. Grante, Jr., decided that the principal magistrate was wrong in law and therefore, he quashed the conviction and the sentence as well as the consequential order of forfeiture passed against Mr. Gaye. The High Court ordered the State to restore to Mr. Gaye his radio apparatus and property within seven days for the radio to resume normal operation. The High Court Judge was of the opinion that Mr. Gaye did not commit the offence of tax evasion and that the act of closing the radio and ordering it forfeited to the state was a clear violation of Mr. Gaye's right to freedom of expression, which in his opinion was not only a fundamental human right but also a basic necessity of democratic governance. The court rightly argued that the work of the media to seek and disseminate information freely is the cornerstone of a democratic system in every civilized country.

In July 2003, the High Court in Banjul dismissed another high-profile case brought by the state against six men. In this case, Messrs. Ebrima Barrow, Momodou Ousman Saho (Dumo), Momodou Marena, Ebrima Yabo, Lieutenant Lallo Jaiteh and Lieutenant Omar Darboe, all accused of treasonable offences and taken to court, were acquitted, and accordingly discharged by the high court in 2003. In his ruling, Justice Ahmed O. Belgore noted that there was no evidence, direct or circumstantial, linking the accused persons to the case filed against them. There was therefore no ground for the court to consider any of the counts contained in the information sheet upon which the accused persons were charged and thus acquitted and discharged them.

In June 2005, the High Court in Banjul dismissed a highly controversial murder case filed by the government against the main opposition leader, Mr. Ousainou Darboe, and others. In this case, the government accused Mr. Darboe and his people of murdering a supporter of the ruling party Alliance for Patriotic Re-orientation and Construction (APRC) while campaigning for the 2001 presidential elections. Despite the fact that senior politicians within the ruling party wanted to see Mr. Darboe and some key members of his party locked up, the high court did not hesitate to dismiss the case simply because the prosecution failed to establish a case against them.

In September 2005, leaders of the four opposition parties in the country obtained a crucial victory in an important court case they filed against the state shortly before the 29 September 2005 bye-elections scheduled to be held in four constituencies. The Independent Electoral Commission (IEC) decided that it was going to allow voters whose names did not appear on the list of the main register of voters to vote at the bye-election if they came with valid voters' cards. The opposition cried foul and argued that such a practice would not ensure genuine elections and therefore, took the matter to court. On 28 September 2005, just a day before the bye-elections, the high court gave a landmark ruling on the practice. While nullifying the practice, the high court in Banjul held that "the decision of the first respondent [the IEC that it] will permit holders of voters cards to vote even if their names do not appear on the register of voters, will not ensure a genuine election and will therefore be an infringement of the right of the applicants herein to stand at genuine election as guaranteed by Section 26(b) of the 1997 Constitution of The Gambia". Consequently, the court ruled against the ruling party. This is because holders of voters' cards, whose names do not appear on the main register of voters, could be holding forged cards and this violates the principle of a genuine election, which in the opinion of the court is a fundamental right of anyone contesting or standing at the elections.

In July 2006, the high court in Banjul invalidated an executive order issued by the Minister for Local Government and Lands dismissing the Mayor of Banjul, Pa Sallah Jeng. The high court ordered that the Mayor be reinstated with immediate effect. In all these and many other cases that have not been mentioned here, the Gambian judiciary had to take a bold stand to assert its authority and independence to uphold the principles of justice, equity, the rule of law and fair play in the governance process. However, as the next section indicates, the cost of fighting to maintain judicial autonomy and independence in The Gambia has been quite significant.

On 11 June 1997, in Drammeh vs. the State (Criminal Appeal No. 25/96, 1997-2000 GR, 21), the Court of Appeals overturned a decision of the high court in 2006, dismissing the appellant's appeal against conviction and sentence by the Trial Magistrate for offences of, inter alia, stealing, housebreaking and escape from lawful custody. This case originated in the magistrates' court where the accused was convicted and sentenced. When he appealed to the high court, the court dismissed the appeal against conviction and sentence. Upon further appeal to the Court of Appeals, the Court of Appeals found that there were several irregularities during the process, which meant that the basis of the high court's 1996 decision was flawed. The Court of Appeals discovered that the record of appeal presented to the high court was bereft of the usual notes of the Trial Magistrate. In other words, there were no statements, no particulars of the alleged offences for which the appellant was convicted, the record of the appeal did not also contain the evidence upon which he was convicted, nor was there a record of the judgement of the trial court. Due to the absence of this critical piece of information, which was crucial to the appeal process, the appellate high court based its decision on a summary of trial proceedings, which the Trial Magistrate was requested to write up three years after conclusion of the trial. All this was in violation of Section 275 of the Criminal Procedure Code (the Cr. P. C, cap 12: 01, Laws of The Gambia), which makes it mandatory that when presented; an appeal should be accompanied by a copy of the judgement or order appealed against. It is from the judgement that the appellate court can discern and determine what evidence was available before the trial court and whether, based on such evidence, the charge or charges of which the appellant had been convicted could or could not be sustained having regard to procedural as well as substantive law relating to the instant case. Thus, it was because of the irregularities highlighted above that the Court of Appeal allowed the appeal against conviction and sentence and consequently reversed the high court's 1996 decision. To conclude, the Court of Appeal's findings in Drammeh vs. the State is a clear testimony that if the independence of the superior courts is compromised by political interferences, executive pressures or by any other means, there is going to be a persistent miscarriage of justice from the lower courts.

Finally, the trend of "continuous struggle" by the judiciary to assert its authority and independence against the wishes of an ever-powerful executive has not yet shown any sign of reversal, although serious concerns have been raised in various quarters over the appointment, by the President in 2006, of the first ever Gambian-born Chief Justice. Since The Gambia became independent in 1965, non-Gambian senior judges have always held the post of Chief Justice. Whether the new Chief Justice will keep or reverse the trend is a critical question that cannot yet be given a definitive answer as the relationship between the new head of the judiciary and the executive is yet to be tested. The appointment of a Gambian Chief Justice by the Jammeh administration is a positive development in the political sense. It is a concrete achievement in the struggle for political emancipation of The Gambia. It enhances the ownership by Gambians of their political institutions in general and the judiciary in particular.

Political and other forms of interference in the Gambian judiciary

The Gambian judiciary has, over the past few years, experienced different forms of political interferences, ranging from dismissal of superior court judges, non-renewal of the appointment of serving senior judges, to violent attacks and intimidation of leading practitioners. In 2001, a Supreme Court judge, Justice Hassan B. Jallow, was sacked under suspicious circumstances after presiding over the court in about three major cases, all of which the government lost to political opponents. The cases included Ousman Sabally vs.

Inspector General of Police in which the constitutionality of the Indemnity Act 2001 was challenged and Kemesseng Jammeh vs. the Attorney General which also involved serious constitutional questions. The dismissal of Justice Hassan B. Jallow was a serious blow to the Gambian judiciary for several reasons, the most important of which are: (1) The dismissal came at a time when Justice Jallow, with his colleagues on the Supreme Court Bench, were struggling very hard to guard jealously the autonomy, integrity and credibility of the country's judiciary and to protect and enforce the supremacy and authority of the 1997 Constitution, the fundamental law of the land. (2) By the time Justice Jallow was dismissed, he was the only Gambian who had made it up to Supreme Court level. All other judges of the highest court in the land were non-Gambians. With the appointment of Justice Savage as the first Gambian Chief Justice and the promotion of Justice Janneh to the Supreme Court, the situation has now changed although, as at now, one cannot certainly judge whether the change is for good or otherwise.

In late 2005, the government did not seek to renew the contract of two Nigerian judges, Justices Tahir and Belgore. These two judges were often described by many as the most decent foreign judges that the Gambian judiciary has ever had. They successfully presided over the high court in several high-profile cases during the course of which, the integrity and credibility of the country's justice system faced crucial tests. The State vs. Ousainou Darboe and Others (Criminal Case No. 14/2000), a case cited above and which was filed by the state against the main opposition leader and, which was dismissed in 2005, is one such high-profile case. The case was presided over and thrown out of court by Justice Tahir. In 2001, too, a senior magistrate, Mr. Borry Touray was dismissed from office for simply deciding a case against the state. In early 2006, the country's last foreign Chief Justice, Justice Allen Steven Brobbery from Ghana, was dismissed under mysterious circumstances. No explanation was given by the government for Justice Brobbery's termination although, independent critics and observers believed that the matter had to do with his latest attempt to redeploy some of the senior judges, including a highly controversial one, from the criminal division to the civil division of the high court. The judge at the centre of a controversy is usually thought to be sympathetic to the state.

Another form of interference suffered by the Gambian judiciary is violent attacks and intimidations of senior practitioners. In December 2003, unknown gunmen shot one of the country's most prominent and leading practitioners, Lawyer Ousman Sillah, several times in front of his home. Mr. Sillah narrowly escaped death. He was immediately flown to Dakar, Senegal, where he underwent major operations after which, his life was saved. The reasons for Mr. Sillah's attack are not yet known. However, many observers believe that Mr. Sillah's involvement in another politically motivated high-profile case instituted by the executive against a former political heavy weight, Mr. Baba Jobe, was probably the cause of the violent attack against him.

Finally, a recent form of interference experienced by the Gambian judiciary is deliberate undermining of court orders by the state. The most recent example of this form of interference came in July 2006 when the high court nullified a dismissal order against the Mayor of Banjul and ruled that the mayor be reinstated with immediate effect. Up to the time this chapter was completed (August 2007) the mayor has not yet been reinstated. Like the previous trend, this present one is showing no signs of reversal. The trend looks set to continue so long as the judiciary continues its quest for autonomy and refuses to be subdued by the state and its agents. Gambian politicians and their counterparts in many West African countries need to recognize the fact that in a truly functioning democracy, the instances of the state or the executive losing major court battles to political opponents or individuals or to non-state entities are inevitable and that, such a loss should be viewed as a positive development which only enhances the country's democratic credentials and therefore a credit for the government of the day rather than seeing it as humiliating defeat at the hands of political opponents.

Power of the Supreme Court to review and depart from a previous decision: a possible ground for interference

There is no doubt that the reconfiguration of the courts system in The Gambia in 1997, with a Supreme Court designated/redefined as the Court of Final Authority for the country replacing the Privy Council in England, was a laudable achievement in the Second Republic. The move was not only cost effective but it was timesaving and more in line with the dignity and integrity of The Gambia as an independent sovereign nation. Moreover, to further safeguard the independence and integrity of the Supreme Court as the country's highest judicial institution, the court is empowered by the constitution to review and depart from any of its earlier decisions when it is determined by the Justices that it is the right thing to do (Section 126 (2). However, despite the merits of the new system, human rights and judicial experts, independent observers, and critics, have expressed a strong opinion that the power of the Supreme Court to review and depart from a previous decision may provide an opportunity for the executive to interfere with the process of an ongoing review and influence its outcome. This opinion is being expressed as a result of the judgement of a review panel of the Supreme Court on 18 June 2002 in which the court's previous judgement dated 5 December 2001 on the constitutionality of the Indemnity Act (No. 5 of 2001) was reversed. This coincided with the arrival of a new Chief Justice for The Gambia from Pakistan, Justice Muhammad Arif, and the first ever non-African judge to head the Gambian Judiciary, since independence in 1965. The fact that Justice Arif was from outside the continent and probably was not well informed on the level of human rights consciousness in Africa and the extent to which the continent's
200

human rights jurisprudence had developed, provided a golden opportunity for the losing side in the 5 December 2001 judgement when it moved to invoke the review jurisdiction of the Supreme Court. The state, therefore, wasted no time to file a petition seeking review of the above-mentioned judgement. Interestingly enough, under the new Chief Justice's leadership of the Supreme Court, the review was allowed and the 5 December judgement reversed. Handing down the court's judgement in the case of Inspector General of Police and others vs. Ousman Sabally (Supreme Court Civil Ref. No. 2/2001), then Chief Justice Arif stated the following as the reasons for his dissenting opinion in the judgement at hand:

- That Subsection (2) (c) of Section 100 of the 1997 Constitution, which was a basis of the 5 December 2001 judgement of the Supreme Court, is a one-sentence provision and therefore must be read together as such before it can form the basis of the Court's finding that the new Legislation (Act No. 5 of 2001) is not within the competence of the legislature to make. Section 100 (2) (c) reads: "The National Assembly shall not pass a Bill to alter the decision or judgement of a court in any proceedings to the prejudice of any party to those proceedings or depriving a person retroactively of vested or acquired rights, but subject thereto, the National Assembly may pass Bills designed to have retroactive effects."

His Lordship explained that in the case of Mr. Sabally, the plaintiff in that case, no decision or judgement was made by the high court in Civil Suit No. 115/2000. Thus, the newly amended Indemnity Act (No. 5 of 2001) did not have the effect of retroactively nullifying or altering the decision or judgement of the court in the proceedings at hand. In other words, the new Act had not violated Section 100(2) (c) of the Constitution. Although, His Lordship may have made a point when he asserted that the high court did not hand down a judgement by the time the matter was referred to the Supreme Court, he should be reminded that the legislature is constitutionally barred from making any retroactive legislation that would deprive a litigant of a vested right or interest even if the matter is yet to be contested before a court of competent jurisdiction. The high court was under obligation to refer the matter (i.e., the constitutionality of the new Act (of No. 5: 2001)) to the Supreme Court for its determination. Thus, the question regarding whether the high court made or did not decide regarding the case in question is irrelevant to the constitutionality of retroactive legislation. Most important is the fact that the new statute, as discussed earlier, would have had the effect of retroactively depriving Mr. Sabally of his vested right to go ahead with the case and obtain the remedies claimed for. To this effect, the new Act violated Section 100(2) (c) of the Constitution and Article 7(1)(a) of the African Charter on Human and Peoples' Rights for blocking the plaintiff from accessing the court, which is a fundamental right enshrined in the international human rights conventions to which The Gambia is a signatory. This brings us to close to understanding Justice Arif's second reason for dissenting in the judgement at hand.

- That the decision of the African Commission of 5 November 1999 on Communication No. 145/95 brought by the Nigerian-based Civil Liberties Organization against Nigeria and which Justice Hassan B. Jallow cited in his 5 December 2001 judgement, is not relevant to the instant case. This is because, according to His Lordship, the Banjul Charter (African Charter) in itself is not a piece of legislation, which can be formed into a touchstone for testing the constitutionality of any provision of the Constitution in relation to its application to legislative measures passed by the National Assembly (Inspector General of Police v Ousman Sabally, Supreme Court Civil Ref. No. 2/2001).

The African Commission was in that case of the opinion that legislative nullification of court proceedings, which retroactively deprive a litigant of a vested right or interest is a violation of Article 7(1)(a) of the Banjul Charter, which guarantees the right of access to the courts in a civil case. The Gambian Supreme Court was convinced

202

(and we agree with the Court) that the Indemnity Act (No. 5 of 2001) would have legislatively nullified the plaintiff's vested right in that case and further that The Gambia was under obligation in international law to respect Article 7(1)(a) of the African Charter and also to make its legislation conform to its international obligations. His Lordship then cited Article 1 of the Charter, although the Article is, by all implications, supportive of Justice Jallow's 5 December 2001 judgement and not that of Justice Arif. Article 1 reads as follows: "The Member States of the Organization of African Unity parties to the present Charter shall recognize the rights, duties and freedoms enshrined in this Charter and shall undertake to adapt legislative or other measures to give effect to them." This provision, as we have already stated, is in line with the Supreme Court judgement that nullified the Indemnity Act on 5 December 2001. In other words, by judicially enforcing Article 7(1) (a) of the African Charter, the Supreme Court was able to achieve what the legislature had failed to do. Likewise, we would beg to differ with His Lordship over his conclusion that the Banjul/African Charter is not a piece of legislation in itself.

Since the advent of the current international political system, with the inception of the United Nations in 1945, treaties have become the overriding source of international law. Today, even the customary rules of international law have been codified or written down in the form of treaties. Thus, all law-making treaties are pieces of international legislation binding on member states. There is abundant international authority supporting the view that states parties to legally binding treaties cannot rely on any domestic consideration such as sovereignty to evade their international obligations under such treaties. In other words, the obligation of a state to fulfil international agreements, like the Banjul Charter, that it has contracted, is a fundamental principle of international law. In the early 1930s, the former Permanent Court of International Justice (PCIJ) made a series of declarations and rulings to that effect. Thus, in its advisory opinion regarding the exchange of Greek and Turkish populations, the then International Court declared that "a State which had contracted valid international obligations was, in international law, bound to make in its legislation such modifications as maybe necessary to ensure the fulfillment of the obligations undertaken."[21.]

Similarly, in the Greek-Bulgarian Communication case in which the former PCIJ – the Permanent Court for International Justice - was asked to interpret the convention between Greece and Bulgaria regarding reciprocal emigration, the court declared that "it is a generally accepted principle of international law that in relations between states, which are signatories to a treaty, the provisions of the municipal law cannot prevail over those of the treaty."[22] In another case concerning the treatment of Polish nationals and other persons of Polish origin in the territory of the free city of Danzig, the Permanent Court of International Justice ruled that a state cannot adduce against another state its own constitution with a view to evading obligations incumbent upon it under international law or treaties in force. In this case, the court further held that "contracting parties to a treaty may intend to create rights and obligations for individuals, which will be enforceable by national courts."[23] Thus, Justice Jallow's judgement of 5 December 2001, invalidating the Indemnity Act (No. 5: 2001) was in line with the principles of international law highlighted in those cases. This brings us to another reason for Justice Arif's dissenting opinion. His Lordship apparently trusted the motive and intention of the legislature when it backdated the date of entry into force of the newly amended Act (of No. 5: 2001) to January 2000 when he observed that, "[a]s regards to the question relating to the nature of the amended provisions of the Indemnity Act, I am of the view that by specifying the date for the application of the law in relation to its taking effect on a specific date in the past, it is in itself, a good testimony to find the intention of the legislature."

Justice Arif also stated that "[t]hat the right of appeal in pending proceedings is not a matter of procedure, it is a right accrued in the proceedings before the court concerned." Thus, in His Lordship's opinion, this right could not be defeated by the legislature. Although His Lordship has made a very important point here, there is no conflict between the principle he has established in this case and Justice Jallow's 5 December 2001 judgement. In fact, that was the very reason why the Supreme Court in that judgement invalidated the newly amended Act. In other words, the Act had the effect of defeating an accrued right and this is something that the legislature is not competent to do.

In this case, Justice Arif was probably influenced by the American theory of mechanical jurisprudence when he said: "I am of the considered view that as required from times immemorial we, the members of the Judiciary are supposed to be wearing the laws of the land on the sleeves of our dresses and can ill afford not to abide by the mandate of the laws passed by the concerned legislature within the contemplation of the fundamental law of the land, i.e., the constitution of The Gambia."[24] We have no problem with the latter part of this statement, particularly, where he referred to the need for the judiciary to abide by the laws passed by the legislature within the contemplation of the constitution. But we would say that the courts in general and the Supreme Court, in particular, should and must be prepared to check on the legislature and rectify such unconstitutional laws. This is exactly what the Supreme Court did in its 5 December 2001 judgement. However, the learned Justice Arif was, obviously, not guided by the principle stated in the later part of that statement. Rather, he was guided by the first part of the statement where he described the members of the judiciary as the wearers of the law on the sleeves of their dresses. As indicated earlier, the learned judge appeared to have been influenced by the concept of mechanical jurisprudence, which is a by-product of analytical positivism and the legal apparatus of the laissez faire doctrine in America. According to the system of mechanical jurisprudence, the judicial function is limited to the judge's mechanical task of finding and declaring the law, as it exists. In other words, judges are not lawmakers and they cannot venture into doing what the political process and the constitution did not do. Rather, their task is strictly mechanical in nature in the sense that they are limited to discovering, declaring, and then applying the law as made for them by the legislature. The rules of law are in a fixed form, which is why the judge has to follow a mechanical process to find those and fix the instant case into such rules.[25]

In this modern age of respect for human rights, the rule of law and the independence of the judiciary as principles of democratic governance, we would rather recommend the system of political jurisprudence and not the mechanical one. According to the latter system, the constitution is a political institution and that judges are policy makers who are not outside the political struggle. Judges are subject to internal and external influences and they are part of the political process. Consequently, the judges should be functioning not only as interpreters of existing laws but also as lawmakers. The system of political jurisprudence appears to have been influenced by the sociological movement in jurisprudence which calls for pragmatism as a philosophy of law and for the adjustment of principles and doctrines to the human conditions.[26]

The system of political jurisprudence is preferred because it encourages judicial activism and creative dynamism in the justice delivery process, which is why it is more responsive to the needs of society than that of mechanical jurisprudence, which encourages judicial passivism and self-restraint. Judicial activism is judicial lawmaking, that is, the employment of legislation as a technique by the judges to expand the jurisprudence of the court in order to better service the interests of society. During this process, the judges would service the interests of the judiciary's constituency in pursuance of its

206

ideology, its conception of state and judicial functions. Thus, an activist judiciary will not hesitate to invalidate or nullify any legislative instrument or executive order that violates the constitution or the fundamental rights of the individual. On the other hand, judicial passivism or self-restraint occurs when the judges uphold the validity of legislative and executive acts of the government of the day even though they may violate the basic rights of the people. This is not in line with the supremacy status that human rights and fundamental freedoms currently enjoy within the state's legal and constitutional order. In 1972, the Supreme Court of India made a landmark ruling on the status of human rights and fundamental freedoms within the structure of the legal and constitutional order of India. Thus, in Kesavananda Bhrati vs. the State of Kerala,[28] in which the Supreme Court of India developed a new concept known as "The Basic Structure Concept" into the Indian Constitution, the court established constitutional limitations to the power of parliament to amend the constitution. According to the court's ruling in that case, the constitution was constructed upon the pillars of a philosophy, which constituted the basic structure of the constitution. This includes fundamental human rights, the constitution's supremacy status, its republican and secular character, the country's democratic form of government based on the Westminster style and the principle of separation of powers. Some of the judges in this case went further by stating that human rights and fundamental freedoms of the individual are not only part of the basic structure of the constitution, rather they constitute the essence or foundation of such a structure. In any case and as a result of this ruling, a fundamental rule of constitutional law was established in the common law jurisdiction, that is, the legislature has no power to amend or tamper with that part of the constitution containing the fundamental rights of individuals. This is because the human rights provisions of the constitution are so entrenched into the structure of the edifice of the constitution that any act of interference by parliament with those rights would amount to an act of rewriting and what parliament or the legislature has under the constitution is the power to amend and not to rewrite the constitution.

This principle later became an important precedent to be followed by different jurisdictions and legal systems of the Commonwealth. It has deeply influenced the thinking of jurists, judicial and constitutional experts, and human rights advocates in many countries across the Anglophone world. Here, in The Gambia, the provision of Section 226(7) (4) of the 1997 Constitution appeared to have been drafted along the lines of the principle established by the Supreme Court of India in Kesavananda Bhrati vs. the State of Kerala. According to s.226(7) of the 1997 Constitution of The Gambia, several provisions of the constitution are identified as forming part of what we may call "the key or entrenched clauses" of the constitution and as Section 226(4) has provided, such clauses or key provisions cannot be amended by parliament through its normal amending procedure. Rather, amendment can only be undertaken through a set of complicated procedures, which include the holding of a referendum on a proposal to amend any of those key provisions. Chapter 4 of the constitution, which provides for the protection of fundamental rights and freedoms, as well as Sections 4, 5(1) and 6(2), which relate to the constitution as the supreme law of The Gambia, are among such key provisions or entrenched clauses. Twenty years after that historic ruling in India and in Justice Arif's own backyard, the Supreme Court of Pakistan invalidated an executive order by the former President of Pakistan, Mr. Ghulam Ishaq Khan, dismissing the Prime Minister, his cabinet, and the entire government of Pakistan including the parliament. In this case, Muhammad Nawaz Sharif vs. Federation of Pakistan [1992], the Supreme Court of Pakistan reinterpreted the right of individuals to freedom of expression to include the electoral process. In other words, when the people of Pakistan went to the polls to elect the Prime Minister and their Members of Parliament, what they exactly did was to exercise their freedom of expression by freely and consciously expressing their choice in the person of Prime

Minister Nawaz Sharif. Thus, the presidential order dismissing him and his entire government without substantial legal or constitutional justifications was unconstitutional and the Prime Minister was therefore reinstated together with his government by the court. Thus, there was abundant legal, constitutional, and judicial authority in support of Justice Jallow's 5 December 2001 judgement when he invalidated the newly amended Indemnity Act (of No. 5, 2001). On the other hand, all the authorities cited here and found elsewhere do not support Justice Arif's 18 June 2002 dissenting opinion and reversal order in Inspector General of Police and Others V Ousman Sabally.

Finally, in light of the above detailed analysis and the principles underlined, we would argue that despite Justice Arif's 18 June 2002 judgement and reversal order setting aside the earlier judgement of 5 December 2001, his dissenting opinion will not be followed by courts in The Gambia. Instead, Justice Jallow's 5 December 2001 judgement will continue to be followed by courts in The Gambia and beyond and will always be cited with support and endorsement by legal researchers, academics, and constitutional and human rights experts.

Furthermore, although the question whether Justice Arif's 18 June 2002 judgement was the outcome of political interference or executive pressure could not be decisively answered in the affirmative. It is obvious that the peculiar circumstances under which he assumed office as head of the Gambian Judiciary made him vulnerable to political pressures and executive interference, as mentioned earlier. Whether Justice Arif's 18 June 2002 judgement was influenced by political pressure or executive interference or not, the fact that the power of the Supreme Court to review and depart from a previous decision is vulnerable to outside influence remains unaltered. Some observers believe that the fusion of the Office of the Attorney General and that of Minister of Justice in The Gambia means that the top law enforcement official in the country would always be a political appointee and would likely attempt to influence judicial proceedings in the country in favour of the government of the day. Thus, to avoid such influence or interference, there is a need to separate the office of the former from that of the latter or to separate the Director of Public Prosecutions from the post of Attorney General. In this situation, the Attorney General or Minister of Justice could continue to be the principal legal advisor of the government through whom the government can sue and be sued. On the other hand, the Attorney General or Director of Public Prosecutions as the case maybe, who is always a neutral person, should be appointed by the National Assembly upon recommendations of the Public/Judicial Service Commission to represent the public interest.

Summary and policy recommendations

This chapter has examined some of the major trends that have characterized the functioning of the judiciary in the Second Republic of The Gambia namely: the judiciary's struggle to assert its autonomy and independence in the face of different forms of political pressures and interferences. Despite numerous instances of interference in the process of the administration of justice, the courts in The Gambia have managed to effectively check on and substantially arrest some excesses of both the legislative and executive arms of government. The overturning by the Court of Appeals in 1997 of treason convictions and death sentences of the men who allegedly led an abortive coup in November 1996, the nullification by the Supreme Court in 2001 of the Indemnity Act (No. 5: 2001), and the court's partial nullification of another Act of Parliament aimed at amending several provisions of the 1997 Constitution, as well as the reversal by the high court in Banjul in 2000, of the judgement of the Kanifing Magistrates' Court in favour of the state in the *Citizen FM* case, are all examples of the effectiveness of the judiciary as a check on executive and legislative excesses.

The trend of executive interference in judicial matters, however, has continued to be demonstrated in various forms, including summary dismissal of both superior and lower courts judges, refusal by the executive to abide by court orders, and violent attacks and intimidations by unknown persons against legal practitioners. The sacking of Justice Hassan B. Jallow, a Supreme Court Judge and Chief Justice Brobbery in 2001 and 2005 respectively, as well as the violent attack against Lawyer Ousman Sillah in 2003 and the government's failure to abide by the court's ruling in Pa-Sallah Jeng's case, provide concrete examples of such continued interference. Losing major legal battles to political opponents and private individuals can sometimes cause frustration and embarrassment to political elites. Consequently, any form of political pressure or interference may follow as a reaction to such a loss. In this modern age of respect for human rights, democratic values and good governance, political elites, and the executive authorities, as well as traditional and other influential leaders across the continent, need to understand that political interference in the process of justice delivery and administration can be counterproductive to a nation's political, social, and economic development.

Concerning the security of tenure of office of judges, this chapter finds that the constitutional provisions on the retirement of superior court judges are quite generous and effective. Section 141 of the 1997 Constitution has provided both for optional and mandatory ages of retirement for superior court judges in The Gambia who are 65 and 70 years respectively. This chapter argues that the period between the normal time to begin a career and 65 or 70 years is fairly long enough for a serving judge to achieve a lot. On the other hand, the security of tenure of superior court Judges is threatened by Section 141(2) (c) of the Constitution, which empowers the President to terminate the appointment of superior court judges in consultation with the Judicial Service Commission. In other words, giving the President power to appoint and terminate superior court Judges compromises the independence of the judiciary as it provides for an unnecessary dependence by the latter on the executive. We believe that this particular situation weakens the autonomy of the judiciary of the executive. Thus, it may be appropriate, in light of the above exposition, to suggest that the power of appointment of superior court judges be vested in the Judicial Service Commission and that the power to remove judges from office be entrusted to the National Assembly as the case is with the removal of such judges on the grounds of inability to function or infirmity body or mind and misconduct.

Despite numerous instances of interference and political pressure on the judiciary, the latter remains, to a large extent, independent or autonomous from the executive. The Supreme Court judgement on the constitutionality of the Indemnity Act (of No. 5: 2005) and the high court's ruling in a 2005 murder case by the state against the main opposition leader Mr. Ousainou Darboe and others as well as several other rulings in which the courts corrected the executive, support the above conclusion.

In conclusion, independence of the judiciary in The Gambia and elsewhere on the continent will be better safeguarded and more effectively guaranteed if we take a rights-based approach to the question. In other words, the key actors, and main stakeholders in governance, particularly the government, civil society, the private sector, and citizens should recognize that to have an independent and impartial judiciary is a fundamental human right and must be protected.

6

International Human Rights and the Law of Nations: A brief analysis of the philosophical foundations, basic premises and historical background of human rights from the conventional and Islamic perspectives

I.   Introduction

This chapter makes a quick attempt to analyze comparatively the theoretical or philosophical foundations of the modern concept of human rights, its basic premises, origin, and historical background from the perspectives of different jurisprudential systems and civilizations. This chapter begins by analyzing the theoretical foundations of law and rights under the parameters of the 17th century natural law philosophy. Consequently, the views and perceptions of some American, European, and other Western leading political philosophers and jurists about law and rights are scrutinized. These include:

- Hugo Grotius, who is generally regarded as the founder of modern international law and of having prepared the ground for secular and rationalistic version of modern natural law (d.1645)
- John Locke, the renowned English political philosopher (d.1704)
- Sir William Blackstone (1723 – 1780) the famous English legal philosopher and jurist
- James Wilson (d. 1798) who was a leading American jurist of the late 18 century
- Jeremy Bentham (d. 1832) a leading and prominent jurist of the utilitarian theory of law and rights
- John Austin, founder and a leading scholar of the Austinian School of Legal Positivism
- The American Theory of Legal Realism
- A. V. Dicey – an English political philosopher of the 19th century

This chapter also examines the philosophical foundations of law and rights within the Islamic system of jurisprudence. This chapter further examines the conceptual foundation of human rights in national legal systems, the origin of domestic human rights and the background of human rights in international law and the nature of international human rights. The socio-economic and political importance of international human rights and the impact of the 1948 human rights revolution on the Muslim world and the political processes of the Islamic countries are also subjected to thorough scrutiny and analysis.

The last question to be addressed by this chapter is the origin of international law in Islamic jurisprudence and the contribution of the early Islamic jurists and Muslim state practice in the evolution and development of the legal rules and principles governing inter-state relations.

Finally, the main objective of this chapter is to study and establish the true nature and real meaning of human rights and law and the extent to which human rights can and should be respected by all within the legal systems and civilizational contexts of the various nations of the modern time despite vast differences in their political, cultural, religious, geographical backgrounds and legal systems.

This chapter then concludes that regardless of all the differences surrounding the modern concept of human rights – be they conceptual, philosophical and historical backgrounds, cultural, religious beliefs, ethnic, geographical and linguistic variations or legal and political systems of nations, there seems to be a consensus among peoples of different civilizations and legal, cultural and political systems that the individual human being needs protection and must be protected against the state and society in general from any act of aggression, abuse and disrespect of his or her dignity and rights.

I.a. Law and rights in general: some theoretical and philosophical foundations

One of the most obvious features of the 17th century natural law philosophy, which has largely influenced the modern concept of law and rights in the West, was the detachment and separation of law from theology and religion. This was accompanied by a great emphasis on the power of reason as one of the distinctive characteristics of human beings. Hugo Grotius (d. 1645), one of the most prominent jurists and legal philosophers of the time who is generally regarded as having prepared the ground for secular and rationalistic version of modern natural law, believed that natural law is a dictate of right reason which measures the quality of moral necessity and legitimacy of an act by the extent of its conformity or otherwise with the rational nature of human beings. So, for him the state was an association of free people who agreed to come together for the enjoyment of their rights and common interests. Thus, the sole purpose behind the creation and formation of the state was to promote, protect and enjoy the natural rights of people who submitted their sovereign power to a ruler. Some of the dictates of natural law in the view of Grotius include the following:

> To abstain from that which belongs to other persons, to restore to another any goods of his which we may have, to abide by pacts and to fulfill promises made to other persons, to repay any damage done to another through fault and to inflict punishment upon men who deserve it. [1]

These, in brief, are the basic moral foundations of modern international law in general and international law of human rights in particular.

For John Locke (d. 1704), the renowned English political philosopher and another believer in natural law, what existed prior to political and any form of social organization or institution was a state of nature under which men lived together according to reason without any common superior authority on earth. He believed that in this state of nature men lived together under the guidance of the law of nature by which their rights and responsibilities were determined. Like Grotius and many other natural law philosophers of the same age, John Locke, it appears, did not recognize the importance of divine revelation to law and to the determination of the rights and duties and responsibilities of individuals vis-à-vis one another and society as a whole. This is because the law of nature according to him was an objective rule and measure emanating from God but ascertainable by human reason.[2] Thus Locke, whose political writings, especially the

216

Two Treatises on Civil Government, are believed to have largely influenced the English Revolution of 1688 which gave birth to the 1688 Bill of Rights and subsequently influencing the American and French Revolutions of 1776 and 1789 respectively, was a strong advocate of the natural and inalienable rights of men and women. He argued that even before government existed, men were free, independent and equal in the enjoyment of those natural and inalienable rights. In his opinion, the most important of such rights were the rights to life, liberty and property. He, however, appeared to have acknowledged the existence of a serious weakness in that state of nature he was talking about. In other words, Locke realized that the state of nature lacked some central and common authority and machinery. So, there was the tendency that everybody would have executive power over the law of nature and this made the whole system prone to injustice and partiality or bias especially when one was to become a judge for one's own case and for those of one's friends. So, for these obvious weaknesses and inconveniences of the state of nature, Locke suggested that civil government was the best and the most proper remedy or solution for that problem. [4]

Sir William Blackstone (1723-1780), another English devotee to the theory of natural law, wrote that the law of nature is that which could properly be thought of as human law. He ruled out any role for human beings in making this law. Instead, Blackstone argued that the law of nature was dictated by God and for that reason it was binding over the entire globe in all countries and for all times. He further argued that the role and task of the judge was to try to discover or find out, and apply, but not to make and create this law, and that human laws contrary to the law of nature are invalid, while the valid human law derived its force and authority from that original law.[5] I have not been able, however, to detect or even sense throughout his discussion of the law of nature, any incline of recognition by Blackstone of the importance of divine revelation or prophet-hood to the process by which the law of nature was sent down to human beings. Blackstone, who believed in the existence of natural law and therefore natural rights, divided rights into two types namely: absolute and relative rights. Relative rights are incident to and due to individuals by virtue of their membership of society. While the absolute rights are those claims, entitlements, and privileges that the individual is entitled to by virtue of being a human being. This is what is meant by natural rights. In other words, they are invested in human beings by the immutable laws of nature. The English jurist and political philosopher thought that the principal aim of society and principal view of human laws was to recognize, protect and enforce such rights and their full enjoyment by every individual member of society. [6]

James Wilson, (d. 1798), an American jurist of the late 18th century and a former associate justice of the United States' Supreme Court, was another advocate of the theory of natural law and therefore natural rights of people. He argued that the main function of the law was to guarantee i.e. safeguard and protect the natural rights of the individual against any encroachment by the government. To him, natural law which provides a basis for natural rights and illuminates the ends of government was a God-created absolute standard against which individual and community acts must be measured. The American natural law advocate then defined what he meant by natural rights as the right of the individual to their property, to their character and reputation, integrity and honour, their right to liberty and safety. All of the above concerns the theory of natural law and natural rights. I now consider other theories of law and rights.

As for the utilitarian theory of law, Jeremy Bentham (d. 1832) held that law is a human creation and that a good deal of law is made by judges. According to his utilitarian theory, law whether made by the judge or the legislature should be in accordance with the Utility Principle and the notion of usefulness, happiness and goodness to

218

society as well as to the individual. So, for utilitarians, every right is an ordinary one. In other words, for the utilitarians, who set out one supreme goal of happiness and preference maximization, they would accept, recognize and respect rights only if they are able to bring about their goal of the maximum satisfaction of preferences or happiness. Thus, under the utilitarian construction, an act of torture might be accepted so long as torturing suspects could bring about happiness to society. [9] On the other hand, the Austinian theory of legal positivism emphasizes the aspect of command and sanction in positive law or the command theory of law and sanction theory of duty.

The positivists believe that the notion of command implies a relation of superiority and inferiority, i.e. law "properly so called" is a command from political superiors to political inferiors which, sanctioned with a threat of evil, has to be complied with or obeyed.[10] Thus, under the Austinian doctrine of legal positivism which he developed in his school of analytical jurisprudence which strictly separates law from ethics and morality, the emphasis is on legal rights and there is no talk of any rights in the absence of clear black letter law giving such rights to the individual. This is because legal rights are conferred by statutes and by the decisions of courts. So, in order for such claims, moral or otherwise, and entitlements and privileges to be given legal force there has to be an enactment of specific legal rights sanctioning or legally recognizing such claims or rights. [11] So, legal rights, according to the legal positivists only exist when there is a specific black letter provision guaranteeing them.

Furthermore, somewhere near the positivist construction, but far away from the naturalist theory of law, stands the American theory of legal realism. This theory rejects the idea that there are rules of law that have weight, authority and force in the law which the judge should look for and apply in any case before the court. Instead, legal realists have placed judges at the centre of law making. They maintain that judges do legislate and that the judicial decision-making process is a creative rather than a mechanical activity. Obviously, the realists would reject the idea of natural and divine law. Rather, they hold the view that judges are not bound by any existing rules, but that a rule of law is made as soon as the judge announces his or her decision. So, the law of a state is that body of rules laid down by judges in the course of their determination of the legal rights and duties of the people vis-à-vis the state and vice versa.[12] So, for the realists, who emphasize the centrality of the legislative role of the judge, rights are actually existent and really meaningful only in the course of the judicial process especially at the moment when the judge decides.[13] Unlike the legal positivists, who attribute the function of law to a central and superior political authority, the legal realists emphasize the central role of the judicial process in making the law and concomitantly giving, defining and protecting the rights of the individual. It is not clear what exactly this school of philosophy is trying to establish. Do the realists want to emphasize the important role of an independent judicial system in the process of defining and determination of human rights? Or are they attributing to the judiciary the legislative role of the legislature when it comes to defining and determining the scope of human rights? What is however clearly understood from the realist construction is the centrality of the role of the judge in the process of adjudication, promotion and protection of human rights.

For A.V. Dicey, another English political philosopher of the 19th century, individual rights were secured not by guarantees set in a formal document but by the ordinary remedies of private law available against those who interfered with those rights. In other words, the common law principles of habeas corpus and action for damages in tort to be declared by common law judges are the basis of actualization by citizens of their rights and liberties.

These differences in the theoretical foundations of law and rights among those leading Western legal thinkers do not very much affect the modern concept of human rights, although some controversy still exists over the precise nature, scope and extent of rights. It goes without saying that the modern concept of human rights has been influenced not only by natural law but also, albeit to a greater or lesser extent, by legal positivism, legal realism and utilitarianism. However, it is believed that somewhere between the 13th and 17th centuries the meaning of the term right, an equivalent of *jus* in Latin, shifted from doing right to possessing, owning and having a right, a claim, an entitlement and privilege. [14] Despite the fact that some theoretical differences exist among legal experts over the conceptualization of the value of rights, they all seem to agree on two important aspects of rights. First, that individuals need protection against the state and the government of the day is elected by the majority and that rights whether legal or moral are a necessary if not a sufficient means of ensuring that protection. Second, those rights are goods which individuals own or have as theirs. [15]

I.b. Legal and moral rights

Rights that are created and conferred by a constitution or a legal system may be termed as pure legal rights i.e. the right to appeal, the right to make a will, the right to dispose of property that is lawfully owned and the like. However, rights that people inherently own or have whether or not they are recognized in a given statute, constitution or a legal system are called moral, fundamental, natural and inalienable rights of human beings. They are also called politico-moral rights. These rights are not created by the legal system but it recognizes them and guarantees their implementation. These rights are said to have possessed a special value because they rest on a moral conception of people as separate individuals of equal worth. They are sometimes called fundamental rights given that they are recognized in the constitution which is the fundamental law of the country. They are for the same reason also called constitutional rights or basic rights of human beings. The civil and political rights invoked by the American Declaration of Independence of 1776 and the French Declaration of the Rights of Man of 1789 belong to this kind of politico-moral rights. We now move on to examine the nature of law and rights in Islamic law.

I.c. Law and rights from an Islamic perspective

The Islamic concept of law and rights is fundamentally different from what I have been discussing above. It is not utilitarian, neither is it positivist nor does Islam recognize such loose concepts as legal realism and the theory of natural law. Islamic law, on the other hand, has in the first instance to be placed, understood, interpreted and applied within the context and bounds of the Divine Revelation. Islamic law is of divine origin and its development or growth and expansion have to be guided by the fundamental principles of that revelation i.e. al-Quran and Sunnah of the Prophet (p.b.u.h [Peace and Blessings of Allah be Upon Him]). Thus, the typical nature of the law of Islam is that it is of divine origin, it is comprehensive and inclusive of all facets and activities of human life, that it addresses itself to both individual interests and those of society at large, that it is suitable for and applicable by all people of all generations and that the Islamic community is under strict divine obligation to put into effect the rules and principles of Islamic law, (albeit every generation of Islam does so in the most suitable way for the solutions of its peculiar everyday problems). To sum up, the practical rules of Shari'ah deduced from the detailed evidence of the divine sources of Islam, constitute the juriscorpos of Islamic law. [17] Consequently, Islam law is the only source of guidance for everything needed and related to the life of Muslims and is the heart of the Islamic system of life. This is why Islamic law has different branches or areas of discipline ranging from the rules of theology, the science of method and sources of the law otherwise known as legal philosophy, to the rules governing family life such as marriage, divorce and maintenance, the rules governing commercial transactions, the law of inheritance, criminal law, laws governing civil matters, the law of evidence and other procedural accepts of the law.

This specific nature of law in Islam, its intimate relation and interconnection with the Divine Revelation or *Shari'ah* and the special position of *Shari'ah* in the structure of Islam as a way of life, has ruled out any possibility for that law to be separated and detached from theology, faith or religion in a true Islamic society.

So, it is this law of Islam which is inseparable from its Divine Revelation that defines and determines the nature and scope of the rights of human beings in that system. It provides the necessary procedure and the right framework and regulates the process of promotion, protection and actualization or realization of those rights. According to al-Shātibī, the overriding objective of *al-Sharī'ah* is the consideration of public interests or *maslahah*. In his famous treatise, *al Muwāfaqāt*, this Maliki jurist identifies five basic necessities of life which are essential to the existence of life and the survival and prosperity of the human being. Their neglect, according to him, would result in total chaos and the eventual destruction of human life on earth. These values, whose preservation and protection is what *Sharī'ah* is all about, are religion (*dīn*), life (*nafs*) intellect (*'aql*) lineage or (*nasl*) or progeny and property (*māl*).[18] These values are to be protected by both positive and negative means i.e. by providing whatever may be necessary for their full realization and enjoyment, on the one hand, and by preventing whatever could cause or lead to their total destruction or disregard on the other.[19]

As for the precise nature of rights in Islam, some contemporary scholars believe that the majority of Muslims jurists did not or have not made any serious attempt to give an exact definition of right or *haqq*. This is perhaps because they feel that the term *haqq* which is the Arabic equivalent of the English word, "right" was so obvious that it did not have to be defined. It *(haqq)* was traditionally used to mean truth, obligation and any benefit or interest and entitlement whether material or spiritual or anything that one legally deserves or is entitled to. It is also defined as meaning both reality and truth. So, anything termed *haqq* must conform to the requirements of wisdom, justice, truth, reality and propriety. It is, however, important to understand, as al-Attas explains, that the term *haqq* or right encompasses both "statement" and "actions, feelings, beliefs, judgements and the things and events in existence."[20] Thus, the values referred to under the concept of *haqq* or right include numerous values and entitlements that are all universal, indivisible and inalienable. These are what we refer to in contemporary times as human rights and fundamental freedoms.

Consequently, I would like to support at this juncture the view held by many that human rights and fundamental liberties in Islam are not mere entitlements and privileges that one has to have, possess and own. Rather, they are necessities of life guaranteed or given not by any human authority but by God the Almighty and must therefore be respected, promoted and protected under all circumstances. [22] Thus human rights, as Islam teaches, must be preserved, promoted and protected under all circumstances for every human being regardless of faith, nationality, social status and of any other consideration. In other words, since human rights are necessities of life, their protection becomes a fundamental obligation falling not only upon the Islamic state but upon each and every individual as well.[23] What needs to be noted in this connection is that the concept of rights in Islam is not only placed within the context of the Divine Revelation but that it also has to be understood, interpreted and promoted or actualized under the guiding principles of Islamic jurisprudence *(Usūl a-Fiqh)*.

I have already stated that the overriding objective of *Sharī'ah* is the consideration, preservation and protection of human interests and the general wellbeing of the people. But what has to be remembered here according to Muslim theologians is that one of the five fundamental values and necessities that *Sharī'ah* aims to protect is *din* or religion and according to al-Attas, there are four primary significations for the term *din*. The first two being indebtedness and submissiveness to the will of God. The state of indebtedness requires that one should abase oneself to the service of one's Master and Creator to whom the debt of creation is owed. This means that the individual must obey the laws and commandments of God the Creator and Sustainer of the universe to whom everyone owes the debt of existence. [24] Similarly, the submissiveness to the will of God means total obedience to God's Law i.e. to observe his commands and avoid his prohibitions. The remaining two primary significations of the term *dīn* are:

iii.   Judicial power i.e. that people's daily routines – commercial and all other transactional activities are to be conducted in accordance with law.

iv.   The natural tendency of *man* to form society and obey laws and establish just governments as well as to obey God the Creator. [25] It, therefore, has to be taken as a fundamental principle of Islamic theology and law that the concept of human rights cannot be separated from and placed anywhere outside the domain of religion.

Consequently, one of the most obvious differences between the Islamic and the Western approaches to understanding human rights is that there is no room for secularism or secularization of human rights in the Islamic system where the whole concept of right is anchored into the heart of Shariah which is the divine law of Islam. This is why Islamic perception of relativism cannot be the same as that of the conventional systems. According to al-Ghazālī, the spiritual and religious affairs of life of every individual believer have to go hand in hand with the worldly and material aspects or affairs. The two aspects cannot be separated because the basic requirements of *din* include both the spiritual and material wellbeing of the individual believers. [26]

Human rights are therefore an integral part of the entire structure and edifice of the Islamic way of life, whereas most conventional political, legal, economic, socio-cultural and state systems of the modern time are premised on the principle of separation of religion from the state and state matters. Finally, what has become clearly visible from this exposition of the nature and the conceptual foundation of law and rights in Islam is that, unlike modern Western and Westernized constitutions and legal systems where there exists the duality of individual rights and state interests, "Islamic law does not proceed from a position of conflict between the respective rights and interests of the individual" [27] and those of the state. Rather, rights of the individual, their promotion and protection form part of the main functions, duties, responsibilities and interests of the state and moreover, both the state are the individual are, on an equal footing, obliged to follow the rules of *Sharī'ah*. Furthermore, that their mutual relationship is to be conducted in accordance with the dictates of that supreme divine law. The quality of *īmān*, or faith in God, together with its concomitant aspects of piety, justice, honesty, sincerity and sense of responsibility, should indeed be the foundation of any bill of human rights in an Islamic state. [28]

This precise and concrete nature of rights in Islamic law was perhaps what had impressed a former judge of the International Court of Justice at The Hague, (the ICJ) when he observed:

> Human rights doctrine in Islam was a logical development from its basic postulates, namely the sovereignty of God and the revelation to the prophet. [29]

The former judge of the ICJ, C.G. Weeramantry, explains that from such postulates, the basic principles of human rights, including those contained in modern international human rights conventions and treaties, followed logically as a necessary part of Islamic law.[30] Finally, a closer look at the five fundamental values that, according to Muslim jurists, *Shariah* has been revealed to protect and preserve, clearly shows that Islamic law has in actual fact adequately guaranteed the protection and ensured the means of actualization of all fundamental human rights and basic freedoms incorporated in the international human rights conventions and treaties of contemporary times i.e. the protection of life, religion, intellect, progeny and property has definitely included all the civil, political, economic, social and cultural rights protected by the modern international law of human rights and various national laws of the nation states of contemporary times.

I.d. Can the concept of human rights be universally and comprehensively Defined? And what significance will that definition make?

As the above discussion of the nature of rights reveals there can be no single universal and comprehensive definition for the concept of human rights. The various philosophical perspectives just highlighted above stand to contradict one another. So, to give a single definition comprehensive enough to be accepted by all is out of the question. Similarly, the continuing debate and controversy between the theories of universality and cultural relativism over the scope and relevance of human rights is another factor ruling out the possibility of providing such a definition. While any definition by the proponents of the universality theory would stress the universal, indivisible, interdependent and interrelated character of human rights and that they have to be placed beyond the limits of domestic jurisdiction, the cultural relativists would advance a definition which emphasizes the need to consider human rights in their ideological, regional and national context and on the principle of respect for and noninterference in the internal affairs of a sovereign state. However, given that the concept or term "rights" is used to describe a variety of relationships the following description of the concept may be recognized (although it sounds influenced by the theory of natural rights): Human Rights are those fundamental values inherent in every individual human being on the basis of humanity and recognized by law both domestic and international.

Human rights in this way mean three things, namely (i) immunities, this refers to civil and political rights which protect against encroachment by the government; (ii) privileges i.e. economic, social and cultural rights for the realization of which affirmative action by the government is necessary; and (iii) power to create a legal relationship. This is a reference to the formal power of the state to pass laws and regulations in connection therewith. As for Islam, just like the case in the conventional sense, human rights define the relationship between the state and the individual and that they serve to limit the power of government. What has become very clear out of this precise exposition of the nature of rights in Islam is that the current phenomenon of rampant violation and sheer disrespect and disregard of human rights in many parts of the Islamic world is purely due to attitudinal rather than doctrinal problems. In fact, it is no secret that most Muslim countries of contemporary times do not follow or apply Islamic law. So, Islam has got nothing to do with what is happening there.

Furthermore, I have already indicated that the Islamic approach does not proceed from a position of duality between individual and state interests. So, the controversy we have seen in the conventional approach will not apply in an Islamic system, because if the

228

government does its duties properly, the rights of the individuals will receive due protection. Although some contemporary scholars have attempted to define the concept of human rights in Islam, many of such definitions are not comprehensive perhaps because they overlook the fact that this concept has to be traced in the concept of *hukmshar'ī* i.e. the communication of the law giver conveyed in the form of a command or a prohibition which regulates the conduct of every legally responsible individual or *mukallaf*. Thus, *hukmshari* is a major concept containing a variety of other concepts including that of rights and obligations. Both the command and prohibition constitute the mandatory rules of *Shari'ah* which may require a certain action or give a choice whether to do it or not. Actions required may be obligatory (*wajib*), recommendable (*mandūb*), permissible (*mubāh*), disapproved (*makrūh*) and prohibited (*haram*). If the enforcement of human rights requires affirmative action they may have to be fitted into one or perhaps all of the first three categories. But if they are to be realized by means of negative action then the latter two criteria may be applied i.e. the obligation to preserve life will fall under *wājib* or mandatory obligation, whereas the prohibition of destroying life falls under *haram* or prohibition .[32] This is why I have referred to al-Shātibi's approach of dividing *maslahah* or human interest into *darūriyyāt, hājiyyāt and tahsiniyyāt* as the best way of explaining the precise nature of rights in Islam. Thus, what matters is not to define the concept of human rights in Islam or to say what they mean but it should be to say what they are, where they should be placed and how they can be actualized in an Islamic state. And for the last one I believe institutions like *Majlis al – shūrā, qādā', and hisbah* can be effective mechanisms of implementation. Before I end my discussion on this issue let me take a brief look at the position of human rights in national and international law in the past.

II. Human rights in national legal systems

Human rights occupy prominent positions in the national constitutions and legal systems of many countries of modern times including almost all Muslim countries. In countries like United States of America, India, Nigeria, Pakistan, Malaysia, Indonesia, The Gambia, Senegal, Guinea Conakry, Mali, South Africa and Ghana, fundamental rights are incorporated into the supreme law of the land or the constitution, and therefore, unchangeable by the executive authorities through an amendment process or by way of executive orders.

II.a. Origins of domestic human rights

Domestic human rights law is said to have emerged in Europe as early as 1215 when the Magna Carta, the Great Charter in which the fundamental rights and privileges of the English people were guaranteed, appeared during the reign of King John and in 1688 when the British Parliament enacted the 1688 Bill of Rights.[11] This was followed later by the American Declaration of Independence and the Bill of Rights and the French Declaration of the Rights of Man of 1776 and 1789 respectively. Unlike domestic human rights law, the international law of human rights is a very recent development. Prior to 1945, it was still not developed because international law was generally not concerned with how states treated their citizens. Such matters were regarded as falling under the domestic jurisdiction of each State. Nevertheless, international human rights have their origins in the 19th century when it can be historically traced to or attached to a number of international legal documents and institutions such as the doctrine of humanitarian intervention, humanitarian law and the League of Nations. [12] These documents and institutions, it must be admitted, were largely limited in scope and to some extent political rather than idealistic in motivation. But with all this their significance in the growth and development of international human rights cannot be underestimated.

However, what you may be interested to know at this level is whether human rights enjoyed any significant position or attention in the domestic legal and political systems of Europe and many other countries in the past. Although attempts have been made by some Western scholars to trace the origin of modern human rights in the ancient code of law of the Babylonian King Hammurabi (about 2130-2088 B.C), some   legal historians of Europe admitted that the sanctions provided by this code to protect the worthy human values and other objectives, such as the administration of justice, marriage and family affairs, were so disproportionately cruel that it is, in our context, preferable not to regard them as being the foundations of this newly developed branch of both national and international law.[34] The same is the case with the Roman Law which guaranteed to the Roman citizen (but not foreigners and slaves) the right to take part in the government of his or her country by way of participating in the exercise of the power of legislation, in the administration of criminal justice, in electing public officials and in having a share in the police power. The common law of Anglo-Saxon countries also has its own criteria, somewhat similar to the Roman law – as to what is just and fair and provides an objective yardstick for measuring people's conduct in the area of individual rights and freedom. But the two systems i.e. Roman Civil Law and Anglo Saxon common law - have maintained institutions and practices which are inconsistent with some of the fundamental concepts of modern human rights.[35] Furthermore, even the English Petition of Rights of 1628, the Bill of Rights of 1688 and, of course, the much earlier document known as the Magna Carta of 1215, though they all contained ideas of rights, they did not define or purport to define the basic and fundamental human rights of every individual irrespective of any consideration.[36] This is why some legal experts maintain that human rights "as a term of art" is of recent origin i.e. it goes back only to the last decades of the 18th century or the 17th century as some others argued.[37] However, there is no doubt that the modern human rights movement has been largely influenced by the Virginia (American) Bill of Rights of 1776 and the French Declaration of the Rights of Man of 1789 both of which symbolized two great revolutions in Western legal, economic and socio-political history. Thus, throughout the 19th and 20th centuries, the American and French examples of providing bills of human rights in their constitutions were followed by a vast number of countries on the continent of Europe and later in the Americas, Asia and Africa.[38] The Russian Revolution of 1917, while following the American and the French precedents by including in the 1918 Constitution some of the rights guaranteed by its Western counterparts, exhibited certain fundamental differences in its pronouncements. The Russian Constitution and, of course, its political system appeared to have viewed such rights as positive rather than negative privileges. i.e. If the American, French and any other Western or Westernized constitution prohibit any violation of the right to freedom of expression, the Russian Constitution holds that for the individual to secure and enjoy the right to freedom of expression, it must abolish the dependence of the press upon capital and that all technical and material means for the exercise of that right i.e. the publication of newspapers, pamphlets, books and similar materials should be handed over to "the working people and the poorest peasantry." Likewise, if the American and French constitutions prohibit any violation of the right to freedom of peaceful assembly, the Lenin 1918 Constitution, in order to secure complete freedom of assembly for the working people and the poorest peasantry offered to guarantee all premises convenient for public gathering, including lighting and heating facilities and furniture. [39]

What has to be noted here is that in the Leninian concept of rights, the so called "working class or poorest peasantry" were not provided the choice of purposes for which such rights to freedoms of expression, assembly and the like were given, rather, it was for the state to make that choice for them. Thus, the basic difference then between the Western capitalist and what used to be the Soviet socialist conceptions of human rights, as seen in their national constitutions, is that while rights in the Western approach are designed in order to prevent interferences, especially on the part of the public authorities, with fundamental rights, the Soviet Socialist approach did not entertain that idea. Rather, it promised to provide and make available all technical facilities for such rights to be enjoyed by the people but it refused to promise freedom in the choice of purpose for which the technical facilities would be used. Another difference in their domestic approaches to human rights is that the West emphasized the traditional civil and political rights. [40] However, what I have tried to explain in this brief discussion is that beginning from the 18th century, the concept of human rights and fundamental liberties started to force its way into the national constitutions and legal systems of many countries of the world including even those of the socialist bloc and Islamic countries. Finally, it should be noted at this juncture that all Muslim countries which have incorporated human rights and fundamental freedoms in their national constitutions have followed the American and the French model.

III. The modern concept of human rights in international law and the nature of international human rights

The relation or connection between international law and the modern concept of human rights and fundamental liberties is a substantial one. Although international law has itself taken from the concept of the right of man, it has given more than it has taken. This is further demonstrated by the addition of the phrase "international" to that of "human rights". Thus, within the structure of the law of nations, human rights as a political concept assumes the name: "International Human Rights" or International Human Rights Law" or International Law of Human Rights. [41] In practice, but not in theory, international law's concern with human rights has manifested itself in two different ways i.e. through the doctrine of humanitarian intervention and the adoption of international treaties. As far as the general concept of fundamental rights of human beings is concerned, it suffices here to say that, starting from the 17th century and throughout the 18th, 19th and 20th centuries, the doctrine of humanitarian intervention was and is still, on a number of occasions, invoked by the major powers, and that international treaties, as they (major power) would argue, were and are still concluded in order to come to the rescue and protection of the oppressed populations and endangered groups, to deal with matters of religious liberty, to combat terrorism, slavery and the slave trade, to improve labour conditions, to arrange for the supervision and administration of certain mandated territories, to provide, under the auspices of the defunct League of Nations or the present United Nations, for the protection of the rights and interests of racial, linguistic, religious or cultural minorities especially in Eastern and Central Europe, Africa, Asia and South America.[42] The military interferences by the major Western powers and their allies, under the auspices of the United Nations, in Bosnia, Somalia and the Great Lake Region of Africa and the intervention by troops of the Economic Community of West African States (ECOMOG) in Liberia, Sierra Leone, Guinea Bissau, the Cote d'Ivoire and Mali provide us with good examples. So, international law has been heavily involved in the refinement and development of many of the basic concepts of fundamental rights of human beings as they exist and are understood in contemporary times.

As for the question of when and how the modern concept of human rights might be said to have originated in international law, it is believed that attempts to discover this i.e. to seek a foundation for the fundamental rights of the individual in the Law of Nations, go back to the early or first half of the 16th century when the Spanish theologian and lawyer, Francisco Devitoria (1480-1546), who in his work, *De IndisNoviterInventis* of 1532, gave a series of lectures about the Indians recently discovered by the Spanish settlers in the Americas.[43] So, by strongly pleading for the rights of the indigenous Indians, Francisco Devitoria did not only influence the growth of the modern concept of human rights in international law, but he is also thought to be the first scholar (in the West) who had attempted to "legal reasoning, moral principle and political courage in support of a cause "which might be considered as" involving human rights as well as international law." [44]

III.a. Nature of international human rights

International Human Rights, which may henceforth be described as that branch of modern international law which is concerned with the protection of individuals and groups against possible violations by governments, other institutions, and individuals internationally recognized rights on one hand and with the promotion of these rights on the other. Expressions like international human rights law, international protection of human rights and international bill of human rights, are sometimes used to refer to this branch of the Law of Nations (LN). The latter expression is, however, confined to major human rights treaties concluded at the level of the United Nations i.e. the Universal Declaration of Human Rights (UDHR), the International Covenant on Civil and Political Rights (ICCPR), the International Covenant on Economic, Social and Cultural Rights (ICESCR) and other subsidiary conventions dealing with human rights promotion and protection.[46] International human rights have, by virtue of its definition, significantly departed from the traditional attitude of international law which is usually defined as the law governing relations between nation states exclusively binding on them in their mutual intercourse.[47] Although, the scope of the definition of international law was somewhat expanded after the First World War to include some of the newly created inter-governmental organizations deemed to deserve some or certain limited rights under international law, individual human beings were still excluded and not deemed to deserve international legal rights as such. Instead, they were said to be objects rather than subjects of international law. Furthermore, the law of Nations was in its very nature still inapplicable to the manner in which a state treated its own people as this was entirely within the state's domestic jurisdiction. Oppenheim did, however, indicate that individuals might, under certain circumstances, be conferred rights and imposed duties of international law. At this point, however, we will conclude by saying that one of the most obvious weaknesses of modern international law is that it addresses itself exclusively to state institutions rather than individuals who make up or create and run these institutions.

This is completely different from the position of the Islamic Law of Nations (ILN) which is an integral part of Islamic law. The Islamic Law of Nations, otherwise known as Islamic International Law, originated in the basic sources of Islam. It is meant for all times and universally applicable to all people and institutions. This argument finds support in the legal meaning of the term *siyar*, the typical name for Islamic International Law. Juridically, it is that branch of *fiqh* or Islamic jurisprudence which regulates the conduct of the Islamic state in its relationship with other states and regulates the conduct of the believers in their relations with unbelievers of enemy or other territories as well as with the people with whom the believers have made treaties either as *mustā'mins* – non – Muslim aliens or *dhimmis*– non- Muslim citizens. *Siyar* also regulates the manner in which Muslims should deal with apostates and rebels or *būghāt*.

While concluding my discussion of the nature of international human rights I must mention that it is, like any other system of law that purports to regulate human conduct, a normative order in the sense that its rules stipulate what ought and ought not to happen and as one expert puts it, "not necessarily what will or will not happen."[51] In other words, law is naturally unable to make things happen or to prevent them from happening. Rather it provides guidelines for the right things to happen in the right manner. It is also described as a primitive law in its early stage of development, intended to govern a society which is in its collective sense, a primitive one possessing only a few centralized legislative, judicial and executive organs.[52] Thus, international human rights has the usual normative character of law and of legal rules i.e. just as there is no guarantee that a law will be obeyed, neither does it follow that all offenders or violators of the law will be punished. In fact, the likelihood of punishing those who violate the human rights law is more remote. This is because the validity of law does not depend on its being obeyed or on whether sanctions will be applied in the event of any disobedience. Instead, a law is valid in the juridical sense if the system recognizes its source as competent. Finally, international law of human rights should not be confused with international humanitarian law (IHL). The latter is concerned with human rights protection during wartime and is thus defined as "The Human Right Component of the Law of War;" whereas the former, it appears, addresses itself to peacetime situations. However, International humanitarian law also has some influence on the latter.

III.b. Socio-political importance of international human rights

The domain of modern human rights is a multi-disciplinary subject. It has been the product of different powerful socio-cultural forces that have come together to constitute and shape human society. Consequently, human rights have become the meeting point of a large number of academic disciplines which sprang out of those socio-cultural forces i.e. historical, philosophical, religious, legal, social, cultural political and economic forces.[55] Thus, it is against this highly exciting background that the importance of international law of human rights and indeed the role of the United Nations and the regional and sub-regional systems in its rapid growth should be valued. Although the development of international human rights norms and standards predate the inception of the United Nations, it is a well-known fact that the end of the Second World War and the subsequent establishment of the UN had substantially contributed to the restructuring, definition and rapid growth and development of international law in general and the development and crystallization of international law of human rights in particular. The period from 1945 to the present day has been witnessing the fast growth and virtual crystallization of a new branch international law which has, in turn, drastically changed and reshaped the field of international legal and political relations among member countries of the community of nations. The long-standing attitude of international law towards individuals as objects and not subjects has virtually been changed and the scope of its traditional doctrines of domestic jurisdiction and non-intervention in the internal affairs of a sovereign state has been drastically limited or narrowed down by the advent of international law of human rights. Since the end of the Second World War, a large number of human rights treaties, both global and regional, have been concluded under the auspices of the United Nations and other regional groupings, and then signed, ratified or acceded to and in some cases incorporated into domestic laws. All those international human rights instruments are mainly concerned with the socio-economic, political, civil and cultural rights of the individual based on the philosophy or fundamental principle of their being a human, their human worthiness and inherent dignity as such. Earlier, the UN Charter was also

238

equipped with comprehensive provisions on human rights which provide the basis for elaboration of the vast materials on international law of human rights that have later been concluded by the United Nations. The human rights provisions of the UN Charter recognize the close relationship and intimate nexus between respect for the human worth of the individual, on one hand, and peace, tranquility and prosperity or socio-economic progress of the individual and society at large on the other.

Likewise, the Universal Declaration of Human Rights recognizes that in order to save humanity from the scourge of wars, from the outrages of barbarism, oppression, racial and ethnic discrimination and other socio-political and economic injustices which sometimes necessitate rebellions and in order to secure and ensure international peace and security, it is necessary to establish a just international order and that respect for human rights should be the paramount and essential foundation for the establishment of that order. In other words, recognition and respect by everyone, of the inherent dignity and of the equal and inalienable rights of all members of the human family is the foundation of peace, freedom, justice and prosperity in the world. This is an axiomatic fact because experience has shown that disregard and contempt for fundamental human rights have often resulted in barbarous and brutal rebellious reactions which ultimately would deeply shock and outrage or injure the conscience of humanity. The internal conflicts that hit the Horn of Africa, the Great Lake regions and North and West Africa regions during the current decade are a good example. In the early 1980s due perhaps to the active involvement by UNESCO and other UN specialized agencies in the promotion of international peace, economic development and education and research, certain values and norms began to take shape within the structure of international law of human rights. These international values or rights, identified by some experts as "the five cardinal human rights" are: "the right to peace, the right to development, the right to a healthy environment, the right to enjoy the common heritage of mankind and the right to humanitarian assistance." In 1986 the General Assembly of the United Nations recognized the right to development as a collective human right. It is, however, important to note that all these five rights are collective rights and those that belong to the so-called third generation rights.

Thus, the importance of the modern international law of human rights to the socio-economic, civil, political and cultural life and development of the individual is clearly visible in the provisions of the Universal Declaration of Human Rights and of the two human rights covenants adopted by the United Nations in 1966 in furtherance of the human rights provisions of the Charter. They have called for and in most of the cases secured for the individual, the precious rights to life, liberty and security of person, the rights against torture, slavery, arbitrary arrest and detention/exile, the right to fair trial, the right to freedom of movement, of thought, freedom of religion and conscience, to freedoms of opinion or of expression, assembly and association and the right to freely participate in the government of one's country.[61] The socio-economic rights they called for and guaranteed for the individual include the rights to work, to an adequate standard of living which ranges from enough food, clothing, housing, medical care and the like, to the right to education etc.[62] On the other hand, the cultural rights include the right to participate in the cultural life of one's community in all aspects, the right to share in scientific advancement and the right to the protection of the moral and material interests resulting from one's scientific, literary and artistic production.[63]

Most of this wide range of rights has now forced its way into many national constitutions and the legal system of many countries. As we already stated in this section, international law of human rights has introduced some drastic changes in the domain and course of international politics. The most obvious of these changes is that the scope of the traditional doctrine of domestic jurisdiction has been

240

severely curtailed so as to exclude gross violations of human rights by states against their own citizens. This has now become a matter of concern for the international community as a whole. Under Chapter 7 of the UN Charter, the Security Council is mandated with the power and authority to take necessary measures to deal with the problem of armed conflicts and any situation or act of aggression that breaches or threatens international peace and security. Today serious denials of human rights or gross violations of fundamental rights by a state of its own citizens are viewed as constituting a cause for armed conflict or a breach or a threat to international peace and security and therefore prompting the UN Security Council and even sometimes, certain major powers and regional groupings to intervene in the internal politics of that country. The civil wars that we witnessed during the last and the present decades in the Balkans, the Great Lake Region, in the Horn of Africa as well as in West Africa, in the Middle and Far Eastern countries, and the interventions of regional, sub regional and other blocs in those conflicts clearly illustrate the point under consideration. Themes like prevention of genocide, war crimes and crimes against humanity, gross violation of fundamental rights of the people and fighting against drug trafficking and international terrorism have been used by major powers like the United States of America and the EU not only to have or maintain strong political influence and secure huge economic and political interest but also to establish military bases and to keep and apply effective strategies in certain strategically important countries in Europe, the Middle East, Asia and Africa.

Similarly, due to the strong impact of the global human rights movement, heinous crimes and inhumane practices like slavery and the slave trade, apartheid, racial segregation and all sorts of racial, sexual and other forms of discrimination which were once legitimized or accepted as part of the political process in countries like the USA and South Africa have now been outlawed at least in theory by international law and their own domestic measures. However, we must admit that such discriminatory practices have in actual practice not completely disappeared in those and many other countries. In the United Kingdom, where the government functions without a completely written constitution and a bill of human rights, relentless efforts are being made for the EU Human Rights Convention to be eventually incorporated into domestic law and thereby providing the British citizens with their first ever comprehensive Bill of Human Rights.[65] Likewise, the Declaration on the Granting of Independence to Colonial Countries and People adopted by the General Assembly of the United Nations in 1960 had an important effect in decolonizing many Afro-Asian Dependent territories of the time. Thus, by becoming independent from Western colonialism and political domination, the peoples of those dependent territories and colonies, especially in Africa and the Caribbean countries, have had the tremendous opportunity to fully enjoy their basic and inalienable right to self-determination i.e. to determine their political fate and to shape and run their political and economic institutions by themselves.

Furthermore, human rights have always gained a prominent and conspicuous position in the foreign policy agenda of the major Western European countries and of the United States government. These countries have always included the promotion of and respect for human rights among their foreign policy objectives. Governments in these countries are sometimes faced with the problem of deciding whether, when and in which country, they would give a higher priority whenever the question of respect for and promotion of human rights of their own people became an issue as compared to others, foreign policy objectives, such as national security, international trade and similar huge economic and political interests and other forms of co-operation.[67] Despite all these problems, the major powers of the world often warn state offenders and violators of human rights that their wrongful acts will not go unchecked and that economic and other benefits may be affected. So, the former Labour government of Prime Minister Tony Blair repeatedly warned that the United Kingdom would not sell arms or give aid nor would she grant licences to export arms and weapons of strategic importance or even to give significant development aid to any state which violates human rights.[68] Some of the major powers would sometimes refuse to give foreign aid or economic and military assistance or to engage in any bilateral or even multi-lateral transactions with countries they accuse of involvement in massive human rights violations against their own citizens. During the Balkan War the United States and her Western European allies imposed wide ranging economic, trade, diplomatic and military sanctions against Serbia for the latter's atrocities and gross violations of human rights in the former Yugoslavia i.e. in Bosnia, Croatia and in the province of Kosovo.

There is, however, a major cause for concern with regard to the use of human rights as a foreign policy objective in the conduct of a country's foreign relations. That is, the major powers sometimes use double standards especially during the days of the Cold War, in their attitudes towards South Africa before the end of the apartheid era and toward the Arab-Israel conflict. The United States, for instance, would be prepared to punish Iraq, Iran, Libya, Sudan Syria and Cuba for what she terms as gross violations of human rights or for failing to honour a UN Security Council's binding resolution, while she would do absolutely nothing against Israel, despite the fact that the Jewish State is always accused of human rights violations. Israel persistently violates international law and arrogantly disregards the UN Security Council's resolutions. Just few years ago, Israel came under severe criticism by the United Nations for the former's continuous use of torture against the Palestinian suspects and detainees. The Jewish State, however, defended itself by describing her action as a legitimate method of interrogation.[69] In the same way, in countries where the major Western powers have maintained huge political and economic interests, such as those of the Arabian Gulf and the Middle East, massive and systematic violations of human rights are often ignored, simply because they do not want to embarrass or anger their political allies in those countries and thereby jeopardizing such economic and political interests. However, in those countries where they have few interests and the rulers are not on good terms with them (the Western powers) especially when they reject the Western version of democracy like Cuba and Venezuela, for instance, every bit of human rights violation is blown out of proportion and reported by the most reputable international media organizations. This kind of double standard is, in my opinion, a result of their over-politicization of international protection of human rights which is doing great harm to the global human rights movement and eventually retarding the rapid development of international law in that area.

We now turn our attention to the impact of the global human rights movement in the Islamic World.

IV.   The impact of the 1948 human rights revolution on the Muslim world

Finally, the global human rights movement has also pervaded almost all parts of the Islamic World. There are several examples showing how the international human rights revolution has left its footprints on various parts of the world. First, most Muslim countries on the three continents of Europe, Africa and Asia have either signed and ratified or acceded to the main international human rights conventions which constitute the backbone of international law of human rights i.e., the UDHR, the ICCPR, the ICESCR and other subsidiary conventions. Human rights movements and associations have been formed in most of these countries i.e. Egypt, Sudan, Pakistan, Malaysia, Nigeria, Turkey, Senegal and the like. Similarly, their respective constitutions have given substantial recognition to most of the modern norms of human rights. The constitutions of Malaysia, the Islamic Republic of Iran, the Islamic Republic of Pakistan and The Gambia's 1997 constitution can be cited examples.

244

Second and more importantly there has been a series of conferences on human rights in Islam held in Tehran – Iran and Cairo – Egypt in recent years. On 29-31 January 1987 the Iranian government organized an international conference on human rights in Islam. At the conclusion of the conference delegates who came from different Muslim countries affirmed in their recommendations that being a way of life that conforms to the nature of human being, Islam has provided its followers with all the necessary human rights and fundamental liberties. These include the right to respect the dignity of the human person, the rights to life, equality and non-discrimination, the rights to freedom and security. Similarly, all Muslim countries in Africa with the exception of Morocco are active members of the African human rights system and signatories to the African Charter on Human and Peoples' Rights.

IV.a.   The Universal Islamic Declaration of Human Rights

Another possible influence of the Human Rights Revolution in the Islamic East (the Islamic World) is the introduction or adoption of the Universal Islamic Declaration of Human Rights adopted in 1981 by the International Islamic Council of Europe in Paris, France. The Islamic Declaration comprises a preamble and 23 articles covering a wide range of human rights which are essentially the same as those found in modern international treaties on human rights. In its preamble the Islamic Declaration emphasizes the divine origins of human rights as they were drawn from *al-Qurān* and *Sunnah*. For this reason, the rights are eternal, inalienable and can under no circumstances be suspended, abrogated and tampered with by any human authority or institution, except only in accordance with strict procedures established by *Sharī'ah*. The Islamic Declaration then affirms in the preamble its conviction that the recognition, respect or acceptance of the rights it declares is a prerequisite for the establishment of a true Islamic society based on the principles of *tawhīd*, (belief in the absolute or oneness of God) justice, equality, the rule of law or supremacy of *Sharī'ah* and equality before the law as well as government by *amānah* or trust and accountability – both to God and to the people. All of these, according to the Declaration, were the foundations of peace and prosperity for the people. The wide range of rights contained in the Islamic Declaration include the following: the rights to life, to liberty and security of person to equality and to equal opportunity for the use of the natural resources by all, the rights to justice i.e. equal and easy access to justice, to fair trial, the right to be protected against the abuse of power by government authorities, the right against torture, the right of the individual against defamation of his /her character, the right of refugees running away from oppression, tyranny and injustices to be granted asylum, the rights of the minorities, the right of the individual to take part in all aspects of public life including of course, the political life, the right to freedoms of thought, belief and expression, the right to freedom of religion, the right to freedom of assembly, association and to take part in *Da'wah* or the propagation of Islam, the economic rights i.e. to work, development, private ownership and to initiate investment projects, the right to establish a family, the marital rights of women, and a number of other rights.

Finally, it should be noted here that Islamic Council of Europe is neither an official organ of the Organization of Islamic Cooperation (OIC), nor does it represent any Islamic country or group of countries and that its declaration on human rights has not yet been adopted by any Islamic country. Nonetheless, the fact that the principles and individual rights established in the universal Islamic Declaration of Human Rights are substantiated in the general principles of Islamic law as stipulated in the Holy Quran and Sunnah of Prophet (SAW) makes it absolutely important and very relevant to and part of the International Human Rights Revolution.

V.   Islam and the origin of international law

Many Western European writers and legal experts often claim that the modern law of human rights, like any other rule of international law, is a pure product of European Christian civilization. According to them, international law is the product of the European mind and beliefs and is therefore based on European state practices developed and consolidated during the last three centuries. The Westerners argue that, due to the impact of colonialism, Asian and African countries lost not only the ancient rules which they used to observe in their inter-state conduct but also lost their international status and personally as members of the family of nations. For this reason, Afro-Asian countries were unable to play any role in the formulation and consolidation process of international law.[89] While Hugo Grotius, a 16th century Dutch jurist, is identified as the founder of modern international law, the modern concept of human rights in the West is claimed to have its origins in the Magna Carta of Britain which contained principles of trial by jury, habeas corpus and the control of Parliament of taxation. However, the claim that habeas corpus has its origin in the Magna Carta is itself debatable. In other words, it might have been taken from religion because as Syed al – Attas says: "The legal concept of habeas corpus (you must have the body) as a fundamental procedure of justice is perhaps only a mere imperfect reflection of awesome and irrefutable procedure to come."[90.]

In this part, this chapter examines Islamic rules of inter-state relations which offer a precedent refuting the above assertion. We do not know what they mean when they claim that international law is a product of Western Christian civilization and that the modern concept of basic human rights originates from the Magna Carta of 1215.

We, in the developing countries, will however disagree with this view, because their ideas in this regard are tantamount to saying that before the 16th century the whole world was steeped in absolute ignorance, barbarism and savagery. This, of course, was steeped in absolute ignorance, barbarism and savagery only in what is referred to, today, as the Western or civilized world but not in the Islamic East. This is because every fair-minded person, Muslim or otherwise, who knows a little about Islam and Islamic history, would readily acknowledge the great contribution that Islam made. They would similarly be aware of Islam's huge impact upon human civilization, cultural refinement and enlightenment through its vast heritage of knowledge and belief – the richest ever known to humanity. As already indicated, it is not correct to generally conclude that before Grotius the world did not know about or have rules of inter-state conduct presently known as the Law of Nations. It is proved beyond reasonable doubt that even in Europe itself there were some people who well before the Dutch jurist spoke about rules of conduct among nations. These included some early 16th century Spanish theologians like Francisco De Vitoria, Francisco Suarez and the Italian jurist Alberico Gentili. As from the Islamic perspective, I would call it an insult to all Muslims to say that their system of belief has not provided clearly defined and cohesive of inter-state relations.

Furthermore, it is confusing to claim that international law is a product of Christian civilization when its founding father Grotius himself admitted that up to the time he was writing his work, Christian people and countries throughout the world had no law regulating the conduct of warfare. He was quoted as saying:

> I observe everywhere in Christendom a
> lawlessness in warfare of which even
> barbarous nations would be ashamed.
> Nations would rush to arms on the
> slightest pretext or even without cause
> at all.

Grotius was referring to the law of war presently known as international humanitarian law which is the backbone of modern international law. The question posing itself here is how is it reasonable to claim that international law is a product of Christian civilization and indeed, which Christianity are we referring to? Is it the original and true one or the Westernized or secularized version of it?

We are saying this because from the Muslim point of view, as Syed Al-attas explains, "there are two Christianities, the original and true one and the Westernized version of it. Original and true Christianity conform to Islam."[93] However, it is worth mentioning at this juncture that the secularization process which Christianity has undergone in the West has its origin not in the biblical faith as one might be deceived in believing, but in the misunderstanding and misinterpretation of the biblical faith by the European philosophers, which is one of the reasons why the difference between Islam and Christianity has become a fundamental one. I would say, with all confidence, that the first scholar to write about international law in the history of human civilization was Imam Muhammad Ibn al-Hasān al-Shājbani, one of the founding fathers and the most authoritative jurists of the Hanafi School. Some Western Scholars, I have learnt, to my astonishment, refer to al-Shāybāni as the Grotius of Islam, although he died almost eight hundred years before Grotius.[95]The reverse would seem to be more apt i.e. Grotius is Al-Shāybāni of the West. This jurist who wrote his work, in the early days of Islam and died in 182 of the Hijrah (d. 804 while Grotius died in 1645) dealt with many aspects of the law of warfare and many other issues relating to mutual legal relations between Muslims and non-Muslims both at state and individual levels.[96]

Similarly, many other Muslim jurists produce extensive treatises on the subject of Islamic International Law. They include IbnHisham, IbnIshaq, Sarakhsi and others. Furthermore, these scholars did not create the rules of Islamic International Law on their own; instead, they deducted them from the most basic sources if Islam i.e. al – Qurān and *sunnah* of the Prophet himself and those concluded at the time of the four rightly guided caliphs.[97] This is because, *siyar* or Islamic International Law is an integral part of *fiqh* or Islamic law. Thus, the only sense in which Western writers could be correct and justified in attributing the growth and development of international law to themselves is, when they mean those rules of inter-state conduct based on the idea of humanism and secular principles which are completely devoid of religious or divine origin, inspiration and guidance.

In another development, it is equally incorrect to claim that human rights are of Western origin and that they are the product of the Western mind and civilization.[98] It is however important to note that Magna Carta came into existence about six hundred years after the advent of Islam. Moreover, it is believed that the principles of basic human rights found in the Magna Carta were included therein unconsciously because until the 16th century no one in the Western world knew that the English Charter contained those basic rights already alluded to.[99] Muslims, on the other hand, had for many centuries before the Magna Carta, been enjoying what are now being called the basic or fundamental rights of human beings. This reality may not be clearly visible to or understood by non-Muslims or Western scholars who fail to realize that in the Islamic system of belief, there does not exist the duality that they have created between religion and state, philosophy and theology or between the spiritual and material life of man. Thus, in Islam, rights are not granted by any king or a legislative assembly or by a dictator. Instead, they are given by God the Absolute Sovereign. For this reason, no king, dictator, legislative assembly or government on earth has the power, right or authority to interfere with these rights. They can, under no circumstances, be suspended, withdrawn or violated in any way. Human rights in Islam, in the words of Maudūdī,

> Are not like those basic rights which are conferred on paper for the sake of show and exhibition and denied in actual life when the show is over; nor are they like philosophical concepts which have no sanctions behind them.[100]

The Islamic principles containing the human or basic rights of human beings are found in the primary sources of Islam i.e. al – *Quran* and *Sunnah* of the Prophet (S.A.W) (Sallallahu Alaihi Wasallam- meaning Peace and blessings of Allah be upon him) as well as the traditions and administrative practices of the four rightly guided caliphs and those of their successors. In the same way, many early Muslims rulers, thinkers or jurists and writers had either spoken or written about people's right to have their dignity, human worthiness and freedom as well as the security of the person and life preserved and respected by others. In *al-Quran* (40:13), Allah says that he created humanity from a single pair of a male and female and that tribes, races, nations into which they are made are just convenient labels by which they recognize each other and identify their differing characteristics and not for them to despise or look down upon one another. Indeed, the verse continues, *he most honoured of mankind in the sight of God is he who is the most pious or righteous of them.* This verse established the most fundamental principle of the rights of a human being to equality, the right to respect one's personal dignity and human worthiness. According to al-Tabarī, to be most righteous means to be punctual, regular and sincere in performing one's obligation imposed by Allah and that it is only this way that one can be better or higher in status than others who are trailing behind.[101] This verse also embodies the right of everybody against discrimination based on sex, race, social status and any other consideration. According to al-Qurtūbī, the verse was revealed on the day of *fat Makkah* or the conquest of Makkah to dismiss any form of discrimination in Islam. He said the whole issue was triggered when some of the companions uttered racist remarks against Billal who was ordered by the Prophet (S.A.W) to call *ādhān* immediately after the conquest.

Al-Qurtūbī quoted one of these racist remarks attributed to al-Harith Ibn Hisham who allegedly said: "Didn't Muhammad find anyone to make *ādhān* except for this black eagle?" (Bilāl). He concluded that by virtue of this verse there can be no grounds for the superiority or preference of one person or group over another just because of race, sex, social status or any other consideration other than that already mentioned i.e. on the grounds of piety and righteousness.[102] In the *sunnah*, there is a large number of traditions embodying the principle of respect for human dignity and for all privileges or rights granted to man by God. Some of these traditions made it clear that, apart from piety or righteousness, there does not exist in Islam, any grounds on which a person or group of persons can claim superiority, virtue or honour over another or the rest. The Holy Quran says: "Your Lord is one, your father (Adam) is one and that an Arab is not better than a non-Arab, nor a non-Arab is better. Likewise, a red (white) man was not better than a black man and nor a black was better than a red man. The best and most honoured among you is he who is the most pious and righteous."

In another tradition reported by al-Būkhārī, the Prophet (S.A.W) said that "the best among all the people is he who is sacrifices his life and Property on the path of Allah."

In similar tradition reported by al-Tabārī, the Prophet (S.A.W) said that no one is more virtuous, privileged or advantaged than others (in
252

the sight of Allah) except by *dīn*. In all these traditions the word "*fadl*" or its derivative "*afdal*" is used and according to IbnManzūr the term *fadl* has got many significations. These include increase, betterment, privilege, advantage, distinct position and a state of being discriminated against or given special favourable treatment. Thus, the principle of equality and nondiscrimination which is one of the pillars of modern international law not only has its origins in the most basic sources of Islam, but was also practically demonstrated by early Muslims rulers, scholars and thinkers. As for the Sahābāh, the four rightly guided caliphs were known to be strict in their adherence to the Islamic principles of justice, respect for human dignity and people's rights and freedoms during their successive administrations. Umar Ibn al-Khatāb, for instance, was famous for being scrupulously strict, just, humble and very keen to see that the rights or interests of the masses were promoted and protected. His rule was just perfect and, as far as I can understand, his administration practically demonstrated the twin principles of responsible and limited government more than anyone else who came after him. In fact, these concepts have remained a mere high idea or dream yet to be achieved by governments of the so-called modern period. The second caliph was one day quoted as saying "why should you enslave the people when they are born from their mothers, free. Umar said these strong words as a warning and admonition to his governor to Egypt, Ibn al – 'As. It is reported that a son of Ibn Al- 'Āas had taken part in a horse racing event with some ordinary Egyptians. At the end of the race, scuffles broke out between the son of the governor and his opponents in the event. Consequently, he beat one of them severely, claiming that he was the son of the honourable (governor). When the whole story was reported to the Caliph, he summoned the governor and his son to his headquarters in Madinah and ordered the victim to take his revenge on both Ibn Al- 'Āas and his son. This is because the latter used and abused the former's power to act aggressively towards others.

Among the early Muslims thinkers and jurists who spoke about people's rights was AbūYūsufYaqūb a co-founder of the Hanafī School. In the introductory part of his book (Kitāb al-Khārāj) he advised the then caliph, Harūn al-Rashīd, to treat his people equally, to protect their rights and interests and make sure his government was founded on the pillars of *taqwā* or righteousness. He warned that any government not built on righteousness would collapse. Similarly, AbūYūsuf warned the caliph against corruption and corrupt practices in the administration. To him, justice i.e. (putting everything in its proper and rightful place) was the only guide for rulers.[110] In view of the above exposition of the position of rights in Islam, I would say that the question is not about their origin but about how they are understood and interpreted in a given context or civilization.

It is my view that the same misunderstanding and misinterpretation that the West had regarding the biblical faith is being repeated with regard to the modern concept of human rights whose contents are considered by Westerners in the context of a purely secular perspective. For this reason, I would suggest the scope of freedom or liberty in the West continue to expand and it is today claimed to have included acts or activities which are quite contrary to God's commandments. Acts like marriage of a couple of the same sex, and the rejection of one's own faith are being endorsed or approved in the West under the pretext of freedom. Human rights campaigners in Britain and Australia have recently been calling their respect governments to decriminalize lesbianism and homosexuality. They argued that the laws penalizing these offences violate people's basic right to freedom. If the concept of human rights understood and interpreted in this way, is what they refer to when they say: human rights are Western in origin, I have no objection because, in Islam rights are weighed against duties and responsibilities.(M. H. Kamali, 1997). They are interpreted in the context of the Divine Revelation from which they have been drawn. Thus, in Islam there can be no right to perform any act or practice which violates Gods commandments, so the scope of freedom in Islam cannot be extended so as to cover any act that goes against Islamic principles. This is because freedom in Islam means that human beings should be consciously and willingly, submit themselves to the will and commands or authority and the law of God. This perhaps is one of the reasons why the Islamic way of life is referred to as *dīn*, a term which in its most basic form reflects in true testimony, the natural tendency in human beings to form societies and obey laws, of course, God's law and to strike for or seek just government. I will conclude my discussion of this issue by registering my subscription to and complete agreement with Syed al-Attas that the problem with Western people is that they are inclined to regard:

> His culture and civilization as man's
> cultural vanguard and his own
> experience and consciousness as those
> [who are] representative of the most
> evolved of the species. So that all the
> people are in the process of lagging
> behind them.[114]

In spite of Islam's unprecedented contribution to the history of the emancipation and enlightened or cultural refinement of humanity and the great importance it attaches to the preservation and protection of people's interests and rights, a considerable number of Muslim countries have been involved in systematic and persistent violations of their people's basic rights. These range from various forms of harassment, arrest and detention, imprisonment, sending into exile and in extreme cases, killing of their political opponents in the name of curbing religious or Islam extremism or fundamentalism. However, the latter term is created by their Western political allies and former colonial powers and therefore alien to Islam. This criticism of Muslim governments does not however, intend to exonerate Western or non-Islamic countries from gross violations of basic human rights. In fact, some of the worst and the most sophisticated violations of human rights take place in those countries often called the major powers of the world. They are often accused of systematic torture of detainees, initiating racially motivated proceedings against certain minorities and the imprisonment of conscientious objectors.

Lastly, it may be pointed out that even some of those at the International Court of Justice in The Hague would acknowledge that Islam has contributed enormously to the development of international law and human rights. A former judge of the International Court of Justice from Sri Lanka believes that this has happened in many ways: first, the relationship between human beings and God is vertical whereas that between human beings and their fellow human beings is horizontal and when human beings' vertical relationship with their creator receives due care the horizontal and when human beings' vertical relationship with their creator receives due care the horizontal relationship between them and their fellow humans, tends automatically to receive due attention. This is because duties imposed by God are comprehensive and all encompassing. In other words, human rights are best promoted and protected through our performance of God's commandments. Second, the principle of trust, amānah, (Trust) is another way in which Islam has contributed to the development of international law, especially the newly emerging international environmental law. By virtue of this principle, human beings are told to use the earth and everything on it as a trust property and should therefore not abuse, spoil or destroy the environment. The exercise of political power or government authority and the conduct of international relations also come under the principle of amānah. Thus, Islam in his opinion fertilizes universal thinking in the field of human rights and international law through many of its notions and concepts i.e. the notions of universalism, communion and solidarity, human dignity, supremacy of the law, limited sovereignty, the right to privacy, presumption of innocence and many more; while other non-Muslim scholars acknowledge that from the very beginning the right to freedom of religion has been entrenched in the Islam tolerated other religions. They concede that Islamic recognition of other beliefs as being of divine origin is the theological basis for its (unprecedented) toleration of non-Muslims. Similarly, African and Asian countries have influenced the growth and development of modern international law and human rights. After gaining independence, Afro-Asian countries have, due to a high level of solidarity and cooperation in a number of important issues, influenced the growth of contemporary international law i.e. rights of refugees, questions of legality and the banning of nuclear tests, reciprocal recognition, the right to self-determination, fighting terrorism, enjoyment of media rights and the like.[117]African cultural tradition is also said to have contained basic norms and ideas of respect for human dignity, rights and liberty.

VI.   Conclusion

In conclusion, the main objective of this chapter was to study and establish the true nature and real meaning of human rights and law and the extent to which human rights can and should be applied and respected by all within the legal systems and civilizational contexts of the various nations of the modern times despite the existence of vast differences in their political, cultural, religious, geographical backgrounds and legal systems. This chapter would, therefore, conclude that regardless of all the differences surrounding the modern concept of human rights - be they conceptual, philosophical and historical backgrounds, cultural, religious beliefs, ethnic, geographical and linguistic variations or legal and political systems of nations - there seems to be a general consensus among peoples of different civilizations and legal, cultural and political systems that the individual human being needs protection and must be protected against the state and society in general from any act of aggression, abuse and disrespect of his dignity and rights under all circumstances. The differences highlighted above in the theoretical foundations of law and rights among nations of different civilizations do not necessarily affect the value, content and usefulness of application and actualization of the values and principles incorporated under the modern concept of human rights, although some controversy still exists over the precise nature, scope and extent of some of the rights guaranteed by the International Human Rights Conventions.

In other words, despite the fact that some theoretical differences exist among legal experts over the conceptualization of the value of rights, they all seem to agree on two important aspects of rights. First, that individuals need protection against the state and the government of the day which is elected by the majority to serve popular interest. Similarly, those rights, whether we call them human, legal or moral, are a necessary if not a sufficient means of ensuring sustainable peace, security and stability of society at large. Second, that human rights are goods which individuals own or have as theirs under all circumstances. As from the Islamic perspective of rights, this chapter has concluded that human rights are an integral part of the entire structure and edifice of the Islamic way of life. This is in total contrast to almost all conventional political, legal, economic, socio-cultural and state systems of contemporary times which are premised on the principle of separation of religion from the state and state matters. According to al-Ghazālī, the spiritual and religious affairs of life of every individual believer have to go hand in hand with the worldly and material aspects or affairs of life in general. The two aspects cannot be separated because the basic requirements of *din* (way of life) include both the spiritual and material well-being of the individual believers. Finally, what has become clearly visible from our exposition of the nature and the conceptual foundation of law and

258

rights in Islam is that, unlike modern Western and Westernized constitutions and legal systems where there exists the duality of individual rights and state interests, Islamic law does not proceed from such a position of conflict between the respective rights and interests of the individual on one hand and those of the state on the other. Rather, rights of the individual, their promotion and protection form part of the main functions, duties, responsibilities and interests of the state and moreover, both the state and the individual are, on an equal footing, obliged to follow the rules of Shariah governing the Islamic obligation of protecting the dignity, human worth, life and basic rights of the individual.

7

Law Faculties, Ethics, and Legal Professionalism: A Contemporary African Perspective

1. Introduction

The judicial system and the legal profession both serve as custodians of the constitution in modern societies. Thus, these institutions are mandated by statute to guard the moral fabrics of modern societies. Within this context, the legal profession draws its legitimacy from the law faculties and law schools through which legal education, practitioner competence, and the ethical standards of the profession are authored and encoded.

Recent events like the well-publicized bribery-for-judgement scandal in the Ghanaian judiciary (The Anas Aremeyaw Anas scandal) and incidents of miscarriage of justice elsewhere in Africa (Ayodeji and Odukoya 2014, Ghana Integrity Initiative 2007, Ellet 2013) have challenged the ability of the legal profession to execute its solemn

260

commitment to high ethical standards and service to society. This is evidenced in this quote by Justice Michael Kirby, *'without a" tip", a file may be lost and will never make its way to a hearing. Without a bribe, a favourable decision may not be assured'*(Kirby 1996, cited in Ghana Integrative Initiative 2007, p. 5). This unfortunate legacy levels direct and implied indictment not just on the moral fortitude of the individuals involved, but also inscribes negative stereotypes and thus challenges the relevance of law faculties and the broader legal educational systems that produced rogue practitioners.

This chapter begins with a highlight of inherited law curricula and legal professionalism as the context of discussion. This section introduces this chapter's perspectives on the need for a re-negotiated law curriculum and how this can revive ethics and legal professionalism in Africa. The next section seeks theoretical support for this chapter's characterization of legal professionalism and offers a critique of ethics and professional ethics in the wider African context. The latter part of section two draws on existing research to conceptualize legal ethics and professionalism; this section further draws on the socio-cultural learning theory to support this chapter's assumptions of the impact of inherited law curriculum on the legal professionalism in Africa. A review of African law faculties is presented in section four. This review is conducted against the backdrop of rising judicial corruption and social and statutory responsibility of law faculties. This is followed by discussion on the changing role of law faculties in a contemporary African context. Using this as a case study, this chapter concludes with an outline of curriculum innovations that are aimed at reviving ethics and legal professionalism within the law faculty of the University of The Gambia.

1.1 The context: inherited law curricula and legal professionalism in Africa

This chapter, therefore, holds the implicit assumption that the onus lies on the academic community and the law faculties in particular to initiate the types of curriculum improvements that would facilitate the production of legal scholars of repute whose deep knowledge of ethics would be symbolic of vicarious professionalism and high ethical standards. As law faculties work to equip legal trainees with the knowledge and personal attributes that are beneficial to society, recent bribery scandals within legal corridors, lend support to the views of those scholars who advance the argument that the inherited legal system in Africa is to blame for the emergence of rogue elements within the legal profession (Joireman, 1999 and 2001).The proponents of this view argue that African societies would be best served when the inherited legal system and its curriculum are imbued with ethical principles that reflect Africa's cultural realities. Drawing on the views of Ayantayo (2011) and Ozumba (1995), who argue that the moral conditioning of African legal practitioners is influenced by their natural right of reason, statutes and common law in Africa need not draw inspiration from local precedents alone (Manchester and Salter 2006); but also draws inspiration from local customs and traditions. Hence, the tension between legal professionalism and African customs and traditions tends to be blamed in part on the inherited legal system from which current legal curricula draw their impetus (Joireman, 1999 and 2001).

This chapter thus aims to interrogate these views and legal practices within the framework of a re-negotiated law education curriculum. The objective here is not to substitute existing curricula with something entirely new, but to stimulate debate on the continuing validity of an undiluted common law system in African. This chapter therefore seeks to pursue a discourse on how legal professionalism in Africa may be enhanced by incorporating into the inherited system ethical principles that promote traditionalism and humanity instead of corrupt tendencies that are currently bedeviling the legal profession in Africa.

2. Theoretical underpinnings

Legal professionalism entails the professionalization of the judicial system to enable judicial actors to function as honourable members of a noble profession (Kahn 2009). Within this context, lawyers and judges and other legal luminaries would be expected to meet society's expectations of them as custodians of high ethical standards. While this expectation may not be based on the philosophical version of "truth," it would however be grounded on upholding the epistemology of service, agency, and professionalism; hence, the imperative to display behaviours that are consistent with the attributes of ethical champions. The professionalization process culminates in professionalism. While professionalism may be defined as ethos, attitudes, competence, and the work practices exhibited by members of a given profession (Burger 1995, Heineman Jr et al 2015); there is no consensus in the literature on how a profession should be defined (Salga 2015).

However, professionalization involves a process by which a particular occupation evolves into a profession, a vocation, or a full-time career. Thus, the pursuit of legal professionalism through the 're-professionalization' of the judicial function in Africa, would mean that lawyers, judges, and other experts on jurisprudence would be governed by ethos that include strict adherence to high ethical standards and codes of behaviour; a commitment to a social ideal that gives priority to service to society at the expense of the personal interests of practitioners; a system for certifying that members possess the required knowledge and skills levels before being licensed to practice; and the existence of a common body of specialized knowledge based on the application of systemic theoretical principles; and a defined system of specialized education and training at the highest levels as well as on ongoing professional development ((Burger 1995, Abdul Barr 2007).

Thus, legal professionalism becomes the function of two interlocking variables: a system of ethical code of practice; and a common body of specialized knowledge that is based on the application of theoretical principles. This understanding thus informs the roles of ethics and law faculties in the re-enactment of legal professionalism in a contemporary African context.

2.1 The wider context of ethics and values

The literature on ethics as an academic concept is cross-disciplinary in nature. While different scholars have investigated the ethics phenomenon within varying disciplinary domains, there is cross-disciplinary consensus on the commonality of its impact on social and professional behaviour (Giles and Jeremy 2001, Ozumba 1005, Omoregbe 1993, Ayatanyo 2011). Hence, Etta and Asukwuo (2012) contend that ethics is a science that is concerned with the formation and dispensation of humanity's moral doctrine. Within the disciplines of philosophy, sociology, jurisprudence, theology, and business management (Van Rooy 1997, Khan 2009, Silvij 1999), the ethics phenomenon has been presented as a science that studies human actions and motives and how the definitions of right and wrong are drawn to influence an individual's moral identity. Based on existing studies (Ayatanyo, 2011, Ozumba 1995), legal practitioners' religious beliefs exert strong influence on their ethical identity. As the dominant religions in Africa espouse social cohesion, through their teachings, Christianity and Islam thus provide ethical reinforcements to members and thus instill moral doctrines that concur in most part with professional norms of behaviour (Abdul Barr 2007). Further to this, Ayatanyo (2011), among several African scholars, advances the argument that the moral doctrine of African professionals may not be shaped by religious beliefs alone but may be shaped in tandem with "the very nature of things" in which the conscience of the professional uses the natural right of reason to build a moral fortitude that facilitates the practitioners' definition of right and wrong.

While these views on the sources of ethics have been widely reviewed in existing research, what still remains unexplained is the extent to
264

which the identified sources of ethics have been successful in reviving legal professionalism in Africa. Based on observable evidence, it could thus be inferred that in the midst of continual religious reinforcements and widespread opportunity for natural right of reason (Ozumba 1995), rampant corruption within the Bench and Bar symbolizes cases of low moral standard. Hence, one can advance the argument that another source of ethics in the legal profession may be the tension between inherited legal curricula and the values of humanity and communalism that are typical of African societies (Kigongo 2000). These values appear to be in constant conflict with the gestalt of Western individualism from which western legal ethics draws its origin (Joireman 2001 and Hofstede 2001). Thus, Africa's communal and humanitarian tradition constitutes what has been named in the literature as African traditional ethics (Ayantayo 2011, Etta & Asukwo 2012). These authors argue that the so-called African traditional ethics can be explored within a defined theoretical frame and used to tackle the social and professional ills of the world. While these scholars have yet to offer how their proposition can be applied to strengthen the moral backbone of the world; their works have, however, drawn an unmistakable attention to the discourse of ethics as a regional or geographic concept.

Currently, there is however no clarity in the literature on the regionalization of the ethics phenomenon (Kignongo 2000). What abounds, however, is the universalism of ethics or moral standards. Within cross-disciplinary contexts, ethics has been identified as a universal phenomenon in which customs and tradition, human conscience, experience, exposure, and reinforcements combine to arbitrate social and professional conduct thus providing the metrics for assessing acceptable behaviour. Furthermore, the universalism of ethics is evidenced in international protocols like the Universal Declaration on Human and Peoples' Rights (Shivji 1989, Nagengast and Turner 1997, An-Na'im, 1999a). Such protocols recognize the universality of ethical mores, while acknowledging that the enforcement of such mores would be hugely influenced by the cultural realities that emerge as the customs and traditions of a group. This argument thus builds the conceptual foundation for this chapter's call for the adaptation of inherited systems of jurisprudence to an African mediated content rather than advocate its absolute substitution with one that draws its content entirely from the branded 'African traditional ethics'.

2.2 The nature of legal ethics and professionalism

Drawing on reviewed literature on ethics in the preceding sections of this chapter (Ayittey 1991, Khan 2009, Kignongo 2000, Fafa Mbai 2013), these scholars maintain that professionalism and legal professionalism is driven by high ethical standards and regulated codes of behaviour. These behavioural codes, which may be written or unwritten, provide the moral pathway for a legal practitioner's dealings with him or herself, his or her clients, adversaries in law, and the courts. Thus, legal professionalism becomes a function of a body binding rules and practices that determine the professional conduct of members of the bar. The implication, therefore, is that the objectives of professionalism have emerged as the honourable intent to maintain the dignity of the legal profession, to pursue friendly relations between the bench and the bar and reinforcing the practitioners' commitment to ideals that prioritize service to society. In highlighting the nature of legal professionalism and legal practitioners' triple obligation, Khan (2009) argues that an advocate's obligation to clients, to the profession itself, and to the courts and the justice delivery process, mandates members of the legal profession to "expose, discourage, and where possible, stop any incident or instance of corrupt or dishonest conduct in the profession". However, recent indictments and consequent convictions of lawyers and judicial officials of corruption charges in some African countries provide evidence of ethical lapses in African judicial and legal institutions.

Despite the sworn allegiance of the indicted individuals to uphold the ethics of the legal profession, wanton violation of professional ethics has been widely documented in both academic and practitioner literature (Burger 1995, Heinemann Jr. et al 2015, Ghana Integrity

Initiative 2007). This evidence thus validates the argument that there could be in existence other sources of ethical identity that are potent but implicit, whose influence tends to override those of religion and natural right of reason (Ayantayo 2011 and Ozumba 1995) informing the moral identity of members of the legal profession. It has not been empirically determined that the inherited legal system and curricula contribute to ethical lapses in Africa's judicial institutions (Joireman 2001). However, having carefully followed rising number of cases of judicial corruption in Africa, this chapter seeks to propose that "the impact of inherited legal systems and curricula on legal professionalism in Africa" be identified as an area for future research. This proposition is made against the backdrop of the outcomes of existing research (Joireman, 1999 and 2001) which has documented the dissonance between pre-colonial judicial institutions and behaviours and those that developed in post-colonial era. Thus, the colonial metropoles' substitution of pre-existing judicial mechanisms with the common law system carries ramifications for both the rule of law and legal professionalism in Africa.

Based on the socio-cultural learning theory (Wertsch 1991, Lantolf 2000, Vygotsky 1997), these authors argue that the human mind is often mediated or interfaced with tools for humans' understanding of the world. Accordingly, Lantolf (2000), draws on the classical work of Vygotsky (1937), to argue that the mediatory tools through which humans develop their subjective understanding of the world may be artefacts that carry the characteristics of specific cultures. These artefacts which can be transferred from one generation to another can thus be modified or reworked to suit the needs of its individuals or communities. In the context of current discourse, the inherited legal system becomes the artefacts that are rooted in Western values but modified and passed on to Africans by colonial metropoles even when such system lacks the perfect blend with African traditional values.

It could thus be argued that the repetitive encounter of African legal professionals with this inherited system and curricula, which draw their inspiration from the individualistic disposition of Western values (Hofstede 2001, 2011), creates moral tension within professionals whose social and ethical mores have a bias for communalism. Following repetition through learning and practice, law students and legal professionals become intimately socialized (Nonaka and Toyama 2003) and thus become conditioned (Field 2005, De Houwer et al 2000) to substitute communalism with individualism as the basis of moral values (Ayantayo 2011, Kignongo 2000). While academic and professional development is encouraged, the inherited legal system and curricula, in this instance, indoctrinates and implicitly acculturates students and practitioners within the precepts of its roots thereby transforming participants from the communally responsible to the implicit and self-serving clones of a system whose values negate Africa's humanitarian tradition. The relevance of education or any other vocation is measured by its ability to empower participants to function as ethical symbols who provide reinforcement to the social mores of their host communities. Hence, any acclaimed good education or professional practice that substitutes rather than reinforces the social mores of its participants will not only disaggregate the identity of its host communities in the long run, but it will also serve as a source of sabotage to its social and economic cohesion. It is based on this premise that the next section of this chapter uses prescriptions and normative considerations to present a narrative on the current and future role of law faculties in promoting legal professionalism in Africa.

3. The curriculum of modern African law faculty

The main purpose of learning has to be to prepare students deliberately with the knowledge and personal attributes that will help them to thrive in complex and changing contexts. Hence, quality education has become a process of acquiring knowledge that is empowering to the learner and of value to society (Hockings 2010, Trowler 2010). Thus, universities through their academic faculties embody a social and statutory responsibility to design and deliver educational experiences that are empowering to the learner and of value to their host communities. Within this context, modern law faculties in Africa must strive to impart specialized legal knowledge that is inspired by local cultures and conditions while adhering to the highest ethical standards and codes of practice. Given the remit of this chapter, the attainment of legal knowledge and professionalism
268

among African practitioners thus becomes the prerogative of law faculties in Africa. While this statement sounds rhetoric, it is however worthy of note that law faculties in African universities have so far failed to deliver on this mandate (Ghana's Integrity Initiative 2007, Ayodeji and Odukoya 2014). While there is a documented increase in the number of law graduates across the continent (Ellett 2013), this increase has not been replicated in legal practitioners' appreciation of professional ethics across the continent (Ayodeji and Odukoya 2014, Ghana Integrity Initiative 2007). This situation thus represents an indictment on law faculties and their inherited curricula across Africa. In buttressing the point on the norms of a relevant legal curriculum, Economides (2010) admonishes that relevant education, regardless of geographic location or ethical background, must demonstrate good grounding in "public law, both constitutional and criminal; private law, concerning obligations, persons and property and at least some elements of commercial law; also, preferably through special courses dedicated to some elements of legal history and of the philosophy and sociology of law". This scholar argues that these principles of jurisprudence must be formalized with the knowledge of law *as* "a domain of practical reason".

This reference to law as a practical discipline draws on an earlier assertion on the responsibility of law faculties to the customs and traditions and the welfare of society. Simply put, there exists the expectation albeit implicitly, that the responsiveness of legal professionalism to local situations should be enhanced beyond the elucidation of such lawyering traits as scepticism, judiciousness, critical thinking and intellectual balance (Burger 1995, Heineman Jr. et al 2015). A re-negotiated legal curriculum would thus highlight the importance of creativity and innovation among legal practitioners with the aim of facilitating practitioners' cognitions of value tensions between legal business and social welfare, between individualism and the community, between delineating inherited legal ethics and the need for a re-negotiated curriculum. Thus, there is the recognition among legal scholars (M'Bai 2013 and Economides 2010) that the re-negotiation of African legal education (academic and professional) be led by law faculties to serve local needs. A response to this call for change can be initiated with curriculum innovations that facilitate a shift from the inherited common law tradition, to give priority to curriculum practices and principles that reflect the systemic and cultural realities of local African communities.

Within this context, African law faculties must therefore accept some responsibilities that reach beyond transmitting technical competence to promoting awareness of public and community interests that transcend servicing the legal needs of fee-paying private clients. This can be achieved not only through traditional lectures based in the classroom but also through working outside the formal environment such as running special programmes like clinical legal education, *pro bono,* and community legal services outside the physical boundaries of the law school. Consequently, innovative law faculties provide the institution for encouraging the good in lawyers and discouraging the bad. Thus, such institutions incentivize practitioners for high ethical standards and thus improve the opportunities for the renewal of legal professionalism in Africa. As Economides (2010) observes, "professionalism is an important value to be nurtured regardless of its significance to the legal profession and civil society. Ethical perspectives also matter when it comes to core academic activities of legal scholarship such as teaching and research." Thus, in the pursuit of a re-negotiated legal curriculum, a course on legal ethics needs to be made mandatory in the undergraduate law curriculum. The expected outcome of this process is the strengthening of the integrity and moral fabrics of future lawyers and judges based on the humanistic African tradition. This would engender local relevance to the curriculum and thus help trainee lawyers connect better with the fundamental values and wider civic responsibilities of legal scholars and practitioners.

4. The role and responsibility of law faculties

Based on its assumption that inherited legal systems are complicit in the declining trend of legal professionalism in Africa, this chapter has thus identified law faculties as the best placed institutions to lead the quest for a re-negotiated legal curriculum and by extension, a re-negotiated legal system in Africa. The implication, therefore, is that law faculties in African universities would assume the dual responsibility for excellence in legal education as well as fostering professionalism in the legal profession. In other words, the law faculty would have the huge task of working to instill professional awareness and commitment in the minds, hearts and attitudes of their students on one hand, and promoting high ethical standards, on the other. Given that law faculties traditionally provide professional education for lawyers, this proposition would certainly draw criticism about its validity in terms of resources and management. However, the case of declining professionalism among legal practitioners ((Burger 1995, Heineman Jr. et al 2015), and rising cases of corruption in African judicial institutions (Ghana Integrity Initiative 2007, Ayodeji and Odukoya 2014), have made the initiation of a new approach to legal education a recurring imperative. Thus, law faculties and other legal institutions would need to do more than just disseminate primary legal knowledge. The proposed role of these institutions would cover responsibilities beyond facilitating law students' acquisition of the core legal competences and include facilitating the acquisition of skills, attributes and capabilities that are complementary to the core curriculum of torts, contracts, civil procedure, criminal law, property, and constitutional law (Economides 2010, Heineman Jr. et al 2015). Arguably, this approach would facilitate a renewal and the inculcation of those traditional values that might have been alienated by the current inherited common law system (Joireman 2001).

5. Legal professionalism through curriculum innovation: the case of the University of The Gambia

The phenomenon of judicial corruption that has been well documented in the literature (Ghana Integrity Initiative 2007, Ayodeji and Odukoya 2014, Ellette 2013), in tandem with a re-awakening for Africa's collectivists tradition (Hofstede 2001) provided the motivation for the Law Faculty of the University of The Gambia to embrace the need for a re-negotiated legal education curriculum within the framework of African cultural realities. The objective at this stage is not to substitute current curriculum with an entirely new one, but to facilitate preliminary understanding on the impact of the inherited curriculum on the professionalism of African legal practitioners. Thus, as part of the pilot phase, a panel would be recruited to facilitate a longitudinal understanding of how a departure from the inherited legal curriculum may influence the professionalism of Gambian legal practitioners. In this effort, the Faculty of Law of the University of The Gambia has made the following adaptations to its inherited curriculum:

1. Legal ethics as a course or subject of study has been incorporated in and made mandatory (a core course) of the faculty's undergraduate law degree programme (the LLB degree requirements).

This course introduces ethical analysis, including the examination of various theories of ethics, the structure of the adversarial system and the role of lawyers, the concept of a profession and the wider responsibilities of lawyers in the community, and the ethical and professional duties of practitioners, legal academics and advisors. The aims set the student to canvass a range of contemporary ethical issues, explore personal perceptions of ethical behaviour, improve their ability to articulate and justify various ideas and arguments. As
272

already alluded to, this is a new approach which represents a major departure from the earlier tradition of legal education according to which legal ethics as a field of study was preserved for the Bar programme only. The new approach will no doubt set high expectations for future lawyers and better expose them to the ideals and principles of professionalism and ethics of the legal profession.

2. Clinical legal education and *pro bono* and community legal services

The first strategy relates to traditional lectures based in the classroom, while the second strategy takes the whole issue outside the physical boundaries of the classroom and out of the law faculty or school. Provision of *pro bono* or free legal services to needy individuals and communities is a special sacrifice by law professionals to render special professional services for the good of humanity. It is a very good forum or method of instilling professional awareness and commitment as well as promoting high ethical standards in the minds, hearts and attitudes of our young lawyers and legal trainees. In view of the fact that the whole exercise is free and absolutely free, the chances of corruption and corrupt practices and ethical lapses are very minimal and it gives the young lawyers a good opportunity to be sensitized to and to adopt the moral qualities of sacrifice, generosity, altruism and serving others to actualize the good and benefit of the community. This is why the faculty of law's clinical legal education *and pro bono* legal services programme is actively utilized as a vehicle to transmit the principles, norms and values of professionalism and high ethical standards to students.

3. Periodic Public Lectures on Ethics and Professionalism

The Faculty of Law of the University of The Gambia is currently running a series of extracurricular activities including periodic public lectures on various contemporary legal issues. The topic of the maiden lecture which was held in 2013 was "Legal Ethics and Professionalism including the African perspective of Ethics and Good Morality" by Hon. Fafa Edrisa Mbai, the former Attorney General and Minister of Justice of the Republic of The Gambia and a leading practitioner in the country. Issues involving ethical leadership and legal professionalism are featured regularly in those lectures and other extracurricular activities of the faculty.

4. Essay writing and Moot Court competitions focusing on professional ethics and responsible leadership are being incorporated into the Faculty of Law's extracurricular activities aimed at promoting good moral behaviour and ethical standard for future lawyers, legal experts, and professionals.

5. The Law Review Journal programme of the Faculty of Law of the University of The Gambia, which was first published 2013, is another mechanism for the faculty to promote the ideals, principles and norms of legal professionalism and ethical leadership. Issues involving legal ethics and professionalism are featured regularly in the journal.

6. Inclusion of short modules on legal ethics in the curriculum or course contents of all the major courses of the LLB degree programme.

In addition to making legal ethics a core course in the faculty's undergraduate degree programme, most of the issues, principles and rules forming part of the curriculum or course content of the legal ethics course are being broken down in the form of short modules and incorporated in the course contents of the main subjects of the LLB programme. Thus, part of the legal ethics course content relevant to criminal law, law of contract, law of evidence, constitutional law, law of tort and so on are incorporated in the course content of the respective courses and activities listed above. Notwithstanding this, legal ethics as a subject of study continues to be a core or mandatory course in the undergraduate programme of the Faculty of Law.

6. Conclusion

This chapter seeks to draw attention to the declining professionalism within the judicial sector in Africa. As highlighted by the number of cases on judicial corruption on the continent, this chapter sets out to stimulate debate on the causes and effects of professionalism and ethical identity on legal practitioners in Africa. Following observable evidence, the incidence of judicial corruption in Africa has become a phenomenon that is not only questioning the ethical identity of the culprits but imposes negative stereotypes on Africa's reputation in general and its judicial integrity in particular. Given the solemnness of the legal profession's responsibility to society, the legacy of judicial corruption is something that should not be tolerated. Hence, this chapter seeks to build intellectual synergy by calling for research efforts to be directed towards understanding the relationship between the inherited legal curriculum and the professionalism of legal practitioners in Africa. Within this context, this chapter conducts a critique of the theoretical foundation of professionalism and the wider context of the ethics phenomenon. Thus, ethics emerged albeit implicitly as a regional phenomenon that is either mediated by practitioners' religious beliefs or their natural right of reason or by a third implicit but potent force that is yet unknown. This understanding thus gives substance to the assumption that the inherited legal curriculum which is incentivized by the Western individualistic tradition may be creating tension within African legal practitioners whose ethical foundation is built around Africa's collectivist tradition. This is a grey research area in which this chapter aims to facilitate preliminary understanding.

This chapter concludes with strong conviction that the law faculties of African universities should lead the effort to revive legal professionalism on the continent. In addition to leading the research effort on the causes and effects of the trend of declining professionalism within the legal profession, this chapter draws on a series of curriculum innovations by the Law Faculty of the University of The Gambia to demonstrate how a renegotiation of the inherited curriculum can be initiated within the context of Africa's cultural realities. While this chapter calls on African law faculties to lead the curriculum re-negotiation effort, it however sees no need for a complete substitution of the inherited legal curriculum. Thus, this chapter aims to rely on using future research outcomes as the empirical basis for the infusion of locally relevant content to the currently dominant common law curriculum. As such, outlined curriculum innovations at the University of The Gambia's Faculty of Law are being used as the means to an end and not the other way round.

Following this example, the curriculum of African law faculties and law schools would need to be structured and administered in a way that will help students develop competences that are complementary to the core lawyering skills and also reflect the true realities of African societies. These competences as may be derived from a re-negotiated curriculum would enable future lawyers to be sensitive e to their responsibilities to government, the private sector, and their clients and to the whole of society in every respect of life particularly when they make decisions that call for the application of morally sound judgement. If the legal education process fails to engage students and the law profession in a way and manner that will help them develop sound ethical identities, then African universities and their law faculties will fail in their obligation to society as well as in the effort to reverse the declining legal professionalism in Africa.

276

8

Harnessing Traditional Governance Institutions to Improve Governance in West Africa: A Case Study of The Gambia

Introduction

Presented in this chapter are the results of the survey on harnessing traditional governance institutions in West Africa, using The Gambia as a case study. This survey was aimed at providing baseline information for traditional governance institutions in The Gambia on their roles, women rights and gender equality, their relationship with the modern institutions so as to revitalize them and make them effective actors of a democratic and developmental system of governance in The Gambia and the sub – region.

Country background

The Gambia is a small country located on the west coast of Africa, surrounded on three sides by Senegal, extending inland widths varying from 24 to 48 kilometres along the banks of River Gambia, with a total area of 10,690 square kilometres. The Gambia has a population of 2 million according to the 2013 Population and Housing Census which is increasing at a rate of 2.7 per cent per annum. It has a fairly limited human capital base with a literacy rate of 52 per cent (2013 Census).

The Gambia has an open economy with limited natural resources and is one of the least developed countries in Africa with a per capita income estimated at present at $300 USD (World Bank, 2006). It was ranked 155th out of 177 in the UNDP Human Development Index (HDI) for the year 2006. The traditional economic activity has been the production and export of groundnuts, although in recent years significant progress has been made in diversifying production and exports towards tourism, trade and services. More than 70 per cent of the population is engaged in agriculture, which accounts for about 30 percent of real GDP; communication 13.6 percent and the trade industry contribute 13.3 percent of value added, with the rest accounted for by services. Regarding recent economic development, official estimates indicated that the Gambian economy would continue to grow at 6.5 percent in 2008 onwards. Inflation has remained at single digit levels over the period and the dalasi has appreciated against major international currencies.

The Gambia is divided into 39 districts and 7 administrative regions namely, Banjul, Kanifing, West Coast Region, Central River Region, Lower River Region, North Bank Region and Upper River Region. All regions are headed by governors, who are appointed by the head of state, whilst Banjul and Kanifing municipalities are headed by mayors who are elected through elections. During pre-colonial times, traditional institutions were involved in governance and chiefs played a crucial and leading role in most communities in The Gambia. The advent of colonial rule introduced Western forms of governance that, today, with their accompanying political and administrative structures, dominate at the national and regional levels. However, at the district and community levels they share the responsibility of governance with traditional authority, mainly that of the chiefs. Within rural communities, for example, inadequate infrastructure and poverty hamper access to modern or state agencies of security, justice and health. In such a situation, the chief assumes a very critical role of serving the people, being therefore, a vital and strategic partner for development. Under colonial and post-colonial governments, traditional institutions of governance suffered erosion of their authority. Now that traditional governments, chiefs and the people were rising to the challenges of modernization, democratization and the role of the chiefs as an agent of development being subjected to close scrutiny by researchers and governance experts from time to time, a new initiative was needed to facilitate and accelerate growth of a system of governance sensitive to the culture and history of The Gambia. This may provide the answer to the question of how traditional governance can contribute more effectively to efforts to bring more stability, by encouraging alternative dispute resolution, peacebuilding, poverty alleviation, income generation and many more.

But while Western institutions of governance have been able to adjust to some of the challenges brought by modernization, traditional forms of governance have been slow to respond to change. Hence this work is concerned with transfusing the positive elements of the two forms / systems to improve governance in West Africa.

Methodology

Some traditional governance structures existing in The Gambia pre-date modern governance structures. The advent of colonialism and Western education has eroded some of these structures and the young generation tends not to be quite knowledgeable about these structures. To have a better insight into these traditional structures therefore, this survey targeted both serving and retired chiefs and elderly people in certain parts of the country. It was felt that the historical perspective of traditional governance institutions was essential for a better understanding of how these structures functioned in the past and their relevance now. The survey team adopted an in-dept interview approach in order to capture the views of respondents on this issue. Respondents chosen for the in-depth interviews were purposively selected considering their knowledge of traditional governance issues and their social status within their communities. Those interviewed were serving district chiefs, ex-chiefs, prominent community leaders or persons living in villages that have been the seat of chieftaincies in the past, career politicians, historians and professional writers on Gambian affairs. After the results were compiled, a focus group discussion was organized to share the findings of the fieldwork with a view to deepening the study and completing the information. Respondents chosen for the focus group discussions were purposively selected as well because of their knowledge of traditional governance in The Gambia.

Using an interview guide with questions related to key issues on existing traditional governance structures, their roles and weaknesses of the institutions, their relations with modern governance institutions and possible strategies and mechanisms to be incorporated in order to harness the roles of these institutions in accelerating socio - economic, cultural and political development in The Gambia and elsewhere in West Africa. This aspect of the study is supplemented with evidence gathered from a literature review which looks at traditional governance institutions from the historical perspective to their relevance in a modern setting.

Limitations of study

In The Gambia only limited studies have been conducted on governance, particularly in the area of traditional governance. The problem posed by such limited research has been compounded by limited availability of literature on traditional governance institutions. In the absence of adequate literacy on the subject one is left with no option but to rely on people knowledgeable in traditional governance to have an insight into this area. Reliance on this source of information can in some instances be problematic since information provided could be subjective sometimes and information from varying sources could be conflicting. Opinion on traditional governance institutions can in some instances be influenced by political affiliation of respondents. This is particularly the case where a family has lost their status as the ruling clan in the pre-colonial era as a result of measures instituted by a post – colonial or post-independence government. Some of these experiences may influence opinion on traditional governance issues.

Introduction

Sub – Saharan Africa is a region best described as the cradle of humanity with a unique and diverse social set up that emerged during the course of human development. The region has assured itself a place in the global historical set-up despite frivolous misgivings about its potentialities by Western critics. By the 7th century Africa and West Africa in particular were engaged in a systematic representative democracy with functional government which modern forms of democracy built on. By the period in question, West Africa had already opened up to settled agriculture and had specialized smiths, cravers, weavers and traders. To show case the traditional democratic system Mansa Musa of Mali established the ministries of fishing – *Hari fama*, forests – *Sao Farma*, Agriculture – *Babili Farma* and finance – *Khalisso Farma*. However, the nature of political theorem in West Africa had encountered changes at various stages of its history as several contacts with outsiders arose. These contacts with the Arabs and Europeans had significantly made landmark changes to the indigenous governance system. Colonialism that followed made a complete overhaul of the indigenous Africa traditions with the European economic and political interest as the overriding principle. Colonialism paved the way for an over diluted traditional rule system. Kinship with all its entrenchments gave way to chieftaincy a subsidiary title, authority and power. Colonialism therefore morally and psychologically bankrupted the indigenous governance system and put forward a system that has downgraded the traditional governance system for good.

In The Gambia, chieftaincy was forced upon the colonizers in the later part of the 19th century. Gambian kings known as 'Mansa' and 'Bur' were undone by the colonialist and the chiefs were appointed in consonance with the indirect rule system. In 1894 the administrator of Bathurst Governor Llewellyn stated that traditional but unsatisfactorily native customs in The Gambia were to be reformed. Subsequently the protectorate system ordinances of 1894 were promulgated that divided the protectorate into districts. It was stated by the ordinances promulgated by successive colonial administrations that "the administrator may, if he thinks fit from time to time subdivide any district into convenient groups of villages and may appoint headmen who are subordinates to the head chiefs to have supervision of any such group. The administrator may dismiss any headman and appoint a successor and may at any time re – arrange the grouping of the villages." This piece of legislation introduced the chieftaincy system in The Gambia.

Conceptual framework and basic premises

Definition of governance and government

Government means the machinery and institutional arrangement for the exercise of sovereign powers for serving the internal and external interests of the communities of the state. In other words, because it is the outcome of a social contract, the government serves the interests of the masses at the domestic level and at the level of international relations as well. On the other hand, governance is the process, as well as the results of making authoritative decisions for the benefit of society. It means the act or process of governing, and specifically refers to authoritative direction and control. "Governance is a broader notion than government, state and regime and it is the interaction between formal institutions and those in civil society" (Mander and Asif 2004: 11). In other words, the process of governing is specifically an act of making authoritative decisions and control. Traditionally, government and governance should refer to both mechanisms and processes of managing the affairs of the people in the past. Whether used in the modern or traditional sense governance is a process in which certain elements in society wield power, authority and influence and make policies and decisions concerning public life and social change. For the World Bank, governance "is the manner in which power is exercised in the management of a country's economic and social resources for development". Thus, governance includes public sector management, accountability, the legal framework, transparency and information handling (Mander and Asif 2004: 12). For the UNDP, governance is beyond the act of mere exercise of power by the state. Rather, it refers to the act of exercising power or authority, whether political, economic, administrative or otherwise to manage a country's resources and affairs. Consequently "governance comprises the mechanisms, processes and institutions through which citizens and groups articulate their interests, exercise their legal rights, meet their obligations and mediate their differences"

(UNDP 2000: 9). The governance process should be a dynamic one because it should be guided by sound and potentially creative policies manned and implemented by leaders who should have the ability to rise above the existing ordinary structures to change the rules of the game and to inspire others to positively contribute in national efforts to move society forward in new and productive directions (Hydon 2000). What all this means is that exercise of power is the central element in the governance process. Power is defined as "the general capacity of a state to control the behaviour of others" (Holsti 1967: 141). The capacity to control behaviour is the fundamental nature of the process of exercise of power and authority. There are three main aspects of power i.e. influence, resources mobilization, and management and relationships. This fundamental nature of the exercise of power is an intrinsic element in the business of governance both in the past and now.

Traditional governance institutions

Traditionally, rulers were the custodians of African culture and heritage. They were the symbols of people's voice and authority. Their prime task was to see that people's rulers and their subjects live together peacefully, smoothly and harmoniously as one family. Traditional chiefs used to preside over dispute settlement cases involving landownership and distribution, marriage, inheritance, divorce, religious ceremonies, administration of justice in accordance with the principles of customary law. Traditional authorities and institutions were instituted, rulers installed, recognized and obeyed and the entire governance process run in accordance with norms and principles of customary law. However, with the advent of Islamic rule in The Gambia around the 8th century AD, Traditional Governance Systems of the people became heavily influenced by the teachings of Islam in almost every aspect of socio-economic, cultural and political life. Today many of the practices referred to as traditional governance practices in The Gambia are essentially Islamic practices.

Throughout the period of traditional rule including the Islamic period, the rulers and the officials drew their legitimacy from the belief of the people who expected them to exist and function not only in theory but in practice as well. Thus, the legitimacy of traditional rulers did not come from an act of appointment by a sovereign political authority; rather it came from the belief and the will of the people.

In the Senegambia region, the situation was the same, traditional rulers were the custodian of people's culture, heritage and authority. The subjects sincerely subjected themselves to the authority of their rulers and whole-heartedly rallied behind them. This high level of support and loyalty to traditional rulers attracted the attention of the 18th century English trader, Francis Moore, when he observed: "If a person wants anything to be done by a good number of people, the best thing is to apply to the 'al cade' (the village head) to make dispatch with it; but if a factor (trader) does not take care to keep in with the al-cade, he will seldom or never gets things done as they ought to be" (quoted in Mahoney 1982: 19). Thus, unlike rulers of the modern sovereign state, traditional rulers enjoyed true legitimacy and honest support of their people.

Governance institutions, systems and practices

There are several actors in governance but the main ones are three i.e. the state, civil society and the market or private sector. Whether at the state level or elsewhere, governance in general varies widely ranging from political, economic and administrative to systemic governance. The latter encompasses the processes and structures of society that guide political and socio-economic relationships and create and maintain an environment of health, freedom, and security and provides the opportunity to exercise personal capabilities that lead to a better life for all people (Mander and Asif 2004: 42 - 43). This type constitutes the conventional governance system, which is the formal institutional and organizational structure of decision-making. Since governance embraces all methods that societies use to distribute power, manage all the affairs of the people in general and manage resources and problems in particular, it may be characterized as "good" or "bad". For the UNDP, governance cannot be sound or good unless it sustains human development. Likewise human development cannot be sustained without good governance. Hence there is need to develop capacities for good governance as an important strategy to eradicate poverty. The modern international human rights systems emphasize the need to respect, promote and actualize basic human rights and fundamental freedoms of the individual. This view therefore calls for a rights-based approach to governance and the governing process. However, whether we take UNDP's or any other approach to good governance, the following factors must be considered if societies are serious about achieving good governance:

- Public resources and problems must be managed effectively and in response to the critical needs of society. In other words, governance processes should be responsive to the critical needs of the people.

- The grassroots people and the masses must be involved in the process in order to ensure responsiveness. This is called "The bottom-up approach" to governance.

- That the outcome of this responsive and participatory approach should be sustainable economic growth, which reaches the people at all levels of society.

Forms / systems of government

In the modern time society is used in several forms or systems of government structures and institutions that include the following:

286

- Democracy, which emphasizes principles and values, like the rule of law, respect for human rights and fundamental freedoms, independent of the judiciary and the legal profession, separation of powers and popular participation. Democratic forms of governance rely on popular participation, accountability and transparency.

- Socialism, which emphasizes the central role of the state in managing and distributing resources. It believes in state ownership, control and complete monopoly of major industries.

- Monarchies: A monarchical system may be constitutional or an absolute one. Constitutional monarchies are usually restricted by written constitutions or conventional legal rules or both. Malaysia is a good example of a constitutional monarchy, while Britain is an example of the latter case. Saudi Arabia and its sister actors in the Arabian Gulf provide examples of absolute monarchies.

- Consultative system: The advent of Islam about 14 and a half centuries ago brought to human political traditions a unique system known as the system of 'Khilapha' or vicegerency or a system of succession based on consultation and administrative centralism. It emphasizes the need to govern in accordance with the teachings of the Divine Revelation as enunciated by 'Shariah', or Islamic law which according to Islam was itself revealed to serve and protect the best interest of mankind and the whole world. (al-shatibi, 1997, 391-328).

- Post-Colonial Africa has since the early days of nationhood been experiencing another form of government known as "military rule and despotism". This happens when the military seizes power in what may either be a bloody or bloodless coup-de-tat. The lifespan of the first republics of Ghana, Congo, Nigeria, Mali, The Gambia and many others was ended by the military in those countries.

Similarly, the English, American and French political traditions have introduced two other systems of government known as parliamentary democracy, which operates in Britain, India and elsewhere in the Commonwealth as well as presidential executive operating in America and France. Under the parliamentary system sometimes referred to, as "The Westminster Style" the head of government who is usually called "Prime Minister" is different from the head of state that may be called "President" or "Monarch". This sounds like a government based on dual authority. However, with the advent of constitutional rule in contemporary times, the competences and responsibilities of the two heads are well defined. Usually, the head of government assumes the substantive powers of the state while the head of state is relegated largely to the position of a nominal head. In Britain, the so-called constitutional conventions are used to demarcate the borderline between the two authorities.

Many Francophone countries in Africa including Senegal, the Cote d'Ivoire and Guinea Conakry somehow combine the two systems in which case the Prime Minister is subject to the authority and control of the President who is the substantive head of both the state and the government of the day.

During the First Republic of The Gambia, the Jawara administration to a certain extent combined the two in the sense that Cabinet Ministers were drawn from Parliament. In other words, the executive to a certain degree was relying on Parliament, which was always controlled by the ruling party. However, Sir Dawda Jawara did not create the position of a Prime Minister, rather he appointed a vice president who served under his direct supervision and control. The

Second Republic has drastically moved away from that tradition. Under the Jammeh administration even though there is a vice president who is appointed and controlled by the President, the executive is structurally independent of the legislature. In the 1997 Constitution, Members of Parliament cannot concurrently serve in Cabinet.

As for traditional governance rules in Africa, it did not have to go through such a delicate complexity of structures and mechanisms particularly in the Senegambia region. The main chieftaincies of the Senegambia region included the 'Wolof' and 'Mandinka' states. The 'Wolofs' are found in the region and once lived to the North of Senegal river but the invasions of Berbers and Fulas of Tekrur (Futa-Toro) drove them Southwards to the region between the Senegal and Gambia rivers, which they now occupy (Mahoney 1982: 16). As for the Mandinkas, they migrated from the Mali Empire to the region. This phenomenon started in the 13th century when the Mali Empire was established. The Mandinka warriors led by 'Mansa' Sundiata Keita (founder of the Mali Empire) gradually occupied and controlled the whole of Gambia valley (except Saloum, which remained under the Wolofs and Foni, which was the home of the Jolas) (Mahoney 1982: 19). The Mandinka rule thus extended over all the territories seized by 'Manding' Warriors including the states along the Gambia Valley such as Baddibou and Barra near the estuary and Kantora in the Upper River Region and Kombo. Unlike the Wolof States, the Mandinka dynasties were subjected to the Mali Empire. Their rulers swore allegiance to the Mansa or emperor of Mali and were obliged to send tribute to him (Mahoney: ibid).

Traditional systems of government

A common characteristic of the Wollof and Mandinka States was centralized government either under a powerful ruler and impressive nobles as the case was with the Wolofs or under chiefs called

'Mansas' and village heads in Mandinka states (Mahoney 1982: pp.16-19). In the Wolof dynasty, the ruler was elected or chosen by a few lords (about three or four) from among the nobles due to his personal qualities. This is because the main task of the Wolof ruler (Bur) was to lead his people in wars and defend his people particularly, the nobles. A Wolof ruler would reign for as long as he pleased the nobles who often dethroned their Kings by force. As for the Mandinka dynasty, great importance was placed on local government under village heads originally called "Foroes". With the advent of Islamic rule, the title for village head was replaced by the Arabic title "al-cadi", which means a judge. These men who belonged to the nobility had played a significant role in the Mandinka state. Indeed, it is often said that the success and prosperity of any Mandinka dynasty depend on the wisdom and competence of its al-cadies. "It was their responsibility to distribute land, administer justice in minor cases, collect the Mansa's taxes and generally oversee the efficient running of their district" (Mahoney: ibid). Thus, what existed under the Mandinka dynasty was slightly similar to the modern concept of 'devolution of power' from the central to local government authorities. Unlike the Wolof 'Bur' every Mandinka ruler was obliged to consult his village heads or al-cadi and elders of the people before laws were legislated or any action was taken on important matters. "Indeed, without the support of the elders, the Mansa was powerless for though he was acknowledged as the head of state and was treated with great respect by his subjects, he had no dictatorial powers according to the customs of the people" (Mahoney: ibid). Hence the system and structure of government in the Mandinka state looked nearer to those of contemporary times. Modern concepts like decentralization, devolution of power and delegation of authority can be slightly felt or seen in the style of governing under the Mandinka state. The Islamic political tradition of governing through consultation is evident in the government of the Mandinka state. Unlike the Wolof state, Mandinka society was patrilineal so that succession to the throne was through the male line and rotational. This meant two things i.e. women were out of it and that different towns of the dynasty took it in turn to provide the candidate for the throne. This rotational system meant that every al-cadi could become a Mansa or a ruler (Mahoney 1982: 20).

For the Wolof dynasty, society was matrilineal, which meant that succession to the throne followed the female line. Thus, the son of one of his sisters always succeeded a Wolof ruler. In fact, there were dynasties where the 'Bur' had to be of noble origin through his mother and the father's status was never considered. It is reported that Jolof was the only Wolof state that was patrilineal in which succession followed the male line (Mahoney 1982: 17). In the Wolof state, women of leading families used to play an important role through the governance process. The mother and sometimes the sister or cousin of the King assumed a special title known as the "Linguerre" meaning Queen or Princess. The Linguerre was the head of all women of a Wolof dynasty and she presided over the law courts, which dealt with women's affairs. In some instances, the Linguerre had villages placed under her which paid her tribute and cultivated her farms. In the coastal states she enjoyed an additional income from the salt and fish trade. Furthermore, in the state of Walo, the Linguerre could even succeed to the throne and assume the title of 'Bur' (Mahoney: ibid). What all this means is that certain women in Wolof dynasties of the past used to play an important political role unlike the situation in Mandinka states. This is another aspect of similarity between traditional and modern governance practices.

Finally, traditional governance systems of the Senegambia region were influenced by Islamic political traditions. The advent of Islamic rule lent them political institutions and practices such as al-cadi system, administrative centralism, the institution of Shura or consultative councils and the application of Islamic legal and moral rules and principles in solving disputes, family matters and in all other areas touching on the business of governance and administration (Senghore, 2007).

Transfusion of traditional systems into the government of the modern sovereign state

Despite the fact that African traditional governance institutions continue to exist in various parts of the continent, they have to a very high degree been incorporated into the government of the contemporary sovereign states. In countries like Botswana, Namibia and The Gambia traditional chiefs are appointed and controlled and their functions determined or limited by the sovereign state government. Although the idea of incorporation or linking traditional governance institutions with those of the sovereign state is what this study tends to encourage and advocate, such linkage or incorporation should not take the form of a knockout game situation whereby one party's gain means another's loss. Rather, the two dimensions of political authority should be regularly bolstered by way of transfusion of institutions and practices from one dimension to the other on the basis of dual authority. This may be done in several ways including the following:

Mode of transfusion

A)   Incorporation

This is a method of creating mixed government based on dual authority, which operates in a way that does not compromise the heightened prestige and normal benefits enjoyed by traditional rulers as expected of them by their devoted subjects. This method of incorporation of traditional and modern dimensions of government into a united system based on dual authority may take various forms such as the following:

ii.   Constitutional recognition of traditional governance
         institutions and reservation of places for traditional rulers
         or their representatives in the main arms of government
         and other administrative agencies of the state. i.e. the
         legislature, the Executive, the Judiciary, the Civil Service
         and Provincial and Local Administrative Bodies.

iii.   The use of traditional assessors by statutory courts to assist
         in the adjudication of cases involving customary or
         religious law. This task may be assigned to the newly
         revived alternative dispute resolution mechanisms
         provided that they are run by traditional mediators and in
         accordance with traditional norms and customary rules
         and values.

iv.   Inclusion of chiefs or traditional rulers within political
         parties and government institutions.

v.   Recognition and inclusion of traditional norms and values
         and system of education and discipline into the sovereign
         state dimension of education.

Finally, it is important to note that the sovereign state badly needs to
obtain political legitimacy from traditional rulers and political
institutions and needless to say this method of incorporation
guarantees it to obtain that legitimacy and unlimited support of the
masses.

B) The system of justice (i.e. courts and the law)

If statutory and customary courts are properly linked they would easily function to maintain the integrity, vitality and stability of political life in both dimensions of government. In the first place, maintenance and preservation of the independence of the unified judiciary will be a priority for such a system where the judiciary is used as a vehicle to link and regulate the relations of the two dimensions of government. The logic behind this is that traditional rulers will be strongly inclined in favour of a situation where there is constitutional rule and prevalence of the rule of law so that they can be saved from executive manipulation and control. This form of inter-dimensional linkage also ensures the prevalence of the rule of law and also the protection of the rights of the people by independent law courts for the same reasons explained above.

One of the major crises of governance in Africa for the past decades is the absence of the rule of law and the occurrence of interferences with the judicial processes. The instance of a political authority higher than the law itself is very common in all parts of the continent. Thus, judicial independence under the unified system of mixed government will be strengthened by the need for judges to harmonize the current systems of statutory, religious and customary law. Such harmonization of laws is absolutely necessary because the traditional order needs to be confident that the system is a non- hostile linkage mechanism which equally ensures the protection of their interest as citizens who identify themselves with the traditional political order and they will therefore better appreciate the values and the practical importance of mixed government. Another aspect of the judicial linkage between the two dimensions of political authority is that it provides a better opportunity of reconciliation or resolution of historic disputes or claims and counter claims between nations, communities and groups across the continent.

C) Inclusion of religious, traditional and other authorities in the business of governing and managing the affairs of the modern state

This method will ensure the restoration of discipline and high moral standards in the governance process. Thus, the system of mixed government based on dual authority could be a special way of decentralizing power and authority in The Gambia and with the best elements of the two systems combined governance will definitely be enhanced. Finally, what African leaders and Africans in general need to do in order to resolve the chronic governance crisis of that continent is to change attitudes at all levels of society. There is no other way of doing away with the major crisis of governance if people have not changed their behaviour or attitude in every domain of life particularly in the governance sphere. For Africa to do away with corruption, nepotism, indiscipline, conflicts, poverty, malnutrition and military rule, the attitudes of its people must completely change.

Section 2

Typology and roles of traditional governance in The Gambia

Sub–Saharan Africa is a region best described as the cradle of humanity with a unique and diverse social set up that emerged during the course of human development. The region has assured itself a place in the global historical set up despite frivolous misgivings about its potentialities by western critics.

By the seventh century Africa and West Africa in particular were engaged in a system of representative democracy with functional government which was improved by the modern sovereign state government. During the period in question, West Africa had already opened up for settled agriculture and had specialized smiths, cravers, weavers and traders. For example, the traditional governance system of Mansa Musa in Mali established the ministries of fishing – Hari fama, forests – Sao Farma, Agriculture – Babili Farma and finance – Khalisso Farma. This is quite similar to the structuring system of the modern sovereign state government.

However, the nature of political theorem in West Africa has encountered changes at various stages of its history. The frequent contacts between the Africans, Arabs and Europeans around the 15th, 16th and 17th centuries had significantly changed the indigenous governance system. The colonialism that followed brought with it a complete overhaul of the indigenous Africa governance traditions with the promotion of European economic and political interests as the overriding principle. Colonialism paved the way for the continent's diluted traditional rule system. Kingship with all its entrenchments gave way to Chieftaincy with its subsidiary titles, authority and power. Colonialism therefore morally and psychologically bankrupted the indigenous governance system and put forward a system which downgraded the traditional governance system for good.

In The Gambia, Chieftaincy was forced upon the colonizers in the later part of the 19th century. Gambian kings known as 'Mansa' and 'Bur' were undone by the colonial powers and Chiefs were appointed in consonance with the indirect rule system. In 1894 Bathurst Governor Llewellyn decided that traditional native customs in The Gambia were to be reformed. Subsequently the protectorate system ordinances of 1894 were promulgated which divided the protectorate into districts.

It was stated in the ordinances that: 'The administrator or the Governor may, if he thinks fit from time to time subdivide any district into convenient groups of villages and may appoint headmen who are
296

subordinates to the head Chiefs to have supervisions of any such group. The administrator may dismiss any headman and appoint a successor and may at any time re – arrange the grouping of the villages. This piece of legislation explicitly introduced the Chieftaincy system in The Gambia.

Typology of traditional governance institutions in The Gambia

Traditional governance system in pre–colonial Gambia presented a centralized and orderly kingship system that maintained traditional values, laws and social order. This system embedded the traditional and social values of the community. By 1902, after the whole of The Gambia was brought under the protectorate system, a hierarchical system in which orders and responses were obeyed and given from governor to commissioner, to chiefs, to village heads and then to the people. The indirect rule system was thus forced upon the people. The British appointed head chiefs were assisted by native authority consisting of elders of the villages as tribunal members. Badge messengers were also appointed as local police to assist in maintaining law and order. It should be noted that this spirit of colonial decentralized traditional rule has been preserved and maintained in both the first and Second Republics of The Gambia. As part of the instant study, data was collected on typology and the roles of traditional governance in The Gambia to supplement the literature review done on this theme. Below are the findings from the survey.

The respondents were asked what type of traditional governance institutions existed in their communities. Divergent views were expressed regarding the types of institutions that existed in the various communities as indicated by the following utterances during the in-depth interviews.

Traditional Governance Institutions as we know them today exist in levels, viz, (i) Kabilos (the coming together of different compounds) (ii) Community Youth Organization (iii) Council of Elders (iv) District Authority (constitutes the chief and alkalos in the district). Highly centralized institutions existed before the colonial era. After colonization a diluted form of chieftaincy was introduced and this type of rule continues until this day. In pre – colonial times, traditional institutions were involved in governance and chiefs played a crucial and leading role in most communities in The Gambia. The advent of colonial rule introduced Western forms of governance that, today, with their accompanying political and administrative structures, dominate at the national and regional levels. As a result, the system was highly centralized but now it is decentralized.

The respondents were also asked if there are any governance institutions that existed in the past that do not exist now. The findings of the survey showed that governance institutions existed in the past that no longer exist. This is made clear in the following statements:

I. *The Association of Youths is most dormant among the ones listed above. This is being revitalized through on-going governance programmes establishing Village Development Committees*

The traditional rulers were in charge of government and all its functionaries in the past but have limited authority over the people.

The institutions of the Mansa's (Kings) no longer exist. They were power chiefs who can go to any settlement abduct women and children and burn the village.

On the issue of why they think these institutions ceased to exist, the responses differ, just as for example:

They primarily ceased to exist due to a change process at the community level. This change process was fuelled by the migration of
298

young people to urban settlements away from their communities to pursue secondary education. This youth migrants who acquired Western education became admirers of Western lifestyles and the Western fashioned elites leading to their shunning of the traditional norms and beliefs which were the very essence and foundation of rural traditional communities.

These traditional rulers ceased to exist after the arrival of the colonial masters. They dismantled the ruling dynasty and established their own system of governance that served their interest.

They ceased to exist because of the importation of foreign culture and values. Secondly, our countries depend on aid and donors always attached strings to the aid given to us.

The colonial masters removed these institutions because the system was in the interest of the people.

Regarding the opinion that there has been any change in the functions of these traditional governance institutions, the findings of the survey indicate there have been changes in their functions. Below are some of the views of the respondents on this issue:

Chiefs have no sole authority over their subject today, the government directly governs or through the local government authorities.

Yes and the following account for the changes:

I. *The legal dimension. Customary law is different from English law. Community leaders were at the forefront of making community laws which adequately served communal interests. Community leaders were the legislators, executives, and the judiciary. Evidently, some noticeable differences could be seen in the way functions and responsibilities were discharged then compared to what obtains in modern democratic societies. For example, in the past, the failure of any community member to behave in accordance with the community norms was handled by calling up a meeting of the Council of Elders where the offender was summoned to attend so that there would be a collective correction of the offence. The drawback in this system, however, is the fact that all the family members of the offender were involved in the litigation involving any one member of the family. Such a system of adjudication was viewed as unfairly broadening the apportionment of blame in any communal resolution of conflict. A person should take full responsibility for his acts in accordance with the principles of natural justice as we know it today.*

Chiefs in the early days were respected as whatever decision they took was respected. But today because of slogans on empowerment, human rights, gender equality among others being promoted by NGOs and Civil Society Organizations this has eroded the powers of the chiefs. Now decisions can be taken without consulting chiefs but in the early days one dared not.

During the data collection for this survey, an attempt was made to solicit views of the respondents on how heads of traditional governance institutions ascend to power. The evidence has shown that ascending to power is no longer through inheritance. Find below some of the opinions transcribed from the discussions.

    (i)   The electoral process (ii) inheritance (iii) as prescribed by the community, or (iv) selection and appointment.

Heads of traditional governance institutions ascended to power through inheritance in the past but now the appointment is done by the president.

In the early days, heads of traditional governance institutions ascended to power through inheritance. Which I think was not fair as one family would rule. This has been the norm until the last two decades when chiefs were elected. Now, the system has changed again and now it is the head of state in consultation with the Secretary of

300

State for Local Government, Lands and Religious Affairs, Governor and the council of elders in that region who appoint chiefs.

The respondents were also asked if the process of succession has changed and about the advantages and disadvantages of the processes. Perceptions of the changes in the succession process from the respondents showed that most people were against the system of inheritance but also had reservations about the election of chiefs as they might be controlled. Varied perceptions are contained in the following statements:

In the past there were ruling dynasties. In Nuimi, for instance, only three surnames were entitled to the throne, namely Jammeh, Manneh, and Sonko. Colonialism, which was a system of coercion and dominance and subjugation of a people used these existing power structures to consolidate power. This system marginalized those families that were not in power at the time as succession to the throne was concentrated on only a few families that were known to the Europeans.

In the First Republic, there was no radical change in the political process surrounding the issue of succession. The only thing that was new then was the extension of a limited franchise to allow only compound heads to participate in the election of traditional rulers. Therefore, compound heads were solely responsible for electing a chief. The implication is that authority may shift from its original custodians depending on the choices of compound heads. The system had the drawback of a limited communal participation in the election of traditional authorities and the government could come in to reduce the number of contesting candidates which resulted in the elimination of the most deserving candidates. Youth and elderly people without compounds were not allowed to vote. The system had the advantage of freeing government from the blame having to do with electing the wrong person.

The Second Republic reformed the process of succession by introducing the selection and appointment of traditional authorities. The selection of the village authority starts from doing the nomination from the founders of the village. However, the nominee must be acceptable to the villagers. This is followed by the recommendation of the chief via the governor to the secretary of state for local government, land and religious affairs. For the appointment of chiefs, the responsibility lies in the President of the Republic. The system has the advantage of minimizing conflicts and tensions at the community level as community citizens do not determine the final accession to power of a district authority. Appointed chiefs cannot blame any set of people for not supporting them during their election campaign. We, therefore, expect the impartiality of chiefs to be very high.

The disadvantage with this system of selection and appointment could be that authority may shift from its traditional custodians.

The process of succession changed as now the chiefs are appointed by the president. Since they are appointed by the president, they might not be independent in the decisions they take.

The process of succession has changed. The system used to be by inheritance but now it is based on appointment. An appointed chief might not be independent in taking decisions. The system should have been based on free and fair elections and the chiefs should be easily removed from power by the executive.

Definitely, the process has changed. Before it was based on inheritance and now it is based on elections. The advantage is one family cannot continue to rule forever and anyone who is interested in the position can compete for it. The disadvantage is that it could divide the communities and could affect the peace and harmony that existed within the community.

Roles of traditional institutions

As shown in Section 1 above, chiefs were the custodians of African culture and heritage and the voice of the people. It was their responsibility to see that people lived together smoothly and peacefully as a unit. They presided over matters affecting land ownership and distribution, marriage, inheritance and had authority over traditional laws and customs.

Role of women in traditional governance system

Generally speaking, and with the exception of a few Wolof dynasties, women had been marginalized economically, politically and socially as a result of age-old discrimination and biases. Economic exploitation was their lot alongside widespread poverty and landlessness. In pre–colonial Senegambia, a woman could rise to the rank of 'Mansa' as had happened in Nuimi, Kombo and Sine. In Wolof states, the Queen mother or the King's sister had a special titled called Linquerre and was responsible for matters affecting women economically and legally. In the social structure, women were responsible for cooking, clearing, sweeping, fetching water, caring for children and many other domestic chores. These unique contributions to the socio–economic development of the traditional social set up continued to exist in the post-independence era. Women are involved in agriculture and other income generating activities such as market gardening, savings clubs, fish marketing and petty trading. Very few women have survived modern economic competitiveness and become successful entrepreneurs. Poverty tends to characterize their life both in rural and urban centres. The traditional governance of the past played an important role in key sectors of development including the following:

Health in traditional governance

In traditional Gambian society, health and orderliness were the basic elements of a woman's survival. Access to cheap medicinal herbs was guaranteed for all. Traditional healers maintained a basic standard of living for a healthy population. Today the rapid economic and social changes have made health delivery very expensive as it depends entirely on modern medication. However, under the sovereign state of The Gambia, the primary health care system with the introduction of traditional birth attendance (TBA) and trained village health workers has improved access to health services and basic health facilities. Furthermore, the government of the Second Republic has significantly improved health facilities and service delivery programs in The Gambia.

Education and traditional knowledge

In traditional Gambian Society, education was centred on traditional knowledge. This indigenous knowledge has been orally passed down for generations. Thise knowledge consists of stories, rituals, mystic healings, circumstances and birth attendance, hunting, legends, folklore, songs and customary laws. The custodians of this knowledge were mandated to preserve and educate successors who would be able to hand them over to the next generation. However, traditional knowledge today has extensively declined as Western education spreads rapidly and widely all over the country. There is no doubt that traditional knowledge needs to be revisited, revived and conserved as a manifestation of national heritage. Beside traditional knowledge, the practice of Islam was accompanied by a comprehensive and rich body of knowledge disseminated through a unique system of learning.

Conflict resolution in traditional governance system

Traditional rulers had a responsibility to the people in maintaining law and order, administering justice and resolving disputes justly and impartially. They had authority over traditional laws and customs and arbitrated with the advice of carefully chosen councils of elders. These elders handled criminal cases within the community before they reached the climax. The social structures established historical associations between families, ethnic groups, villages and between regions throughout history. Such associations permeated all spheres of life and reinforced dialogue, peaceful coexistence and love for one another. It is the author's view that such associations known locally as 'Dankuto' and 'Sanawuya' should be reinforced and nurtured by all in modern times, as they go a long way towards fostering trust and understanding among communities. Chiefs also performed the function of Ombudsman at the grassroots and served as guardians of the community based on freedom, peace and justice. Disputes were resolved through open discussions with the complainants leading to consensus and collective decisions acceptable to all parties.

Relationships between traditional and modern government institutions

There exists a conducive political environment between traditional and modern state institutions. In post- independence Gambia, local government assumed greater responsibility in relation to the administration of local authorities. At village level, the Alkalo is chosen by the people, endorsed by the chief and confirmed by the governor. In representative democracy the political order started at the lowest unit with Village Development Committee. Above this, is the Ward Development Committee supervised by the Ward

Councillor at the district level. The Ward Councillor represented the ward at the Area Council at regional level.

The collection of taxes, levies and dues which were formally under the prerogative of the chiefs in the colonial era are now handled by the local authorities. Traditional authorities fulfilled their role as custodians of traditional customs and cultural heritage. The constitution guarantees the institution of chieftaincy as the symbols of traditional laws and customs with overriding responsibility for matters affecting land ownership and distribution, issues involving family feuds such as marriage, divorce, inheritance, communal disputes and a broad pattern of magisterial authority including presiding over District Tribunals or courts in all cases except murder. Their role as intermediaries between the central government and local people created by the colonialists continues to be relevant in the local government system of contemporary Gambia.

Traditional governance and modern political parties

The role of Seyfolu and Alkalou as mediators and arbitrators in dispute resolution and crime management, and as the symbolic voice of the people, requires them to maintain a particular political lifestyle. As government officials they must preside over all sorts of state functions at district and village level. Their role as adjudicators teaches them to respect diverse political opinions in a democratic system of people belonging to different political dispensations. They are therefore not expected to participate in politics or accept political positions. They should also have no political ambition or political clout. The principle of moral or ethical order militates against their participation in political activities.

Also, as part of the current study, data was collected on the relationship between traditional governance and political parties to supplement the literature review. Below are the findings from the survey:

The institutions of chiefs and village heads which existed prior to the colonial era were retained by the colonial government. The colonial government used these existing structures as a tool to ease the administration of the colonies. Through what was known as indirect rule the colonial government administered the regions through the chiefs and village heads. These traditional rulers in addition to representing the colonial government in the regions and villages also collected revenue from their subjects. They also played a key role in the promotion of the cultivation of cash crops meant for export such as peanuts and cotton. They also played an important role in law enforcement and the administration of justice.

Legislation related to local government provides for most of the traditional governance institutions. The Local Government Act of 2002 provides for traditional institutions such as chieftaincies and the village heads (Alkalolu). With the attainment of independence, these structures were retained as an arm of central government, mainly for the purpose of taxation and the administration of justice. In the absence of modern governance structures at the village level, village heads have been used for the collection of rates and taxes within their communities. Revenue collected by these heads was then paid to revenue collectors who are often based with the district chiefs. This arrangement enables local government authorities to monitor compliance with the payment of these rates and taxes.

The 1997 Constitution of the Gambia provides for the office of the chief's involvement in the dispensation of justice. Chiefs are largely empowered to adjudicate civil matters. Cases they mainly preside over relate to marriages, inheritance and land disputes. Since a number of these cases hinge on traditional norms and values, Chiefs are assisted by a group of wise men (Council of Elders) in their court proceedings. The Gambia being predominantly Muslim and the country's legal system premised on customary, Islamic and modern laws, the group of elders advise the chief during court proceedings and even adjudicate in cases before the district tribunals. District tribunals refer cases beyond their jurisdiction to higher courts for arbitration. The role of the group of elders within the district tribunal is not limited to presiding over cases brought before the tribunal but they are also instrumental in matters of dispute resolution. With dwindling agricultural land in the country, land disputes are common and offices of the chiefs have often played an active role in resolving such disputes. It is common for these elders to intervene in marital disputes with a view to amicably resolving such disputes.

In the area of development, the Government of the Gambia recognizes the need for community ownership of development initiatives. In a quest to promote ownership of development programmes, the government has sought the input of communities in the planning of development projects through the Village Development Committees (VDCs). These committees work with the chieftaincies and the village heads at all levels of development endeavour. Traditional institutions have also worked with central government in sensitizing their communities on national development initiatives.

As de facto representatives of government in the districts, the chiefs have since independence been largely allied to government. This has mainly been because, despite being elected officials in most cases, the power of the executive to install and remove chiefs has made occupants of this office subservient to the executive. Notwithstanding this state of affairs, chiefs have and continue to play a key role in the governance of The Gambia. During the First Republic chiefs had a representative in parliament in the form of a nominated member of parliament. This was aimed at affording them the opportunity to promote the interest of the office of chief in the national parliament. Since 1994, however, chiefs have ceased to be represented in the National Assembly although they continue to play an active role in national politics. During electioneering chiefs are involved in canvassing for votes for the incumbent and have been quite influential in rallying support for the governing political party.

Largely as a consequence of colonial experience, chiefs have largely sided with government in electioneering. Support for an opposition candidate in any election by a serving chief is confidential for fear of reprisals from the executive. The Chief's involvement in party politics has often been queried by opposition parties in view of their influence on the electorate. Apart from the potential negative effects on democratization, the involvement of chiefs in party politics has an additional potential of the populace losing confidence in their impartiality in the dispensation of justice, particularly where litigants and defendants identify themselves with opposing political parties. Such questions of impartiality may dissuade the populace from seeking redress from the district tribunals. Due to the increased politicization of the office of chief even elders nominated to the district tribunals tend to largely identify with the ruling party.

In The Gambia, the relationship between the political parties and the traditional authorities has not been cordial particularly with the opposition and this date back to the First Republic. During the First Republic, although the chiefs were elected they dare not stand on a political platform to support the opposition and in fact they always do their best during either local government elections, presidential or parliamentary election to ensure that the opposition does not win. These traditional authorities always marginalize members of their communities who support the opposition. If chiefs do not interfere in politics and allow their subjects to use their franchise, their relationship with the political parties particularly with opposition would be very cordial. They have the right to join any political party, but do not have the right to go out openly and campaign for any political party. It is also important to note that before the Second Republic, Chiefs were represented in parliament through nomination but today this no longer exists. Just like the colonial era, and the First and Second Republics, most of the time Chiefs are appointed and removed by the executive and as such they also sided with the ruling government for fear of reprisals and as such are likely to lose respect from the opposition parties. Also, a non - partisan chief was likely to lose respect of the members of the community who support the opposition as the chiefs might not be able to arbitrate in an impartial manner.

The institution of chieftaincy through protection system ordinances of the British colonial administration

Gambian states and kingdoms from Kombo to Kantora were ruled by kings and queens who enjoyed full sovereignty with total control of customary and statutory powers. These powers were bestowed on them by their people without outside interference. However, after the British hegemonic control in 1894, states and kingdoms lost their authority and sovereignty. The first Protectorate System Ordinance to be promulgated in 1894 was a piece of legislation that divided the protectorate into chieftaincy districts headed by British appointed head chiefs (Gailey 1987). The appointment of head chiefs was to manage the day-to-day affairs of the protectorate in line with the British idea of maintaining law and order and flourishing of trade. Two travelling commissioners were also appointed for the North and South Bank of The Gambia to reinforce imperial authority over the protectorate. The Second Protectorate Ordinance passed in 1902 sub-divided some districts into convenient groups of villages with new head chiefs. Such sub-divisions affected Niumi, Badibu into lower and central Badibu, Kombo into Kombo North, South, Central and Eastern. The ordinance also brought Fulladu under the British rule. Another significant ordinance was passed in 1913. This ordinance further outlined the administrative powers of travelling commissioners and introduced reforms that abolished internal slavery and new forms of taxation such as the yard tax according to which every yard was supposed to pay (Southern 1952). A further significant Ordinance was the Native Administrative Ordinance promulgated in 1933. This ordinance created native authorities and empowered native tribunals to have full control over traditional laws and customs. It also outlined the chief's administrative and managerial powers (Gray, 1966). An annual chiefs' conference was held every year from 1947, as a forum for political, economic and development debate in the protectorate. Chiefs, as the mouthpiece of the rural majority, used this forum to transmit rural opinion to government. At the 1959 constitutional conference in Brikama, chiefs insisted that the protectorate should be represented by its own people. Therefore, in the newly formed House of Representatives or Parliament eight chiefs were indirectly elected to represent the rural majority (Hughes 2006).

Changes to chieftaincy in the First Republic

The coming of independence was not a good thing for chiefs. In the absence of protectorate parties during the colonial era, chiefs remained the dominant element in the political affairs of the protectorate. When the former People Progressive Party (PPP) came into limelight chiefs were threatened by the rural political elites who undermined their status as rural authorities. The chiefs' outright support of some chiefs to United Party (UP) eroded their sense of impartiality and compromised their status as traditional rulers. They suffered political intrigues and intimidation by the newly formed PPP government in 1965. Rural political elites usurped their customary and statutory powers by giving them little say in rural political and development activities. Chiefs no longer served as the mouthpieces of the rural population and were not allowed free rein in rural activities. The newly created Ministry of Local Government and Lands dismissed or retired 14 chiefs by March 1965. The provincial governors who replaced the white commissioners used coercion and patronage in dealing with chiefs. They were forbidden to support the opposition and were either to keep out of politics or support the ruling PPP. Chiefs therefore became the losers in their traditional and customary heritage (Wright 2004).

Changes to chieftaincy in the Second Republic

The Second Republic introduced new legislation in the 1997 Constitution in order to maintain the process of manipulation of chiefs. The law on election of chiefs was amended and replaced by a new enactment whereby the President is empowered to appoint Chiefs (see section 58 of the 1997 Constitution and section 133 of the Local Government Act 2002). Any bona fide resident of a district can be appointed as chief. Traditional ruling family does not count as well as being founding lineage of a settlement. This amendment, nonetheless, has weakened the position of chieftaincy as traditional rulers as anybody can be appointed chief. Notwithstanding, district chiefs are no longer the mouthpieces of the rural population but party bigwigs. Political coercion and monitoring of their activities by the ruling party stalwarts undermined and compromised their status as traditional rulers. On the positive side, their judicial powers were enhanced and as district tribunals they can administer laws pertaining to civil and criminal cases such as family feuds, land disputes, order damages from offending parties, treason, felony and all other criminal offences except murder. All in all, chiefs are still the losers in the Second Republic as they were in the First Republic considering their status and authorities as traditional rulers.

Main characteristics of traditional rulers

- Chiefs are the representatives of the government in all districts.
- They are the custodians of traditional and cultural heritage.
- They supervise the administration of the district.

- They serve as chief magistrates in administering civil and criminal cases in the District Tribunals
- Chiefs consult with Alkalolous and council of elders before decisions are taken.
- Chiefs are peace brokers between individuals, families and communities within the district.
- Chiefs and Alikalolu constitute the body of the politics of traditional rule in The Gambia and District Authority

Enhancing traditional rule system in The Gambia

Traditional governance in The Gambia has a significant place in modern representative democracies. Chiefs and Alkalolu are still significant in the traditional governance system. It is the view of the author that they should therefore be exposed to and acquainted with broad patterns of cultural, legal and political norms of their community. Governments must provide basic training to traditional rulers in order to build their legal capacities and provide them with human right principles. It is suggested that there must also be a widespread improvement of their service conditions in terms of salary, allowances, pensions and mobility. This should also apply to members of the district tribunals and badge messengers. 'Alkalou' should also be on salary rather than receiving annual commission of twenty to thirty percent on the total amount of rates and taxes collected in their villages. The role they play in society today needs to be preserved and nurtured in the multi-party democracy. Decentralization of the local governance system should promote the concept of democratic decision-making processes for chiefs.

The social expectation of central government to protect the citizenry and provide them with the basic needs of life cannot be achieved without the support of the traditional government authorities. Government must develop a national policy framework in building the capacities of traditional rulers as well as devolving the participation of ordinary citizens in decision-making processes. The traditional and social values of the community should be brought in consonance with democratic principles. The decentralization of local governance must allow religious tolerance, freedom of speech and discourage arbitrary rules. Seyfolous' role as the custodians of the traditional cultural heritage must not be eroded but strengthened, preserved, maintained and sanctified in order to enhance their full participation in democratic decision – making processes.

Finally, it should be emphasized that in traditional systems, Chiefs and Alkalous are not the ultimate decision makers, rather decisions come from the consensus of the tribunals and the council of elders at village level respectively. The adage that all are born equals encourages certain people to believe that choosing one family alone as successive rulers in a community perpetuates inequalities. They therefore call for the ballot box in a democratic election. They argue that one family alone should not rule forever without the consent of the ruled. Notwithstanding, in order to ensure the survival of the cultural heritage, traditional rulers must be indigenes of the area of their jurisdiction. This will give them greater acquaintance with the norms and values of their community. They must know their subjects, their ways of life, family units, Kabilo and lineage heritages, customs of landownership, village boundaries and ethnic set up. They must be bred and known in their community to give them recognition, support and legitimacy as the mouthpieces of the people. It is undisputed that traditional rulers are popular among the people and command a great deal of respect and influence.

Internal traditional governance systems in The Gambia

Structure of internal traditional governance system

Pre-colonial period

The pre-colonial Traditional Governance System in West Africa was based on centralized government under powerful rulers who had both executive and judicial powers (Buah: 1986). These powers were not absolute powers but were guarded by checks and balances that prevented the rulers from becoming too powerful and oppressive. In this regard, a functional and well-coordinated government was established that controlled trade and revenue, social and religious activities and fostered unity of all people within the state (Buah: 1986). In pre-colonial Gambia the governance systems of the Wolof, Mandinka and Fula were uniform in nature with similar power structures. The Mansa or Bur had responsibility as leader to maintain peace and stability and uplift the socio-economic status of the people (Curtin: 1975). It goes without saying that Islam had a formidable appearance in the 19th century and transformed the governance structure of Gambian states. Aristocratic power declined as Islam became dominant among the common people who became loyal to the new religion. Islam also preached equality and fairness to all people and these undermined the authority of the rulers (Searing: 1988). The animosity between Islam and the aristocratic class was centred on the latter's fear of losing their privilege and power, which led to the downfall of the old aristocracy to new Muslim families.

POLITICAL HIERARCHY

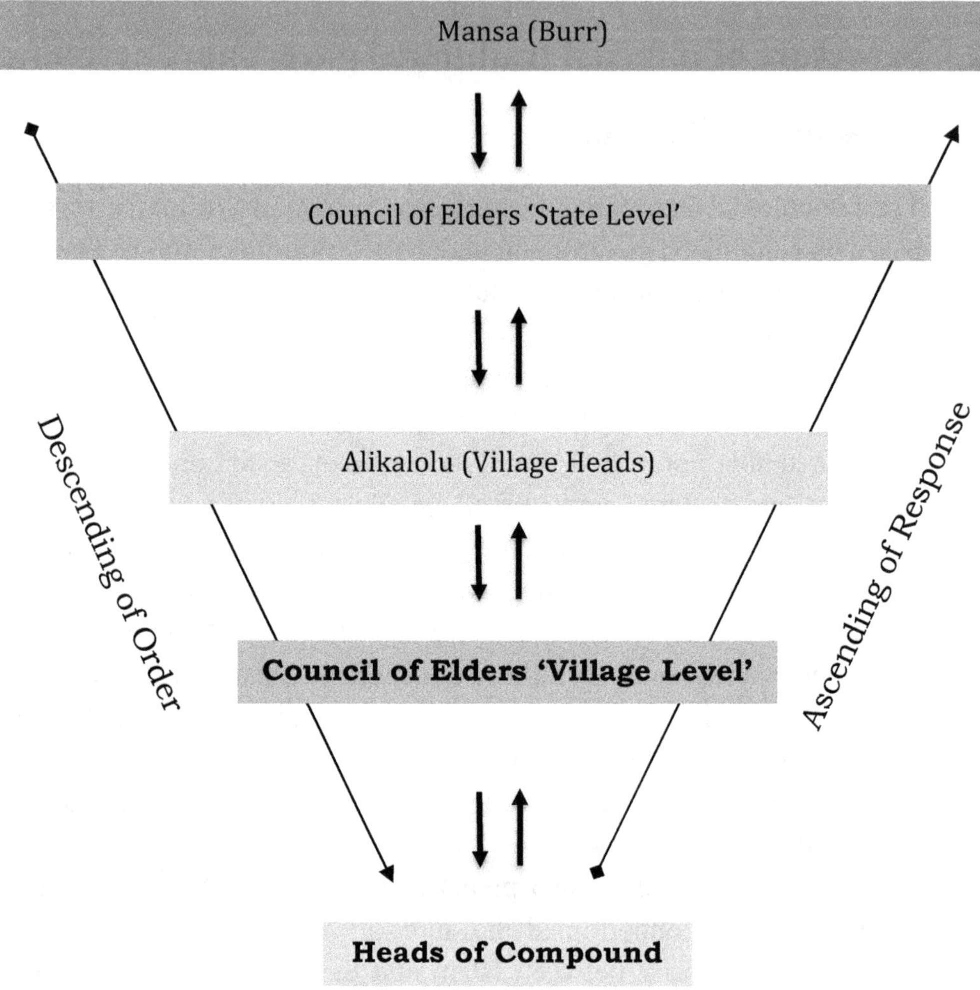

Colonial period

The dichotomy between pre-colonial and colonial traditional governance systems was the ultimate control of the political and economic lives of the people by colonial officials. Governance structures were framed in ways that favoured colonial control of trade and revenue (Gailey: 1987).

Colonially appointed District Chiefs remained the mouthpieces of the rural majority. Besides, the annual chief conference was used as a forum for political debate and the transmission of rural opinion to government. (Hughes: 2006). The indirect rule system, which was a cheap way of ruling the protectorate, established the Native Tribunal System that spelt out the jurisdiction of District Chiefs, which involved the dispensation of justice, collection of taxes and the control of both resources and markets within the district (Gary 1966). Unlike the centralized structure of pre-colonial system, the hierarchical system of giving orders and responses to orders differed tremendously. The protectorate was divided into divisions and then into districts, which were made of towns and villages under local rulers.

Traditional governance hierarchy

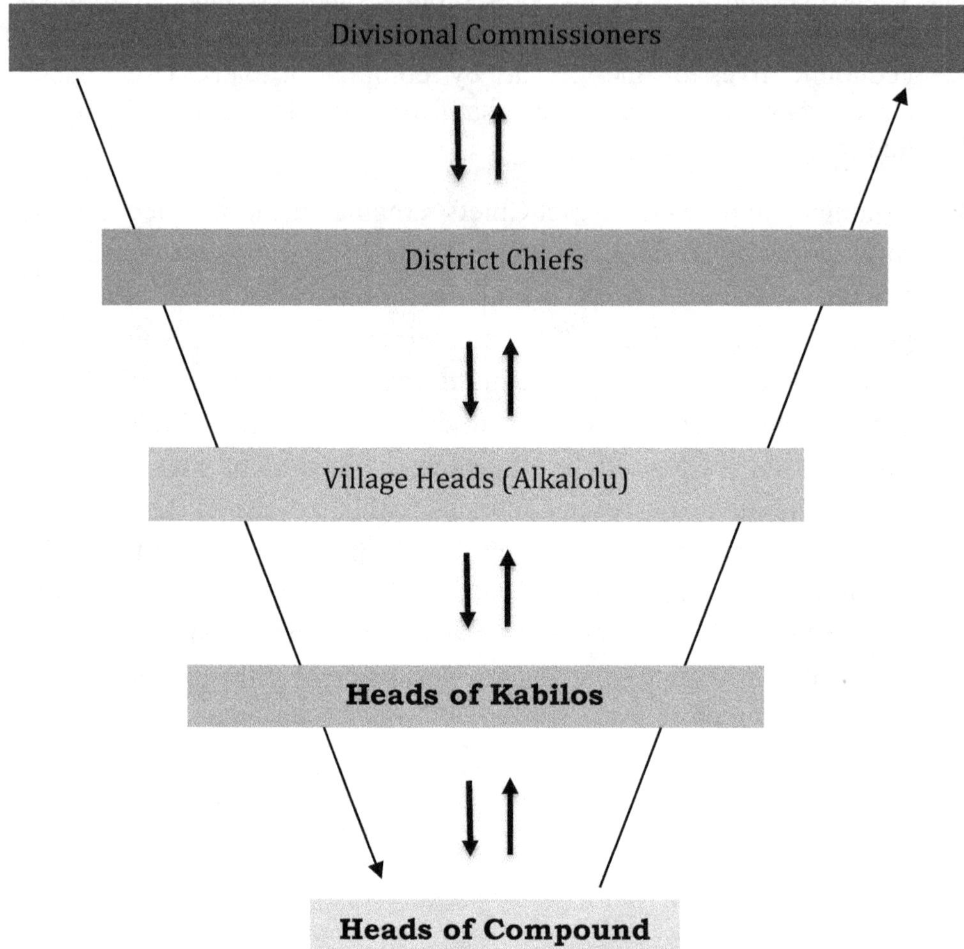

Post-colonial period

It can be noted that the nomenclature and jurisdiction of traditional authorities remained the same from colonial to post-colonial era. The 1960 Constitution which created the House of Representatives empowered eight chiefs nominated by chiefs themselves as members. The 1970 Republican Constitution reduced the number to three. However, the 1997 Constitution of the Second Republic outlawed the representation of chiefs in the House. The hierarchical structure remains the same.

Management of power and decision-making processes in traditional governance

The process of decision-making in the traditional governance system goes through a tier. At the top was the ruler who served as chief executive officer but had no dictatorial powers and had to consult the council of elders before laws were made or important decisions were taken. The Alkalolu as representatives of the ruler at village level were responsible for disseminating information and decisions to their communities. Without the full support of the council of elders and the Alkalolu the ruler's position would be weakened and without authority (Mahoney: 1982).

As part of the study, data was collected on management of power and decision-making processes in traditional institutions. Below are the findings from the survey:

Management of traditional governance institutions in The Gambia is at two levels. The first is management of these institutions by the Ministry of Local Government and Lands through Regional Governors and secondly management structures that exist at the grassroots level. Management through the Ministry of Local Government and Lands is formal with legislative provisions made in the Local Government Act for the management of these structures. At the grassroot level, however, management of traditional institutions is informal and based on cultural norms and values. The council of elders plays a pivotal role in the management of these structures providing the checks and balances to regulate the operations of the structures. When necessary the council of elders provides governors with information on governance matters related to the chiefs and village heads and may even advice on possible remedial measures to identify problems. Chieftaincies and village headships wield a lot of power and command respect from their communities. Notwithstanding their powers, these institutions have placed a lot of importance on the involvement of communities in the running of the institutions. To facilitate community involvement in the governance activities of these traditional institutions, councils of elders have been established at regional, district and village levels to provide advice to leaders of these institutions. Traditional leaders consult these councils in any major decisions taken. As indicated earlier, these councils service as juries in district tribunals and take centre stage in the resolution of disputes within their communities. On matters related to development, although heads of traditional governance institutions are consulted, decisions are often made by the Village Development Committees (VDCs).

Transfer of traditional power within the governance institution

Transfer of power in traditional governance system passed from one ruling family to another. In some areas there were multiple ruling families which rotated the kingship among themselves. Leadership shifted from one ruling family to another, for example, in Niumi, leadership rotated between the Jammehs, Mannehs and Sonkos. In Kombo, Muslim Jihads ousted the traditional rulers and a new form of ruling family emerged (Mahoney: 1982). In the Second Republic, the President appointed and dismissed Chiefs as stipulated in the laws of The Gambia. This issue is explained in more detail in the section

320

below. In determining the position of traditional governance towards conventional governance it could be said that it serves to diffuse traditional values and cultural norms into the norms of the same traditional system. These values are reinforced by the dynamics of the decentralization process. This reinforces democratization. Democratization moves towards decentralization of local governments, which demands popular participation in the decision-making processes. It also reinforces social control and development, order and stability, which are fundamental to good governance. The intertwining of conventional governance with traditional governance transcends all sectors of life be they economic, social or political.

As part of the instant study, data was collected on the transfer of power within the governance institution. Below are the findings from the survey:

As has been the case in many African countries, the offices of traditional governance institutions have been used by colonial governments as an arm of government under the indirect rule, to maintain law and order within the colonies, protect the economic interest of the colonialists and mobilize labour. To accomplish this objective colonial governments recognized the structures that existed before their arrival.

Since ascension to the traditional positions such as chief and village head was largely based on lineage, these were largely maintained in the interest of maintaining acceptability and respect for the institution amongst local communities. During the colonial era, although traditional institutions such as that of the chief continued to be respected they were largely not accountable to the populace and their survival in power depended mainly on the satisfaction of the colonial government with their rule. This made the chief very powerful and in most cases autocratic in their dispensation of justice. With independence and the maintenance of the office of chiefs in the country, although successive post-independence governments have made major gains in introducing democracy into the establishment and functioning of the office of chiefs, the legacy of the pre-colonial and colonial period continues to influence the functioning of this office. Although some chiefs ascend to power through a democratic process and others are appointed by the President, often whether covertly or overtly the lineage of nominees for the position of chief is considered to ensure a popular choice. Where such considerations are flouted, a nominee faces the potential of rejection by the populace and is likely to face problems within their communities.

Neo-traditional form of chieftaincy

The above analysis of the legal regime governing traditional governance institutions and structures in The Gambia since the colonial days to the present time clearly shows that chieftaincy of post-colonial Gambia is a neo-traditional form of chieftaincy. The chiefs of independent Gambia, like those of the colonial days, play a hybrid role in nation building. On one hand, they are imposed by the government of the modern sovereign state to enforce its laws, policies and implement its decisions taken at the central level. On the other hand, and in a very limited capacity, the chiefs serve the interest of the people over whom they preside and exercise traditional authority. The 1997 Constitution has not precisely defined the position of traditional rulers within the overall structure of political power and authority in The Gambia. Section 193 (3) of the Constitution states that an Act of the National Assembly shall make provision for the functions, powers and duties of Local Government Authorities including provision for the participation of the inhabitants in the development and administration of the area and also the promotion of Gambian culture and traditions.

However, the Constitution is emphatically clear and decisive in subjecting traditional authority to that of the government of the modern sovereign state. Sections 58 and 59 of the 1997 Constitution have in actual fact incorporated the Traditional Governance System in The Gambia into the governance system of the modern sovereign state. According to Section 58, the President shall appoint District Chiefs in consultation with the Minister for Local Government and Lands, while Section 59 vests the power of appointment of village head persons in the Minister of Local Government and Lands in consultation with Regional Governors. However, section 59 (2) has mandated the Minister for Local Government and Lands to consider traditional lines of inheritance in making such an appointment. (Also see sections 133 and 141 of the Local Government Act – 2002).

Furthermore, it worth noting at this juncture that the regime of Local Government Authorities in The Gambia is constituted by city councils, municipalities, area councils and districts. The latter is the power base for traditional rulers. It appears from the wordings of Section 132 of the Local Government Act 2002 that Traditional Political Authority in The Gambia is constituted by and probably limited to District Chiefs and Village Head Persons (Alkalolu). Thus, according to section 132 of the Act, a district authority for each district is constituted by the Chief of the District as its Chairperson and all Village Head Persons within the District. Similarly, section 136 of the Act provides that District Chiefs can be removed by the President while sections 137 to 140 define the powers, functions, duties and benefits of traditional Chiefs.

Despite all these drastic changes in the chieftaincy system in The Gambia, successive governments from the colonial period up until now have continued to reorganize and emphasize the importance of the role of traditional rulers in the political, cultural, economic, social and spiritual life of the Gambian people. Thus, in 1942 the Colonial Administration headed by Governor Hilary Blood convened the first conference of traditional rulers "Mansa Bengho" or Chiefs' Conference. The conference took place at Janjangbureh, provincial capital of the Central River Region of The Gambia under the auspices of Commissioner Letch Ward. From 1942, the Conference of Traditional Rulers or Mansa Bengho as a political mechanism became part of the overall structure of the chieftaincy system in The Gambia and a tradition conducted every year until 1990, after which it became dormant for more than one decade. In 2001, President Yahya Jammeh revived the tradition of Mansa Bengho with a view to redefining and strengthening Gambia's traditional governance system, structures and practices and also to giving more recognition and support to the cultural significance and historical role of traditional rulers. The concept of Mansa Bengho as perceived by the colonial administration, which created it, was not necessarily in line with the policies of the Jammeh administration towards reviving traditional governance systems, structures and practices in The Gambia. Thus, President Yahya Jammeh established a new traditional governance mechanism known as the National Council of Traditional Rulers (Sefolu) to replace the conference of traditional rulers as a common central political forum for the traditional chiefs. This new mechanism was to be headed by a Paramount Chief – another new position created by the Jammeh administration within the power structure of the chieftaincy regime of The Gambia. The Local Government Act – 2002 was amended by the National Assembly in the later part of 2007 to create the new position of a Paramount Chief who would head the newly introduced mechanism of the National Council of Chiefs. The government believes that the Paramount Chief and his Council will provide the much-needed forum for traditional rulers to discuss openly and critically various topical issues of life and state matters ranging from governance, culture, upholding the rule of law, maintenance of law and order, internal security and also to disseminate information, to deliberate on policies and issues touching on the economy and sustainable development.

The new Paramount Chief Mr. Demba Sanyang who is also the Traditional Chief of Kombo North District of the Western Region was inaugurated by President Yahya Jammeh on Friday, 29th February

324

2008 in Brikama, the provincial capital of the region. Addressing the National Council of the Chiefs and the first Paramount Chief to be inaugurated in the history of the Gambian chieftaincy, the President explained the nature of the type of chieftaincy that he had envisaged to operate in modern Gambia. He explained that District Chiefs are the Executive Authorities in their respective areas and that therefore, it was important for all of them to work together in harmony for the benefit of the people and their development. The President told the traditional chiefs that as President he was under the law. Thus, all traditional rulers and indeed all other authorities in the country are governed by and subject to the law of the land. This was a direct warning to the traditional chiefs that under no circumstances they should undermine or disobey the laws of the modern sovereign state, which in many cases reduce traditional rulers to mere instruments and mouthpieces of the government of the day.

Finally, although the government of the Second Republic is putting a lot of efforts in trying to revive the tradition of chieftaincy in The Gambia, there is no guarantee that this important traditional political institution, which will continue to be controlled by the government of the modern sovereign state as it had always been during the days of colonial rule and throughout the lifespan of the First Republic, will be able to regain its pure traditional character. Thus, chieftaincy in The Gambia is no more traditional in the real sense of the term; rather, it is a neo-traditional form of political system and institutions.

Roles of traditional governance institutions and their contributions in promoting socio-cultural, economic and political development of The Gambia

Regarding the roles of traditional governance institutions in the social, cultural, economic and political development of the nation, some of the respondents are of the view that traditional governance institutions do have a role to play. This is evident from the remarks of the respondents presented below:

Traditional governance institutions contribute immensely to the political, cultural, social and economic life of a nation.

As is amply evident in society, traditional norms and values continue to influence our daily practices including how occasions such as naming ceremonies are conducted. Traditional leaders are viewed as custodians of our culture. All major decisions affecting communities are taken under the stewardship of village heads [Alkalolou]. For example, when a difference emanates between any two parties the verdict that Alkali passes, becomes binding on both parties in settling the dispute thus guaranteeing a semblance of social stability. The traditional leader in a similar vein plays a crucial role in coordinating matters surrounding community development.

Traditional leaders can influence political outcomes. It is for this reason that competing political parties try to win the support and sympathy of traditional rulers or leaders. In the First Republic it was not uncommon to see a whole community siding with a particular political party. Those who in the community decided for one reason or the other to express dissenting views got marginalized due mainly to their political beliefs. Therefore, politics became a source of political conflict.

The contribution of traditional governance institutions in national development covers a lot of sectors. Community efforts such as cleaning the environment help reduce diseases such as malaria. Other positive contributions in the area of health include sanitation and the provision of clean drinking water.

Education has long been valued and cherished under all forms of traditional settings. Community members are given training on all aspects of human relationships such as respect for elders, methods and signs of communication, etc. It is a widely held belief that the erosion of traditional values and norms is directly linked to the dwindling importance of traditional schools. Traditional institutions are partners in education through the mobilization of community support toward the construction of schools and help increase enrolment in schools by making sure that all the children who have reached the school going age are in school.

Land is communally owned and its management rests on the shoulders of the community elders in traditional societies. Upland areas are mainly managed by men as opposed to lowland areas which are managed by women. User rights and the need to consult on matters relating to let us say transfer of land were meant to be observed and practised.

The management of the environment is given a lot of prominence in traditional settings because it was viewed as a source of sustainable livelihood, viz food, clothing, and shelter.

On the human rights dimension the protection of children was guaranteed through all the elders taking full responsibility for correcting the undesirable behaviour of the children. These corrective measures were effected by ensuring that children become aware of their responsibilities.

The traditional setting has mechanisms in place for conflict prevention, management, and resolution. The council of elders is an important and effective institution in this respect. The adoption of this institutional framework in the Second Republic has reduced the number of cases dealt with by district tribunals by effectively managing conflicts.

The empowerment of women is nothing new in traditional communities. Despite our communities being patriarchal, history has taught us that women have always been in the forefront in many communal matters including becoming leaders of dynasties.

Coming back to the most recent developments in The Gambia, women continue to play significant roles in national development by holding responsible positions including the positions of Vice President, Secretaries of State, National Assembly Members, etc., in the current administration.

They serve as a means through which society is united. They preserve the traditional and cultural values and practices. They maintain law and order, distribute land and represent the central authority at the community level.

On the issue of women having a role to play in traditional governance in The Gambia, all the participants were of the opinion they have a role play but only on issues that affect them. This is an indication that women still have limited role to play in our societies. This is amply made clear in the following statements:

They have an important role to play particularly in issues affecting them.

Women's role was most seen in a wide range of food production. This enables the kingdoms to be self-reliant. This trend continues as women are involved in almost all sectors of socio – economic development. Therefore, they have a role to play in traditional governance in The Gambia.

Women have a role to play in traditional governance but on issues that concerns them like female circumcision. This is the tradition we inherited from our parents and this is what is practised today.

On the question of whether and why it is acceptable for women to take a leading role in traditional governance similar sentiments have been expressed as to whether women have a role in

traditional governance in The Gambia. Most of the respondents were of the view that it is acceptable for women to take a leading role in traditional matters that concern them. Find below transcripts of some of the interviews:

In general matters women can be listened to but cannot take leading roles. They can be left to lead where the matters to be dealt with affect only women. That notwithstanding, women are today becoming traditional leaders (Alkalolou).

Women can take the lead in matters that concerns them like female circumcision.

In our communities, women only take a leading role in issues that concern them. This is what we found our ancestors have been doing and whatever they were doing was based on a reason. Going by our religion, women are only supposed to take the role in what concerns them as well. So, in traditional governance, women will take the leading role on specific issues only.

The political system has long been dominated by men because it is men dominated society. This does not mean a total denial of women's right to take a leading position in the traditional governance as women Alkalolou and opinion leaders have been registered with resounding success. This means that women can take a leading role in traditional governance when necessary.

Opinions were given during the interviews on the relationship between political parties (ruling and opposition) and traditional governance institutions. The findings of the survey indicate that the relationship between the traditional governance institutions has only been cordial with the ruling party and not cordial with the opposition. This is attributed to the fact that since the chiefs are appointed by the ruling government, they fear losing their

position if they associate with the opposition. These were some of the opinions expressed during the interviews:

The kinds of political programmes being sold by political parties determine the kind of relationship between political parties and traditional governance institutions. Most political parties believe that the traditional governance institutions always side with ruling parties. For this reason, these institutions have always been the subject of negative attacks by opposition parties. Among all the traditional institutions it is only the Alkalo who receives a lot of influence from the government. Since the Alkalo cannot all by himself wield a lot of power to determine political outcomes; the accusations of the opposition parties are unfounded. The chief has influence over Alkalolou but not so much of influence to sway the decisions of the council of elders. To validate this statement, it is not unusual today for traditional leaders such as Alkalolou to side with opposition parties.

Chiefs are seen as responsible for the upkeep of the traditions and social values of communities and are not expected to be involved in party politics and should maintain neutrality in all political activities. The relationship between the traditional governance institutions and the opposition has been cordial because they are always accused by the opposition of siding with the ruling party.

The relationship between the traditional governance institutions and the ruling party has been very cordial. This is attributable to the fact that the ruling party is the government of the day and if the chief did not side with them, they could be removed from power. Their relationship with the opposition has not been good as they are always accused of supporting the ruling party. This is why there should be a chieftaincy act, which protects the chiefs from victimization because of party affiliation.

The respondents were also asked how traditional governance institutions contributed to the area of politics and democratization.

Chiefs cannot be excluded in the democratization process as they deal with ordinary citizens. District tribunals remain important in the administration of justice and a large proportion of cases concerning the ordinary citizens are presided by them.

In the area of politics, chiefs most of the time side with the ruling party, even if they did not subscribe to the ideals of the ruling party. In the area of democratization, they have not contributed much although they facilitate meetings of the opposition parties in their communities provided they have permission from the government.

The respondents were also asked about the role the population plays in decision making within the traditional governance institutions. Some of the respondents reported that the population has a role to play in traditional governance institutions. Below are some of the transcripts from the interviews:

Traditional governance institutions are driven by the population in an all-inclusive manner.

The population also does participate at village and district level in the governance process through village and ward development committees and at the regional level through elected councillors.

The population plays a very important role in decision making within the traditional governance institutions. As the chiefs are their representatives, they are always consulted by the councils of the elders or 'Kafos' on issues affecting their livelihoods. If they are not consulted and a decision has to be taken, it could lead to grievances and could lead to unrest in the community and the chief could be removed. Knowing this danger, they are always involved in the decision-making process.

The population doesn't have any say in the decision-making process. When a decision has been taken by the government, it will be communicated to the chief, who will in turn communicate it to the people through the council of elders or the 'Kafo's' and they take it or leave it.

Criticisms and limitations of traditional governance institutions:

Weaknesses and challenges facing traditional governance institutions.

Interviewees were asked about their opinions on the weaknesses of the traditional governance institutions associated with any of the following areas: health sector, education, land management and the environment, protection of human rights, conflict prevention and resolution, women's empowerment, gender equality and the democratization process and transparency and accountability.

There could be serious health hazards emanating from the practices of traditional governance   institutions. For example, circumcisions done in traditional settings are sometimes used by the application of unscientific processes and procedures that could seriously undermine the health of those to be circumcized.

The basic instrument of judicial governance in a traditional setting is the district tribunal. This tribunal operates on the basis of the English legal system, customary law, and Islamic law (Sariyah). The applicability of the English legal system can sometimes prove difficult at the local level as most district chiefs are not literate. These illiterate chiefs in such circumstances have to rely on their court clerks who sometimes are not fully conversant with conventional legal matters. Moreover, even those chiefs who are literate are not or may not know anything about English law.

Powerful traditional leaders who are feared by most members of their communities will always have whatever verdict they pass on conflicts fully respected. This opens the adjudication process at the local level on conflict resolution vulnerable to unfair judgment, favouritism and personal bias.

The small size of the country makes decentralization not as important as it is presumed to be. Wherever one is located in the country, one can access central authority within a reasonable period of time. Therefore, if the people were involved in decentralization or otherwise, some valid arguments would have been advanced against decentralization.

The Area Councils which are the local implementing institutions identified under the decentralization framework do not have the capacity to implement a successful and viable decentralization programme.

Health, education, land management, conflict resolution, women empowerment, and the like are lifelong processes that need the attention of everyone. However, the modern state institutional structures have limited the role of traditional institutions. The primary health care system has given maximum participation of the people.

Female circumcision is widely practiced in our communities and in this era of sexually transmitted diseases if we do not sterilize the blades we use or use different blades we might infect our people. Therefore, we need to be vigilant in what we are doing.

On education, we thought there was no need to send our children to Western schools as they might be converted to Christianity, whilst today we are reaping the benefits of our children being sent to school.

They get education and are not converted to Christians and are able to support us.

On the issue of human rights, traditional governance institutions have been doing well. As before the issue of human rights, particularly the rights of the child, became a subject of discussion, we were able to discipline our families but today because of the issue of human rights, we can no longer control our families. Therefore, one could say that in the area of human rights, it is the modern institutions that have weaknesses not the traditional system.

For conflict prevention and resolution, I think traditional authorities have been doing well. We have a council of elders and chiefs who can resolve an issue amicably without seeking redress from the courts. At times a serious problem could occur at night and before daybreak the issue is resolved without the knowledge of many people

Women's empowerment and gender equality is another burning issue just like the right of the child. Women have a role to play in households and should be honoured. Before the advent of issues related to gender equality, we ran our homes without any problem but so many marriages are having problems now as a result of this call for equality. This will affect our families as it could lead to splits among the children.

On the issue of democratization, traditional institutions have been doing very well to involve and respect people's voice.

There is no weakness of the traditional institutions on any of these issues. We have been following what our ancestors left here and we have not seen any weakness in that.

On the issue of factors that facilitate or hinder the traditional institutions from playing a more important role in the development process, the results of the survey indicate that traditional authorities do not get the recognition they deserve as

they are not consulted on certain issues affecting their communities. This is reflected in the transcripts below:

Traditional authorities still do not get the recognition they deserve from the development players. Non-Governmental Organizations (NGOs), for example, in pursuing their development work have been known to be using alternative structures as opposed to using the traditional authorities as an entry and rallying point for executing their mandates at the local level. In the education sector, you will hardly find a headteacher consulting with the local authority on matters pertaining to the running of their schools. All of them would prefer limiting their consultations to the Parent-Teacher Associations.

Central government has given the traditional institutions the authority to handle all cases except murder.

Traditional institutions should be consulted in all decisions that affect their communities. They should be involved in all projects in their communities from the planning to the monitoring and evaluation stage.

In our present society, people are working towards their personal gains and therefore traditional authorities are not respected. Secondly, as they lack independence and might not be consulted on certain issues, they might not be able to play an important role in the development process.

Regarding the relevance of traditional governance institutions in The Gambia, all the respondents are of the view that traditional governance institutions are relevant to The Gambia as they complement modern governance institution in their functions. These were some of the opinions expressed during the interviews:

Of course, traditional governance is relevant to The Gambia. Certain issues like marriage, land and other social issues are better resolved at the community level than at courts or police stations. Also, the administrative and transaction costs of handling these cases will be less than they would have been if handled by modern governance institutions. This will enable the government to focus on more pressing governance issues.

Yes, traditional authorities are very relevant in today's Gambia. In societies with traditional governance settings, people mostly come together through combined efforts for their betterment both as individuals and as a community. To achieve this, they are better off being guided by chiefs than other government officials.

These institutions are very relevant. The proper functioning of most public institutions depends on their ability to get the cooperation of traditional institutions. The Police Force, for example, is today using concepts such as Community Policing which requires the input of traditional governance institutions to maintain and keep the peace. The Police Force cannot maintain peace in this country all by itself considering their numerical strength.

Traditional governance is no longer relevant in today's Gambia. Now they cannot take independent decisions as they are elected.

Section 3

Relationships between Traditional and Modern Governance Institutions e.g. the state, related institutions, political parties

On the relationship between traditional and modern governance institutions in The Gambia, all the respondents were of the view there is a relationship between the two but there were divergent views about their relationship. These are some of the views expressed by the respondents during the interview:

This relationship is characterized by both conflict and conformity. The only way to do away with the conflict between the two institutions of governance is to make sure that the level of participation of traditional governance institutions is not diluted by the modern governance institutions.

The relationship was much more cordial in the old days than now. Now the government is putting in a lot of efforts so that issues like marriage, land among other disputes are handled by the chiefs so that these issues can be resolved amicably without reaching the courts.

The inter–relationship between central government and traditional authority remains unchanged since the two complement each other in participatory democracy.

You know traditional governance institutions are not very functional in modern governance environment.

The relationship between the two institutions is good but it is the modern institutions that benefit much from the relationship. As you know, modern governance institutions are in the hands of people with Western education who at times are not trustworthy. At times they come up with policies and programmes which we are not familiar with and have no option but to endorse it.

On the issue of how modern governance institutions have been helpful to traditional institutions in their fulfilment of their roles and responsibilities, some of the respondents reported that modern governance institutions have been helpful. Below are some of the transcripts from the interviews:

To a large degree, modern governance institutions are facilitating the realization of the roles and responsibilities of traditional governance institutions. It is important to empower and recognize the traditional institutions of governance and to sensitize public agencies who deal with the public directly such as the Police Force about the need to collaborate with local authorities in ensuring the execution of their assigned responsibilities.

Modern governance institutions have been helpful in assisting traditional governance institutions in fulfilling their roles and responsibilities. The government has been giving us support in the settlement of land disputes, conflicts within communities and giving us the leading role to administer aid in case of disaster like fire or floods in our communities.

Maintaining chiefs and giving them the mandate to execute their duties is one of the ways governments is helping traditional governance institutions in fulfilling their roles and responsibilities. Government has also been creating a conducive environment that enables the chiefs to embark on their development projects for the benefit of their communities.

Regarding how independent traditional governance institutions or authorities are to modern governance institutions or authorities there were divergent views from the respondents. Below are some of the views expressed by the respondents:

Traditional governance institutions have been destroyed as they can no longer take independent decisions.

Traditional governance institutions/authorities enjoy a considerable degree of independence from modern governance institutions/authorities.

They have some degree of independence from modern governance institutions.

Traditional governance institutions are independent as they have been given the mandate to handle issues in their communities. In certain issues, the modern governance institutions have to intervene to avoid abuse of power.

Their decisions should be in line with the constitution and the opinion leaders within their communities also play a vital role in influencing their activities. This shows that they do not take independent decisions and do not act independently.

On the issue of changes in the relationship between modern and traditional governance institutions in the past, there were divergent views from the respondents regarding the changes.

There is a change in the way traditional positions are assumed now. In the early days, eligibility to become chief was limited to certain families. Thereafter it was based on elections and now it is the head of state that is empowered to appoint chiefs.

There are many changes now. During the colonial era up to the last three decades collection of taxes and control of revenue was in the hands of the chiefs as well as land administration and distribution but now all these issues are handled by the government.

There has not been any significant change from the past as chieftaincy still exists. But the number of chiefs that existed in the past has increased. Also, chiefs at times are not consulted in certain decision making.

Traditional governance institutions no longer exist and as such one cannot measure whether there is any change in the relation between the two institutions.

On measures that can best improve the relationship between modern and traditional governance institutions, the findings show that one of the ways of improving their relationship is through consultation as indicated by the following quotations:

A consciously planned programme of developing a governance policy should allow for good representation of the traditional authorities. There can be instances where the views of traditional authorities are not fully incorporated into governance policies. There is the need for balanced interaction and effective cooperation which will greatly improve policy formulation and implementation.

We should always be consulted by modern governance institutions particularly on issues pertaining to traditional governance. In the past we used to settle disputes of any nature without any problem. Even if the matter is a modern governance institution issue but has taken place in our communities, the issue should be discussed with us rather than taking unilateral decisions.

Modern governance institutions should contact the traditional institutions regularly so that decisions are reached by consensus. This mechanism ensures that government does not rule arbitrarily, particularly, on issues of traditional governance.

There should be a Memorandum of Understanding (MoU) between traditional and modern governance institutions. Modern government should recognize the existence of traditional governance institutions and seek advice from us on any issue. We should also be part of the legislature.

Section 4

Strategies and mechanisms to harness the role of traditional governance institutions in accelerating the social, economic, cultural and political development and in ensuring good governance in West Africa in general and in The Gambia in particular.

The in-depth interviews included a question on what can be done to make traditional governance institutions in national development (in all sectors) more effective. It was no surprise that prominent among

340

the factors identified was the issue of consultation when it comes to decisions affecting their communities. This was raised by all the respondents interviewed, as indicated below:

Traditional governance institutions are firmly entrenched in Gambian society. They continue to play a pivotal role in the socio-political lives of the people. Most of these structures pre-date the post-colonial period and both colonial governments and post-independence governments recognized their importance and made legal provisions for their existence alongside modern institutions. These institutions continue to serve in the areas of the dispensation of justice and other national development endeavours. Notwithstanding their continuous importance, modernization has taken its toll on the public's recognition and appreciation of the importance of these institutions.

As the country continues to enhance her democratic credentials, traditional governance institutions are undoubtedly relevant in the attainment of national development objectives. In the area of the dispensation of justice, for example, the critical problem facing the sector is the backlog of cases in the courts. This can mainly be attributed to the increased reliance of the populace on conventional courts for the dispensation of justice. In the recent past, however, the government has instituted measures to reduce the backlog of cases in the courts. In addition to instituting measures to expedite court proceedings, the government has also initiated alternative dispute resolution which is aimed at encouraging litigants to settle their cases out of court amicably. Traditional institutions can play a key role, as they did in the past, in the management of cases to ensure speedy resolution of conflicts. Disputes within communities can be effectively resolved with the intervention of Alkalolu and where they fail such matters can be forwarded to the chiefs who can then negotiate a resolution of the matter or arbitrate between the parties. This is one area where traditional institutions can effectively contribute to law enforcement, hence the promotion of good governance.

In the area of development, community participation is key in the attainment of national development goals. The involvement of traditional governance institutions in all stages of development endeavour is essential in promoting both ownership of development initiatives and ensuring that such initiatives are relevant to the aspirations of the people. Village Development Committees (VDCs) have in the past been quite instrumental in the initiation and implementation of development initiatives at the grass-root level. Such structures if harnessed could contribute more effectively in national development and governance.

For traditional governance institutions to continue to be effective partners in national development, society needs to continue to accept and recognize their contribution to national development. With increased democratization in the country, acceptability of these institutions is contingent on the involvement of the populace in the management of the institutions, decision making and transfer of power within the institutions. It is essential, therefore, that the populace is involved in the selection/election of officials of traditional governance institutions and where the process is stalled by disagreement, a democratic process of electing members should be embarked on to ensure acceptability by all and sundry. The free and fair election of officials of traditional governance institutions is particularly critical in alkaloship and chieftaincy positions. This is because over the years democratic processes have become increasingly entrenched in Gambian society and where communities have disagreed on alkaloship or other traditional leadership positions this has often been amicably settled through an election.

One way of aiding the development process is to involve chiefs. There is a general consensus that traditional leaders such as chiefs have a role in the governance of the state.

In The Gambia, traditional authorities play an important role in the socio – economic development of The Gambia particularly in the rural communities. They play a significant role in socio – economic activities involving the use of environmental resources. Traditional authorities are the first to know when there is a problem within their communities, be it bush fires, or conflicts involving the use of natural resources such as forests and land. They therefore will be the first to stop such abuses if they are formally empowered to do so.

Traditional authorities definitely have an important role in providing leadership in community development provided the necessary resources and capacity to enable them support and lead the processes for community development has been provided. Therefore, there is the need for the modern state to provide institutional support to traditional institutions to strengthen their capacity to lead their communities in their development efforts. Support in the form of workshops and conferences that enable the chiefs to engage with government on important policy issues should be organized. This will enhance their capacity to enable them to play an important role in the development process at that level. It makes them more effective in terms of being responsive to the needs of their people. In this way, traditional governance will more effectively contribute to ensuring good governance.

There should be a constitutional provision to specify the powers and responsibilities of chiefs both at the community and national levels. The chieftaincy institutions should be allowed to play their judicial roles and as such there is the need for legal backing for traditional authorities in judicial matters.

Chiefs must be made part of decision-making processes at all levels and therefore should be represented at Parliament to take part in decision making. This lack of institutional representation will limit the influence of traditional authorities at the national level and could affect their capacity to the processes of enhancing the participation of the rural poor in local development.

Disputes within the communities can be resolved by the Alkalolou and the chiefs in the form of community courts that can handle minor civil cases. For example, in conflict resolution, traditional authorities intervene in a wide range of issues. They play important roles in land issues, family matters, etc. In all these matters, the traditional authorities are a key node in a network of institutions that may include the district or even the provincial courts, the police, etc. Sometimes they are the first venue sought for by the parties, in other times they function as appeal institutions, and in other cases they provide advice, or evidence in cases being dealt with by other institutions.

There is the need for traditional governance institutions to be consulted particularly those traditional authorities with a demonstrable knowledge of both the traditional and modern ways of governing. Leaving everything to technocrats when it comes to policy development will lead to under-achievement due to the lack of sufficient knowledge about traditional settings.

The existence of traditional governance institutions should be acknowledged by the central government. They should be consulted on all issues pertaining to their communities be it health, education or any other issue, so that they will feel being part of the process thereby supporting any activity that is being undertaken in their communities.

Chiefs' roles as custodians of the traditional heritage must not be eroded, but they should be strengthened and preserved to enhance their role in decision making processes. They should be recognized, empowered and given their due respect. They should also be given some degree of independence and their positions should not be politicized.

The maintenance of good governance in any country is not the sole responsibility of central government. In a country like the Gambia where modern governance institutions are either non-existent or weak in certain localities, there is need for traditional governance institutions to complement modern institutions in the maintenance of good governance.

In The Gambia traditional governance institutions have played a pivotal role in the governance of the country as early as the colonial period. As indicated earlier, chiefs and village heads had during this period served critical roles in the administration of justice and had been used by the colonial administration as agents of development within their communities. In the early days of the introduction of Western education in The Gambia, for example, the colonial administration was faced with stiff resistance from indigenes. To engender acceptance of Western education therefore, chiefs had to serve as role models by enrolling their children in school. As a result of this move, the first Gambians within rural communities to accept Western education were the chiefs. In addition to this measure, chiefs also embarked on sensitizing communities to the importance of sending their children to school, which eventually resulted in increased enrolment in all parts of the country. With independence, chiefs and village heads continue to assume their traditional roles in the governance of the country. Chiefs continue to serve in their law enforcement capacities and also continued to partake in the development agenda of their communities. At the village level, village heads arbitrate minor disputes and where necessary resolve disputes within their communities. Cases of crime or dispute beyond the jurisdiction of the village heads are either referred to the chiefs or to the police. Most civil cases within rural communities are often presided over by the village heads or the chiefs. With independence and the institutionalization of democratic governance, traditional governance institutions began assuming key roles in electoral processes. These roles range from the help they provide in the registration of voters prior to elections, the role they play in maintaining peace during elections to their actual participation in electioneering.

Good governance includes sustainable development. Traditional institutions are, therefore, expected to contribute to its advancement by providing timely and accurate information on environmental protection and promotion of the idea of sustainable development within the communities they serve. Traditional institutions are an important aspect of the democratization process because they provide a vital link between the rural population and the modern state. It also provides an environment that can be used to enhance community cohesion and decision – making. Information is vital to civic participation and also encourages its development. When people get better informed, they are most likely to participate in policy discussions and communicate their ideas and concerns freely. The development of an informed citizenry is one of the basic functions of the modern state.

Section 5

Conclusion

Evidence from the results of the survey has shown that during the colonial era, The Gambia had a centralized form of governance in the past but now a decentralized system is in place, although the decentralization process is incomplete. At the regional level, governors are in charge of the day-to-day running of their regions. Within the regions chieftaincies at district level are in charge of administration at that level and chiefs also administer the settlements through the village heads that also have structures such as Village Development Committees through which settlements are administered. Regarding succession, the results show that succession is no longer through inheritance, because it is the head of state who now appoints the chiefs and this being the case, they may not be independent in the execution of their duties. This has been manifested in the survey results and the Focus Group Discussions in the relationship between the traditional governance institutions and the modern state as well as the ruling and opposing political parties. Most of the respondents reported that chiefs always side with the ruling party and antagonize the opposition and cannot take independent decisions for fear of losing their positions. Results of the survey show that women have limited powers in traditional governance institutions. Although the evidence seems to suggest that gains have been made in the increased empowerment of women in governance institutions, males continue to dominate the leadership of governance institutions. Decision making is largely dominated by men and women only decide on matters affecting them.

Traditional institutions which in the past operated in an undemocratic environment seem to be increasingly entertaining democratic tendencies. Many traditional institutions have been consultative on issues related to governance and a number of institutions are being constituted through democratic processes. The election of officials to bodies such as development committees is common. Village heads even go through an electoral process where communities disagree over succession to headship. The election of such officials has resolved conflicts within communities and made leaderships more acceptable, a recipe for good governance. Collaboration between traditional governance institutions and modern institutions is strong and government of The Gambia has effectively used these structures to reach out at communities in remote parts of the country. Evidence from this survey indicates that traditional governance institutions are quite relevant in the modern state. It is, however, evident that in the interest of acceptability, these institutions need to democratize.

Regarding the relationship between the traditional institutions and political parties, evidence from the survey has shown that the relationship has not been cordial particularly with the opposition parties and this dates back to the colonial era. This is attributable to the fact that even if the Chiefs are elected as in most cases, it is the executive who has power to appoint and remove Chiefs thereby making them subservient to the executive. Evidence from the results of the survey indicate that traditional institutions have a role to play in ensuring good governance. Chiefs and village heads play a critical role in the administration of justice in their communities. In most rural communities, modern institutions are either weak on non – existent as a consequence of this, most people living in the rural areas of the country report to the Chiefs in matters of dispute pertaining to domestic and non–domestic conflict situations, rather than to the law courts or the police station.

FGD – validation of the survey results

After the in-depth interview, results from the field were compiled. A Focus Group Discussion (FDG) was organized to validate the results of the survey. All the data collected was discussed and below is the summary of the discussions that emanated from the FDGs:

Types of traditional governance institution

The structures mentioned above are indeed the ones that are on the ground. However, in addition, community women's association also existed (and still exists). This structure is responsible for decisions on issues that concern women such as female circumcision and other traditional functions. During the colonial era the system was highly centralized but now it is decentralized. Today's Gambia has a decentralized form of traditional institutions in the form of *Kafos,* council of elders and youth development organizations, etc., unlike the pre – colonial system which was highly centralized. Another governance structure within rural communities is the Village Development Committees (VDCs). These committees are constituted

348

at the village level through a selection or election process with the general endorsement of the villagers. The VDCs have been instrumental in coordinating village development initiatives working with government and NGOs. These have been set up within communities to identify their development priorities and mobilize resources and manpower towards development programmes. The government has been quite supportive of VDCs and has channelled most development initiatives through them.

Governance institutions that existed in the past but do not exist now

Some of the traditional governance institutions still exist but in diluted and less authoritative nature (almost dormant). For example, *kabilos*, community youth organizations, council of elders and community women's association used to have a lot of authority over the community but now, due to westernization and urbanization, these institutions are barely struggling for existence. In this era, they are more pronounced in the rural than the urban settlements. In the colonial period there was in addition to the chief, a native authority which included elders from various villages, not merely the chief himself, and local treasuries were established to demonstrate that monies in the fund now belonged to local units and not the central government. The native authority assisted the chief to decide how funds collected through taxes were to be used. Also, the annual conference of chiefs started in 1944; it provided an opportunity for all chiefs to meet, listen to the policies proposed by the government officials, and respond to their views. This no longer exists as a governance institution.

On why these institutions ceased to exist

The reasons for the non-existence of the institutions have been addressed to a good extent. However, one can add that the more developed settlements are inhabited by people from different and very diverse cultural backgrounds. Therefore, the culture of one or a few groups cannot be embraced by all. In such areas one would find village development committees and ward development committees that are geared more towards development rather than traditional governance.

Has there been any change in the functions of the traditional governance institutions?

Most of the changes in the functions of the traditional governance institutions are largely to do with their effectiveness rather than their existence. Almost all the traditional institutions still exist but they do not serve the ultimate objective for their formation.

How heads of traditional governance institutions ascend to power

Ascending to power through inheritance is now history at chieftaincy level. The practice, however, still obtains at the level of Alkalolou. In recent years, politics and government interference has changed the situation in many communities with Alkalolou and chiefs coming to power through appointment. During the colonial era, the chiefs were appointed by the governor, upon recommendation of the commissioner in charge of that province. Each chief had its own court, with members coming from other prominent villages. Now the system has changed completely. Before the accession was based on inheritance and election but now they are appointed by the executive.

Changes in the process of succession

The theme has been adequately dealt with. The colonial governments used some of the traditional structures that they found in existence. For example, in Niumi, the three surnames, Jammeh, Manneh, and

Sonko were already entitled to the throne. In Fulladu, Musa Molloh was on the throne when the colonialists arrived. His descendants continued to occupy the chieftaincy until the Second Republic, when chiefs are now appointed by the executive. Yes, the process of succession has changed. Now one family has not clinched power for decades. When there is a vacuum, the executive will decide who should fill it. The advantage is that one family will not rule forever. The demerit is that the chief might not get the support of that family and might not be independent in taking certain decisions as he or she is appointed by the executive.

Roles of traditional governance institutions in national development

Their roles in national development have been limited by their inability to enforce full authority in their communities. Most of the time, they are informed instead of consulted on the development activities taking place in their communities. Traditional governance institutions have an important role to play in national development provided their authorities are respected. Traditional governance institutions play a pivotal role in the socio-economic development of The Gambia. These institutions have played an important role in the politics of the country. Some of these structures have been inherited from the colonialists who had used them to perpetuate their rule. Due to the inherent influence of the state on these structures, they have often been used as an extended arm of government, hence their inclination to defend the political interest of government. Due to their importance in politics, governments try to ensure that leadership of such structures largely consists of governing party supporters. In rare instances, some of these traditional governance institutions clandestinely work with opposition parties to avoid reprisals.

Women's Role in Traditional Governance

When women cannot resolve serious disputes or conflicts they turn to the council of elders, who are most of the time men, to take the final decisions. Female genital cutting, a traditional practice with far reaching health consequences, is an entrenched tradition with structures in place within the traditional setting for the administration of the practice. Females play a leading role in this practice but are also supported by the male folk both morally and financially. Women are usually relegated to the backseat in traditional governance because of traditional reasons. However, they are usually influential in the background. They are key actors who organize and facilitate functional governance institutions. However, it is still unusual for women to be IN the forefront of traditional governance. For instance, there are no female chiefs and of all the village heads in this country, only two are women. Kinship structures such as *kabilos* are also rarely headed by women.

Is it acceptable for women to take a leading role in traditional governance?

Women in traditional leadership positions may be confronted with challenges from men who are firm believers in patriarchal society. Often tradition and religion are used to support their position. In pre – colonial Wolof society, the Linguerre or Queen mother was a powerful voice in the running of the state. War could not be fought without the sanction of the Queen mother. The wives of local Gambian chiefs like Matarr Ceesay, Mama Tamba Janneh also held court and settled disputes while the chief was away in Bathurst (now Banjul). Today women alkalos are leading in few villages such as Juffureh. The Alkalo of Juffureh, the most famous village in The Gambia is a woman, Tako Taal. She epitomizes the emergent role of women in traditional authority. Until recently women, trailed behind in traditional governance. Women have in general not been allowed

352

to assume leading roles in these institutions and have had limited say in decision-making processes. In the recent past, however, with increased collaboration between modern and traditional governance institutions and increased democratization of traditional institutions, women have increasingly been given prominent roles in the running of these institutions. It is not uncommon for women to assume membership of the executive committees of development committees.

Relationship between political parties and traditional governance institutions

This is true of all the chiefs since the post-colonial era. Chiefs have been removed not only for supporting the opposition but also for not doing enough to ensure that the opposition does not have significant support in their districts. As regards the dilution of the institution of chieftaincy, it has to do with the dismissal and retirement of chiefs and *Alkalolou* by the then People's Progressive Party (PPP) government after independence in 1965. Chiefs who were suspected to be close to the opposition were summarily dismissed. This marked the start of the destruction of the governance institution of chiefs. In the First Republic (1962 – 1994), the PPP regime was openly hostile to the chiefs whom it suspected of siding with the opposition United Party (UP). In 1963 and March 1965, more than 20 chiefs were retired or dismissed on such grounds. The relationship between the chiefs and the political parties has not been cordial. Chiefs most of the time openly support the ruling party and also try to victimize families who support the opposition. Whenever meetings are held in their communities by the opposition, they use all means possible to make sure that the meeting is a failure.

Contributions of traditional governance institutions in the area of politics and democratization

Their contribution has always been in favour of the ruling parties which are not truly democratic. Traditional governance institutions have not been doing much in the area of politics and democratization as they always support the ruling party and antagonize the opposition. At times they took this stance because of fear of losing their positions. The increased democratization of many traditional governance institutions meant lineages which had traditionally ascended to power in the past through inheritance have lost it. In some instances, this has not been quite acceptable to the traditional ruling class who has often posed a challenge to such rulers. Their contribution usually lies in the organization and mobilization of supporters. They lay the groundwork for campaigns at their various localities by preparing meeting grounds, food, and shelter and in some instances fund raising for the ruling party.

Role of the population in decision making within the traditional governance institutions

Generally, the population is hardly consulted on day-to-day decision making in these institutions. Even when there is need for any input from the population, it is the civil society leaders who are most of the time males that are consulted on behalf of the population. However, with the advent of village development committees, a community-based organization established by an Act of Parliament, and found in virtually all settlements in the country, there is an attempt to foster inclusive decision making. This is supposed to be a representative of a cross-section of communities, through which decisions could reflect their opinions. However, it remains to be seen how effective the VDC is with regards to representing the interest of communities.

Weaknesses in the traditional governance institutions

The theme has been adequately dealt with.

Factors that facilitate or hinder the traditional institutions from playing a more important role in the development process

The theme has been thoroughly discussed. Creating an enabling environment and giving logistical support are some factors that help traditional institutions play a more important role in the development process. On the other hand, the lack of adequate consultation as well as their inability to take independent decisions limits their roles in the development process

Relevance of traditional governance institutions in today's Gambia

Traditional governance institutions are relevant to The Gambia. However, they have to be a hybrid of tradition and modern governance systems to be responsive and acceptable to the population. This is the only way they can gain the desired recognition in a rapidly developing society. Yes. The Gambia still has a largely rural population that is why traditional authority is still relevant in the rural communities. The high illiteracy rate also means the traditional governance still counts a lot as it is such institutes which matter most to the provincial people. The use of alternative dispute resolution mechanisms to build social cohesion and dispense justice, a major preoccupation of traditional chiefs is another indication of the relevance of traditional governance institutions in today's Gambia. The modern governance institutions cannot do it all particularly at the community. Issues like environment, land management and conflict resolution are better handled by the communities themselves than the modern state. Therefore, traditional governance institutions are relevant in today's Gambia. Traditional governance institutions are relevant in today's Gambia as they are intermediaries between the modern state institutions and the local people. Chiefs can also assist in maintaining peace and order within their communities.

Relationship between traditional governance institutions and modern governance institutions

There is a conflict in the relationship between the two institutions. This is because of the inability of traditional institutions to adapt to the rapidly changing development in human rights issues such as empowerment, rights of the child, gender equality, freedom of expression and association etc

Although there are advantages associated with the collaboration between modern and traditional governance institutions, the downside of it is the increased interference of central government in the running of traditional governance institutions. These interferences border on traditional ascension to power, and increased reliance on modern institutions for arbitration and conflict resolution.

Have modern governance institutions been helpful to traditional governance institutions in their fulfilment of their roles and responsibilities?

Modern governance institutions have been helpful in many ways by supporting traditional institutions with human and material resources necessary for an enabling environment. They also ensure that there is no abuse of power at the traditional institution level. Difficult community cases are also handled by the modern system.

Independence of traditional governance institutions/authorities from modern governance institutions/authorities

Nowadays traditional governance institutions have some degree of independence as long as their decisions are not viewed as abuse of power by the government or contravene the policies of the ruling party.

Relationship between modern and traditional governance institutions in the past

One significant change in the relationship between the two institutions is the lack of consultation regarding development projects in the communities, which weakens the position among the population. Another change is government allowing people to bypass traditional structures and launch complaints directly at the modern courts or police.

Measures that can best improve the relationship between modern and traditional governance institutions

Government should ensure that there are proper consultations with traditional governance institutions prior to the implementation of any development projects in the communities. Also, through sensitization, the government should encourage people to use traditional institutions to resolve issues like land disputes, conflict resolutions among others rather taking these matters to the modern institutions directly.

What can be done to make the contribution of traditional governance institutions in national development more effective?

Traditional institutions should be the link between government and development agencies on the one hand and the communities on the other hand. Any failure to pass through the link would be seen as undermining the traditional structures and therefore weakening their authority.

As traditional institutions can dispense justice and resolve conflicts at community level; in order to make their contribution more effective to national development, they should have clear definition of their authority.

9

Towards Arab-African Integration in the Struggle against Western Hegemony and Imperialism:

A Critical Perspective

i)   Introduction

While colonialism takes place when a country is dominated politically by another developed country, imperialism broadly means an imposition of the stronger nations' will or rule over the weaker nations by means of force or threat to use force or otherwise. Imperialism goes with serious territorial, political, economic, social, religious and cultural implications. Once the will or rule of the stronger nations is established or imposed over the weaker nations, the consequences of this unfortunate development could be seriously devastating as the victim nation automatically loses its sovereignty, cultural and religious identity and the sovereign right of the people to self-determination (A.K. Chaturvedi, 2006).

The advent of political independence around the middle of the 20th century did not necessarily prevent the continuation of imperialism throughout the African continent. One of the most interesting stories of Western colonial rule and imperialism in Africa is that the colonial powers deliberately and strategically left their languages, their political, economic and legal systems behind, thereby denying the Africans the golden opportunity to return to the roots of their civilization as well as moral and cultural values. What further complicated the situation is the fact that the first generation of leaders in post-independence Africa were trained, oriented and strategically directed to protect the economic, political and strategic interest of their foreign masters or Western allies. This explains why colonialism is referred to as one of the worst and the most inhuman forms of socio-political and cultural injustice that humanity has ever committed against their fellow human beings (A.A Senghore, 1999).

Colonialism is, in my humble opinion, a crime against humanity because it did not only distort but it effectively ended the history and destroyed the identity of the colonized peoples whether they are African or otherwise. It so happened that both African and Arab nations found themselves in this unfortunate situation which has left long lasting devastating effects on their respective cultures, economics, social organizations and the regions particularly Islam which brings together millions of Arabs and Africans across the African continent and beyond. This is why the two peoples who share a lot in common including their destiny need to come together to rescue the current situation and while doing so, cultural integration could be a good option.

In fact, Arab-African integration started in the early days of Islam when the Prophet was still alive. Africa was Islam's second destination after Makkah. About eight years before Prophet Muhammad migrated from Makkah to Al-Madinatu Munaw-wara, 10 senior companions (Sahabahs) led by Ousman Bun Afan and his wife

Roqiya Bint al-Rasul (SAW) and Abdu Rahman Bun Awf migrated to Abesainiyah where the ruler Al-Najjashiy greeted them with warm welcome (Al-Min 1993: 7). Islam remained Africa's main and only heavenly religion for about 11 centuries before the arrival of other faiths and denominations from outside the continent. Today, more than half of the people living on the continent profess Islam and about 25% of the Muslims of the World live in Africa (Robinson 2004: 27). This chapter critically examines the prospects of a future Arab African integration in a bid to challenge Western/European hegemonic and imperialist policies and conspiracies against the Arab Africans. The question of Arab African cultural interaction is a comprehensive one because it will have to deal with a period of more than 1400 years, a huge continent and millions of people of different socio-cultural, ethnic, political and economic backgrounds. However, Arabs and Africans after having lived together as Muslims or otherwise for more than 14 centuries are no strangers to each other, the two peoples share a lot in common including the important factors, values and the most solid foundations of integration. Such unifying factors and values include the following:

• Common grounds for integration

❖ **Religion:** The majority of Africans, Arabs and non-Arabs alike, profess Islam both as a religion and way of life. Since the spread of Islam into Africa, communities, tribal and ethnic groups as well as individuals across the continent started to adhere submissively to its fundamental teachings, obligations and institutions. Thus, after professing Islam for more than 14 centuries, Islam becomes a natural part of African identity.

❖ **The Arabic Language:** Arabic was the language of revelation of Allah to Prophet Muhammad (SAW) and consequently, the language of the Sacred Book (The Holy Quran), the Law (al-Shariah) and Prayers (al-Salat wa Du-a). Although most African Muslims continue to speak their respective languages and vernaculars, Arabic remains the primary language of Islam as a religion and civilization, it became dominant in North Africa and much of the Sahara region. Arabic words spread into the languages of many African societies particularly in describing matters of religion, governance, warfare, trade and Muslim diplomacy (Robinson 2004: 27). The Arabic language continues to win high respect and admiration in hearts of millions of Muslims throughout the length and breathe of the continent. Several major African languages are heavily influenced by the Arabic language to such an extent that the percentage of Arabic words in some of those languages could be as high as 75% or 80% while in some others; it could be as high as 40 – 50%. Hausa, Swahili and Somali are good examples of the first category, whereas 'Fulani and Mandinka' stand for the second category. Thus, like Islam as a religion and way of life, Arabic is another crucial unifying factor that could perpetually bring Arabs and Africans together as common people.

❖ **Arabs and Africans share a heritage of Western European colonial past:** Using several methods and features of subjugations, European imperialists occupied many African territories and areas to bring them under colonial rule. The methods used were military conquest, threat otherwise known as 'Gunboat diplomacy' and peaceful signing of treaties where in most cases, the rulers involved did not know the implication of the treaties they were signing. Countries/nations like Algeria, Morocco, Egypt, Ghana, Nigeria, Niger Tunisia, Uganda and the Senegambia Region and Mauritania are among those Arab African nations that went through the bitter experiences of European imperialism and colonial past (Barkindo 1994: 28 – 38). Similarly, the two peoples have so much in common that they strongly challenged and successfully ended their long history of European imperialism and colonial rule (Abdullah 1989: 17 – 35).

❖ **Victims of Western hegemonic policies and aggressive wars**: Another important experience that Arabs and Africans shared in common is that they were on different occasions victims of the Western/American hegemonic policies and wars of aggression. Egypt, Algeria, Libya, Sudan and several Muslim territories in West Africa particularly the 'Fulani' Kingdom led by Ousman Dan-Fodio, the 'Tuklor' Kingdom led by Sheikh Omar Futi, the Senegambia Region, the Samouri Touray Dynasty on the Niger River and the Fadlullah Dynasty in Central Africa i.e. Lake Chad, were all victims of European imperialist and hegemonic policies and long and protracted wars of aggression. Palestine, Iraq, Syria, Iran and Afghanistan in Western and South Asia have also been subjected to the same hostile and aggressive policies of European imperialism and hegemony. America and its Western allies have always used their position as permanent members of the United Nations Security Council, their veto power on the Council and their influence over international financial institutions like the World bank, the IMF and GATT (WTO) to perpetuate their domination of the so-called "Third World" countries including African and Arab nations. The current international economic system was created by the agreement at Britton Woods in the United States. It rests on three pillars:

iii.   The International Monetary Fund (IMF)
iv.   The World Bank and
v.   The General Agreement on Tariffs and Trade (GATT), which has now been replaced by the World Trade Organization (WTO). The declared Objectives of these international economic institutions are as follows:

"The IMF was designed to deal with currency exchange and balance of payments problems stemming from international trade."

"The World Bank was created to assist in the development process of Member-States especially to arrange for loans to facilitate economic projects."

"GATT (now WTO) was the mechanism by which states could resolve disputes and increase volume of international trade through the lifting of national restrictions" (Diehl 1997: 199).

There is no doubt that the objectives highlighted above are noble ones and the institutions concerned respectively functioned towards achieving such noble objectives. However, it is also an established fact that the major international financial institutions do carry out and perpetuate their hegemonic policies against the Third World countries.

- **The Arabs and Africans belong to the same category of nations referred to in the international system as "Third World Countries".** On this forum too, Arabs and Africans share a lot among themselves including their common desire to have more power over international economic regimes in order to assure that the so-called 'Third World Countries' get all the advantages of the international economic system and financial institutions and also to take part in the creation, maintenance and governance of the international economic regimes (Murphy M. 1997: 210 – 214).

- **Common membership in global organizations**: Arabs and Africans share a common membership in several international intergovernmental and non-governmental organizations. These include the United Nations and its affiliate agencies, the Islamic Conference Organizations, the Arab League, the African Union and the Group of 77.

Thus, the values and institutions highlighted above and possibly several others are critically important factors that could constitute a common ground for Arabs and Africans to forge an effective union in their struggle against Western hegemony and imperialism. However, there are diametrically opposing forces operating on the ground, which could and would definitely block any efforts by Arabs and Africans to form a united front of any kind against Western interests. Such forces are deeply seated in the minds and hearts of Arab Africans who are either unable or unwilling to part with them. Therefore, in this section, we will consider some of the most important factors that may work against any meaningful Arab African integration with a view to forming a united front against Western imperialism in the present international political system.

- **Obstacles to Arab African Integration**
- **Colonial Legacies**

The advent of independence from colonial rule around the middle of the 20th century did not usher in a complete break with colonial institutions and legacies. One of the most difficult obstacles that impeded Africa's integration in the post-colonial period is the impact of different legacies left behind by colonial powers. English and French colonial rules, for instance, left behind their respective legacies in the legal and economic systems, political institutions and other aspects of Western civilization. The existence of bitter rivalry and imperial ambitions among European nations and rulers seeking to occupy different portions of African territories resulted in the apportionment of the continent by the colonial powers into so many colonies, protectorates and settlements. Since the colonial powers came from different socio-cultural backgrounds, spoke different languages and followed or applied different practices and systems of government and administration, it was inevitable that they would leave behind different legacies in their respective colonial territories. These differences in their colonially inherited values and systems impeded efforts aimed at nation building, economic progress and political integration on various parts of the continent. Issues like language and colonial partition of territories constituting the same geographical, historical and ethnic region and planting the seeds of separatists' movements in some regions are among the Western colonial legacies that continue to effectively prevent any form of serious economic and political integration across the African continent. Let us take the Senegambia Region and the State of Cameroon as examples.

Sene-Gambian integration: A lost cause

Senegal and The Gambia constitute one natural geographical unit, they belong to the same geographical, historical, cultural and ethnic region given that Senegal actually sandwiches the tiny but naturally beautiful Republic of The Gambia. The two entities therefore have every opportunity to be united and as Awasom aptly argues that "The Gambia is right inside the belly of Senegal and nowhere else is union more required and easier to achieve in Africa than between these two States given that almost every Gambian has a Senegalese blood relative" (Awasom 2006: 94 – 95). But due to marked differences in their colonially inherited values and legacies i.e. languages and economic and political systems, the question of union between the two states has proven to be out of the question. The Senegambia region was carved into two distinct territories by the French and British colonial authorities in 1889 and placed under separate administrations (Awasom 2006: 95).

During the few years that preceded The Gambia's political independence from Britain, many efforts were made on both sides to integrate the two entities and such efforts were apparently supported by the two colonial powers particularly Britain. But such efforts ended in vain because the parties were not prepared to make the

366

sacrifices necessary for the success of such a laudable venture. Gambians were not willing to surrender certain principal areas to the proposed union executive. They made it clear that in the event of union with Senegal the key areas of internal administration, the police, the civil service and local government matters, the legal and educational systems and the question of maintenance of close ties with Britain and the Commonwealth were to remain under Gambian control (Awasom 2006: 97). Senegal too was not prepared to part with any of the main colonial values it has inherited from France for the sake of a union with The Gambia. On the other hand, one could also ask whether Britain was really genuine in her support for The Gambia to be united with Senegal. This is because The Gambia achieved its independence from Britain in 1965 and full sovereignty with republican status in 1970 without the question of integration with Senegal being given a definite answer or addressed in any concrete form. Thus, despite signing dozens of collaborative treaties by the two countries since The Gambia became independent in 1965 and despite making a concrete attempt to establish a form of loose union between them in 1982, that was when the Senegambia Confederation was formed, Senegal and Gambia are still far apart. As the two countries continue to guard jealously their respective colonially inherited values and systems, there is, as yet no sign of readiness and sincere commitment on both sides to integrate into a single union republic.

The case of Cameroon

The state of Cameroon was subjected to the same European experiences starting from the last quarter of the 19th century when it became a German protectorate in 1884. Awasom explains that "during the First World War in Africa, German Cameroon was conquered by the Allies and divided disproportionately into the British (Western) and French (Eastern) spheres" with Britain acquiring just one-fifth of the territory formally occupied by Germany

(Awasom 2006: 90 – 92).   Many of the ethnic groups of Cameroon
who are separated by the Anglo-French partition of the country are
situated on both sides of the territory particularly in the Anglophone
North-West and South-West provinces and the Francophone West
and Littoral provinces (Awasom 2006: 91) Thus the Anglo-French
partition of Cameroon and the differences in their colonially inherited
values and systems have created difficult identity crises, which pose
a serious threat to efforts aimed at nation building, economic progress,
maintenance of peace and order and sustainable development in that
part of Africa.

- ## The experience of other African countries

In North-East Africa, Somalia and Sudan were subjected to similar
European colonial or imperialist experiences.   Somalia was
partitioned into five territories namely, British Somaliland, French
Somaliland, Italian Somaliland, the North Frontier District in Kenya
and Ogadin in Ethiopia.   This was followed by the Italian
proclamation in 1936 of the establishment of Italian colony in East
Africa, which was called "Africa Orientale Italiana" or the Italian East
Africa. The move merged and reconfigured the territories of Eritrea,
Somalia and Ethiopia along ethno-linguistic lines into one colony
(Zewde 2006: 54 - 55). Elsewhere in Sudan, the British government,
which was said to have supported the unification of Somalis, followed
a diametrically opposite policy. There, Britain planted the seeds of
separatism in Southern Sudan, which after independence became one
of Africa's longest and most destructive civil wars. The British
government effectively sealed off Southern Sudan from the northern
part of the country and the northern traders were barred from the
South. Their declared objective was to protect the Southerners from
the habitual raids and exactions of the Northerners. In pursuance of
this hegemonic policy, the British government excluded Arabic
language in favour of Southern languages, and mother tongues, closed
Islamic schools and banned Muslim preachers in the South. At the

368

same time, Christian Missionaries were encouraged and given every available opportunity to flourish in Southern Sudan.

However, it was later understood that the real objective of the colonial administration in Sudan was to stop the spread and prosperity of Islam in the South and also to ultimately sow the seeds of Southern separatism (Zewde 2006: 56). In this part of the continent religion was used by the colonial authorities to divide the Africans in Sudan and keep them apart. This policy, arguably, did not serve the interests of the two religions (Islam and Christianity) separating the two peoples in Sudan. Rather the policy only brought about confusion and misunderstanding among a people who belonged to the same ethnic, cultural and geographical identity. With southern Sudan achieving independence in July 2011, the war of independence, which was waged by the South against the North, was over and one would have thought that the two independent countries would now put their bitter and painful history behind them and lead their peoples into a new era of peaceful coexistence, good neighbourliness and friendly bilateral relationship. However, it is very unfortunate, devastating and heart breaking to watch the South and North Sudanese begin a new era of wars and conflicts between their two sovereign states. This time is not a war of independence but rather a war or conflict over borderlines separating the two countries. It is another destructive war over who owns what territory and who should have a legitimate claim and sovereign right over a few oil fields and other natural resources along the borderlines separating the two countries.

Finally, the present configuration of the African continent into so many nation states is another legacy of Western colonialism, which like those highlighted above will definitely block any serious effort or attempt to actualize any meaningful form of Arab African integration aimed at making a united stand against Western hegemony. Thus, unless Arabs and Africans who happened to be victims of Western colonial rule are willing and morally prepared to break with the values and systems they have colonially inherited from the West, they will never be able to unite themselves and their efforts to challenge effectively Western hegemonic and imperialist policies against Islam and the Islamic world in particular and the African people in general.

Let us now move on to consider another difficult issue, which like colonial legacies will definitely be a major obstacle to Arab African integration as it has been proven to be in the past when efforts were made to achieve regional or sub-regional integration in many parts of the continent. That is the issue of identity and politics of belonging. This is what the next section explores.

Identity and politics of belonging

Ethnic and regional politics are increasingly an ongoing phenomenon in Africa's political processes. References to race, ethnicity, religion, political ideology, people of different backgrounds, district or province of origin have in many cases prominently featured in the daily languages of politicians and political elites, community leaders and the main actors of other interest groups in African societies. Trade unions, political parties, service delivery organizations, socio-cultural groups, economic interest groups and political and think-tanks on various parts of the continent have always been dominated by a particular ethnic, tribal or religious group or proponents of a given political ideology. In Africa today, the politics of identity and belonging has even entered the realm of African academia. Some Cameroonian academics argue that democracy in Cameroon should be more of an ethnic right than simply an issue of one man one vote. That is because there are small and big tribes and small and big ethnic groups all over the continent. Thus, as a real entity, each of these groups should be taken into consideration in a well-conceived democracy. A Cameroonian academic argues that when a demographically superior ethnic group is part of the picture, there is a big temptation that in applying the principle of democratic free choice the ethnic multitude would express itself in favour of the strong ethnic group, which in this way would stifle those ethnic groups who are demographically weak (Mono Ndjona 1997: 102 – 103). The argument is that although it may be fair enough to recognize the one-man-one-vote democratic principle, this democratic principle would defeat itself when, through that vote, only one ethnic group expresses its hegemony. This amounts to self-contradiction since democracy in this sense would be serving the totalitarian interests of those it has enabled to raise (Nyamnjoh, 2006). Academics are among the cream of society not only in Africa but elsewhere too and if some of them are beginning to envisage a democracy of ethnic groups as long as those groups remain a reality, that shows how seriously the continent is affected by the politics of identity and ethnic belonging.

Many parts of Africa particularly, the North-eastern, Central and Western regions, have been ridden with inter-state and intra-state conflicts since the beginning of the second half of the last century due mainly to the clash of identities and excesses of the politics of belonging. The Rwanda-Burundi conflicts, the wars that ravaged Liberia and Sierra Leone in the 1990s, the Eritrea-Ethiopia conflicts and the ongoing Darfur conflicts are good examples of inter-state and intra-state conflicts caused mainly by the clash of identities and the excesses of the politics of belonging. Somalia represents the most unfortunate case of all these conflicts. This is perhaps the only African country where the population is constituted by the same people (black Africans) speaking the same language (Somali) and they profess the same religion (Islam), follow the same school of thought in Islamic jurisprudence and located within one geographical unit. Somalis are bound together by the necessary elements or values that constitute the major expressions of identity (i.e. religion, language and ethnic origin). Thus, as it was observed regarding the

Senegambia case, in Somalia too, I would say, 'nowhere is unity more required, urgent and easy to achieve in Africa than in that country.'

Elsewhere in Northeast Africa, the conflict in the Western Sudanese province of Darfur is another unfortunate mark in African political history. Like Northern Sudan, the Western part of the country has a Muslim majority population, the so-called Arab African divide is invisible and where it exists it does not justify the war of unprecedented ferocity characterized by massive destruction of life and property and mass displacement of people and animal that the conflict has led to. Thus, the question as to "What unique identity or set of values are the warring sides in Darfur defending or protecting against each other" has not been and probably will never be satisfactorily answered. Similarly, identity politics lay at the root cause of the prolonged civil war that ravaged the Southern part of Sudan. Finally, with the politics of identity and ethnic belonging still raising its ugly head all over the continent, any meaningful form of Arab African integration aimed at making a united front to challenge effectively Western hegemony is very unlikely to happen.

Arab disunity

With Arabs deeply divided over several key questions in international relations such as the Palestinian and Iraqi conflicts, the Arab Israeli relations and America's attitude toward the Islamic World, there is little hope that they will ever be in a position to form a united front with their fellow Africans to effectively face the challenge of Western hegemony. The inability of Arabs to agree among themselves and make a united stand in the international political arena is one of the saddest stories of their contemporary history. Arabs are held by non-Arab Muslims in high esteem, they see them as role models and look to them for an Islamic global leadership that will one day free Muslims, their political leaders and service delivery institutions from the conspiracies and hostile policies of European and Western hegemony. One would often ask why is it that the North Africans are still unable to unite themselves into one Great Maghreb Union despite the fact that they have every opportunity to do so? With the exception of Libya, the North African Arabs do not have different colonial legacies rather they were all colonized by France and therefore their colonially inherited values and systems are one and the same, they share the same language (Arabic), religion (Islam), ethnic origin (either Arab or Berber) and constituted by the same geographical unit. Despite possessing all the necessary unifying elements or values, which are the major expressions of a nation's identity, there is no sign of the North Africans' readiness or even willingness to form one Great Maghrib Union. Thus, unless Arabs particularly African Arabs are able to put their house in order, there is no hope of realizing any form of an Arab African union, which can realistically stand up to face the enormous challenges posed by Western hegemonic and imperialist policies and conspiracies against them.

Poverty and Corruption

The existence of abject poverty and widespread corruption in many parts of the continent raised serious moral questions about Africa's readiness to form a viable alliance with their fellow Arabs to challenge effectively Western hegemonic policies. It is almost certain that money was used and would continue to be used by the West to pursue its colonial and imperialist objectives.

The ineffectiveness of international organizations

There are few international inter-governmental and non-governmental organizations comprising only Arabs and Africans in their membership. The existing organizations of this type, such as the Organization of Islamic Conference, the Arab League, the African Union and the Group of 77 are so weak and ineffective in the international political arena that their voices are not heard at all in the world's major political events. They cannot make any impact on or influence decisions and major events in the international system, neither can they shape major policies and processes of today's international politics and global governance. Modern international organizations are playing a major role in the current international political system. The more usual image of the role of international organizations today is that of an instrument being used by members for the articulation of specific objectives. This is particularly the case with international intergovernmental organizations where members are sovereign states with powers to do many things to serve the interest of their respective people. Another important image of the role of international organizations is that they can be used as an arena or forum within which members can act in pursuance of their own interests. In this case, the organizations provide meeting places for their members to come together to exchange views and pursue their respective interests (Archer 2006: 68 – 96). Thus, in this modern age of global governance, international organizations do not only assist the functioning process of the international political system but also they are capable of bringing huge returns and benefits to their members. In conclusion, with the type of weak and ineffective international organizations of Arab Africans of today, it is clear from the above exposition that there is little chance for them to be able to use those organizations as an instrument or arena for the articulation and eventual realization of their common objectives in the international political system. In view of this political reality of the Arabs and Africans one may be justified to suggest that one important step in their drive to tackle collectively the difficult question of Western hegemony and imperialist policies and conspiracies against them is to strengthen those international organizations by way of making the sacrifices and concessions necessary for the effective functioning of such institutions in the modern world.

Lastly, another major issue which can be considered a critical and fundamental obstacle to the realization of Arab African integration is the presence of different faiths and beliefs throughout the continent. Undoubtedly, the West which is largely Christian would attempt to exploit this Muslim-Christian divide among Africans to perpetuate its hegemonic and imperialist presence on the continent. Notwithstanding that in some part of the continent, like the Senegambia region African Muslims and Christians have been leaving together in peace and harmony for several centuries.

Absence of political will and effective leadership in the Islamic world

There is almost a total absence of sincere commitment, political will and effective political leadership in Africa and the Arab World to organize Arabs and Africans into a viable force capable of challenging Western hegemony and European economic imperialism in the present international political system. The former Libyan leader Muamar Ghadafi was known for his pan-African's tendencies and attitudes in the continent's contemporary politics and development drive. He loved Africa and the African people and his country spent billions and billions of United States dollars in the cause of the continent's development and possible unification. Ghadafi lacked the necessary support from his fellow African leaders and the necessary moral legitimacy and credentials to actualize the long-awaited dream of Africa's integration and eventual unification. Most importantly, he missed the opportunity to actualize his dream of a United States of Africa. Now that Ghadafi is gone the continent is waiting to see the birth of a new pan-Africanist who will succeed the likes of Nkrumah, Patrice Lumumba and Muamar Ghadafi of Ghana, the Democratic Republic Congo and Libya respectively.

Endless domestic conflicts and the ensuring crisis

The seemingly endless conflicts and the ever increasing political and governance crisis that these conflicts have resulted in continue to be another serious hurdle or obstacle to regional and sub-regional integration across the continent. Unless such conflicts are completely or substantially resolved and the political climates in various countries stabilized, integration of any kind will simply be out of the question. The paragraphs that follow give a very brief but clear picture of the domestic conflicts, some of the consequences and the ensuring crisis that have engulfed various parts of the continent.

In the few years preceding independence and self-rule in Africa many Africans and their friends all over the continent and beyond had high hopes and expectations that with political independence and liberation there were numerous opportunities for the indigenous leaders to prove the worth and dignity of the African people. They expected the entire continent to enjoy the fruits of an effective economic and political governance system which would have ensured sustainable economic growth, lasting peace and security and that eventually the African people would fully realize all the potential that God has bestowed on them as a great continent. However, ordinary Africans are bewildered and seriously disappointed by the outcome of several decades of self-rule which is nothing but gross mismanagement of economic resources, rampant corruption, nepotism, political insecurity, decline of state power and authority, endless coups and coup attempts, abject poverty, military and autocratic rule, overstaying in power and many more. These and other crises have dominated the economic, political and socio-cultural environment in post-colonial and self-governing independent Africa. In fact, the crises have now become the order of the day across the length and breadth of the continent. It is very obvious that the majority of West Africans are now lost or are losing faith and

376

confidence in their political leaders and government systems. These disappointing results and experiences have indeed raised serious questions about the quality of the character, mind and leadership attitude of the post independent African leaders (Obadina: 2008). The most frustrating of all obstacles and problems of African Governance are its persistent and chronic domestic conflicts and leadership disputes which have eventually destroyed the foundations of the state in countries like Guinea Bissau and Somalia today, Liberia, the Cote d'Ivoire, Rwanda and Brunei and Sierra Leone in the recent past.

Some consequences

Economic exploitation, political repression and the eventual failure of the social welfare and public service delivery systems throughout West Africa

Millions of Africans are exposed to severe economic hardships, political instability and socio-economic insecurity

Electoral malpractices, disputes over election results, persistent refusal by incumbent leaders to share power with political opponents,

The spread of civilian led autocratic rule and military dictatorships which block all means of democratic and peaceful leadership succession, military coups like the recent coups in Mali and Guinea Bissau,

The unprecedented rise of the cost of living and basic commodities at a time when only 4% of national budgets are currently spent on agriculture, as well as the dramatic increase in the cost of fertilizer,

The continuous rise in the cost of fuel, the instances of daily power cuts because of inadequate generating capacity or the inability of the state to provide enough fuel for power generators,

The absence of potential foreign investors from many countries in the sub-region due to poor infrastructure and communication facilities, and poor human rights records of governments across West Africa.

The senseless war that Boko Haram is waging against the Nigerian federation represents a new method, level and timing of religious and ethnic violence in the sub-regional.

These and many other problems continue to obstruct and sometimes derail the governing process in Africa South of The Sahara, where the removal of entrenched autocratic civilians and military dictators has become an impossible task.

Efforts aimed at the eradication or even substantial reduction of corruption, nepotism, favoritism and other administrative mall practices have all turned out to be a formidable task holding back socio-economic development and progress in the whole of the West Africa Sub-region. In view of this background the realization of any meaningful Arab – African integration whether economic, political and cultural integration, becomes virtually impossible (Senghore, 2013)

- The Crisis in Northern Mali
- The current conflict in North Mali could constitute a special obstacle to Arab African mutual understanding and interaction at various levels particularly within the West African Sub-region. The main players in the conflict and the leading actors of the current international global political system as well as the African sub-system continue to blame the Islamists in Northern Mali as being the cause of the conflict. However, there is a very strong opinion which refuses to attribute the cause of the Mali conflict to religion or more especially to the so-called Islamic fundamentalism. This opinion which seems

to be the most realistic of all the opinions on the cause of the Mali conflict squarely laid the blame for starting the Mali crisis on ethnicity and racism. Ethnic and racial differences are in actual fact lying at the bottom of the Northern Mali crisis. In other words, the so-called Arab-Tauoregs who are a distinct ethnic or racial group from the black Africans are no more willing to live together with their fellow Africans under the banner of the same state. Thus, they are fighting for the creation of an independent Arab –Tuareg nation in Northern Mali to be called the "State of Azawad" (Diakete, 2013).

The section below gives a brief but clear picture of the Mali crisis and the ensuring consequences of that conflict.

Mali crisis

Since Mali become independent from France in 1960, the West African country has suffered from various destabilizing events which include droughts, a series of coups, 23 years of military dictatorship, internal conflicts and rebellions spearheaded mainly by Tuareg rebels in the North and being completely saddled with a chronic budget deficit making it heavily dependent on foreign aid and the money sent home by millions working overseas. With all these problems the former Western Sudanese republic (now Republic of Mali) had made significant successes in food production and democratization. Mali is said to be self-sufficient in food production. This is mainly due to the fertile Niger River basin in the southern and Eastern Parts of the country.

Regarding democratization, Mali was able to break with its long years of military rule when it successfully conducted its first democratic election in 1992. Thus, the first democratically elected president of Mali took power in 1992 and since then the country's democratic credentials and development achievements have continued to grow from strength to strength until the 22nd of March 2012 when Africa's most senseless coup took place in that country.

This coup has completely destroyed Mali's new democratic achievements. One of the reasons that make the coup puzzling is that it came only a few weeks before the country's next democratic elections. The coup leaders justified their action by citing the country's inability to defeat the Tuareg rebels in the North. In other words, the coup came in the aftermath of a series of losses suffered by the Malian Army in the face of the Tuaregs, who were apparently strengthened following an influx of weaponry from Libya transported there by the Tuareg rebels who were fighting for Colonel Ghadafi until his death in 2012.

("Timbuktu's Sidi Yahia mosque attached by Mali Militants", BBC news, 2 July 2012; "Mali Tuareg rebels declare independence in the north", BBC News, 6 April 2012, Security Council Press Statement on Mali, 10 April 2012, "Senior UN official condemns 'alarming reports of sexual violence in Mali," UN News Center, 10 April 2012, UNHCR deeply concerned as Mali crisis worsens).

The biggest question here is whether the new military rulers who were now heading to northern Mali have been able to reverse the series of losses the country's army had been suffering, before the coup, at the hands of the Tuareg rebels. The answer is obviously a definitive "NO;" in fact, the Tuaregs had registered significant successes in the days, weeks and months that followed the coup as a result of the confusion in which the central government in Bamako has been thrown and which seriously weekend it. Demoralized and rendered ineffective by the absence of a strong, strategically focused and capable political and military leaderships, the Malia Army continued to suffer significant losses until the time France decided to intervene.

Thus, on 6th April 2012, the National Movement for the Liberation of Azawad (MNLA) formed in 2011 mainly by armed Tuareg fighters returning from Libya, proclaimed independence. The MNLA fought together with the Islamist group, Ansar Adin, virtually captured most of the territories in the North, including the cities of ancient Tumbuckutu, (Tmbukutou), Kida, Gau and other towns. It is worth mentioning at this juncture that the Tuareg rebels engaged the Malian in a series of skirmishes in the vast desert of the nation in the 1960s, the early 1990s, and again in 2006. To conclude, the 22 March 2012 coup has definitely and woefully failed to achieve its stated objective. As a result of the coup and the ensuing developments relating to the country's chronic leadership crisis, this vast West African country has again been condemned to its usual status of being one of the world's poorest nations despite being Africa's third biggest gold producer. The people of Mali have again suffered serious setbacks in their continuous struggle to end the ever-escalating militancy by the Tuareg rebels who took up arms demanding greater rights for their people since the 1960s and 1970s. As a result of the renewed conflict and the leadership crisis, the human rights situation in Mali remains in dire situation with latest reports revealing terrible incidents of violations and atrocities against both sides, interference with the rights of individuals and groups, the right to liberty and security of persons, the right to privacy, the right freedom of movement, assembly, association, freedom of speech and other rights violations committed during the renewed fighting in the Northern part of the country (Senghore, 2013). France and its allies have so far failed to bring back stability and return Mali to normalcy and to democratic constitutional rule while the sub-regional grouping is still undecided about what to do exactly to once and for all and the crisis in that country (Timbuktu) Sidi Yahia mosque attached by Mali Militants," BBC news, 2 July 2012; "Mali Tuareg rebels declare independence in the north," BBC News, 6 April 2012, Security Council Press Statement on Mali, 10 April 2012, "Senior UN official condemns 'alarming reports of sexual violence in Mali," UN News Center, 10 April 2012, "UNHCR deeply concerned as Mali crisis worsens"). The problem in Northern Mail is further complicated by the fact that some of the neighbouring countries like Mauritania and Algeria which share the same root as the Mali Tuaregs do not seem to be very clear on their stand on the conflict. They have not come out clearly with any serious statement either condemning or supporting the war in this West African vast country. Thus, if proper care is not taken by the stakeholders both within and outside Africa, the Mali crisis could further develop into a form of racial or ethnic tension between the Arab –Tuareg of North and West Africa on one hand and the black Africans of Mali and West African on the other (Senghore, 2013).

Conclusion and suggestions

This chapter has examined the problems and difficulties that a future Arab African alliance to counter Western hegemony and imperialism will face in the process of global governance, which is basically the sum effort of managing global affairs (Archer 2006: 108). Despite sharing some major values and cultural traditions that constitute a natural basis for unification and despite being subjected to bitter experiences in the past that make the issue of integration very urgent and easily achievable, the Arabs and Africans are still apart. This chapter argues that different colonial legacies, the deeply seated politics of identity and ethnic belonging, the Arabs' disunity, poverty and rampant corruption, weak international intergovernmental organizations and the absence of political will and exemplary leadership, constitute major obstacles on the road to a future Arab African integration. Thus, if the Arabs and their fellow Africans are serious about integration with a view to tackling collectively Western hegemony and imperialism they may be advised to do the following:

1. The Arabs and Africans, who badly need each other, must forge some form of relevant economic and political union/integration for the betterment of their peoples and communities. For this to happen they must be prepared to make a complete or substantial break with their colonial past

and substitute the colonially inherited values with those that they share among themselves. As shown above, the ongoing ideological, intellectual and systemic problems being experienced in many African societies are due, mainly, to the introduction of Western ways of thinking, judging, believing and managing the affairs of people by the colonialists into those societies. Muslim scholars, intellectuals and political leaders who have been unduly influenced by the Western civilizations, its scientific and technological advancements and other colonially inherited values were very instrumental in spreading and enhancing European values and colonial legacies in the Muslim world (Attas 1993: 15). The noble goal of doing away with Western colonial legacies cannot be achieved without big sacrifices on both sides and in fact, the process could be costly to some leaders as they may be removed from office. At this juncture, it may be relevant to remember the experience of the Turkish Islamists when they won the elections in that country in the 1990s. Upon becoming Turkish first Islamist Prime-Minister in the modern time, Mr. Najmu al-din Arabakan declared his intention to create one Islamic common market, bringing together the leading economies and major powers of the Islamic world. Arabakan was convinced that Muslim countries had huge natural and material resources, which enabled them to create a common market of their own and circulate such resources among themselves without Western or European interferences. To concretize his dream, he called for a summit of Islamic countries referred to as the "D-8" or the developing eight countries. However, as a result of Western hegemonic policies and imperialist conspiracies, Mr Arabakan could not achieve his dream; he was overthrown by the Turkish Army and later banned from politics in that country. Consequently, Turkey's first Islamist Prime Minister of the modern times became a victim and major casualty of Western hegemony.

2.   The Arabs and Africans need to do away with the politics of identity and ethnic, regional or ideological belonging.
3.   Arabs need to be more visible in many parts of the continent where there is large concentration of African Muslims.

4. Arabs need to take a leading role in global efforts aimed at solving Africa's chronic problems such as poverty, corruption, killer diseases and bad governance. In this case, it will not be enough only for the Arabs to send aids and material assistance but they should also be physically present in many parts of the continent so as to influence the transition morally culturally.

5. Arabs must stop their differences and disagreements with immediate effect.

6. The Arabs also needs] to pay equal attention to Africa's non-Muslim communities and try to contribute in a very significant way to the solution of their socio-economic and political problems

7. Racial discrimination must be rooted out of the Arab African communities.

8. They should strengthen their common intergovernmental organizations and make them more responsive to their needs in the international political system.

9. Islamic teachings in the areas of economic and political governance, interstate relations, intra-Muslim relations and forms of socio-cultural relations or interactions must be enforced.

10. Most importantly, political, religious and community leaders of both sides must be sincerely committed and willing to forging an African alliance to challenge Western hegemony and economic imperialism.

11. Textbooks and other materials taught or used in schools, colleges and universities must be revisited so that the teaching and learning processes would reflect the new desire for integration and to correct the misconceptions and wrong understanding that the two peoples have about each other's cultures, ethnic origin and social settings and values.

12. There is need to encourage and indeed actualize inter-Arab African trade, investments and cultural exchanges.

10

Responsible Leadership and Effective Governance: A Prerequisite for Peace, Stability And Sustainable Development in Africa

I.   Introduction

In the few years preceding independence and self-rule in Africa many Africans and their friends all over the continent and beyond had high hopes and expectations that with political independence and liberation, opportunities would abound for the indigenous leaders to prove the worth and dignity of the African people. They expected that with responsible and committed leadership across Africa, the entire continent would enjoy the fruits of effective economic and political governance systems, which would have ensured sustainable economic growth, and lasting peace and security, so that eventually the African people would fully realize their potential in all spheres of life. However, most Africans have been disenchanted with the outcome of several decades of self-rule, which has come to be nothing but gross mismanagement of economic resources, rampant corruption, nepotism, political insecurity, devastating ethnic, religious, sectarian and political conflicts, decline of state power and authority, endless coups, counter coups and coup attempts, abject poverty, military and autocratic rule, and many other aberrations. These and other crises have dominated the economic, political and socio-cultural environment in post-colonial and self-governing independent Africa. In fact, the crisis has now become the order of the day across the length and breadth of the continent.

Following, the adoption and introduction of two powerful international legal instruments on democracy and democratization in Africa, - the first being the African Union's (AU's) *Charter on Democracy, Elections and Governance* of 2007 (henceforth *The Charter*) and the second being Economic Community of West African States (ECOWAS's) *Protocol on Democracy and Good Governance* of 2001, (henceforth *The Protocol*) genuine hopes were raised from various parts of the continent that Africa's long-standing problem of military coups and military rule in general was now going to be a thing of the past. These two instruments, plus the constructive role played by ECOWAS that was strongly supported by the United Nations, the AU, the European Union (EU) and other Western countries in decisively ending the conflicts in Liberia, Sierra Leone, Guinea Bissau and most recently in 2016, and finally, the political impasse in The Gambia followed by successful restoration of democracy in these countries, gave the impression that military rule was definitely on its way to becoming a thing of the past, and potentially even outlawed in Africa, especially in the West Africa sub-region.

However, the most recent events in Mali, Guinea Conakry, Burkina Faso, the newly independent state of South Sudan, the Darfur region of the Republic of Sudan and in the troubled Tigray region of Ethiopia, - the current host of the African Union's headquarters- plus the ongoing conflicts in Libya and the political instability in Algeria and Tunisia have all contributed to dashing away any hopes that effective structural changes could be enforced anytime in the near future. In fact, It has now become very obvious that the majority of Africans have actually lost or are losing faith and confidence in their political leaders and government systems. These disappointing results and the unsatisfactory experiences of political independence and self-rule throughout the continent, have indeed raised serious questions about the character, intentions and leadership capabilities of most post-independence African leaders (Obadina: 2008).

The most frustrating of all obstacles and problems within the current African Governance systems are the persistent and chronic domestic conflicts and leadership disputes, which in the recent past have devastated the foundations of State in countries including Guinea Bissau, Rwanda and Burundi Somalia, Liberia, Libya, Cote d'Ivoire, and Sierra Leone. Since becoming independent a few years ago, the Republic of South Sudan, - Africa's newest state - is still struggling to stand on its own feet, and efforts to build the foundations of statehood for itself as an independent sovereign nation are slow-coming. This is due to the ongoing, ravaging ethnic conflict that continues to destroy the country's much needed human and material resources.

This chapter seeks to discuss some of the major issues pertaining to the principle of responsible leadership and effective governance as a prerequisite for sustainable peace, stability, security and development in Africa. It attempts to do so by firstly defining the concepts of governance, accounting, in the process, for the different global and regional definitions and approaches, including both the African and the Islamic approaches to governance. In the final analysis, a brief discussion on a few selected strategies of conflict and crisis prevention is provided.

This chapter now turns to examine the concepts of governance and leadership including the principles of responsible, effective and legitimate governance and exemplary leadership firstly from a general, secondly from an African and finally from an Islamic perspective.

What is governance?

The term governance is mainly used to refer to the manner in which power is exercised in the management of a country's social, economic and human resources for development. Governance thus refers to the ways in which "those with power use that power" (Asian Development Bank, 2007 - quoted in Sh. Ismail Al – Qudsy & A.

Abdrahman: 2011). John Graham, Bruce Amos and Tim Plumptre, provide a more elaborate definition arguing that governance is "The art of steering societies and organizations. [It] is the interactions among structures, processes and traditions that determine how power and responsibilities are exercised, how decisions are taken, and how citizens or other stakeholders have their say. Fundamentally, it is about power, relationships and accountability. More precisely, it is about who has influence, who decides, and how decision-makers are held accountable. The concept may usefully be applied in different contexts – global, national, institutional and community" (quoted in Sh. Ismail Al – Qudsy & A. Abdrahman: 2011).

The Organization of Economic Co-operation and Development in Europe (OECD) describes the concept of governance as "the use of political authority and exercise of control in a society in relation to the management of its resources for social and economic development. This broad definition encompasses the role of public authorities in establishing the environment in which economic operators function and in determining the distribution of benefits as well as the nature of the relationship between ruler and ruled" (The Organization of Economic Co-operation and Development, 2008 quoted in Sh. Ismail Al – Qudsy & A. Abdrahman: 2011).

Several other definitions of governance from various international organizations are presented here to give a more nuanced understanding of how the term is used in various ways but for the same or similar purposes. For the World Bank, Governance refers to "the manner in which power is exercised in the management of a country's economic and social resources." This definition by the World Bank identifies three distinct aspects of governance: (a) that it is the form of a political regime; (b) that it is the process by which authority is exercised in the management of a country's economic and social resources for development; and (c) that it denotes governments' capacity to design, formulate and implement policies and discharge functions (quoted in Sh. Ismail Al – Qudsy & A. Abdrahman: 2011) also (A.A. Senghore: 2010)

The Canadian Institute of Governance in Ottawa elaborates that "governance comprises the institutions, processes and conventions in a society, which determine how power is exercised, how important decisions affecting society are made and how various interests are accorded a place in such decisions" (quoted in Sh. Ismail Al – Qudsy & A. Abdrahman: 2011).

The Brussels-based International Institute of Administrative Sciences describes governance as "the process whereby elements in society wield power, authority, and influence and enact policies and decisions concerning public life, and economic and social development. Governance is a broader notion than government. [It]involves interaction between these formal institutions and those of civil society" (quoted in Sh. Ismail Al – Qudsy & A. Abdrahman: 2011) also (A. A. Senghore: 2010).

Finally, the Tokyo Institute of Technology refers to the concept of governance as "the complex set of values, norms, processes and institutions by which society manages its development and resolves conflict, formally and informally. It involves the state, but also the civil society (economic and social actors, community-based institutions and unstructured groups, the media, etc) at the local, national, regional and global levels" (quoted in Sh. Ismail Al – Qudsy & A. Abdrahman: 2011)

The African perspective of governance

II- 1.a Legitimate governance under the African Charter on Democracy, Elections and Governance and the ECOWAS Protocol on Democracy and Good Governance

It would be useful now to comparatively consider the above definitions with the African perspective on the approaches to governance, that is, to gauge the ways in which African views fit into the broader, more global theoretical models, some of which have been highlighted in the above section. This current section considers how conflict prevention can be attained through legitimate governance practices. It focuses here on two of the most renowned and revolutionizing international legal instruments of the African systems, these are *The ECOWAS Protocol on Democracy and Good Governance*, and *The African Charter on Democracy, Elections and Governance (ACDEG)*

The two instruments address the main issues and provide solutions for some of the most difficult and complex issues of governance in modern-day Africa. The wide range of governance issues as well as the development and peace strategies addressed within these two instruments are comprehensive and have the ability to pull the continent as a whole, and the West African sub-region in particular, out of its multifaceted problems of mismanagement which have plagued African populations for a very long time.

The two instruments are identical in almost every respect and therefore supportive and complementary to each other. The only difference between them is that the Charter is a continental or an African Union instrument whereas the Protocol is a sub-regional or an ECOWAS instrument. Furthermore, all member countries of the Economic Community of West African States (ECOWAS) are also members of the African Union. The combination of these factors thus renders the two instruments very solid pieces of international legislation, binding on all signatory states. With these considerations in mind this chapter will now focus more specifically on West Africa, firstly dealing with the question of legitimate governance as envisaged by the *African Charter on Democracy, Elections and Governance (ACDEG)*.

The African Charter on Democracy, Elections and Governance

Article 32 of the African Charter on Democracy, Elections and Governance describes governance as a process that entails eight (8) outlined principles. These principles provide a general framework of the attributes that are usually present in well-functioning political, economic and corporate governance practices. They are detailed as follows:

- Accountable, efficient and effective public administration
- Strengthening the functioning and effectiveness of parliaments
- An independent and impartial judiciary
- Relevant reforms of public institutions including the security sector
- Harmonious relationship in society including civil – military relations
- Consolidating sustainable multi-party-political systems
- Organizing regular, free and fair elections
- Entrenching and respecting the principle of the rule of law.

These principles are expanded upon in Article 33 of the Charter which focuses more specifically on the principles of good economic and corporate governance under the guidance of an efficient administration, it elaborates as follows:

- Effective public sector management
- Promoting transparency in public finance management
- Preventing and combating corruption and related offences
- Efficient management of public debts
- Prudent and sustainable utilization of public resources
- Equitable allocation of nation's wealth and natural resources
- Poverty alleviation
- Enabling legislative and regulatory framework for private sector development
- Providing a conducive environment for foreign capital inflows
- Developing and applying tax policies that encourage investment, especially foreign investments. It is worth

mentioning at this juncture that an efficient and effective tax system must be premised upon transparency and accountability
* Elaborating and implementing economic development strategies including private public sector partnerships

Upon reviewing the two articles of *the* Charter, one comes to the realization that the African approach to the definition of good governance is more elaborate than the definitions of the World Bank and other definitions of the term in this section. The African definition also obviously recognizes the clear distinction between the systemic and the managerial aspects of governance and further argues that in order to ensure good governance the two aspects must be adequately addressed. The principles of governance and administration that constitute a democratic system such as free, fair and periodic elections, multi-parti-ism, constitutional rule, respect for human rights and fundamental freedoms, the rule of law, an independent and impartial judiciary, decentralization and devolution of powers and authority, and finally transparency and accountability, represent, to a large extent, the systematic aspects of governance, whereas the remaining highlighted principles are mainly related to managerial issues.

Yet, one also comes to the realization that while the Charter offers theoretically sound solutions, the elaborate provisions therein are largely removed from the political and social realities on the ground. In fact, it becomes quite apparent that a huge gap exists between theory and practice when it comes to the procedures of good governance in many African countries. There are serious issues with the electoral systems and laws, transparency and accountability, with human rights and many more issues of misgovernance across the length and breadth of the continent, as already alluded to in my introduction..

II.2.a Legitimate Governance under the ECOWAS Protocol on Democracy and Good Governance

The ECOWAS Protocol on Democracy and Good Governance views the following principles not only as ingredients of a democratic system of government but also as effective strategies and mechanisms for conflict prevention and resolution.

1. Constitutionalism

The Protocol tasks the member states of the ECOWAS to incorporate in their constitutions and declare as constitutional principles the following:

- Separation of powers between the executive, the legislature and the judiciary
- Empowerment and strengthening of parliaments and guaranteeing parliamentary immunity
- Independence of the judiciary and the legal profession
- Freedom of the members of the Bar must be guaranteed. However, this shall not prejudice their penal or disciplinary responsibility in the event of contempt of court or breach of the law or of code of professional conduct
- Organizing periodic elections which must be free, fair and transparent
- Total rejection of any unconstitutional means of change of government or transfer of power and authority
- Popular participation in decision making, strict adherence to decentralization of power and all other principles of democratic governance at all levels of governance
- The armed forces must be apolitical and be under the command and control of legally constituted political authority

- Secularism and neutrality of the state in all matters relating to religion
- That people are effectively protected from all forms of discrimination
- Political parties shall be formed and given the right to carry out their activities freely within the limits of the law
- That the formation of political parties shall not be based on ethnic, religious, racial, regional and similar divisive considerations
- The freedom of the opposition and the people's free participation in the political process must be guaranteed
- Member states are urged by the Protocol to adopt a consistent and fair system of financing political parties in accordance with criteria to be defined by the law
- To guarantee freedom of association, expression and press freedom as well as the individual's rights to freely assemble and organize peaceful demonstrations
- Former heads of state shall enjoy special status including freedom of movement. They should also enjoy special benefits compatible to their status as former heads of state

2. Reasonable and fair electoral laws

According to Article 2 of the Protocol member states must, in their electoral laws, account for the following strategies:

- No substantial modification or amendment shall be made to the electoral laws in the six (6) months prior to elections, except with the consent of the majority of political parties particularly, the opposition
- Dates and periods of the election must be fixed by the constitution or the electoral laws

- Women should have equal rights with men to vote and be voted for in elections and decision making
- Election management bodies must be independent or neutral and have the confidence of all political parties
- Each member state must establish a reliable central registration of births and deaths
- Voter's list should be prepared in a transparent and reliable manner with the collaboration of political parties including the opposition
- The preparation and conduct of elections and announcement of results should be done in a transparent and reliable manner
- Adequate arrangements must be made to hear and resolve all petitions and complaints relating to the conduct of elections, counting of votes and the announcement of results
- Civil society organizations that are involved in the electoral process to educate and enlighten the people on the need for peaceful elections and avoid all forms of violence and conflict should be engaged
- Candidates who lose the elections must honourably concede defeat to the winning candidates / party
- All holders of public office or power must at all levels refrain from all acts of intimidation, or harassment against defeated candidates or their supporters

3. Election observation and monitoring

The *Protocol on Democracy and Good Governance* encourages member states to approach the sub-regional body and seek its assistance in the conduct of national elections of any kind i.e. whether presidential, parliamentary, local governmental, in the first and second or final round elections. The assistance that a member state may seek from the ECOWAS system may take any form, particularly in terms of observation and monitoring of elections. The sub-regional system may dispatch an observation or a monitoring team to a member country for the purpose of proper observation or monitoring during the election process, to ensure its proper conduct.

Election observation or monitoring could serve as an effective strategy for the prevention of post-election conflicts. In most cases, observation or monitoring missions, which are always requested or invited by the country concerned, are commonly acceptable to all stake holders including, most specifically, opposition political parties.

Therefore, if the observation or monitoring exercise is conducted according to internationally accepted standards, the verdict or views of observers / monitors on the outcome of the election are bound to be accepted by all or at least the majority of political parties involved.

Articles II – 18 of the Protocol provide provisions on how ECOWAS should assist the country concerned. These articles elaborate on how to go about providing observation / monitoring missions and how election observation missions should conduct the observation exercise.

4. Keeping neutral and nonpartisan armed forces, the police and security forces

Articles 19 – 24 of the Protocol deal with the role of the armed forces, the police and other security apparatus of the State. According to the Protocol, the army, the police and security agents of the state must remain neutral, non-partisan and loyal to the nation as a whole.

- The role of the armed forces must be to defend the independence and the territorial integrity of the state and its democratic institutions and not the ruling parties and their elites alone.
- As for the police and other security agencies, their role and responsibility shall be the maintenance of law and order and protection of persons and their properties.

- The police and other security apparatus of the state must be under the authority of a legally constituted civilian authority.
- The rights and freedoms of members of the armed forces, the police and other security agencies, as part of the citizenry, must be protected as provided for by the constitution and the international human rights conventions.
- No member state is allowed to use arms to disperse non-violent meetings / assemblies and demonstrations.
- However, when a demonstration becomes violent, the state can only use minimal or proportional force to restore calm peaceful order.
- Torture and all other forms of cruel or inhumane treatment must be forbidden and offenders of such crimes should be duly held to account for their actions.
- While carrying out investigations the security forces shall not disturb or arrest innocent family members and relatives.
- During their training, the armed forces, the police and other security agents must receive instructions on the constitution, their obligation to respect its authority and supremacy, to respect all ECOWAS Principles and regulations, international human rights and humanitarian provisions and principles and to respect all the principles of democratic governance.

5. **Poverty alleviation and promotion of social dialogue**

Member states of the Economic Community of West African States signatory to the sub-regional Protocol on Democracy and Good Governance have recognized the fact that poverty alleviation and social dialogue are essential ingredients and fundamental requirements for the prevalence of peace and security in any country.

Thus, member states have undertaken as per the provisions of Articles 25 – 28 of the Protocol to develop and implement relevant policies and measurers specifically designed to substantially reduce poverty and promote social dialogue. Such measures shall include the following:

- Provision of basic human needs for the population
- Creating an environment conducive to private investment and the development of a dynamic and competitive private sector
- Job creation and development of the social sector as a priority
- Ensuring equitable distribution of resources and income in order to consolidate national unity and solidarity
- Creation or organization and strengthening employers' associations and trade unions in each member state and at the level of ECOWAS
- As a way of promoting social dialogue in each member country, employers' associations and workers unions should be allowed to hold regular meetings and consultations amongst themselves and with the political and administrative authorities so as to prevent conflict and maintain peaceful relations and social order

6. Promotion of education, cultural exchanges and religious dialogue or consultation

The provisions of Articles 29 – 31 of the Protocol tasks the secretariat of the sub-regional organization to adopt and implement appropriate measures or policies aimed at promoting the following:

- Education particularly women education at all levels and in all fields of training.
- Regular exchanges of students and academics between member states
- The respect and development of the culture of every group of people in each member state
- The promotion, through periodic meetings, of consultations and dialogues among various religious groups of member states

This particular strategy is integral, because as already indicated in the introduction, education, culture and religion are essential factors for peace, stability and development in our sub-region and beyond. Many of the conflicts of the modern time are either religiously or culturally motivated or have very strong religious or cultural dimensions. So, if ECOWAS is able to mobilize its members and engage its governance institutions to promote education, cultural exchanges and religious dialogue, the sub-regional organization would be recording huge successes in its continuous struggle to prevent social strife in West Africa.

7. Respect for rule of law, human rights and ensuring good governance

The Protocol on Democracy and Good Governance as per the provisions of its Articles 32 – 39 recognizes the fact that prevalence of the rule of law, respect for and the promotion of human rights, ensuring good governance and guaranteeing press freedom are essential factors for the preservation of social justice, the prevention of conflict, and the guarantees of political stability, internal security, comprehensive, sustainable and lasting peace, strong democracy and for the good and smooth management of the state apparatus in general.

To ensure that the rule of law is applied, it would be necessary to do the following:

- Promulgation and enactment of legislation of good, reasonable, just and fair laws
- Such laws must be in conformity with the provisions of the constitutions, the international human rights instruments, and the county's international obligations including those that are in the ECOWAS Protocol and the remaining sub – regional instruments, the African Charter on Human and Peoples Rights, the African Charter on Democracy, Elections and

Governance, Constitutive Act of the African Union and similar AU and other international instruments

* Running an impartial and reliable judicial system
* Maintaining an effective system of administration and the efficient functioning of a state's legal and administrative instruments.

* Member states must ensure accountability, professionalism, transparency and expertise in the public and private sectors
* Member states should encourage the establishment of independent national institutions to promote and protect human rights.
* The Protocol has undertaken to adopt and implement measures aimed at strengthening the capacities of national institutions
* Member states must institutionalize national mediation systems in order to encourage swift or quick settlement of disputes, particularly those that are potentially dangerous
* Each member state must work towards ensuring pluralism of the information sector and the development of the media
* Each member state is urged to give financial assistance to privately owned media organizations through an independent national body or through a body freely established by the journalists themselves.
* Member states must take appropriate measures to fight corruption and manage their national resources in a transparent manner and distribute them equitably
* That the ECOWAS's Community Court of Justice should be reviewed so as to give it the necessary powers to hear inter-alia, cases relating to violations of human rights, after all attempts to resolve such violations at the national level have failed.

8. **Promotion of the development and progress of women, the education of children and youth development**

The Protocol on Democracy and Good Governance, under the provisions of Articles 40 – 43, draws the attention of all stakeholders working to ensure sustainable peace, security and development in West Africa, that the development and promotion of the welfare of women, the provision of basic education and training to children and youth are essential factors for sustainable development, progress and peace in every human society.

Thus, to adopt effective measures to ensure peace and security and to prevent conflict, each member state must undertake to:

- Eliminate all forms of discrimination, harmful and degrading practices against women
- Guarantee children's rights and give them full access to basic education
- To protect children against trafficking, child prostitution and child labour
- Put in place at the level of each member state and at the level of the ECOWAS Secretariat all necessary structures to ensure the effective implementation of common policies and programmes relating to the education and the promotion of the welfare of women and youth in the whole of the sub-region

To conclude, the Protocol on Democracy and good Governance provides us with strategies and mechanisms that are more than enough for the West African sub-system to substantially do away with its chronic crisis, particularly its governance and leadership conflicts. If member states are to apply the provisions of the Protocol as highlighted above, to the letter, then West Africa would be bound to emerge out of the current problems of mal-administration, poor governance, insecurity, instability, widespread corruption and poverty in which Sub – Saharan Africa is currently entirely engulfed.

It is, therefore, strategically important for ECOWAS to consolidate its powers, policies and laws, its governance institutions and instruments as a supranational authority so as to bring all member states closer together under its umbrella and ensure that the various strategies and mechanisms of peace and development as well as those of conflict prevention and resolution are adhered to and fully implemented. If this is achieved by the West African sub-system then it will record unprecedented achievement and successes in the history of international inter-governmental organizations of the modern time.

The concept of effective governance in Islam

Given the relevance of Islam in West-African culture, it is instructive at this point, to consider how Islam explains governance both theoretically and practically. The concept of effective governance in Islam is embodied in the Islamic governing principle of *al-siasah al-shar'iyyah*. (shar'iyyah oriented policies) The word *siasah*, which is derived from the Arabic root of *sasa*', meaning politics or to arrange, manage and to rule. The basic purpose of *siasah* or politics in Islam is to arrange, manage and use political wisdom to achieve certain objectives in accordance with the principles and basic tenets of shar'iyyah. The following paragraphs quoted from Sh. Ismail Al – Qudsy & A. Abdrahman: (2011), give a perfect explanation of the Islamic political/governing concept of *al-siasah al-shar'iyyah* and how it can lead to the realization of effective governance in an Islamic system

"Conceptually, according to Ibnu Qayyim al-Jawziyah (1961), *al-siasah al-shar'iyyah* is an act of providing human benefits and protecting them from any destruction, even if the action is not specifically mentioned by Prophet Muhammad (p.b.u.h) and revealed by Allah the Almighty." Ahmad Fathi Bahansi (1965) states that "*al-*

402

siasah al-shar'iyyah is the management of Muslim benefits in accordance with the principles of Islamic law (*shariah*)." Abdul Wahab Khallaf (1984), meanwhile, explains the concept of *siasah* as a "means to administer general matters for an Islamic state including promoting benefits and protecting society from any harm, in line with Islamic law."

While in more general terms, al-Maqrizi defines *siasah* as the action of carrying out good purposes. He also divides the idea of *al-siasah* into two categories, firstly, "fair or good governance" in accordance with the rule of *siasah* known as *al-siasah al-shar'iyyah* and secondly, and contrary to the first, that which is explained as as "bad or unfair governance," or *al-siasah al-zalimah* (Al- Maqrizi).

According to Fathi Uthman (1979), however, *al-siasah al-syar'iyyah* is a term that refers to the practice of administration and constitutional law, as well as the authority of government, which entails accountability for the ruler (*caliph*), *members of the* consultative council or parliament (*ahlul-halli wal-Aqdi*), rights of the individual, public interest (*maslahah ammah*) and others. In this respect, all of these are closely related definitions and they indicate that one of the main focuses of *al-siasah al-shar'iyyah* is the management of government institutions and state resources for the interests and benefit of the public, in line with the rules of *shariah*.

In understanding Islamic administration or management as a sub-concept and practice of *al siyasah*, Al Buraey (1985) states that the Holy Quran used the term *yudabbiru* in several places. The general meaning of the term is to order, lead, operate, manage, plan, steer, or to arrange. This can be applied both for economic planning as well as for performing business. According to him, Islamic administration essentially operates through the mutual understanding of both the government and the people, or what modern political science terms democracy." (quoted in Sh. Ismail Al – Qudsy & A. Abdrahman:

2011). Therefore, in order to realize effective governance in Islam, the following standards must be met:

First: to enable effective governance, the system must ensure basic cooperation between three components, the ruler, the administrative system and the citizen. In fact, the major objective of al-*siasah al-shar`iyyah* is to attain *al-falah* or lasting happiness. It also seeks to avoid destruction or evil (*al-fasad*) as emphasized by the Holy Quran when Allah says:

"And let there be such a group among you, that they may call towards goodness and command what is just and forbid evil. And the very same attained to their goals." (Ali-Imran (3):104).

Second: the governance structure, processes and institutions must be guided and based on the following values (*Akhlaq*):

- *Al-Iman* which is the faith or belief in the sovereignty of Allah and His Messenger
- *Al-Amanah* or trust and accountability
- *Demonstration of and adherence to all* good moral and ethical values
- *Al-Shura or* mutual consultation
- *Al-Hisbah* or prevention and forbidding wrongdoing on one hand and commanding good on the other
- Honesty and integrity in all dealings
- Fair, reliable, impartial and honest administration of justice
- Loyalty to the state and the people
- The principle of personal responsibility
- Mutual cooperation

Finally, in Islam, poor or unfair governance practices are not judged based on public compliance or noncompliance with the specified indicators *per se,* but rather, on their noncompliance with the standards of *Shariah* and the principles of *al-siyasah al-shar`iyyah*. Bad governance is therefore considered sinful.

Responsible leadership and governance in Islam

The concept of responsible leadership and good governance together with its component rules, principles, mechanisms and institutions was epitomized or incorporated in the maiden speech delivered by Abubakar al Siddique (RA) when he was elected, after the death of Prophet Mohammed (SAW), to succeed the Prophet (SAW) as the first *Khalifah* (leader of the Muslim community). Most of the conventional principles of responsible leadership and the liberal democracy principles of democratic governance were in one way or the other embodied in that historic speech given by the first *Khalifah* of Islam.

Thus, modern concepts like constitutionally sound governance, respect for human rights and fundamental individual freedoms, independence of the judiciary and the legal profession, transparency and accountability, popular participation, devolution of power and decentralization of authority, responsiveness to the basic needs of the masses, etc. were directly or indirectly included in Abubaker al Siddique's speech, which by all accounts could be described as the first major policy speech by a *Khalifah* in the political history of Islam. The speech reads as follows:

"I have been chosen to rule over you, though I am not the best among you. Help me if I am right; correct me if I am wrong. The weak among you will be strong until I have attained for him his due, and the strong among you will be weak until I have made him give what he owes. Obey me as long as I obey Allah and His Prophet; if I do not obey them, you owe me no obedience" (Ibn Hisham, 1995). Also, see (I. Sacranie: 2003) and (Subhi Salih: 1965).

According to Iqbal Sacranie this was a remarkable statement for any leader to make. In the case of Abubakar, he defined a unique form of an Islamic social contract vis-a-vis his citizens. He set out the basis and the limits of his authority as well as the duties of his citizens" (Ibn Hisham: 1995) and (I. Sacranie: 2003). Sacranie believes that the speech highlighted several important pillars or areas which are critical to effective governance and responsible leadership. These themes constitute the main framework within which the Islamic polity operates.

First, in this speech, the newly elected Khalifah accepted the position of a leader of the Islamic world with remarkable humility as demonstrated by the following paragraph of the speech, "I have been chosen to rule over you, though I am not the best among you."

In this statement, Aboubacar Siddiq did not only define the basic principles of leadership, but he also acknowledged his role as but one of many companions of the Prophet, all of whom had the same worth in terms of qualities. So, his statement intended to emphasize that his selection to the role of leader did not make him a better Muslim or a better person, rather, that this was a heavy responsibility for him to carry and respect.

Second, the new *Khalifah* defined governance as an on-going relationship between a leader and members of the *ummah*. Leadership creates duties for the citizens as well as obligations to their leader. In his speech, he proclaimed, "Help me if I am right; correct me if I am wrong." In other words, he was keen to emphasize that governance is a participatory process, which entails a mutual interaction between governors and governed, such that the governed are active participants in the governing process. The speech can thus be considered progressive in terms of its views on open government, transparency on the part of the leader, the free flow of information, the integration of an informed and educated public and the institution of mechanisms and processes of accountability, as prerequisites or necessarily elements of responsible leadership and good governance

Abubakar's polity, as Iqubal has observed, "requires genuine engagement and partnership between a ruler and a citizen. It is a system of mutual obligations and duties that recognizes rights and responsibilities. In short Abubakar [called] for a society that incorporates the essential building blocks of democracy yet expands beyond the forms we have become used to. It challenges us to go further to achieve distinctive ongoing forms of participation" (I. Sacranie: 2003) and (Subhi Salih: 1965).

Third, this part of Abubakar's speech, "The weak among you will be strong until I have attained for him his due, and the strong among you will be weak until I have made him give what he owes" shows that delivery of social justice is a central concern and a major priority of Islamic governance. In other words, a "just and cohesive society cannot be maintained in the face of glaring inequalities – whether in economic resources or access to services." (I. Sacranie: 2003). Thus, Islamic governance calls for a government of laws and responsibilities and not that of strong, irresponsible and selfish individual and groups.

 A good example of this is the institution of *zakat*, which is a tax on wealth to help the less fortunate. This principle, alongside that of justice, requires that all should be equal under the law, regardless of their wealth or status (I. Sacranie: 2003).

Fourth, the last part of Abubakar's speech recognized the concept of a limited government and thus set out the basis and parameters of his own authority. "Obey me as long as I obey Allah and His prophet; if I do not obey them, you owe me no obedience." The new Khalifah affirmed in this part of the speech that his authority as head of the Islamic state derived from his implementation of the commands of a higher authority. Thus, he argued that so long as he successfully fulfilled his part of the contract, then he deserved support and loyalty, but if he were to deviate or fail to deliver, he should be held to account by those under his authority.

To conclude, Abubakar's speech clearly established the fact that there could be three potential major challenges facing Muslim leaders of the modern time. They are, firstly, the challenge of leadership legitimacy; secondly, effectiveness in working to achieve national development - economic, intellectual, political and cultural progress. Thirdly, the challenge of failure to deliver their people or communities from injustice, and lastly, the challenge faced by Muslim governments and their international and inter-governmental, and non-governmental organizations of effectively addressing the seemingly endless injustices committed against Muslims in Palestine, Kashmir, Chechnya, Iraq, Bosnia and elsewhere across the globe (I. Sacranie: 2003)

II.   Conclusion

This chapter has raised serious concerns about the seemingly endless and unresolvable national and trans-national conflicts and the ensuing leadership and governance crisis, mainly, of the West African sub-region.

The apparent inability of the major players and the leading actors of the contemporary international political system such as the United Nations, the African Union, the ECOWAS and the former colonial powers of the countries engulfed in the crisis, to contain the situation decisively and comprehensively or substantially is another great concern raised by this chapter.

This chapter, therefore, concludes that an appropriate, effective and everlasting solution to the crisis must be found by all means and under all circumstances. This, arguably, is an absolutely necessity so that the multifaceted and multi-dimensional problems of leadership and governance in West Africa will go for good and be replaced by internal security, political stability and comprehensive lasting peace accompanied by sustainable economic growth or national development and prosperity of all individuals and groups in Africa - South of the Sahara Desert.

This chapter also clearly recognizes the fact that whether by accident or by design or by an act of God, the West African sub-region is inhabited by people of multicultural, multireligious, multi-racial backgrounds and people of different ethnicities, political ideologies and even colonial legacies which have become deeply entrenched in their way of life. The current geo-political, ecological and demographic realities of West Africa are a hard fact that its people have to live with.

In view of the above arguments and given the urgency of the need for a solution to be found, this chapter is proposing some solutions to the problem and while doing so, the article identifies four strategies that it believes could be used as effective strategies of conflict prevention. The proposed strategies are:

- Effective Governance
- Legitimate Governance as envisaged by both the African Charter on Democracy, Elections and Governance and the ECOWAS Protocol on Democracy and Good Governance
- Protection of Minority Rights
- De-politicization of Ethnicity and Religion

This chapter argues very strongly that if these strategies are incorporated into the political processes, the governance structures and the enforcement mechanisms and institutions of the West African sub-system, particularly at the level of the individual member states, the conflicts and the ensuring crisis will definitely completely or substantially disappear forever. However, the proposed solutions and strategies advanced by this chapter are obviously premised on the assumption that the people of sub-Saharan Africa in general and their leaders in particular would have changed or at least are prepared to change their attitude to life generally and the way they relate to each other and do things together as a people living within the same geographical unit especially. In other words, without any meaningful and positive change of attitude by the majority of the people no number of principles, strategies or values, no matter how effective, will work or do anything meaningful to solve the current crisis in our sub-region.

Finally, this chapter calls for ECOWAS's mechanisms, their implementation and enforcement institutions to be strengthened and enhanced. The best and the most realistic way of ensuring this is for the member states particularly, the leading actors, to increase, regularize and   strengthen their commitment to provide the necessary material, financial, moral and political support to the sub-regional government and also for the latter to consolidate its authority and supremacy over all individual governments of each and every member state. Thus, the sub-regional government and central authority must be better empowered and more equipped financially, materially, politically, institutionally and morally.

****

Conclusion

The common theme that unifies the collection of essays which
makes up this book is good governance and responsible leadership
in Africa, with particular focus on The Gambia. These chapters, in
varied degrees and emphases, are concerned with the feasibility of
good governance and responsible leadership in Africa: its drivers
and drawbacks. In the process, the good governance project in
Africa comes across as dialectical, not linear: it is characterized by
cycles of peaks and valleys, gains and setbacks. It waxes and wanes
with neither condition being final or permanent. Mali, Guinea
Conakry, Burkina Faso, Niger, the Republic of the Sudan and the
Republic of South Sudan are examples of emergent democracies that
appear to be steadily sliding into authoritarianism and anarchy or
even civil wars as the case is in the latter two examples. Senegal,
which was once the beacon of democracy and good governance in
West Africa, now totters on the brink of despotism and what could
eventually turn out to be a bloody uprising or even internal conflict.
In early 2017, illiberal tendencies threatened The Gambia's first-
ever democratic transition of power in the wake of the December 6,
2016, electoral defeat of the then ruling party Alliance for Patriotic
Re-orientation and Construction (APRC) by an opposition alliance
in the smiling coast of Africa. Similarly, the December 22, 2022,
controversial coup attempt against the Barrow administration has
raised alarm and stoked fears in various quarters about the fate of
the new democratic dispensation in The Gambia. The underlying
thesis, therefore, is that good governance only thrives when it is
rooted in accountability, transparency, and equitable distribution of
the common patrimony within the framework of a strong and
impartial judiciary coupled with a free, independent and pluralistic
media which hold (political) power holders to account.

While the performance of the judiciary in The Gambia has been
called into question in some quarters, particularly during the first

half of the last decade, it has largely given a good account of itself in dispensing justice without fear or favour, ill will or affection, even in cases involving the executive arm of government. The marked improvement in general legal education in the country, due mainly to the establishment of the faculty of law within the University of The Gambia, together with the dramatic upsurge in universal access to education with the advent of the Second Republic, holds the potential to impact positively on the business of state management in general and the administration of justice in particular, in The Gambia.

In the same vein, the resilience of the independent news media in The Gambia in the face of massive repression and gross undercapitalization, in some instances, has contributed in no small measure to the prospects of good governance and democratic accountability in the country. The independent news media in The Gambia has consistently upheld its statutory obligation and professional commitment to foster good governance and responsible leadership by holding power holders to account for their stewardship in the management of state affairs. In the process, the independent news media have had to contend with a range of constraints and sometimes life-threatening challenges including frequent dismissals from work, cold-blooded murder, disappearances, arbitrary arrests and imprisonment of outspoken journalists. Yet, the news media rise like a phoenix from the ashes, evolving and thriving. In the wake of the digital revolution, the news media practice scene in The Gambia has increasingly become robust with two accredited schools for journalism education up to university level such as the School of Journalism and Digital Media of the University of The Gambia, The Gambia Press Union School of Journalism (GPU J-School), and a profusion of news outlets, most notably online broadcast stations.

Additionally, the doctrine of separation of power, a central pillar of democratic governance, is a norm in The Gambia. This is further strengthened by the protection of basic liberties and fundamental rights in the 1997 Constitution that inaugurated the Second Republic. The provision of these fundamental freedoms and rights has largely served as a bulwark against entrenched autocracy in the country. These structures together with the fact that multi-party elections in The Gambia are mostly peaceful, free, fair and credible render The Gambia, arguably, a democratic state both in theory and practice.

However, given the fact that the African condition is shaped by diverse cross-cultural encounters, notably from both the West and the East (that is, influences from Western and Eastern civilizations) it is important therefore to develop a more nuanced conception of good governance in relation to Africa. The African democratic project stands to be enriched by distilling the virtues of both the Western and Islamic conceptions of good governance and then integrating them into a workable framework that prioritizes the needs and concerns of the African people without having to reject either paradigm wholesale. Relatedly, traditional African governance institutions are pivotal to the ongoing democratization process in Africa. Some of the positive and workable elements of traditional African governance such as background checks and the legitimacy principles need to be incorporated into the core of contemporary African governance. In the past African kingmakers used to do background checks on the incoming ruler to ensure that the new monarch was physically, morally, ethically and emotionally fit to govern. This practice also assured and confirmed the legitimacy and popular acceptance of the new rulers. The common inclusive approach, advocated here, is doubly advantageous. For one thing, it has the great merit of ensuring and preserving the diversity which is the hallmark of the African condition and experience. For another, it strengthens good governance and promotes effective leadership through (popular) participation.

Notes

Introduction

1. Ake, Claude. 2000. *The Feasibility of Democracy in Africa.* Dakar, Senegal: Council for the

     Development of Social Science Research in Africa (CODESRIA)

2. Nyamnjoh, Francis, B. 2005. *Africa's Media: Democracy & the Politics of Belonging.* London &

     New York: ZED BOOKS

3. Zakaria, Fareed. 1997. "The Rise of Illiberal Democracy." *Foreign Affairs.* Vol. 79, No.6 (Nov.-

     Dec. 1997), pp.22-43

4. Herman, Edward S., and Noam Chomsky. 1988. *MANUFACTURING CONSENT: The Political*

     Economy of the Mass Media. New York: Pantheon Books

Chapter 1

1. A.A. Senghore (2010) The judiciary in Governance in The Gambia and the Quest for Autonomy on the Second Republic – Published in New Jersey USA, by the Journal of the third world studies (Journal of The Third World Studies, Vol. 27, No. 2(Fall 2012), pp. 215-248)
2. A.A. Senghore (2012) Press Freedom and Democratic Governance in the Gambia: A right based approach – Published in South Africa by the University Of Pretoria African Human Rights Law Journal Volume 12 No 2. 2012

3. Ahmed B. (2005) The Stone of Justice, Blog at Word Press.Com
4. Ahmed N. ( ) Omar Iban al-Kattah
    http://historyofislam.com/contents/the-age-of-faith/omar-ibn-al-khattab-r/

5. Al-Attas S.M.N. (1993) Islam and Secularism, Kualalumpur: International Institute of Islamic through and Civilizations (ISTAC)
6. Al- Qudsy Sh. H. S.I & Abdraham A. (2011) in (n.e.d.n) European Journal of Social Sciences, Vol.18 United Kingdom: PP. 612 – 624.
7. Beekun R. & Badawi J. (1999) The Leadership Process in Islam
    http://www.google.gm/url?sa=t&rct=j&q=the%20leadership%20proce
    ss%20in%20islam&source=web&cd=1&cad=rja&ved=0CCsQFjAA&
    url=http%3A%2F%2Ffecon.uii.ac.id%2Fimages%2FHand_Out%2FA
    kt%2FSKI%2Fldrpro.pdf&ei=bFBlUda9K66V7Aa3r4CwBg&usg=AF
    QjCNGamRU0ehERBaxtCy_j2-H7Y-
    mrcQ&bvm=bv.44990110,d.d2k

8. Cameron K. & Caza A. (2013) "Development Strategies for Responsible Leadership" Paper Presented at the University of Michigan in 2013
    http://www.google.gm/url?sa=t&rct=j&q=developing%20strategies%2
    0for%20responsible%20leadership&source=web&cd=1&ved=0CDoQ
    FjAA&url=http%3A%2F%2Fcompetingvalues.com%2Fcompetingval
    ues.com%2Fwp-content%2Fuploads%2F2009%2F07%2FDeveloping-
    Strategies-for-Responsible-
    Leadership.pdf&ei=KkJlUb7zHMvY7AarzYCoBA&usg=AFQjCNH
    NDbv70y8vGiqixJ_fPqARBemh7w&bvm=bv.44990110,d.d2k

9. Dassah M.O. (2010) "Responsible leaders: What it takes in a Multi Challenged Global Business Environment". Paper Presented at the First International Conference on Responsible Leadership, University of Pretoria in South Africa, 18-20 May 2010
10. IDC Herzlila, International Institute for Counter Terrorism (2012) ICT's Jihadi Website Monitoring Group
    http://www.marefa.org//index.php/%da%a8%d9%88%d9%a3%d9%a8
11. Junaid. S.W (2004) "The Concept of Leadership And its Application in the Sakkwato Caliphate" Paper Presented at the Conference of Ulama Organized to Commemorate the two Hundred years of the Sokoto Caliphate Held at the Attahiru Dalhalu Bafarwa Institute of Quranic and General Studies, Sokoto, 23-25 of July 2004

12. Mufuruki A. (2008) is there a Crisis of Leadership in Africa?
http://www.africaleadership.net/new005.htm 10/8/ 2008 P.P. 1-4

13. Obadina T. (2008) Africa's Crisis of Governance
http://www.afbis.com/analysis/crisis.htm

14. Pruzan P. & Miller W.C. (2005) "Spirituality as the basis of Responsible Leaderships and Responsible Companies", In Thomas Maak and Nicole M. Pless (eds.) Responsible Leadership, Routledge Publishers, London, 2005 (WWW. Rouledge.com)

15. Sacranie I. (2003) "the Challenges of Leadership in Islam: East and West" Paper Presented at Top Management Programme Conference held in London in 2003
http://www.google.gm/url?sa=t&rct=j&q=the%20challenge%20of%20 leadership%20in%20islam%3A%20east&source=web&cd=1&cad=rja &sqi=2&ved=0CCsQFjAA&url=http%3A%2F%2Fwww.mcb.org.uk %2Fdownloads%2FTMPC.pdf&ei=BkFlUabyOaj07AbIzIGwBA&usg =AFQjCNHzZXxJ700Em_yxyuqZ9oTAZpdxSg&bvm=bv.44990110, d.d2k

16. Sanyang A. (2012) "The Crisis in Guinea Bissau: In Search of a Sustainable Solution" in Aff'a – M'ndzie, Mireille (eds). African Views Intelligence Analysis, N.P.P:

Chapter 2

1. A.A. Senghore, PhD The Judiciary in Governance under the Second Republic of The Gambia – The Quest for Autonomy under the Second Republic", Journal of Third World Studies, Vol. 27, No. 2(Fall 2010), pp. 215-248

2. A.A. Senghore, PhD The Islamic System of Administration and its Capability to ensure lasting peace and sustainable development: A case study of Omar Ibn al Khatab's Style of Administration (Arabic) Paper presented at the International Conference on the Islamic Civilization and its Effectiveness for Muslims to Face the Challenges of the Modern Time held in Nouakchott – The Islamic Republic of Mauritania from the 12th – 14th February 2011.

3. Ake, C. (1996), Democracy and Development in Africa (Washington, DC. Brookings Institution)

4. Archie Mafeje, (1999) Democracy, Civil Society and Governance in Africa

5. B. Holden (1974) the Nature of Democracy, London Thomas Nelson

6. Bo Li, What is Constitutionalism? Perspectives, Vol.1, No.6 Democracy and Governance in Africa: Conclusions and papers presented at a conference of Africa Leadership Forum, Ota, Nigeria, 29 November-1 December 1991.

7. David Beetham (1993), "Auditing Democracy in Britain", Democratic Audit paper No. 1, London, Human Right Centre, University of Essex p.6.

8. Michael Seward (1994), "Democratic Theory and Indices of Democratisation", Defining and Measuring Democracy, SAGE Modern Politics Series, Vol 36, pp. 6— 21.

9. Holden (1974), The Nature of Democracy, London: Thomas Nelson, p. 7-9.

10. Mander Harsh and Asis Muhammed, Good Governance Resource Book, Banglor, Books for Change, 2004

11. Mummer Al Gathafi The Green Book: The Solution to the Problem of Democracy, the Economic Problem and the Social Basis of the Third Universal Theory Tripoli – Libya, World Center for the Study and Research of the Green Book (2005-latest edition 2008)

12. R. S. Kilcullen, Liberal democracy, 2000 (No place and date of publication indicated)

13. Rod Hague and Martin Harrop Comparative Government and Politics: an introduction – sixth edition New York USA, Palgrave Macmillan (2004)

14. Tumkumbi, Lumumba-Kasongo, (2005), Liberal democracy and its Critics in Africa: Political dysfunction and the struggle for social progress.

15. US State Department website (www.state.gov)

Chapter 3

1. Bodenheim Jurisprudence – The Philosophy and Method of the Law 36 (1974). For further detail see   Ibid., 37-57.
2. Locke, *The Second Treaties of Government* 4 – 11 (1952).
3. Abdal Rahim, "Fikrat Huqūq al-Insān Bāyn al-Mabd'a wa'l Tatbīq 11-26 (1968).
4. Locke, *Second Treaties*, 15-30
5. 1 Blackstone, *Commentaries on the Laws of England* 38 – 39 (1979).
6. Ibid., 119-121.
7. Hall, *The Political and Legal Philosophy of James Wilson – 1742 – 1798* pp. 35-36 (1966)
8. Bentham, "From An Introduction to the Principles of Morals and Legislation", Utilitarianism and Other Essays 62-63 (1987)
9. Ibid. Also see Fenwick, *Civil Liberties* 6-7 (1995).
10. Austine, *The Province of Jurisprudence Determined* 35-38. For further detail see 39 – 102 (1911).
11. Ibid.
12. This view or theory of law and its process is held by American Jurists like, Oliver Wendell Holmes, Joseph Bingham,
13. Jerome Frank, Eugen Ehrlich, and Karl Le Wellyn. See Benditt, Law as Rule and Principle – Problems of Legal Philosophy. 22-42 (1978)
14. Bodenheimer, Jurisprudence, 128 – 133. Also see Wade & Philips, constitutional and Administrative law, 87-89 (1977)
15. Kerruish, Jurisprudence as Ideology 141 (1991)
16. Ibid.
17. Ibid., 140. Also see Davis, Jurisprudence: Texts and Commentary 230 (1991). And Reiss (ed.) and Nesbet (tra.) Kant Political Writings 132-154 (1991).

18. Al-Ghāzāli, Al-Mustasfā 4-5 (N.D.). Also see 1 Al-Zūhayly, Al-Fiqh al-Islāmi wa Adillatūh 15 – 28 (1989).
19. Al – Shātibi, Al-Mūwāfaqāt fi Usul al-Sharī'āh 8 – 112 (N.D.).
20. Ibid.
21. Al-Attas, Islam and The Philosophy of Science 18 (1989). Also see,
22. Kashāf Istilāhāt al-Fūnūn. S. V. "Haqq", by al-Tahānawī.
23. Qutūb Muhammad Qutūb, Islam wa Huqūq al-Insān-Dirāsatun Muqārānah 32-34 (1984).
24. Al-Māwardi, Al-Ahkām al – Sultāniyyāh. 319-322 (1985).
25. Amrah, Al-Islām wa Hūqūq al-Insān: Darūrātun la Hūqūq 14-17 (1405 A.H./1985).
26. Ibid. Also see: Maudūdi, "Human Rights, The West and Islam" Human Rights in Islamic Law 1 – 3 (9993); Khan, "The Universal Declaration of Human Rights and the Human Rights in Islam – A comparative study, Ibid., 65 at 69.
27. Al – Attas, Prolefomena to Metaphysics of Islam – An Exposition of the Fundamental Elements of the World View of Islam 41 – 69 (1995)
28. Al – Attas Ibid.
29. Al – Ghazālī, Al – Iqtisād final – I'tiqād 135 (N.D.).
30. Kamali, Freedom of Expression in Islam 18 (1994).
31. Al-Mawardī, Adāb al Wazīr 3 – 4 (1994)
32. Weeramantry, "Islam and Human Rights," *Human Rights in Islamic Law* 3.
33. Fukuyama Francis: What is Governance? A working paper 314 January 2013, Centre for Global   Development,201
34. Ibid
35. World Bank Poverty Reduction Strategy paper (n.d):
36. OSCE: Democratic Governance. Office for Democratic Institutions and Human Rights, Austria, 2016
37. Dahrendorf R. The Challenge for Democracy// *Journal of Democracy*. 2003. № 14 (4). – 107.

38. Holden B. *The Nature of Democracy*. 1974, London: Thomas Nelson, p. 7-9.

39. Beetham, D, "Auditing Democracy in Britain," 1993. Democratic Audit paper No. 1, London, Human Right   Centre, University of Essex p.6.

40. Michael Saward, M. "Democratic Theory and Indices of Democratisation," Defining and Measuring Democracy, SAGE *Modern Politics Series*, 1994. vol 36, pp. 6— 21.

41. Ibid.

42. Ibid

43. Ibid. 6-20

44. Tan, S., and Bridge, J.W. 2008. *Democracy as Culture: Deweyan Pragmatism in a Globalizing World*. New York: State University of New York Press

45. Kim, S. 2014. *Confucian Democracy in East Asia: Theory and Practice*. New York: Cambridge University Press

46. Ibid

47. Ousman Sabally Vs The Inspector General of Police (2000) (Gambia Law Report [1997 2001] GR pp.878 - 883)

48. *Constitution of the Republic of The Gambia* (1997)

49. Wade E.C.S. and Philips Godfrey. 1997. *Constitutional and Administrative Law*. Third Edition. London and New York: Longman Group.

50. Nyamnjoh B. Francis. 2005. *Africa's Media, Democracy, and the Politics of Belonging*. London and New York: Zed Books.

51. Ibid, p.44-45.

52. Senghore A.A. (PhD) (1999) *Problems Concerning the Application of International Law of Human Rights by National Courts: A Critical Study of the Anglo-American and Indian Judicial Approaches*, (a PhD. Dissertation), The International Institute of Islamic Thought and Civilization of the International Islamic University, Kuala Lumpur, Malaysia.

53. Section 100 of *Constitution of the Republic of The Gambia* (1997)

54. Ibid

55. *Constitution of the Republic of The Gambia* (1970)

56. Ibid.

57. Coneley Marshall (1996) Human Rights, Development and Democracy Governance, Democracy and Human Right, *Canadian Journal of Development Studies*, vol. special issue, 99. 19 — 33.

58. H. Mander and M Asif. 2004. *Good Governance*. Bangalore: Books for Change

59. Mare Karl 2003: Legal Theory and Democratic Reconstruction. *American University International Law Review*, vol. No. 19, No. 2 pp.338 — 342.

60. Article 21 (3) of the Universal Declaration of Human Rights (1948) and Article 13 of the African Charter on Human People's Rights (1981). Also M. Garling and Chidi N. Odinkalu (2001), Building Bridges for Rights - London, Inter rights, pp. 14-16.and Momodou Jobe Vs The Attorney General (1984), Appeal cases, 689, 700. Judgement by Lord Diplock.

61. Ibid

62. Ibid

63. Quoted in Ibid.

64. Donnelly Jack 2003: 'Universal Declaration of Human Rights in Theory and Practice," *American University International Law Review*, vol. 19, No 2, pp. 552-553. And *The Constitution of the Republic of The Gambia 1997*

65. World Bank. 2004. State-Society Synergy for Accountability: Lessons for the World Bank. *World Bank Working Paper* No. 30, 2004. Washington: World Bank.

66. Younis, T.A. and Mostafa I.M.D. 2000. *Accountability in Public Management and Administration in Bangladesh*. England: Ashgate Publishing Ltd

67. Morachiello, E., Nicolau, D. and Hegbor, C.K (2015) Public Expenditure and Financial Accountability (PEFA) Assessment 2014, Project No. 2014/337137/1, The Gambia Final Report, 8 January 2015 EU.ACE/KPMG

68. Mulgan, Richard 2000: "'Accountability': An Ever-Expanding Concept," *Public Administration* Vol. 78 No. 3, pp. 555-573. And Ebrahim, A. 2006. Placing the Normative Logics of Accountability in "Thick" Perspective. MA: Harvard School of Government. *Working Paper Series* no.33.2,

69. Bovens, M. 2006. 'Analysing and assessing public accountability: a conceptual framework. *European Governance Papers* No.C-06-01.

70. *Asian Review of Public Administration.* Vol 12, No.2 (July – December 2000)

71. Mulgan, R. 2003. *Holding Power to Account: Accountability in Modern Democracies.* Basingstoke: Palgrave.

72. Pollitt, C. 2003. *The Essential Public Manager*, London: Open University Press/McGraw-Hill.

73. Ibid

74. Ibid

75. *The Constitution of The Republic of The Gambia 1997* and Ministry of Finance, GOTG 2014

76. Ibid. See: Morachiello, E.,Nicolau,D. and Hegbor, C.K (2015) Public Expenditure and Financial Accountability (PEFA) Assessment 2014, Project No. 2014/337137/1, The Gambia Final Report ,8 January 2015 EU.ACE/KPMG

77. Wehner, J. 2001: "Reconciling Accountability and Fiscal Prudence? The Budgetary Role and Impact of the German Parliament," Legislative Studies Vol. 7 No. 2, pp. 57-78.

78. Ibid. See: *The Constitution of The Republic of The Gambia 1997* and Ministry of Finance, GOTG 2014

79. Jammeh 2012: President's State of the Nation Speech

80. Mulgan, R. 2003. *Holding Power to Account: Accountability in Modern Democracies*. Basingstoke: and Palgrave. And Wehner, J. 2001: "Reconciling Accountability and Fiscal Prudence? The Budgetary Role and Impact of the German Parliament", Legislative Studies Vol. 7No. 2, pp. 57-78

81. White, F., Harden, I. and Donnelly, K. 1994: "Audit, accounting officers and accountability: the Pergau Dam affair", Public Law, pp. 526-534.   And White, F. and Hollingsworth, K, 1999. *Audit, Accountability and Government*. Oxford: Clarendon Press.

82. Kromann, J, Kristensen, B., Groszyk, W.S and Bühler, B. 2002: "Outcome-focused Management and Budgeting", *OECD Journal on Budgeting* Vol. 1 No. 4, pp. 7-34.

83. Thatcher, M. 2002: 'Delegation to independent regulatory agencies: pressures, functions and contextual mediation,' *West European Politics* 25: 125–147.

84. Ibid. See: Kromann, J, Kristensen, B., Groszy, W.S and Bühler, B. 2002: "Outcome-focused Management and Budgeting", OECD Journal on Budgeting Vol. 1 No. 4, pp. 7-34.

85. Ibid: See: Morachiello, E., Nicolau,D. and Hegbor, C.K (2015) Public Expenditure and Financial Accountability (PEFA) Assessment 2014,   Project No. 2014/337137/1, The Gambia Final Report, 8 January 2015 EU.ACE/KPMG

86. Ibid

87. Adhikari, Gautarn 2000: "From the Press to the Media," *Journal of Democracy*, vol. 11, No. 1, pp. 56-63. Administration Vol. 78 No. 3, pp. 555-573.

88. Aidoo, Akwasi 1993: Africa: 'Democracy without Human Rights" *Human Rights Quarterly*, Vol. 15 No. 4, pp. 703-715

89. Ansu-Kyeremeh K. 1999. "The Challenges of Surveying Public Opinion in an Emerging Democracy." *International Journal of Public Opinion Research*, Vol. 11 No. 1, pp. 59—72.

90. Article 19 of the International Covenant on Civil and Political Rights

91. Article 19. 1991. *Truth from Below: The Emergent Press in Africa*. Article 19 publications (Censorship Report).

92. Article 21 (3) of the Universal Declaration of Human Rights 1948; and Article 13 of the African Charter on Human People's Rights 1981: Also M. Garling and Chidi N. Odinkalu 2001: Building Bridges for Rights - London, Inter Rights. pp. 14-16.

93. *Asian Review of Public Administration*: July –December 2000: Vol. 12, No.2

94. Baboucar Gaye Vs. Inspector General of Police H.C 2000: 8 *Weekly Law Report of Nigeria* pp. 189 — 200.

95. Beetham D. (1994) Key Principles and Indices for a Democratic Audit. *Defining and Measuring Democracy*, Vol. 36, PP. 25— 41.

96. Bovens, M.2006: 'Analyzing and assessing public accountability: a conceptual framework

97. Budgetary Role and Impact of the German Parliament," *Legislative Studies* Vol. 7

98. Cairncross Francis. 1998. *The Death of Distance: How Communications Revolution Will Change Our Lives*. London: Orion Business Books

99. Coneley Marshall. 1996. "Human Rights, Development and Democracy:

100.   Governance and Contextual mediation'," *West European Politics* 25: 125–147.

101.   Democracy and Human Right, Canadian Journal of Development Studies, vol. special issue, 99. 19 – 33

102.   *Daily Observer* newspaper; Banjul, The Gambia. June 2, 2004.

103.   David Beetham 1993: "Auditing Democracy in Britain," *Democratic Audit Paper* No. 1, p.6. London, Human Right Centre, University of Essex.

104.   Donnelly Jack 2003: 'Universal Declaration of Human Rights in Theory and Practice." *American University International Law Review*, vol. 19, No 2, pp. 552-553.

105.   Dubnick, M.J. 2002. "Seeking salvation for accountability." A paper presented at the 2002 Annual Meeting of the American Political Science Association, Boston.

106.   E.C.S Wade and G. Godfrey Philips. 1977. *Constitutional and Administrative Law*. Ninth Edition. New York: Longman Group.

107.   Ebrahim, A. 2006. Placing the Normative Logics of Accountability in "Thick" Perspective. MA: Harvard School of Government. Working Paper Series no.33.2

108.   Eko, L. (2004) 'See All Evil, Hear All Evil, Rail Against All Evil: Le Messager and the Journalism of Resistance in Cameroon', The leadership challenge in Africa: Cameroon Under Paul Biya, pp. 123–51 in John Mukum Mbaku and Joseph Takougang [Eds.]. Africa World Press, Inc & The Red Sea Press, Inc. Trenton, New Jersey.

109.   European Governance Papers No.C-06-01

110.   Faye Sulayman, et al. 2004. "Monitoring Progress in the Practice of Good Governance in the Gambia." A Consultancy Report, Banjul, The Gambia.

111.   Feltoe Geoffrey. 1993: "Institutionalizing Press Freedom and the Role of a Free Press in the Promotion of Human Rights." *The Institutionalization of Human Rights in South Africa*, pp. 165 - 186.

112.   "Focused Management and Budgeting" *OECD Journal on Budgeting* Vol. 1

113.   Francis B Nyamnjoh. 2005. *Africa's Media, Democracy, and the Politics of Belonging*. London and New York: Zed Books.

114.   Fukuyama Francis. 2000. "The March of Equality." *Journal of Democracy*. Vol. 11, No. 1, pp. 49—55.

115.   Garling Marguerite and Odinkalu, A. Chidi. 2001: Building Bridges for Rights, The International Centre for the Legal Protection of Human Rights.

116.   Goetz, A. M. and Jenkins, R. 2001. "Hybrid Forms of Accountability: Citizen Engagement in: GOTG 2004:

117.   The Office of the Ombudsman (pdf), The Republic of The Gambia. Banjul: Accessed at Website: www.gambia50.gov.gm/files/pdfs

118.   GOTG 2007: *The Constitution of The Republic of The Gambia*. Banjul: GOTG

119.   GOTG 2014: *The National Medium Term Development Plan* (PAGE), GOTG/MOFEA

120.   Government of Philippines, 1987. *Constitution of the Philippines*, Republic of Philippines. Accessed atwww.ombudsman.gov.ph on January 1, 2016.

121.   Griffith, John. 1993. *Judicial Politics Since 1920*. Oxford, UK and Cambridge, MA: Blackwell.

122.   Grey-Johnson, Nana, 2004. *The Story of the Newspaper in The Gambia - An Interpretive Account of the History and Development of Newspaper Journalism in the Gambia*. Kanifing South, The Gambia: BPMRU.

123.   Wade, H.W.R. 1974. *Administrative Law*. Third Edition. Oxford, UK: Clarendon Press.

124.   Holden B. 1974. *The Nature of Democracy*. London: Thomas Nelson.

125.   Hyden Goran 1993: "The Challenges of Domesticating Rights in Africa." Human Rights and Governance in Africa, pp. 257-278.

126.   Institutions of Public Sector Oversight in India," *Public Management Review*, Vol. 3, Issue 3, pp. 363

127.   International Press Institute. 2004. *World Press Freedom Review*, December 2004

128.   Islam Nasir and Morrison R. David. 1996. Governance, Democracy and Human Rights. Canadian Journal of Development Studies, vol.7 no special issue 1996, pp. 5— 16.

129.   Remarks by President Yahya Jammeh, A.J.J (2012)

130.   Kaba Jallow Vs the Attorney General (1972) (not yet reported).

131.   Kromann, J, Kristensen, B., Groszyk , W.S and Bühler, B. 2002: "Outcome-Kumar, C. Raj. 2003. "National Human Rights Institutions." *American University International Law Review,* vol. 19, No. 2, pp. 283-288.

132.   Mare, Karl. 2003. "Legal Theory and Democratic Reconstruction." *American University International Law Review,* vol. No. 19, No. 2 pp. 338-342.

133.   Michael Saward 1994: "Democratic Theory and Indices of Democratization", Defining and measuring Democracy, SAGE Modern politics series, Vol. 36, pp. 6 - 21.

134.   Momodou Jobe Vs The Attorney General 1984: Appeal cases, 689, 700. Judgement by Lord Diplock.

135.   Morachiello, E, Nicolau, D. and Hegbor, C.K. 2015. Public Expenditure and Financial Accountability (PEFA) Assessment 2014, Project No. 2014/337137/1, The Gambia Final Report, January 8, 2015, EU.ACE/KPMG

136.   Mulgan, R.2003: Holding Power to Account: Accountability in Modern Democracies, Basingstoke: Palgrave, GB.

137.   Mulgan, Richard 2000: "'Accountability': An Ever-expanding Concept", in Public Administration and Management, 78.3, pp. 555–573.

138.   Ngoh V. Jolius 2004: "Biya and the Transition" *The Leadership Challenge in Africa - Cameroon under Biya, pp. 427 - 428. No. 2, pp. 57-78. No. 4, pp. 7-34.*

139.   "Negotiating Party Politics and Traditional Authority: Obafemi Awolowo" in *Ijebu-Remo. Nigeria, 1949-1955 ... The Dynamics of Power and the Rule of Law, 2003. 7 ...*

140.   Ousman Sabally Vs The Inspector General of Police 2000: *Gambia Law Report* [1997 2001] GR pp.878 - 883) Palgrave.

141.   Pollitt, C. 2003. *The Essential Public Manager*. London: Open University Press/McGraw-Hill.

142.   Sections 4, 7, 17—38,60,139—159,76,100, 120and42—45, 145— 148, 131 — 133 and 163— 165 respectively of the *1997 Constitution of the Republic of The Gambia.*

143.   Presentation on the case involving "National Alliance for Democracy and Development Vs the Independent Electoral Commission" Monday 22 June (2005)

144.   Senghore A.A. 1999*: Problems Concerning the Application of International Law of Human Rights by National Courts: A Critical Study of the Anglo-American and Indian Judicial Approaches, (PhD Dissertation)*, The International Institute of Islamic Thought and Civilization of the International Islamic University, Kuala Lumpur, Malaysia.

145.   Senghore A. A. 2005 "Contribution of the Human Rights Revolution to the Promotion *of Gender Development and Equality." A paper presented at the Management Development Institute in Kanifing, The Gam*bia.

146.   Sklar Richard 2003: *The Premise of Mixed Government in African Political Studies; Indigenous Political Structures and Governance in Africa.*

147.   Thatcher, M.2002 ''Delegation to independent regulatory agencies": *pressures, Functions and The Criminal Code Act (2005 amendment).*

148.   *The Europa World Book.* 1990. London: Europa Publications.

149.   *The Gambia News and Reports* magazine - December (2002)

150.   The Independent newspaper issues from 23 - 25th July 1999. 19 - 22 August 1999, 21 - 23, 28-30, July and 27 - 30, November 2000. Also, 16-19, 20 - 22 July 2001, 17-19 August and 23 - 25 November 2001. Also, 13-16, January and 22 - 25 September

2003. And 16 - 18, January and 8 -11 April 2004. Also, 24 - 27, October 2005. [This list is not exhaustive but showing example of all the issues surveyed]

151.   The National Media Commission Act (2001) of The Republic of The Gambia (Now repealed)

152.   The Newspaper Act 1944: The State Vs. A.N.O Ousainou Darboe and others June (2005) (Not yet reported)

153.   The Telegraphic Stations' Act 1913:

154.   US Department of State (n.d): Diplomacy in Action, United States of America. Accessed at: http://go.usa.gov/ on December 31st, 2015

155.   Wade E.C.S. and Philips Godfrey. 1997. *Constitutional and Administrative Law*. Third Edition. London and New York: Longman Group

156.   Wade H.W.R. 1974. *Administrative Law*. Oxford.

157.   Reconciling Accountability and Fiscal Prudence? A Case Study of the Budgetary Role and Impact of the German Parliament J. Wehner Pages 57-78 | Published online: 08 Sep 2010 Cite this chapter https://doi.org/10.1080/714003876

158.   White, F. and Hollingsworth, K. 1999. *Audit, Accountability and Government*. Oxford: Clarendon Press.

159.   White, F., Harden,I. and Donnelly,K. 1994: "Audit, accounting officers and accountability: the Pergau Dam Affair," *Public Law*, pp. 526-534.

160.   World Bank: State-Society Synergy for Accountability: Lessons for the World Bank. *World Bank Working Paper* No. 30, 2004. Washington: World Bank.

161.   World Bank Institute (n.d): The Role of Ombudsman Offices in Promoting Good Governance and Effective Service Delivery. Washington DC: World Bank Institute Nordic Trust Fund

162.   Younis, T.A. and Mostafa Iqbal, M.D *2000: Accountability in Public management and administration in Bangladesh-Routledge* Revivals.

163.   Constitution of the Republic of the Gambia (1970)

164. Constitution of the Republic of the Gambia (1997)
165. The Criminal Code Act (2005 Amendments)
166. Decree No 71 1996: Amending the Newspaper Act.
167. The Gambia Radio and Television Services (GRTS) Act
168. The National Media Commission Act 2001: (Now repealed).
169. The Newspaper Act 1944: and as amended in 1996 and 2004.
170. The Telegraphic Stations Act (1913)
171. The Special Criminal Court Act (1979)
172. The African Charter on Broadcasting adopted at Windhoek in 2001.
173. The African Charter on Human and People's Rights (The Banjul Charter).
174. Article 19 (March 2003 issue)
175. Charter of the (former) Organization of the African Unity (Now defunct)
176. Charter of the United Nations Organization
177. Charter of Fundamental Rights of the European Union (December 2000)
178. The Constitutive Act of the African Union
179. The Declaration of Principles on Freedom of Expression in Africa (2001)
180. The European Convention on Human Rights and Fundamental Freedoms
181. The General Principles on Freedom of Expression and Broadcasting Regulations
182. The Inter-American Convention on Human Rights and Fundamental Freedoms
183. The International Covenant on Civil and Political Rights (1966)
184. The International Covenant on Economic Social and Cultural Rights (1966)
185. The Universal Declaration of Human Rights of (1948)
(Numbers 163-171 are selected Gambian statutory instruments,

whereas numbers 172 - 185 are selected international legal instruments)

Chapter 4

1. Aboubacarr A. Senghore (2005) "Contribution of the Human Rights Revolution to the Promotion of Gender Development and Equality," paper presented at the Management Development Institute in Banjul, The Gambia.

2. Also, presentation on National Alliance for Democracy and Development Vs the Independent Electoral Commission Monday 22 June (2005).

3. Article 19 of the International Covenant on Civil and Political Rights.

4. Articles 21 (3) of the Universal Declaration of Human rights (1948) and 13 of the African Charter on Human People's Rights (1981) Also M. Garling and Chidi N. Odinkalu (2001), Building Bridges for Rights - London, Inter rights, Pp. 14-16.

5. Baboucar Gaye Vs. Inspector General of Police H.C (2000) 8 Weekly Law Report of Nigeria pp. 189 — 200.

6. The *Daily Observer* newspaper — June 2, 2004.

7. David Beetham (1993), "Auditing Democracy in Britain," *Democratic Audit Paper* No. 1, London, Human Right Centre, University of Essex p.6.

8. E.C.S. Wade and G. Godfrey Philips (1977) *Constitutional and Administrative Law*, Ninth Edition, New York, U.S.A.: Longman Group.

9. *Europa World Yearbook* (1990) Vol. 1, London: Europa Publications Limited

10. Francis B. Nyamnjoh (2005) *Africa's Media: Democracy and the Politics of Belonging*, Zed Books, London and New York.

11. Geoffrey Feltoe (1993), "Institutionalizing Press Freedom and the Role of a Free Press in the Promotion of Human Rights," the *Institutionalization of Human Rights in Southern Africa*, pp. 165 - 186.

12. International Press Institute (2004) *World Press Freedom Review,* December 2004. IPR, Vienna, pp. 31 —32.

13. Holden (1974) *The Nature of Democracy,* London: Thomas Nelson, pp. 7-9.

14. H.W.R. Wade (1974) *Administrative Law,* third edition, Oxford, UK, Clarendon Press.

15. Kaba Jallow Vs the Attorney General (1972) (not yet reported).

16.Michael Saward (1994) "Democratic Theory and Indices of Democratization" *Defining and Measuring Democracy,* SAGE Modern Politics Series, vol 36, pp. 6— 21.

17. Momodou Jobe vs. The Attorney General (1984), Appeal cases, 689, 700. Judgement by Lord Diplock.

18. Nana Grey Johnson (2004) *The Story of the Newspaper In the Gambia: An interpretive Account of the History and Development of Newspaper Journalism,* Kanifing South, The Gambia, BPMRU.

19. Ousman Sabally vs. The Inspector General of Police (2000) (*Gambia Law Report* [1997 2001] GR pp.878 - 883)

20. Sections 4,7, 17—38,60,139—159,76,100, 120and42—45, 145— 148, 131 — 133 and 163— 165 respectively of the 1997 Constitution of the Republic of The Gambia.

21. Sulayman Faye *et al.,* (2004) *Monitoring Progress in the Practice of Good Governance in The Gambia,* a consultancy report, Banjul, The Gambia.

22. The Criminal Code Act (2005 amendment).

23. *The Gambia News and Reports* magazine - December (2002).

24. The *Independent* Newspaper issues from 23 — 25th July 1999. 19 — 22 August 1999, 21 — 23, 28-30, July and 27 —30, November 2000. Also, 16-19, 20 — 22 July 2001, 17-19 August and 23 —25 November 2001. Also,

13-16, January and 22 —25 September 2003. And 16 — 18, January and 8-11 April 2004. Also, 24-27, October 2005. This list showing various issues of the *independent* newspaper is not an exhaustive one. Rather, it is only an example of all the issues surveyed.

25. The National Media Commission Act (2001) (Now repealed)

26. The Newspaper Act (1944)

27. The State Vs. A.N.O Ousainou Darboe and others June (2005) (Not yet reported)

28. The Telegraphic Stations' Act (1913)

29. Adhikari, Gautarn (2000) "From the Press to the Media" *Journal of Democracy*, vol. 11, No. 1, pp. 56-63.

30. Aidoo, Akwasi (1993) "Africa: Democracy without Human Rights" *Human Rights Quarterly*, Vol. 15 No. 4, pp. 703-715

31. Ansu-Kyeremeh K (1999) "The Challenges of Surveying Public Opinion in an Emerging Democracy" *International Journal of Public Opinion Research*, Vol. 11 No. 1, pp. 59—72.

32. Article 19 (1991) *Truth from Below*

33. *The Emergent Press in Africa* (Article 19 publications - censorship report).
34. B. Holden (1974) *The Nature of Democracy*. London: Thomas Nelson.

35. Beetham D. (1994) "Key Principles and Indices for a Democratic Audit" *Defining and Measuring Democracy*, Vol. 36, pp. 25— 41.

36. Cairncross Francis (1998) *The Death of Distance: How Communications Revolution Will Change Our Lives*, Orion Business Books - London.

37. Coneley Marshall (1996) "Human Rights, Development and Democracy Governance, Democracy and Human Right", *Canadian Journal of Development Studies*, vol. special issue 99, pp. 19 — 33.

38. Donnelly Jack (2003) 'Universal Declaration of Human Rights in Theory and Practice", American University *International Law Review*, vol. 19, No 2, pp. 552-553.

39. Eko Lyombe (2004) "Hear all Evil, See All Evil, Rail Against all Evil: le Message and the Journalism of Resistance" *in Cameroon The leadership Challenge in Africa- Cameroon under Biya.*

40. *The Europa World Book* (1990) London: Europa Publications.

41. Fukuyama Francis (2000) "The March of Equality," *Journal of Democracy*, vol 11, No. 1, pp. 49—55.

42. Garling Marguerite and Odinkalu, A. Chidi (2001) "Building Bridges for Rights," *The International Centre for the Legal Protection of Human Rights.*

43. Hyden Goran (1993) "The Challenges of Domesticating Rights in Africa," *Human Rights and Governance in Africa*, pp. 257-278.

44. Islam Nasir and Morrison R. David (1996) Governance, Democracy and Human Right, Canadian Journal of Development Studies, vol. no special issue 1996, pp. 5— 16.

45. Mare Karl (2003) "Legal Theory and Democratic Reconstruction," *American University International Law Review*, vol. No. 19, No. 2 pp. 338 — 342.

46. Kumar, C. Raj (2003) "National Human Rights Institutions," *American University International Law Review*, vol. 19, No. 2, pp. 283-288.

47. Ngoh V. Julius (2004) "Biya and the Transition, The Leadership Challenge in Africa - Cameroon under Biya", pp. 427 - 428.

48. Nolte Insa (2003) "Negotiating Party Politics and Traditional Authority: Obafemi Awolowo" in *Ijebu-Remo, Nigeria 1949 — 1955", The Dynamics of Power and the Rule of Law.*

49. Senghore A.A. (1999) "Problems Concerning the Application of International Law of Human Rights by National Courts: A Critical Study of the Anglo-American and Indian Judicial Approaches" (a PhD Dissertation). The International Institute of Islamic Thought and Civilization of the International Islamic University, Kuala Lumper, Malaysia.

50. Sklar Richard (2003) *The Premise of Mixed Government in African Political Studies Indigenous Political Structures and Governance in Africa:*

university of California, Los Angeles.

51. Wade E.C.S. and Philips Godfrey (1985) *Constitutional and Administrative Law*, tenth edition, Longman group, London and New York, U.S.A.

52. Constitution of the Republic of The Gambia (1970)

53. Constitution of the Republic of The Gambia (1997)

54. The Criminal Code Act (2005 Amendments)

55. Decree No 71 (1996) Amending the Newspaper Act

56. The Gambia Radio and Television Services (GRTS) Act

57. The National Media Commission Act (2001) (Now repealed)

58. The Newspaper Act. (1944) and as amended in 1996 and 2004

59. The Telegraphic Stations Act (1913)

60. The Special Criminal Court Act (1979)

61. The African Charter on Broadcasting adopted at Windhoek in 2001

62. The African Charter on Human and People's Rights (The Banjul Charter)

63. Article 19 (March 2003 issue)

64. Charter of the (former) Organization of the African Unity (now known as the African Union)

65. Charter of the United Nations' Organization

66. Charter of Fundamental Rights of the European Union (December 2000)

67. The Constitutive Act of the African Union

68. The Declaration of Principles on Freedom of Expression in Africa (2001)

69. The European Convention on Human Rights and Fundamental Freedoms

70. The General Principles on Freedom of Expression and Broadcasting Regulations

71. The Inter American Convention on Human Rights and Fundamental Freedoms

72. The International Covenant on Civil and Political Rights (1966)

73. The International Covenant on Economic Social and Cultural Rights (1966)

74. The Universal Declaration of Human Rights of (1948)

(Numbers 52 -60 are selected Gambian statutory instruments, whereas numbers 61 – 74 are selected international legal instruments)

Chapter 5

NOTES

1.   Justice Brobbery is the former Chief Justice of The Gambia. See A. S. Brobbery, "The Judiciary as a Vehicle for the Realization of the Millennium Development Goals: Ensuring the Rule of Law in Sustainable Economic Development," *Paper presented at a United Nations Development Program (UNDP) Workshop on Law, Development and Governance, Kairaba Beach Hotel, Banjul, The Gambia, 2005.*
2.   John Griffith, Judicial Politics Since 1920 (Oxford, UK and Cambridge, MA: Blackwell, 1993), p. 1.

Chapter 6

1. Bodenheimer (1974) *Jurisprudence* – The Philosophy and Method of Law 36. For further detail see Ibid., 37-57.

2. Locke (1952) *The Second Treaties of Government* 4 – 11

3.   Abdal   Rahim   (1968)   "FikratHuqūq   al-InsānBāyn   al-Mabd'awa'lTatbīq 11-26

4. Locke, *Second Treaties*, 15-30. Also, Muhammad Hashim Kamali (1997) Freedom of Expression in Islam, Cambridge Text Society, UK.

5. Blackstone, Commentaries on the Laws of England 38 – 39 (1979).

6. Ibid., 119-121.

7. Hall (1966) *The Political and Legal Philosophy of James Wilson –* 1742 – 1798 pp. 35-36

8. Bentham (1987) "From An Introduction to the Principles of Morals and Legislation," *Utilitarianism and Other Essays* 62-63

9. Ibid. Also see Fenwick, Civil Liberties 6-7 (1995).

10. Austine (1911) *The Province of Jurisprudence Determined* 35-38. For further detail see 39 – 102

11. Ibid.

12. This view or theory of law and its process is held by American Jurists like Oliver Wendell Holmes, Joseph Bingham, Jerome Frank, Eugen Ehrlich and Karl Le Wellyn. See Benditt (1978) *Law as Rule and Principle – Problems of Legal Philosophy*, pp. 22-42

13. Bodenheimer (1974) *Jurisprudence*, pp. 128 – 133. Also see Wade & Philips (1977) *Constitutional and Administrative Law,* pp. 87 89

14.   Kerruish (1991) *Jurisprudence as Ideology* p. 141

15.   Ibid.

16.   Ibid., 140. Also see Davis, Jurisprudence: Texts and Commentary 230 (1991).   And Reiss (ed.) and Nesbet (tra.) Kant Political Writings 132-154 (1991).

17.   1 Al-Ghāzāli, Al-Mustasfā 4-5 (N.D.).   Also see 1 Al-Zūhayly, Al-Fiqh al-IslāmiwaAdillatūh 15 – 28 (1989).

18.   2 Al – Shātibi, Al-Mūwāfaqāt fi Usul al-Sharī'āh 8 – 112 (N.D.).

19.   Ibid.

20.   Al-Attas (1989) *Islam and The Philosophy of Science* 18. Also see,

    i.   1 KashāfIstilāhāt al-Fūnūn. S. V. "Haqq", by al-Tahānawī.

    ii.   Qutūb Muhammad Qutūb, Islam waHuqūq al-Insān-DirāsatunMuqārānah 32-34 (1984).

21.   Al-Māwardi, Al-Ahkām al – Sultāniyyāh.319-322 (1985).

22.   'Amrah, Al-IslāmwaHūqūq al-Insān: Darūrātun la Hūqūq 14-17 (1405 A.H./1985).

23.   Ibid. Also see

    i.   Maudūdi, "Human Rights, The West and Islam" Human Rights in Islamic Law 1 – 3 (9993).

    ii.   Khan, "The Universal Declaration of Human Rights and the Human Rights in Islam – A comparative study, Ibid., 65 at 69.

24.   Al – Attas (1995*) Prolefomena to Metaphysics of Islam – An exposition of the Fundamental Elements of the World View of Islam* 41 – 69

25.   Al – Attas Ibid.

26.   Al – Ghazālī, Al – Iqtisād final – I'tiqād 135 (N.D.).

27.	Kamali (1994) Freedom of Expression of Expression in Islam 18.

28.	Al-Mawardī, Adāb al Wazīr 3 – 4 (1994)

29.	Weeramantry, "Islam and Human Rights", Human Rights in Islamic Law 3.

30.	Ibid

31.	Dixon and McCorquodate, Cases and Materials on International Law 192 – 94 (1995). Also see, Australian Legal Dictionary, S.V. "Human Rights".

32.	Kamali, Freedom of Expression of Expression, 18. Also, Mahmasani, Falsafat al – Tashrī fi al Islām 14 – 17 (1946).

33.	See Arts 6, 13 and 8 of the American, Indian and Pakistani Constitutions respectively. Also Sec. 4 of the Gambian Constitution article 7.

34.	International Encyclopaedia of Social Science, (1972 ed.) S.V. "Human Rights", by Schwelb.

35.	This is a reference to the practice of slavery under Roman and the absence of a written constitution and a Bill of Human Rights which limit the powers of modern government, as well the notion of parliamentary supremacy under English common law. See Ibid.

36.	See these documents in Gisbert's Constitutions of the Countries of the World 71 – 151 and 273 (1997).

37.	Schwelb, Human Rights, 540

i.	Abdal Rahim, FikratHūqūq al Insān, 40.

ii.   Harries, "Human Rights in Theological perspective", Human Rights for the 1990s (1991).

38.   Schwelb, "Human Rights", 541.

39.   Arts 39 – 69 of the Russain Constitution of 1918 as amended in 1977.   See Simons (ed.)   The Constitutions of The Communist World 343 at 362 – 368.

40.   Schwelb, "Human Right", 541.

41.   Lautherpacht, International Law and Human Rights 115 (1968).

42.   Schwelb, "Human Rights", 541.

43.   Lautherpacht, International Law, 115 -118

44.   Schwelb, Passim., 541. For further detail see Lautherpacht Ibid.,

45.   Beurgenthal, International Human Rights in A Nutshell 1 (1988).

46.   Such as The Genocide Convention 1948, The U.N. Convention on the Elimination of All Forms of Racial Discrimination, The Convention on the Suppression and Punishment of the Crime of Social and Cultural Rights: A perspective on its Development 7 (1995).

47.   1 Oppenhein's International Law 4 (1992)

48.   Glahn, Law Among Nations – an Introduction to Public International Law, 235 – 236 (1992).

49.   Ibid., 4.

50.   Al-Shāybānī, Al-Siyārcomm.. Al-Sarakhi,(Maji-Khadduri Islamic Law of Nations 8 and 39 – 40 (1986).

440

51.	Humphrey, No Distant Millennium – The International Law of Human Rights 15 (1989).

52.	The is a reference to the United Nations and its component organs, Ibid.

53.	For further details about the nature of the I.L.H.R. see Ibid., 15.

54.	Buergenthal, International Human Rights, 14.

55.	Weeramantry, Justice Without Frontiers: Furthering Human Rights 4 – 5 (1997).

56.	Byrnes and Chan (Eds.) Public Law and Human Rights: A Hong Kong Source Book 233 (1993).

57.	Arts. 1,2,3 (1), 55,56,62,68 and 76 of the U.N. Charter.

58.	See The Preamble of the U.D.H.R.

59.	Mishar, "Cardinal Principles of Human Rights", 10 (1) Indian Bar Review 44 – 45 (1993).

60.	Quoted in Ibid.

61.	Arts. 3,4,5,9,10,13,17,18,19,20 and 21 of the U.D.H.R and the corresponding articles of the International Convention on Civil and Political Rights 1996 (The I. C.C.P.R.)

62.	Arts. 23,25and 26 of the U.D.H.R and the corresponding articles of the International Convention on Economic Social and Culture of 1996 (The I.C.E.S.C.R)

63.	Art. 27 of the U.D.H.R and the corresponding articles of the I.C.E.S.C.R.

64. Baily, The U.N. Security Council and Human Rights 123 – 142 (1994).

65. Sedley, "Human Rights: A 21st Century Agenda", Human Rights for the 21st Century 1- 8 (1997).

66. U.N Reso. 1514 (tv) see BrownLie, Basic Documents on Human Rights 28 1992). It is interesting to note that when this declaration was being adopted the major colonial powers i.e. U.S.A., U.K, France, Spain and Portugal abstained from voting. See Ibid.

67. Baehr, The Role of Human Rights in Foreign Policy 23 (1994).

68. B.B.C "News Hour", January 1998.

69. Idem. May 1998.

70. See the U.N.'s Chart of Ratification issued in 1996. Also see Human Rights in Islam Papers Presented at the 5th Islamic Thought Conference in Tehran – Iran, from January 29 – 31st 1987 p. 10 (1978).

71. Att. 1

72. Art. 2

73. Art. 3

74. Art. 4

75. Art. 5

76. Art. 6

77. Art. 7

78. Art. 8.

79.   Art. 9

80.   Art. 10

81.   Art. 11

82.   Art. 13

83.   Art. 15

84.   Art. 14

85.   Art. 15

86.   Art. 19

87.   Art. 20

88.   The remaining three articles 16,17 and 18 deal with the rights of the individual against any encroachment on or interference with his or her property, except only in accordance with procedure established by Shari'ah or Islamic law and the rights of employers and employees as well as the right of the individual to be provided with the basic necessities of life and a fairly adequate standard of living by the government or at least to be given the chance to achieve that standard of living by his or her own effort and respect.

89.   Anand, Origin and Development of the Law of the Sea 1 (1983).

90.   Al-Attas, Islam and Secularism, 77 at F.N. 82 (1993). This important point has been brought to my attention by Prf. Dr. Wan Muhammad Nor Wan Daud, Deputy Director of ISTAC, in a private discussion I had with him.

91   In his work, *De IndisNoviterInventis* Franscisco Devitoria spoke about the rights of native Indians discovered by the Spanish settlers in the Americas, whereas Franscisco Suarez in his work De Bello et de Indis (on war and the Indians spoke about sovereign equality between Spain and the recently discovered Indians, see The New Enclyclopaedia Britanica (vol. II 1986 ed.) S. V. "Suarez". As for the Italian jurist Aberico – Gentili (1552 – 1608), in his 1598 work, *De Jure Belli* (on the law of war), Gentili spoke about certain norms of international law by induction from the observable practice of states rather than by deduction from the theological moral principles. Such norms included humanity and justice in warfare. See Encyclopaedia America (Vol. 12), S.V. "GentiliAlberico".

92   Knight, The Life and works of Hugo Grotius 194 (1962).

93   Al – Attas, Islam and Secularism., 20.

94   Ibid., 20 -22.

95   ĀyyatullahYazdi, "Human Rights in Islam" paper presented at the Meeting of Human Rights in Islam, Tehran – Iran, 26 – 28 December 1989.

96   1 Al-Shaybānī, Al-Siyar, comp. Al – Sarkhāsi, Al-Siyar al-Kabir; al-Shaybāni'ssiyar 133, 145 – 9, 252 – 370 and 466 (1981).

97   Moin al-dīn, The Charter of the Islamic Conference and Legal Framework of Economic Co – operation Among its Member State 16 (1987).

98   Baehr, Role of Human Rights, 15.

99   Maudūdī, "Human Rights in Islam", Al-Tawhid. 59 at 61 (1981).

100   Ibid.

101   11 Al _ Tabarī, Jami' al-Bayān fi Tafsir al-Qurān 89 (1980).

102   16 Al-Qurtūbī, Al-Jami' li Ahkāmal-Qurān 341 (1967).

103   5 IbnHanbal, Al-Musnād 411 (1995).

104   2 Al-Būkhari, Sāhīhāl al-Būkhārī 407 (1987).

105   Al-Tabari, Tafsir al-Qurān, 89.

106   5 IbnManzūr, Lisān al-'Arab 3428 – 3429 (N.D.).

107   For further details about Omar's style of administration see 1 Sayf al-din, 'Alām al-Sāhābah 546 (1981),.

108   1 'Aqād, Al-'Abqariyyāt al-Islāmiyyah 421 (1983).

109   Ibid.

110   AbūYūsufYa'qūb, Kitab al-Kharāj 67 – 72 (1980).

111   B.B.C. "News Hour", April 1997.

112   Al-Attas, Islam the Concept of Religion and the Foundation of Ethics and Morality 12 (1992).

113   Ibid., 4.

114   Al-Attas, Islam and Secularism, 25.

115   For further detail see Amnesty International Report 186 – 268 (1985).

116   Weeramantry Justice without Frontiers, Furthering Human Rights 126 – 140 (1997). Also see Enclyclopaedia of Religion And Ethics (1971, ed.,) S.V. "Toleration", by Arnold.

117   Elias, News Horizons in International Law 29 – 43 (1992).

118   Thiam, "Human Rights in African Cultural Tradition, Human Rights Teachings 4 – 10 (1997).

Chapter 7

1. Abdul Barr IB. (2007) – Al-Kafly fee Fiqh Ahlil Madinahal – Maliki, Al-Maktabah al – Assriyah: Beirul – Lebanon

2. An-Na'im, A. (1999a) 'Introduction', in An-Na'im, A. (ed.) *Universal Rights, Local Remedies: Implementing Human Rights in the Legal Systems of Africa*, Interights: London, 1-21.

3. Ayantayo J.K (Dr) (2011) "*African traditional Ethics and Transformation: Innovation and Ambivalence involved, and Modification for sound Second 21st Century African Intellectual Scholarship*".Available at http://www.codesria.org/IMG/pdf/ayantayo.pdf}. Accessed: March 2015

4. Ayittey G.B.N (1991) Indigenous African Institutions, American University: Washington D.C

5. Ayodeji, G.I and Odukoya, S.I (2014) *Perception of Judicial Corruption: Assessing Its Implications For Democratic and Sustainable Development in Nigeria*; Journal of Sustainable Development in Africa (Volume 16, No.2, 2014)

6. Burger,W.E. *The Decline of Professionalism*, 63 Fordham L. Rev. 949 (1995).Available at: http://ir.lawnet.fordham.edu/flr/vol63/iss4/2.Accessed:August 2016}

7. De Houwer, J., Baeyens, E., Vansteenwegan, D. & Eelen, E. (2000) "Verbal evaluative conditioning in the picture-picture paradigm with

446

random assignment of conditioned stimuli to unconditioned stimuli " *Journal of Experimental Psychology: Animal Behaviour Processes*, 26 (2), 237-2428.

8. Economides. K (2010) *"The Role of Law Schools in Founding and Reviving Legal Professionalism – The Need for Ethical Leadership."* Paper presented at a Public Lecture at The Faculty of Law of the University of the Gambia in 2010: Banjul - The Gambia.

9. Ellett, R. (2013) *Politics of Judicial Independence in Lesotho.* South Africa: Freedom House

10. Etta, E.E. and Asukwo, O. O (2011). Nature Of African Ethics. *INTERNET AFRREV: An International Online Multi-disciplinary Journal Vol.* 1(2) June 2012:55-60. Available at{afrrevjo.net/journals/internetafrrev/vol1_no2_art9_etta&asukwo_af ricanethics_june2012.pdf}. Accessed: August 2016

11. Ghana Integrity Initiative (2007) *Report on Judicial Corruption Monitoring Exercise in Ghana;* Accra-Tema, and Kumasi: Ghana Integrity Initiative.

12. Field, A.P. (2005) in Wills, A.J. (Ed.) New Directions in Human Associative Learning Mahwah, New Jersey Lawrence Erlbaum Associates.

13. Giles, M. and Jeremy. H (2001). "Human rights and development in Africa: moral intrusion or empowering opportunity?" *Review of African Political Economy*, 28(88) pp. 177–196.

14. Heineman, Jr. B.W; Lee, W.F. and Wilkins, D.B (2015) "Lawyers as Professionals and as Citizens: Key Roles and Responsibilities in the 21[st Century]." Center on the Legal Profession at Harvard Law School

15. Hockings, C. (2010) *Inclusive learning and teaching in higher education: Synthesis of research.* Available at {www.heacademy.ac.uk/evidencenet}. Accessed: {August 2016}

16. Hofstede, G. (2001). *Culture's Consequences: Comparing Values, Behaviors, Institutions and Organizations across Nations.* Thousand Oaks, CA: Sage (co-published in the PRC as Vol. 10 in the Shanghai Foreign Language Education Press *SFLEP Intercultural Communication Reference Series*, 2008)

17. Hofstede, G. (2011). *Dimensionalizing Cultures: The Hofstede Model in Context*. Online Readings in Psychology and Culture, 2(1). Available at{ http://dx.doi.org/10.9707/2307-919.1014}.Accessed:{August 2016}

18. Joireman, S. F. 1999. *Legal Institutions and the Rule of Law: comparing the effectiveness of common law and civil law countries.* Paper read at American Political Science Association Annual Meeting, at Atlanta, GA.

19. Joireman, S. F., (2001) *"Inherited Legal Systems and Effective Rule of Law: Africa and the Colonial Legacy"* Political Science Faculty Publications. Paper 113.Available at: http://scholarship.richmond.edu/polisci-faculty-publications/113.Accessed{August 27th 2016}

20. Khan S. (2009) *"Ethics of Legal Profession"*. {Available at: file:///C:/Users/hp/AppData/Local/Temp/Rar$EX00.833/Dr.%20Seng hore!/ethics-of-legal-profession-1275306.html}.Accessed: March 2015

21. Kigongo J.K. (2000) *"The relevance of African Ethics to Contemporary African Society"* {Available at: file:///C:/Users/hp/AppData/Local/Temp/Relevance%20of%20Ethics-1.htm}.Accessed March 2015

22. Kirby M. (1996) *"Legal Professional Ethics in Times of Change"*. Paper Presented at the *St. James Ethics Centre in Sydney on 23 July 1996. In:* Ghana Integrity Initiative (2007) *Report on Judicial Corruption Monitoring Exercise in Ghana;* Accra-Tema, and Kumasi: Ghana Integrity Initiative

23. Lantolf, J.P., (2000) *Introducing sociocultural theory. In:* Lantolf, J. P., ed. *Sociocultural theory and second language learning.* Oxford University Press, 1-26

24. Manchester, C. and Salter, D. (2006) *Exploring the Law: The Dynamics of Precedent and Statutory Interpretation (3*[rd] edn). London: Sweet and Maxwell

25. M'Bai F.E (2013) "Law and Lawyers in A Changing Society" *Paper Presented on the Occasion of the First Call to the Bar*

Ceremony by The Gambia Law School, at Paradise Suit Hotel in Banjul on Friday 18th January 2013

26. Nagengast, C. and Turner, T. (1997) '*Introduction: Universal Human Rights Versus Cultural Relativity'*, Journal of Anthropological Research, 53, 269-272.

27. Nonaka, I., and Toyama, R. (2003). 'The knowledge-creating theory revisited: knowledge creation as a synthesizing process'. *Knowledge Management Research & Practice*, Vol 1, pp 2-10.

28. Omoregbe, Joseph (1993). *Ethics: A Systematic and Historical Study*. Lagos: Joja Press Limited.

29. Ozumba, G. O. (1995). *"African Ethics"*. Ed Uduigwomen, A. F. *Footmarks on African Philosophy*. Lagos: Oborah and Ogbinaka Publishers.

30. SALGA (2015) *Professionalization of Local Government Sector*. Pretoria: Salga

31. Shivji, I. (1989) *The Concept of Human Rights in Africa*, Dakar: CODESRIA.

32. Shivji, I. (1999) '*constructing a New Rights regime: Promises, Problems and Prospects'*, Social and Legal Studies, 8, 2, 253-276.

33. Van Rooy, J.A(1997) *Scriptural Ethical Principles and African Traditional Ethics. In die Skriflig 31(1 & 2):93-106*

34. Vygotsky, L. S. (1997). *The collected works of L. S. Vygotsky, Vol. 4: The history of the development of higher mental functions (R. W. Rieber*, Vol. Ed; M. J. Hall, Trans.). New York: Plenum Press. (Original work published 1941)

35. Wertsch J. (1991). Voices of the mind: *A Sociocultural approach to mediated action*. Cambridge, MA: Harvard University Press.

36. Vicki Trowler, V. (2010) *Student engagement literature review*. Lancaster: HEA/Lancaster University

Chapter 8

1. Bakindo B. et al., (1994) *"Africa and the Wider World" African Since the Scramble.* Longman: Nigeria.

2. Buah F.K (1986). *A History of West Africa From AD1000* London: Macmillan Publishers

3. Crowder Michael, (1977). *West Africa: An Introduction to its History,* London: Longman Group Ltd.

4. Curtin Philip D (1975). *Economic Change in Pre-colonial Africa: Senegambia in the Era of the Slave Trade.* Madison: University of Wisconsin Press

5. Gailey Harry A (1987). *Historical Dictionary of the Gambia,* London: The Scarecrow Press Inc

6. Gray G M (1966) *History of the Gambia,* London: Frank Cass Ltd.

7. Hughes Arnold and Perfect David (2006). *A Political History of the Gambia 1816 – 1994,* Suffolk: University of Rochester Press.

8. Mbai Fafa Edrissa (1992). *Senegambia Insight,* Surrey: Unwin Brothers Ltd.

9. Mahoney Florence (1982). *Stories of Senegambia,* Banjul: Government Printer

10. Searing James (1988). "Aristocrats, slaves and peasants: Power and Dependency in the Wolof states 1700-1850." *The International Journal of African Historical Studies* Vol. 21, No. 3

11. Southern Lady (1952). *The Gambia – The Story of the Groundnut Colony,* London: George Allen Ltd.

12. Webster J. Betah (1980). *The Revolutionary Years: West Africa Since 1800.* London: Longman Group Ltd.

13. Wright Donald R (2004) *The World and a Very Small Place in Africa – A History of Globalization in Niumi The Gambia.* London: ME Sharpe.

14. Mander Harsh and Asis Muhammed (2004). *Good Governance Resource Book.* Banglor: Books for Change

15. Constitution of The Gambia, 1997

16. Local Government Act of The Gambia, 2002

Chapter 9

1. Amin, Jabrullah Omar and Ismael Madbouli (1993/1414 AH), Harb al-Tanssir Fi Afriqia, al-Dammam: Daral Dhakhaer Litawzie Wa-n Nashr.

2. Archer, Clive (2006) *International Organizations*, Third Edition, London and New York: Routledge Taylor and Francis Group.

3. Attas, M. Naquib (1993) *Islam and Secularism*, Kualalumpur: Istac.

4. Awasom, Nicodemus Fru (2006) "Anglo-Saxons and Gallicism in Nation Building: The Case of Bilingual Cameroon and Senegambia Confederation in the Historical and Comparative perspective" in Anthony I. Asiwaju (ed.) *Afrika Zamani Dakar: CODESRIA* pp. 86 – 112.

5. Barkindo B., Omolewa M. and Babalola (1994) *Africa and the Wider World.* Lagos: Longman, Nigeria.

6. Diakite, Ibrahim "Causes of the Crisis in Northern Mali." Paper Presented at an International Colloquium on the Contribution of the Gulen Movement, held in Dakar, Senegal from the 8th to 9th February 2013.

7. Diehl, Paul F (ed.) (1997) The Politics of Global Governance…

International Organizations in an Independent World. Clorado & London: Lynne Reinner Publishers, Murphy Craig N. (1997)

"What the Third World Wants: An Interpretation of the Development and Meaning of the New International Economic Order, Ideology" in Paul F. Diehl (ed.), The Politics of Global Governance… International Organizations in an Independent World Pg. 201 – 214.

8. Nyamnjoh, Francis B. (2005) *Africa's Media: Democracy and the Politics of Belonging*. London & New York: ZED BOOKS.
9. Obadina, T. (2008) Africa's Crisis of Governance http://www.afbis.com/analysis/crisis.htm

10. Robinson, David (2004), *Muslim Societies in African History*, Cambridge: Cambridge University Press.

11. Senghore, A.A. (2013) "Some Strategies Of Conflict Prevention And The Need For Responsible Leadership In Human Organizations With Reference To The Recent Conflicts In West Africa: A Comparative Perspective" Paper Presented At The 10th Doha International Interfaith Dialogue (Conference) From 23rd To 25th April 2013 Doha Qatar Organized By The Doha International Centre For Interfaith Dialogue
12. Zewde, Bahru (2006) "Embattled Identity in Northeastern Africa": A *Comparative Essay in Anthony I Asiwaju (ed.), Afrika Zamani pp. 49 – 63.*

Chapter 10

1. Ahmed B. (2005) *The Stone of Justice*, Blog at Word Press.Com
2. Ahmed N. ( ) Omar Iban al-Kattah http://historyofislam.com/contents/the-age-of-faith/omar-ibn-al-khattab-r/

3. Al-Attas S.M.N. (1993) *Islam and Secularism*, Kualalumpur: International Institute of Islamic thought and Civilizations (ISTAC)

4. AlBuraey, M.(1985) *Administrative Development: An Islamic Perspective.* London: Routledge.

5. Al Maqrizi.(1994) *Mamluk Economics- A Study and Translation of Al Maqrizi's Ighathah- by Adel Allouche,* Salt Lake City: University of Utah Press.

6. Al- Qudsy Sh. H. S.I & Abdrahaman A. (2011) in (n.e.d.n) *European Journal of Social Sciences, Vol.18 United Kingdom: PP. 612 – 624.*

7. Beekun R. & Badawi J. (1999) *The Leadership Process in Islam*

    http://www.google.gm/url?sa=t&rct=j&q=the%20leadership%20process%20in%20islam&source=web&cd=1&cad=rja&ved=0CCsQFjAA&url=http%3A%2F%2Ffecon.uii.ac.id%2Fimages%2FHand_Out%2FAkt%2FSKI%2Fldrpro.pdf&ei=bFBlUda9K66V7Aa3r4CwBg&usg=AFQjCNGamRU0ehERBaxtCy_j2-H7Y-mrcQ&bvm=bv.44990110,d.d2k

8. Cameron K. & Caza A. (2013) "Development Strategies for Responsible Leadership" *Paper Presented at the University of Michigan* in 2013
    http://www.google.gm/url?sa=t&rct=j&q=developing%20strategies%20for%20responsible%20leadership&source=web&cd=1&ved=0CDoQFjAA&url=http%3A%2F%2Fcompetingvalues.com%2Fcompetingvalues.com%2Fwp-content%2Fuploads%2F2009%2F07%2FDeveloping-Strategies-for-Responsible-Leadership.pdf&ei=KkJlUb7zHMvY7AarzYCoBA&usg=AFQjCNHNDbv70y8vGiqixJ_fPqARBemh7w&bvm=bv.44990110,d.d2k

9. Dassah M.O. (2010) "Responsible leaders: What it takes in a Multi Challenged Global Business Environment". *Paper Presented at the First International Conference on Responsible Leadership,* University of Pretoria in South Africa, 18-20 May 2010

10. Hughes, Arnold (2000) "Democratization Under The Military in The Gambia: 1994 -2000" *Common –Wealth & Comparative Politics*, 38:3, 35 - 52

11. İbn Hisham Abdul Malik(1*995) Siratu- Al- Nnabiy, vol.* 2, Tanya Egypt: Darius- Sahabah Liturath.

12. IDC Herzliya International Institute for Counter Terrorism (2012) ICT's Jihadi Website Monitoring Group.

http://www.marefa.org//index.php/%da%a8%d9%88%d9%a3%d9%a8

13. Junaid. S.W (2004) "The Concept of Leadership And its Application in the Sokoto Caliphate" *Paper Presented at the Conference of Ulama Organized to Commemorate the two Hundred years of the Sokoto Caliphate Held at the Attahiru Dalhalu Bafarawa Institute of Quranic and General Studies, Sokoto, 23-25 of July 2004*

14. Mufuruki A. (2008) *Is There a Crisis of Leadership in Africa?* http://www.africaleadership.net/new005.htm 10/8/ 2008 P.P. 1-4

15. Obadina T. (2008) *Africa's Crisis of Governance* **http://www.afbis.com/analysis/crisis.htm**

16. Pruzan P. & Miller W.C. (2005) "Spirituality as the basis of Responsible Leaderships and Responsible Companies", In Thomas Maak and Nicole M. Pless (eds.) *Responsible Leadership, R*oulege Publishers, London, 2005 (WWW. Rouledge.com)

17. Sacranie I. (2003) "the Challenges of Leadership in Islam: East and West" *Paper Presented at Top Management Programme Conference held in London in 2003* http://www.google.gm/url?sa=t&rct=j&q=the%20challenge%20of%20leadership%20in%20islam%3A%20east&source=web&cd=1&cad=rja&sqi=2&ved=0CCsQFjAA&url=http

%3A%2F%2Fwww.mcb.org.uk%2Fdownloads%2FTMPC.pdf&ei=BkFlUabyOaj07AbIzIGwBA&usg=AFQjCNHzZXxJ700Em_yxyuqZ9oTAZpdxSg&bvm=bv.44990110,d.d2k

18. Salih Subhi (1965) Al-Nuzum Al-Islamiyah, Beirut: Darul' ilmi Lil Malaiyee .

19. Sanyang A. (2012) "The Crisis in Guinea Bissau: In Search of a Sustainable Solution" in Aff'a – M'ndzie, Mireille (eds). *African Views Intelligence Analysis, N.P.P:*

20. Senghore A.A. (2012) "The judiciary in Governance in The Gambia and the Quest for Autonomy under the Second Republic" – *Journal of The Third World Studies*, Vol. 27, No. 2 (Fall 2012), pp. 215-248) New Jersey, USA.

21. Senghore A.A. (2012) Press Freedom and Democratic Governance in The Gambia: A right- based approach – Published in South Africa by the University Of Pretoria *African Human Rights Law Journal* Volume 12 No 2. 2012

Index

A

Abdoulaye Wade: 19,
Academic Ethics: 244
Adaptation Strategies: 252-254
African Charter on Democracy, Elections, and
Governance (ACDEG): 364, 365, 373, 384
African Governance: 360, 361, 364, 384, 387
African Growth and Opportunity Act (AGOA): 60
African Unity: 42, 149, 150,207
African governments' attitude: 170
al-Attas: 77-78, 224, 232
al-Ghazālī: 79, 206, 234
al-Quran: 75
al-Shāṭibī: 78, 204, 207
Alliance for Patriotic Reorientation and Construction
(APRC): 139
American Declaration of Independence: 75
American Theory of Legal Realism: 73
Amie Bensouda: 107
Annan, Kofi: 157
An-Na'im, 1999a: 240
Ansaruddin: 15
Anti-Personnel: 88
Arab Disunity: 346
Arab-African Integration: 335-337, 344-346, 356-358
Archie Mafeje: 41
Arif, Muhammad: 183-185, 187, 190, 191
Assaraddine: 15
Assassinations: 123, 126
Attas, Syed al-: 224, 232
Austrian Theory of Legal Positivism: 72

B

Baboucarr Gaye: 130, 142, 143, 145
Baba Musa Tarawallie: 141, 143
Bakau: 132, 130
Banjul: 132, 134, 138, 141, 144, 145
BBC Banjul Correspondent: 126, 130
BBC Focus on Africa: 123
Beetham: 42, 43
Belgore: 168, 181
Bentham, Jeremy: 73, 199
Bilateralism: 232
Blackstone, Sir William: 196, 199
Boko Haram: 10, 16, 351-352
Bove vs. Baldeh: 174
Bridge: 84
Brobbery: 158, 182
Buundung Police Station: 124
Burkina Faso: 360, 384

C

Cadi Court: 169
Capital FM: 132
Carbon Emissions: 252
Cassen and Clairmont: 58
Charter on Democracy, Elections, and Governance: 360, 384
Civil Government (Locke): 70
Claude Ake: 3, 60, 61
Closing Radio Stations: 142
Community Radio: Brikama, 132; Farafenni, 132; Gunjur, 132
Constitutional Liberalism: 3
Constitutional Provisions: 162, 183, 190

Constitutional Rule: 85, 116-117
Constitutional Supremacy: 85
Constitution of The Gambia (1997): 145, 153
Corruption: 142, 360, 374
Courts of The Gambia: 96
Criminal Code Amendment Bill 2004: 123
Criticism of the Independent: 127-128

D

Daily Express: 133, 141
Daily News: 133
Daily Observer: 120, 123
Darboe, Ousainou: 178, 181, 193
Declaration of Independence: 210
Declaration of Rights of Man: 210
Democracy in Africa: 360, 361, 384
Democracy in The Gambia: 66-67, 81-84, 106-113, 117-119
Democratic Governance: 98-105, 115-116
Democratic Institutions: 84-85
Devda Hydara: 123, 126
Devitoria, Francisco: 213
Dicey, A.V.: 74
Divine Revelation: 75
Drammeh vs. the State: 179, 180

E

Ebrima Sillah: 126
Economides: 2010, 244
ECOWAS Protocol on Democracy and Good Governance: 360, 367, 384
ECOWAS: 2
Edward Herman: 5
Education: 372, 373, 375

Elections: 369, 370, 387

Ellett, 2013: 236, 243

Endless Domestic Conflicts and Ensuring Crisis: 349-350

European Union (EU): 21, 49, 114, 147, 360

European Union's Economic Partnership Agreements (EPAs): 60

F

Fair Electoral Laws: 369

Fareed Zakaria: 3, 6

Fajara: 135

Faye, J.C.: 135

Field, 2005: 242

FMB: 132

Forster, Sam J.: 147

Free Press: 108-109, 112

Freedom of Expression: 108-110, 111, 144, 145, 146, 147, 153

Francis B. Nyamnjoh: 5

Francis Fukuyama: 82

G

Gaddafi: 14, 59, 60, 63

Gambia Daily: 134

Gambia Info: 133

Gambia News & Report Magazine: 133

Gambia Outlook: 133, 134

Gambia Press Union: 138, 144, 151

Gambia Times: 134, 135

Governance: 1, 2, 4, 5, 7, 8, 82-83, 99, 112-113, 159, 360, 361, 362-368, 374, 376, 378, 379, 384, 387

Governance Crisis in West Africa: 9-13

Governance Institutions: 259

Government of The Gambia: 90-91
Grant, W.G.: 141
Grotius, Hugo: 68, 196, 198, 224

H

Habeas Corpus: 73
Haqq: 76-77
Hassan B. Jallow: 168, 181, 193
Heritage of Western European Colonial Past: 336-337
Holden: 42, 43, 109-110
Hofstede, 2001: 240
Human Rights: 6, 7, 9, 10, 66-67, 77, 79, 80, 87, 114-115, 196, 200, 201, 205, 207-209, 213-220, 225-234, 373, 380, 384
Human Rights Defenders: 155
Humanitarian Law: 215
Huntington, Michael: 57

I

IMF/World Bank: 43
Independence of the Judiciary: 96-97, 117, 193, 194
Independent news media: 88-90, 107, 120-122, 129-130
Indemnity (Amendment) Act: 153
Inspector General of Police (IGP): 141, 142
Intimidation of Press: 124
International Financial Institutions: 337-338
International Law of Human Rights: 69, 213-214, 224-226, 230
Islamic Governance: 376, 377, 378, 379, 380, 381, 387
Islamic Law: 75-80
Islamic Perspective: 203-206

J

Jallow, Alhagie Yorro: 123, 124
Jallow, Baba Galleh: 123, 124

Jammeh Administration: 127
Jammeh, Yahya: 1, 138, 143, 159, 176, 182
Judiciary: 86-87, 93-97, 157-158, 160
Judicial Corruption: 236, 249
Judicial Service Commission: 166, 167
Judiciary Independence: 6
Juridically: 214
Jurisprudence: 3, 66, 81, 188
Justice: 153

K

Kahn, 2009: 238
Kanifing: 132, 138, 145
Kesavananda Bharati: 189
Kim: 84
Kignongo, 2000: 240, 243
Kololi: 132
Kofi Annan: 157
Kuko Samba Sanyang: 141
KWT: 132

L

Law, Rule of: 373
Leadership: 359, 360, 361, 378, 379, 380
Leadership Crisis: 9, 11, 12, 13
Legislation of The Gambia: 123
Liberal Democracy: 41, 42, 43, 44, 45, 46
Licences: 123
Locke, John: 69-70, 196, 198
Lomé, Togo: 2

M

Mafeje, Archie: 41
Macky Sall: 3
Magna Carta: 210, 224

Majlis al-shura: 208
Mander and Asif: 47, 112-114, 160
Manufacturing Consent (book): 5
Maslahah: 78, 204, 206
Media Commission Act (2001): 138
Media in The Gambia: 88-90, 107
Michael Kirby: 236
Michael Huntington: 57
Modou Jobe: 86, 97, 166
Modern Concept: 213, 214
Momodou Jobe: 166
Multiparty Elections: 1, 3, 4, 6
Multipartyism: 57, 58
Muslim Rights: 222-223
Musa SaidyKhan: 125

N

National Agency Against Trafficking in Person (NATIP): 88
National Agency for Legal Aid (NALA): 88
National Census of The Gambia (2003): 58
New Gambia: 134, 141
Newspaper Act (1944): 137
Newspaper Amendment Act 2004: 123
Noam Chomsky: 5
Nyamnjoh, Francis B.: 5
Nyato: 134
Nyangnjob: 90, 120-121

O

Office of the Ombudsman: 88
Oliver de Sardan: 58
Omoroebe, 1993: 238
Ousman Sillah: 182, 193

Ousman Sonko: 3
Ownership of Media: 120

P

PAC/PEC: 100-104
Paradise FM: 132
Peace: 359, 361, 372, 375, 384
Physical Assault on Journalists: 124
Police: Inspector General of Police (IGP), 141, 142;
Superintendent of Police, 141
Political Authority: 72
Political Independence: 359, 360
Post-colonial Africa: 9-10
Poverty and Corruption: 347
Press Freedom: 88-90, 106-107, 120-122, 135, 136, 144-147
Print Media: Table B, 133
Private news media: 126
Principles of Islamic Jurisprudence (Uṣūl al-Fiqh): 77
Promotion of Social Dialogue: 372
Protection of Minority Rights: 384
Public Financial Management: 100-101

Q

Qur'an: 75

R

Radio Syd: 132
Realist Construction: 73
Reorientation and Construction (APRC): 139
Responsive Rule: 81, 83-84
Responsible Leadership: 359, 361, 378, 379
Rights, Legal and Moral: 74
Rule of Law: 85-86, 116, 373

Rumours: 151

S

Sabally v Inspector General of Police: 85, 116, 165, 171-176, 183-185, 191
Sallah, Halifa: 164, 177
SAPs (Structural Adjustment Programmes): 60
Saward: 83, 109-110
Scepticism: 153
Security Forces: 370, 371
Senghore, A.A.: 117, 128
Separation of Powers: 90-92, 117
Seward: 42, 43, 44
Sharia Law: 16
Shari'ah: 75-80, 203-206, 209, 223-224, 234
Shatibi, al: 204, 207
Sierra Leone: 9, 360, 361
Silviji, 1999: 239
Socialism: 261
State, Civil Society, and Market: 259
Structural Adjustment Programmes (SAPs): 60
Sud FM: 132, 143
Supreme Court of The Gambia: 138, 141, 145, 153
Sustainer: 205
Sylvanus Olympio: 2

T

Table A (Radio Stations): 132
Table B (Print Media): 133
Tan: 84
Tenure of Office of Judges: 167
The Bathurst Observer and West African Gazette: 121
The Feasibility of Democracy in Africa (book): 3
The Gambia Echo: 121

The Gambia Independent: 127-128
The Gambia Weekly News: 121
The Independent: 123-128
The Nation: 134, 141
The Point: 133
The Rise of Illiberal Democracy (article): 3
The Standard: 133
The Torch: 141
The Vanguard: 134
Tocqueville: 107
Today: 133
Traditional Governance Institutions: 258-259
Tribunals: 162
Tuareg Rebels: 13-15

U

UDHR (Universal Declaration of Human Rights): 66, 214, 216, 218, 222
UNESCO: 151
Universal Declaration of Human and Peoples' Rights: 240
Universal Islamic Declaration of Human Rights: 223
Utilitarianism: 73
Uṣūl al-Fiqh: 77, 204

V

Vibes: 132
Victims of Western Hegemonic Policies and Aggressive Wars: 337
Violence against Press: 124
Vulnerable Groups: 87
Voting Rights: 369

W

Wade and Philips: 87, 116-117

Webster's Dictionary: 47
Weeramantry, C.G.: 80
West Africa Magazine: 141
West African Governance Issues: 351-352
Wilson, James: 71, 196, 199

Y

Yahya Jammeh: 1

www.ingramcontent.com/pod-product-compliance
Lightning Source LLC
Chambersburg PA
CBHW051947050225
21485CB00039B/1283